# Hiking the California Coastal Trail

Volume One: Oregon to Monterey

**To**

Eden Marguerite Lorentzen
*who came into this world on a wave of joy as this book was being created,*
*— B.L.*

Brenda Nichols
*to whom I am forever grateful for being my best friend and hiking partner*
*as we explore the natural world,*
*— R.N.*

*the many volunteers who make Coastwalk a wonderful*
*grassroots organization,*

and

*all the people who have fought hard to save the California coast.*
*— B.L. and R.N.*

# Hiking the California Coastal Trail

## A Guide to Walking the Golden State's Beaches and Bluffs from Border to Border

### Volume One: Oregon to Monterey

## Bob Lorentzen and Richard Nichols

Forewords by
Peter Douglas, Executive Director, California Coastal Commission
and
Donald Murphy, Director, California State Parks, 1990-1997

BORED FEET PRESS – MENDOCINO, CA
COASTWALK – SEBASTOPOL, CA
SECOND EDITION, 2002

© 1998, 2002 by Robert S. Lorentzen and Coastwalk
Second Edition, June 2002
Printed in the United States of America
on acid-free, not-less-than minimum 30% recycled paper (30% post-consumer)

Cover and interior design by Elizabeth Petersen, Fort Bragg, California
Maps by Marsha Mello
Edited by Donna Bettencourt

Co-Published by

Bored Feet Press
Post Office Box 1832
Mendocino, CA 95460
(707)964-6629, (888)336-6199, www.boredfeet.com

    and

Coastwalk
7207 Bodega Avenue
Sebastopol, CA 95472
(707)829-6689, (800)550-6854, www.coastwalk.org

Distributed by Bored Feet Press

**Library of Congress Cataloging-in-Publication Data**
Lorentzen, Bob, 1949–
    Hiking the California Coastal Trail : a guide to walking the Golden State's beaches and bluffs from border to border / Bob Lorentzen and Richard Nichols : forewords by Peter Douglas and Donald Murphy : [maps by Marsha Mello]. — 2nd ed.
        p.    cm.
    Includes bibliographical references and index.
    Contents: v. 1. Oregon to Monterey
    ISBN 0-939431-24-6
    1. Hiking—California—California Coastal Trail—Guidebooks.
    2. Trails—California—California Coastal Trail—Guidebooks.
    3. California Coastal Trail (Calif.)—Guidebooks.  I. Nichols, Richard, 1942–   . II. Title.
GV199.42.C22C235 1998
796.51'09794—DC21

10 9 8 7 6 5 4 3 2

# Contents

# Feature Articles

# Foreword

*Executive Director, California Coastal Commission*

THE CALIFORNIA COAST IS MANY THINGS — it sustains a remarkable variety and abundance of life, it fires the imagination, sparks dreams, inspires creative expression, and offers sanctuary for body and soul. It is a place of unmatched natural magnificence, of mystery and power where the drama of beginnings and endings is perpetual. Yet for all its grandeur and potency, it is a fragile environment whose integrity and vitality depend on wise human stewardship.

California's story, accentuated by glory and shame, is inextricably linked to its seacoast where powerful forces collide with unpredictable regularity and spectacular and often terrible consequences. Over time, residents and visitors have forged an enriching and enduring bond with this bountiful and tantalizing reach of geography. Both home and resource, the coast is coveted by many who compete fiercely for a piece of the action and their own brief moment in the sun.

Those who take the time to walk the coast can most closely listen to and hear its stories wrapped around human and natural history. Every cove, beach, stretch of rugged cliffs and mountains, expanse of dunes, forest, scrub and grasslands, and each settlement of people along the way has a storied past whether great or small. Coastwalk is dedicated to exposing people to opportunities to hear and feel these stories, the poetry, the songs, and the passion of the coast.

The coast, like every unique piece of geography on Earth, is never finally saved. It is continually being saved. That is why public understanding and active support for coastal conservation is critical. People have the ability to destroy the coast — we have been fairly adept at that by eliminating nearly all coastal wetlands — but we must recognize the opportunity, indeed the obligation, to protect its natural and human community values through preservation and restoration. As a seasoned observer and participant, I am acutely aware of the power of even one individual committed to doing good works, not to mention the impact of many dedicated to the cause of environmental stewardship for the benefit of current and future generations. There is no better way to expand the cause of coastal conservation than to increase opportunities for people to get to, learn about and experience firsthand the wonders of the coast. By taking the time to go out and be with it, the traveler will learn about the opportunities to conserve this precious resource as well as the potential to do harm.

Coastwalk is a vision whose time is here. Formed by individuals who walk often in nature, the group is committed to the realization of a dream: a continuous coastal trail or series of linked ways making it possible for current and future generations to hike the length of California's coastline from Oregon to Mexico. Although not yet complete, the coastal trail is coming into being and long segments can be traversed by people with a spirit of adventure who are able to walk along the shore. This book is more than a useful guide for those who hike the coastal trail. It is a key to understanding and awareness that the coast is a delicately balanced ecosystem whose future well-being rests in our care.

As you use this guide, remember that the spectacular land- and seascapes you observe, the thriving natural habitats you visit, the physical and visual access you have, the quality of your recreational experience, and the public amenities offered by human communities along the way are all results of a protracted and intense struggle waged by environmentalists to "save the coast." California's world leadership in coastal conservation was brought into being by citizen activism and involvement. In 1972 California voters approved against powerful opposition a citizen's initiative that established our strong and effective coastal protection law. When threatened, as it has been many times, the public has effectively rallied to its defense. More than any environmental program I know, California's coastal protection law is a populist law. We must not take for granted the coast as it exists today. Only public initiative, support and activism are responsible for the coast we know today. Remember too, the greatest accomplishments of coastal conservation are the things you do **not** see — the views **not** spoiled, the public access **not** lost, the wetlands **not** filled, the urban sprawl **not** permitted, the natural landforms **not** destroyed, the agricultural lands **not** converted.

The greatest threat to the coast is public ignorance and apathy. That is why environmental education and public participation in coastal stewardship are so important. This book will help you find your way along the California coast, but more significantly, it will ignite awareness of your opportunity to help protect this marvelous natural heritage with which we are blessed.

*San Francisco*
*December 1997*

# Foreword

*by Donald W. Murphy*
*Director, California State Parks, 1990–1997*

ON THE FIRST DAY OF JUNE 1996, I stood on a beach with a group of Coastwalkers at the Oregon-California border. Actually it was just a line our hike leader Richard Nichols drew in the sand with his hiking stick, but we knew the border was somewhere nearby.

Six in the group would be hiking all the way to Mexico on a dream coming true called the California Coastal Trail, and some of us, including myself, would be walking only about 80 miles down the coast to Patrick's Point State Park. We ranged in age from 20 to 70. The group of hikers going all the way to Mexico averaged around 60 years young. Most of them were women. I was privileged to share most of my hike with Bob Lorentzen, co-author of this book. I know of no individual more dedicated to hiking and to accurate trail guides.

For me, hiking the California Coastal Trail was a rare opportunity to see the coast up close. One of my fellow hikers, Bill Kortum, described our coast as a commons for the people of California. Not only would I be seeing so much of the coast on foot, but I would have the chance to interact on a daily basis with ordinary citizens who love parks and the California environment.

I remember how immediately upon hiking time was suspended. I marveled at the way the fog interacted with the land, making the ocean and the land one. The continuous roar of the ocean found a resonance deep within me. It was real soul music. While I did not dance outwardly my spirit danced inwardly. The long talks I had with my companions illuminated my own life and fostered a deeper understanding of the importance of human relationships. When I saw people searching for agates, I thought how silly to hunt for a shiny piece of rock. But later I was reminded that this quest, though not of great monetary reward, fulfilled the human need for discovery. Likewise, the Coastal Trail provides the perfect opportunity for the human spirit to continue its evolutionary quest, to discover the unique, to connect with the unknown.

The dream of a Coastal Trail from the Oregon border to the Mexican border is a step closer to becoming reality. However, the journey that we embarked upon revealed the need to work harder to acquire the necessary land and rights of way to insure access to the entire coast of California.

As you use this guide, I hope that you become committed to the cause of seeing that the California Coastal Trail is completed. I also hope you will find the connections to our natural world that will bring you a deeper understanding and appreciation of life and the human spirit.

*Sacramento*
*December 1997*

# Preface to the Second Edition

OUR GROUNDBREAKING FIRST EDITION became the first guidebook to present the California Coastal Trail route in detail. Now four years later, although the route hasn't changed drastically, much has changed both in the CCT's official standing and in public perception of the trail.

This second edition reports all changes that have occurred on the CCT north half since 1998. It also adds information about the many changes due in the near future. Almost 60% of the pages have changes. While many are minor adjustments or corrections, the revised text and maps reflect over thirty major changes, including new trail mileage and/or land acquisitions at Westport, Caspar and Point Arena in Mendocino County, near Bolinas in Marin County, at Pacifica, Montara and Half Moon Bay in San Mateo County, and in Santa Cruz County.

Before our book came out in June 1998, the majority of hikers were unaware of California's Coastal Trail, and those hikers who had heard of the CCT had little idea about details of the trail. Yet shortly after Volume Two documented CCT's southern half in May 2000, a *Backpacker* magazine survey of readers ranked the California Coastal Trail among the nation's top twenty long-distance trails.

The CCT gained attention in spring 2000 when California voters passed a parks bond measure that included the first specific state funding ($5 million) for the CCT. In autumn 2001, the governor signed Senate Bill 908, officially recognizing the CCT and initiating planning for its completion. Coastwalk and state agencies are now working together to make a specific plan for the CCT.

While the CCT's biggest changes and improvements will come over the next six to ten years, the public can find all 1200 miles of the current route and hike them using information contained in our two-volume set. Both volumes of *Hiking the California Coastal Trail* are fast becoming an essential reference source for coastal hiking and coastal access, and they provide the only extensive information on the CCT.

Let's envision the Coastal Trail as it nears completion. By 2010, we expect the CCT to be well signed, with large access signs both at access points and on nearby highways to entice drivers out of their cars. Smaller signposts along the trail will show trail users the right path.

We expect the CCT to be a braided network of interconnecting trails and routes spanning California's entire coast. Some strands of the braid will be improved multiple-use trails open to hikers, bicyclists, equestrians and mobility-challenged users. Some will be less developed and for lighter-use, especially in sensitive habitats. Some will be rugged wilderness paths, others unimproved routes along beaches. Some may even require special permits and/or guided hikes. The latter model is already in place on PG&E's Diablo Canyon property, although a through route still must be developed there. The special permit/guided hike options may also be the way to get the CCT established on coastal military bases and in places where large parcels are owned by corporations or individuals willing to open access to their property on a limited basis.

In short, the California Coastal Trail, already a wondrous route open to hikers and other users with help from our guides, will become ever more accessible and complex as the braids of the network grow and develop. Take a hike on the California Coastal Trail this week!

Please note that further updates on the CCT will be available at www.boredfeet.com.

# Imagine a California Coastal Trail

**I**MAGINE A TRAIL ALONG THE ENTIRE LENGTH OF THE CALIFORNIA COAST, a diverse route from border to border that explores beaches, bluffs, headlands, bays and coves, staying as near the shore as possible for 1200 miles. Visualize a route that passes through wilderness areas, towns and cities, climbs over high ridges, and crosses dozens of streams ranging from seasonal trickles to year-round creeks to major rivers.

Happily the California Coastal Trail (CCT) is no longer all in the mind, but too few people realize the CCT already exists, as diverse a long distance trail as you'll find on the planet. The CCT has been being created, designated and built for twenty-five years. Finishing it will take several more years of dedicated work, but other long distance trails have also taken years to complete. The Pacific Crest Trail has taken twenty-nine years to become almost complete since the first guidebook appeared and it's still not done. The Appalachian Trail took even longer.

The biggest advance for California's Coastal Trail since this book's first edition in 1998 came in autumn 2001 when the state legislature approved SB 908. That

*California's official coastal access logo was rejected as the official CCT logo, but we'll still use it until a new logo is approved.*

legislation formally established the California Coastal Trail, mandating the Coastal Conservancy to work with other state agencies to develop a plan and cost estimates for its completion.

Coastwalk and Bored Feet continue to educate the public about the CCT. We're working toward that goal on three fronts. First, since 1983 we've been telling people about the CCT, leading hikes along it every summer, and working to complete the trail.

Second, we've created and published two comprehensive guidebooks for the CCT. You hold the second edition of the first volume, covering from the Oregon-California state line to Monterey, in your hands. We published *Volume 2: Monterey to Mexico* in 2000.

Third, we're working on a study of the CCT in cooperation with the Coastal Conservancy, Coastal Commission, and State Parks Department to map the best routes and uses for the trail, identify major gaps and the opportunities for filling them, and make a budget estimate for its completion. We'll also field check the route using Global Positioning System technology and photography to identify significant features. Also included in the study is the development of a signing program and creation of a website focused exclusively on the CCT. When the study is completed in 2003, efforts will begin to build missing links, acquire land for conservation and trail use, and install signs clearly identifying the CCT. The goal is to have significant new portions of the trail built and signed by 2008.

In the meantime, our guidebooks help you find and follow the California Coastal Trail wherever you choose, for as many or as few miles as the spirit moves you. Be forewarned, though, that hiking the CCT can be contagious.

## The Wondrous California Coast

California is both a land of superlatives and a land of extremes. It not only has the largest population and third largest land mass of the fifty states, it also has the longest coast of all the states except Alaska. The California coastline stretches, sprawls and twists for 1200 miles from the rain forest north to the desert south.

The CCT attempts to visit as much of the coast as possible while traversing the length of the Golden State in a reasonably efficient manner. In some places, topography prevents the CCT from passing directly along the shoreline. In other places, private or restricted property keeps the trail from the coastline. The Coastal Trail takes the through route along the coast, walking a fine line between the practical and the ideal. The CCT strives to see as much of the coast as possible without going far out of the way without good reason. In many places where the CCT misses a corner of the California coast, we'll tell you about a side trail you can take out to a point, down to a pocket beach or to another worthy feature.

# State of the Trail

Does the California Coastal Trail run all the way along the coast? The answer is both a resounding **yes** and a qualified **no**. Yes, it starts on the beach at the Oregon-California line and ends, also on the beach, at the California-Mexico border. The CCT, however, hasn't yet been completed — it's a work-in-progress. In this book and *Volume Two: Monterey to Mexico*, we present the trail as it now exists.

Roughly 62 percent of this current route follows existing trails and beaches. Much of the other 38 percent of today's CCT follows road shoulders on a provisional route that gets you from point A to point B, but isn't in most cases the ideal CCT route. Most of the 20 percent of CCT currently on back roads is reasonably safe to follow. This means that about 82 percent, or around 978 miles of the 1197-mile route (492 miles of the 600 in this volume), is currently recommended as reasonably safe and worthwhile to follow. The other 18 percent follows highway shoulders, and while you can follow the CCT along these highway miles, we present them here more to point out that these parts of the real California Coastal Trail are missing and need to be created than to suggest that you walk them.

Of course, if you feel compelled to follow the entire CCT, you can with extreme caution walk the highway segments. Coastwalk's Whole Hike did so successfully in 1996 and we expect to do it again in 2003. One man ran the entire CCT in 1999. Alternately, until the Coastal Trail is complete, you can bicycle these legs or follow them in a vehicle. If you choose to walk or bike any of the highway portions of the CCT, please follow the safety rules later in this chapter.

# Day Hikes or Long-Distance Trek? You Choose

Basically you have three ways you can hike the California Coastal Trail. The first and most popular way is to day hike any portion of the CCT whenever you choose. Even if you only walk a mile or two you can still have a quality experience, a little taste of the Coastal Trail.

On the other extreme, we know that a few people will want to through-hike the CCT, that is to walk continuously along the entire 1200-mile trail. Such an undertaking should not be considered lightly. Modified types of through-hiking include hiking half the CCT, hiking a set number of miles, whether 50 or 500, walking from Oregon to San Francisco or San Francisco to Monterey, or hiking the CCT through the county you live in or your favorite coastal county. Before doing any through-hike, read *Through-Hiking the CCT* in the back of the book.

The third way to hike the CCT is to make it an ongoing project. Hike a section whenever you can and keep a checklist of what you've done. Perhaps someday you'll head out to hike that final section, and after it's done, you'll be able to take pride in the fact that you've hiked the entire California Coastal Trail.

# The Rules of Road Walking

The most basic rule is "If you don't have to road walk, don't!" but when you do road walk, be careful, and follow these safety rules.

1. Always stay off the road and on sidewalks where available. When you must walk on the road shoulder, stay as far from moving traffic as possible.

2. Always walk with a friend or in a group. This considerably increases your

visibility to drivers. Always walk single file. When in a group, the lead walker and the one bringing up the rear should carry a **caution** or **slow** sign.

3. Always wear bright and/or reflective clothing. Your best bet is to wear bright clothing **and** a day-glo reflective highway vest.

4. When you must cross the road, do so with extreme caution, always looking twice for traffic in both directions. When a group is crossing, they must cross together. Choose a perceptive and responsible group leader and follow their lead.

5. It's usually best to walk facing oncoming traffic (bike in the same direction as traffic). In fact California state law says to walk facing traffic, but in many places where the highway's left shoulder has poor visibility or where no left shoulder exists, it can be safer to walk along the right shoulder of the road.

6. Always pay attention to oncoming vehicle traffic. Many drivers slow for walkers beside the roadway, but all too many do not. Be aware of what approaching drivers are doing. Be especially careful of speeding vehicles, vehicles passing other vehicles, erratic drivers, wide vehicles and trucks. With the latter two, watch for wide side-view mirrors like many RVs have.

7. Never challenge vehicles for the right-of-way or do anything to unnecessarily distract drivers from their complex multiple tasks. That includes clowning around. If you're grouping up to take photos or observe nearby wildlife, make sure you're well off the roadway and not creating a hazard to traffic.

8. Never road walk at night. It's far too dangerous. Even twilight is a particularly hazardous time to be walking any road shoulder.

# How This Guide Works for You

Given the immense and diverse nature of the California Coastal Trail, we've broken the guidebook into two volumes, this one for the northern half of California, Volume Two for the southern half. We've divided the CCT into easily accessible sections you can hike whenever you're in the area. Almost every section has road access to one end or the other and most have vehicle access to both ends. This volume covers 85 CCT sections ranging from 2¼ miles to 19½ miles in one-way length.

The book describes the CCT from north to south because the coast generally unfolds better when you're walking south. The north to south orientation also lets the prevailing winds push gently or firmly at your back. Be aware, however, that if you're walking south with a strong wind at your back, you'll likely need to walk into the wind if you're returning to your starting point.

We provide detailed access information at the start of each section. At a glance you can tell the section's length in either miles or kilometers, how to get there, whether it's only open to hikers or also to bicyclists and equestrians, and what kind of surface the CCT section follows. The access information also tells you whether the section is easy, moderate or strenuous, and what the total elevation gain and loss are to walk it in the direction described. We tell you any cautions specific to that section and who to call to get more information. The access information also details the section's facilities—water, restrooms, phones, picnic areas—and where to find the nearest campgrounds, lodgings and hostels.

Every section's access point is at its northern end, or at least leads to its northern end in the shortest possible fashion. Each section also has a southern

## Map Legend

**Ⓐ** Access – CCT Trail Section Trailhead

**⟨Ⓐ⟩** Alternate Access

**▬▬▬▬** California Coastal Trail

**━ ━ ━ ━** Alternate Trail/Access Trail

**• • • • •** Side Trail

**ooooo** Water Crossing

**Ⓟ** Parking Area

**Ⓣ** Trailhead

**⬗** Hostel/Accommodations

**▲** Campground/Site

**☐** Place of Interest

**⟨ ⟩** Private or Protected Area

**o—o** Gate

**◊** Spring

**⋀** Summit/Peak

access point which, unless we state otherwise, also starts the following section.

We describe every section in enough detail that you can clearly follow it from our text. We also point out what's special about each section and provide some human or natural history to give a sense of the place. Our thirty-six feature articles expand on the cultural and physical aspects of the coast.

We show every CCT section on a map created for this guide. Artist Marsha Mello drew the maps to scale from USGS topographic maps. Instead of showing contour lines, we show the features most useful to find your way along the coast. The map legend at left will help you read the maps. Each map indicates north and the scale. While the book's maps thoroughly support the text, if you feel naked hiking without topographic maps, by all means invest in them and take them on your trip. These would be most useful in the steepest terrain like the Lost Coast.

Of the 85 CCT sections in this volume, four-fifths are less than nine miles long and offer good day hikes. Of the remaining eighteen sections that are nine or more miles long, three along the Lost Coast and one at Point Reyes are best done as backpack trips, although you can day hike portions of these sections from a road at one end or the other. Most of the rest of these longer sections include considerable road mileage. We hope to improve these parts of the CCT in coming years by getting them off the road.

## Have a Safe Hike
### The Ten Commandments for CCT Hikers

1. **Never turn your back on the ocean** when you're in the tidal zone or on the bluff's edge directly above it. **Oversized rogue or sleeper waves** can strike the coast at any time. **Watch for them. They have killed people.** They are especially common in winter but can occur in any season. **Changing tides** offer the other big danger when walking near the ocean. When walking the coast, carry a current tide table for the area and know how to read it. Don't let rising tides trap you. **Dangerous undertows and rip currents** can occur anywhere along the California coast, and can pull anyone in the water out to sea. The farther north you go in

California, the colder the ocean is. Especially along the north coast, the ocean is icy and unforgiving, generally unsafe for swimming without a wetsuit.

2. **Stay back from cliffs.** Coastal soils and rocks are often unstable. Don't get close to the cliff's edge, and never climb on cliffs unless there is a safe trail.

3. **No trespassing.** Property owners have a right to privacy. Please stay off private property. There are enough public places without walking through someone's yard.

4. **Wild animals** range from very tiny to large. **Ticks** are the most persistent pest, especially in winter and spring. Deer ticks, the smallest of ticks, may carry Lyme disease. It can be a nasty and persistent problem if a Lyme disease carrying tick attaches to you for 24 hours or more. **Mosquitoes** may be a problem any-where, and wasps, biting spiders, scorpions, and even rattlesnakes occur in coastal areas. In tidal areas, watch for **jellyfish** washed up on the beach and **sea urchins** in tidepools—both have painful stinging spines. On the wild north coast you may encounter **bears, mountain lions** and **elk**, always potentially dangerous. Bears are most often a problem when you're in camp, so keep all food and uten-sils put away when not in use. If you encounter a mountain lion on the trail, don't run. Make eye contact and make yourself appear larger by spreading your arms or raising your hiking stick over your head. Elk should never be approached on foot, especially during mating season in autumn when bulls may charge on a whim, running up to 35 miles per hour. Skunks and raccoons can also be a prob-lem, but they're generally not life threatening like the larger animals. The bite of any mammal may transmit deadly rabies.

5. **Watch for poison oak.** It takes many forms growing on coastal bluffs. Any contact can cause an itching rash. Remember, leaves of three, let it be! In winter, poison oak's bare branches can still cause a rash. **Stinging nettles** can cause seri-ous if temporary skin irritation when touched. Also be careful with **mushrooms** and other plants you don't know since poisonous species occur in coastal areas.

6. **Crime.** Be sure to lock your vehicle when you park it at a trailhead. Leave valuables out of sight, at home, or take them with you. When camping, try not to leave valuables unattended. Some criminals prey on coastal campgrounds.

7. **Stream crossings** or fords can be deadly. Deep or rushing waters can over-come even the strongest, most experienced hikers. Never ford a creek or river if it seems unsafe. Always use a hiking stick or two and proceed carefully when you cross moving streams. If you're wearing a backpack, undo waist belt and loosen shoulder straps before crossing. We try to mention in specific trail sections when a stream ford might be dangerous, but even small creeks can become dangerous after rainstorms. High tides and changing tides can also affect coastal stream crossings. In addition, this book includes crossings of five rivers, two bays, a har-bor and a lagoon where you must either hire a boat to take you across or make a long road detour. Never attempt those crossings without a boat of sufficient size.

8. **Be careful with fire.** Always extinguish campfires until cold to the touch. You generally need a campfire permit (free) to have a fire outside a developed campground. Never start a fire in an unsafe spot. Fires may be banned altogether during the dry season.

9. **Trail safety and courtesy.** Never cut switchbacks. Equestrians always have the right of way on trails, because you can move aside for a horse much more easily than its rider can yield to you. When you yield to horse traffic, always

## Please Don't Trash Our Coast

*Most litter, other than that poorly placed banana peel, is not immediately dangerous to humans. Litter does have serious costs, however. It not only degrades the beauty of the natural environment, it also pollutes the ocean and can be deadly to wildlife. Even something as small as a cigarette butt, the filter of which doesn't break down, can be lethal when eaten by a marine organism or bird. Many people toss their orange peels onto the natural environment, but an orange peel can take years to decompose.*

*If you think litter is a minor problem, consider that each September more than 40,000 volunteers comb the coast for California Coastal Cleanup Day, collecting more than a half million pounds of trash and fifty tons of recyclables. In 1996 they collected 153,000 cigarette butts.*

*Most of the California coast remains relatively unspoiled. Do your part to keep it that way by not littering. Even better, show your appreciation for Mother Nature by hiking with a trash bag and using it to collect trash you find in otherwise pristine places, even little things like cigarette butts, orange peels, bottle caps and pull tabs.*

*When we request that nobody trash our coast, we also mean preventing unnecessary development on the the bluff's edge, in fragile dunes, wetlands, and other sensitive habitat. That includes no new offshore oil drilling or seabed mining.*

stand as far off the trail as possible and speak in a calm, normal voice to the rider to assure the animal that you are a human being. Bicyclists on trails must yield to hikers and horses and slow to walking speed on blind corners.

10. **Always take responsibility for yourself and your party.** The authors and publishers cannot and will not be responsible for you on the trail. Information contained in this book is correct to the best of the authors' knowledge at press time. Authors and publishers assume no liability for damages. **You must take responsibility for your safety and health while on the trail.** The coast is still a wild place. Safety conditions of trails, beaches and tidepools vary with seasons and tides. Be cautious, heed all warnings and cautions in the book, and always check on local conditions. It is always better to hike with a friend. Know where you can get help in case of emergency.

OTHER THINGS TO REMEMBER WHEN HIKING THE CCT: 1) Always park off roadway facing in direction of traffic. 2) Never park blocking a gate or road.

## How's the Weather on the Coast?

The climate of the California coast can best be described as Mediterranean, although it varies greatly from north to south. Warm dry summers and temperate wet winters characterize this Mediterranean climate found no where else in the United States. The dry season, generally from May through September, offers the best season for hiking, especially in the far north where the rains may linger for a month longer. On the California coast, dry is a relative term since fog and low clouds also characterize the summers, with more persistent and cooler fog in the north than in the south. The persistence of the marine moisture in the north also moderates the temperatures there with Eureka's average August high temperature of 61 degrees contrasting with San Diego's 77 degrees.

During the rainy season from October through April, the California coast still offers excellent hiking opportunities, especially between storms. You'll find, however, that stream fords and river crossings may be more difficult or even impossible during this wet season, especially after big storms, so plan accordingly. You may also encounter beaches eroded of their sand and swamped by high tides and storm-driven waves. Like the temperatures, the amount of precipitation varies greatly from north to south. Crescent City averages 70 inches of rain annually, while San Francisco gets about 20 inches and San Diego typically only 12 inches. Expect higher precipitation where the coast is backed by mountains, like on the Lost Coast which averages around 100 inches each year. Winter temperature variations from north to south are generally less than in summer with Eureka's January average of 47 degrees not that different from San Diego's 55 degrees.

Keep in mind that the California coast typically experiences cycles of drought and flood so that averages may not mean much in a given year. Also, the powerful moderating influence of the ocean limits coastal temperatures to a relatively narrow daily and seasonal range with freezing temperatures in winter and temperatures above 90 degrees in summer uncommon. When the California Coastal Trail meanders as little as two or three miles inland, the ocean's moderating influence is lessened significantly.

Always bring layered clothing when hiking along the California coast so that you can add or subtract layers as the weather and your activity dictates. Shorts and T-shirts may be appropriate in summer, but always have enough layers along so that you won't freeze your buns if a big thick, damp gray fogbank moves in from the ocean. You'll want to add waterproof clothes and boots to the mix when hiking in winter.

## Preparing for Your Hikes

You can day hike the California Coastal Trail for a mile or two, you can hike entire sections, or you can walk the whole CCT from Oregon to Mexico. The longer your hike, the more gear you'll want to consider taking. If you're making an extended CCT trek, be sure to read *Through-Hiking the CCT* in the back of the book. Here we'll only discuss what to take if you're day hiking.

### ESSENTIALS TO TAKE ON YOUR HIKE:
· Layered clothing: T-shirt, long sleeve shirt, shorts, long pants, sweater, sweatshirt, windbreaker, rain gear
· Sunscreen
· Insect repellent
· Sunglasses
· Small first aid kit, including moleskin for blisters
· Current tide table
· Hat with a brim

### HIGHLY RECOMMENDED FOR ALL BUT THE SHORTEST HIKES:
· Water container
· Water filter or purification tablets
· Flashlight or headlamp, extra batteries

· Matches and fire starter
· Pocket knife
· Extra food
· Map and compass
· Watch

### ADDITIONAL SUGGESTIONS:
· Spare socks
· Bandanna
· Toilet paper and plastic trowel
· Binoculars
· Camera
· Field guides to wildflowers, birds, trees, seashore life, insects

# Del Norte County

**H**ERE IN CALIFORNIA'S FAR NORTH, you'll find the California Coastal Trail at its most complete. In fact, of all the fifteen coastal counties in the Golden State, only in immense Humboldt County immediately to the south, in the hiker's mecca called Marin County, and in tiny San Francisco County will you find the Coastal Trail anywhere near as complete as it is for the 56 miles along the Del Norte coast. Here you'll also find both some of the easiest and some of the most strenuous sections of the CCT.

Not only is Del Norte's Coastal Trail virtually complete, it also offers a wondrous diversity of scenery. Along the northern two-thirds of California's coast, only in Del Norte is the Coast Range absent, here replaced by the often snow clad Siskiyou Mountains. As you traverse the northernmost coastline in California, you'll walk beaches (of course), ancient vegetated dunes, rocky bluffs, marine terraces, virgin redwood forests, high prairies, and only about 10 miles of road, none of it highway and all of it scenic and lightly traveled. Of course this total depends on your finding the appropriate low tides and making two boat crossings of major rivers, but that's the nature of the California Coastal Trail. Almost half the 10 CCT miles along roads in Del Norte County follow splendid Coastal Drive, a lightly traveled back road in Redwood National Park, with another 2 or 2½ miles on Crescent City's scenic Pebble Beach Drive where most of the walking is on ample shoulders and sidewalks with stunning coastal views.

What else does Del Norte's CCT offer? In remote corners of Redwood National Park, Del Norte Redwoods State Park, and virtually unknown Tolowa Dunes State Park (formerly called Lake Earl State Park) and Lake Earl Wildlife Area, you'll have some of your best opportunities to view abundant wildlife. You'll also pass through two county parks and a state beach, plus enjoy the pleasant walk through small town Crescent City. All of these splendid places beckon hikers, walkers, nature lovers and explorers to walk the California Coastal Trail.

By the way, locals pronounce it Del Nort.

# SECTION 1
## Oregon-California Border to Yontocket, Tolowa Dunes State Park

**DISTANCE:** 7½ miles or 17⅜ miles with detour to cross Smith River (12.1 or 28 kilometers).

**OPEN TO:** Hikers, equestrians.

**SURFACE:** Beach, trail.

**ACCESS POINT:** "WELCOME TO CALIFORNIA" sign at Oregon-California border.

**HOW TO GET THERE:** Drive Highway 101 to the Oregon-California border, 21 miles north of Crescent City, 7 miles south of Brookings, Oregon.

**OTHER ACCESS:** Pelican State Beach, Kamph Memorial Park, Smith River County Park, and Ship Ashore Resort.

**DIFFICULTY:** Easy.

**ELEVATION GAIN/LOSS:** 120 feet+/80 feet-.

**CAUTIONS:** You must hire a boat to cross the Smith River. Contact Ship Ashore Resort (707)487-3141. Otherwise a 13-mile detour along roads is required.

**FURTHER INFORMATION:** Pelican State Beach, Tolowa Dunes State Park (707)464-6101, ext. 5151, Del Norte County Parks: (707)464-7230.

**FACILITIES:** None at access point. Phone .3 mile south at California State Inspection Station. Restrooms, water, phone and picnic area at Kamph Memorial Park. Picnic area at Yontocket.

**CAMPGROUNDS:** Kamph Memorial Park has a small camping area. Ship Ashore Resort has a private campground. Ruby Van Deventer County Park and Jedediah Smith State Park, a few miles upriver, and Harris Beach State Park north of Brookings also have camping. A walk-in campground is ⅝ mile south of Yontocket.

**LODGING:** Pelican Beach Motel and Ship Ashore Resort are on the route. More lodgings are in Smith River and Crescent City to the south or Brookings to the north.

Welcome to the Oregon-California border, beginning and end of the California Coastal Trail. If you're from south of here, this may seem like a vast wilderness. If you're from the north, you're probably wondering where all the cars on the highway came from. The truth lies somewhere in between.

Symbolically this section of CCT is a great beginning. Just 500 feet from a busy U.S. highway, you can look south even on a clear day and feel as if you are in a wilderness, except for a few nearby houses. The broad beach arches south to the triple cones of Hunter Rock and Prince Island offshore and Pyramid Point along your route.

What you cannot see lurking just beyond the point is the forceful mouth of the Smith River, California's largest undammed river and one of its finest. **Where CCT meets the river, you can only cross the river with a boat.** Without a boat you have two choices: retrace your steps for a pleasant day hike, or detour 13

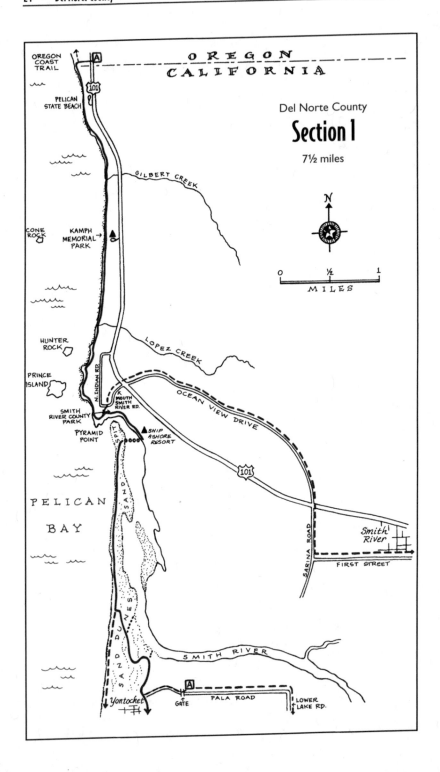

OREGON COAST TRAIL

PELICAN STATE BEACH

OREGON
CALIFORNIA

Del Norte County
**Section 1**
7½ miles

N

0    ½    1
MILES

GILBERT CREEK

CONE ROCK

KAMPH MEMORIAL PARK

HUNTER ROCK

LOPEZ CREEK

PRINCE ISLAND

N. INDIAN RD.

MOUTH SMITH RIVER RD.

OCEAN VIEW DRIVE

SMITH RIVER COUNTY PARK

PYRAMID POINT

SHIP ASHORE RESORT

SPIT

SAND

PELICAN

BAY

SARINA ROAD

Smith River

FIRST STREET

SAND DUNES

SMITH RIVER

Yontocket

GATE

PALA ROAD

LOWER LAKE RD.

miles on road shoulders to cross the river on the highway bridge and reach CCT south of the river. If you choose the detour, you'll find it described at the end of this section.

The California Coastal Trail actually begins 50 feet north of the "WELCOME TO CALIFORNIA" sign where a path heads through alder/spruce forest onto the broad sandy beach. Walk about 900 feet to the tideline where you'll have to visualize your own Oregon-California border in the sand. Turn south and follow the firm sand along the high tideline.

Pass through undeveloped Pelican State Beach around ½ mile where a road to the east leads to Highway 101. Continue down the beach as it veers southeast, drawing near the highway briefly, then turn south to ford Gilbert Creek at 1⅜ miles.

Beyond the ford the beach straightens out, passing through Kamph Memorial County Park at 2 miles where Cone Rock lies offshore. A phone, tiny camp-ground, picnic tables and restrooms stand atop the bluff to the east. CCT leaves the tiny park, continuing south along the tideline.

By 2⅜ miles the beach narrows and becomes steeper. After the ford of Lopez Creek around 2⅞ miles, the beach narrows again. You pass the twin cones of Hunter Rock offshore. Follow the beach out to a rocky point at 3⅜ miles, then continue south with Prince Island offshore. As you pass the island, the beach swings southeast toward Pyramid Point past many offshore rocks.

When you reach Pyramid Point at 3¾ miles, turn east just before the sandy beach ends, climbing along the west face of a rock outcrop and crossing the bluff on a grassy trail around the ocean side of a private residence to overlook the mouth of the river. Before 3⅞ miles a rough trail descends to the pebble beach of Smith River County Park, a good turnaround point for day hikers not planning to cross the river. If you have a boat lined up for the crossing, follow the north bank of the river east and southeast to Ship Ashore Resort then to the boat dock at 4⅜ miles. If you can't arrange a boat, see **Alternate Route A**.

You want the boat to drop you on the sand spit just south of the river mouth. Walk to the west side of the spit and follow the Pacific shore south about 1½ miles, 5⅞ miles from the border if the boat dropped you near the river mouth. Look east toward the dunes for a bright orange triangle. It marks the CCT route south where it enters the dunes of Tolowa Dunes State Park. Walk to the triangle and take the path into the dunes (Alternate Route B stays on the beach). Follow the sandy path east and south. Stay to the right at a trail junction (the left fork heads to the Smith River). Follow the path into dunes of increasing size. By 7 miles a high, wooded dune is to your west, and your trail has become a double track. Continue south to the junction where the double track from Pala Road enters from the left. Turn right and walk uphill past old apple trees. At 7½ miles you reach the top of the hill, site of the Tolowa village Yontocket where a Tolowa cemetery is on your left.

**ALTERNATE ROUTES:** If you haven't arranged a boat shuttle across the Smith River, you need to take CCT Alternate Route A which follows roads on this 13-mile detour. Head northeast to Highway 101, then cautiously cross the highway and walk the shoulder of Ocean View Drive southeast to Sarina Road. Cross the highway and

# The California Coastal Trail Whole Hike
## of 1996

On National Trails Day, June 1, 1996, six hikers rendezvoused at the Oregon-California border to begin a hike of nearly 1200 miles along the spectacular, diverse California coast to Mexico. When they completed the trek three months and three weeks later, this remarkable journey became the first group hike of the entire California Coastal Trail. Hundreds of coast lovers joined the six "Whole Hikers" for anywhere from a few miles up to half the CCT. They included Coastwalk organizers, trail activists, housewives, mothers, students, reporters and four published authors. Donald Murphy, then theDirector of California State Parks, hiked the first eight days. That first day more than three dozen supporters came to cheer them on.

Of the six who planned to do the Whole Hike, remarkably all six succeeded*. These four women and two men ranged from 44 to 68 years of age, came from all over California and included one Oregonian. Some of them were lifelong hikers. One even described herself as "Not a hiker at all," but that would change by the trip's end. In fact the Whole Hike was a life changing journey for virtually everyone involved, and this marathon walk would forever alter the public perception of the California Coastal Trail. This book grew directly from that Whole Hike.

Without numerous support people both on and off the trek, the Whole Hikers never would have made it. Most notably the Ford Motor Company provided a grant and two support vans. Volunteer drivers helped shop and cook, meeting the weary hikers at the end of each day to shuttle them to campground, hostel or community center for the night. One van pulled a trailer with the heavy gear, so hikers could carry only a daypack.

The group walked 1156 miles in the 112-day trek along California's varied shore. They averaged a bruising 12.4 miles a day, not counting 16 rest days. Twice the group covered 20 miles in a day, the longest being 21 miles from Surf to Jalama Beach on the Santa Barbara coast, but the hardest being the 20-mile day from Palomarin at Point Reyes National Seashore up, down and around the rugged Marin Headlands to the Golden Gate Hostel overlooking San Francisco and the Golden Gate Bridge. Their brisk pace covered 15 miles or more on a dozen days.

The most frightening experience? Chest high waves swamped the hikers at a low-tide-only point near remote Cape Mendocino, then the incoming tide trapped them for four hours in a tiny cove. There the drenched, demoralized hikers huddled by a smoky fire and wondered if their luck had run out barely a tenth of the way through their ambitious trek. But the group escaped to become closer and more determined.

Highlights? Too many to mention, but they included backpacking the Lost Coast through southern Humboldt and northern Mendocino counties, crossing the Golden Gate Bridge into San Francisco, rounding Point Conception, and completing the thousandth mile at Santa Monica in Los Angeles County. But the biggest thrill of all was walking up to the Mexico border on the 112th day, each of the Whole Hikers proudly knowing that she/he had completed the Journey of a Lifetime, walking the entire California Coastal Trail.

The event won the Trails for Tomorrow Award from the American Hiking Society, one of ten given, and the Trail Merit Award from the California Trails Conference.

---

*One hiker completed the final 300 miles on his own.

take Sarina Road south ½ mile, then turn east and follow First Street into the town of Smith River. When First Street ends at Fred Haight Drive, take the latter south until it returns to Highway 101. Follow the highway south across the river, then turn right onto Lake Earl Drive. Go west to Bailey Road, turn right and head north briefly, then head west on Moseley Road to its end. Turn right and follow Lower Lake Road north to Pala Road, then follow Pala Road west to the gate at Tolowa Dunes State Park boundary. From there it is ½ mile to Yontocket, about 3 miles north to the Smith River mouth. **Alternate Route B** stays on the beach south of the Smith River all the way along the western edge of Tolowa Dunes State Park. It meets the end of Kellogg Road about 5 miles from the mouth of Smith River.

**SUGGESTED ROUND TRIPS & LOOPS:** The 3¾ miles of beach between the border and Pyramid Point offer a pleasant walk. From Yontocket north to the river mouth offers another pleasant 3 miles, especially the 1⅝ miles through the dunes.

## SECTION 2
## Yontocket, Tolowa Dunes State Park, to Kellogg Beach

**DISTANCE:** 3⅜ miles (5.4 kilometers).

**OPEN TO:** Hikers, equestrians. Dirt roads south of Yontocket open to mountain bikes.

**SURFACE:** Dirt roads, paved road.

**ACCESS POINT:** Yontocket Trailhead.

**HOW TO GET THERE:** Turn west off Highway 101 onto Elk Valley Cross Road .6 mile north of the Highway 199 interchange north of Crescent City. Turn right on Lake Earl Drive in .9 mile. At 2.9 miles from Highway 101, turn left on Lower Lake Road and drive to its end, then go left on Pala Road for one mile to the trailhead at a white gate.

**DIFFICULTY:** Easy.

**ELEVATION GAIN/LOSS:** 200 feet+/180 feet-.

**CAUTIONS:** Portions of trail may be wet in winter and spring.

**FURTHER INFORMATION:** Tolowa Dunes State Park 464-6101, ext. 5151, Lake Earl Wildlife Area (707)464-2523.

**FACILITIES:** None at access point. Yontocket has a picnic table. Near Kellogg Road Trailhead are Environmental Camps with tables and chemical toilets.

**CAMPGROUNDS:** Six pleasant Environmental (walk-in) Camps are located just east of Kellogg Road Trailhead. You must call first (ext. 5151). A Hike/Bike/Horse Camp ⅝ mile south of Yontocket has tables, toilets, non-potable water, a fireplace and corral. Car camping available at Jedediah Smith Redwoods State Park east of Highway 101.

**LODGING:** Many motels in Crescent City.

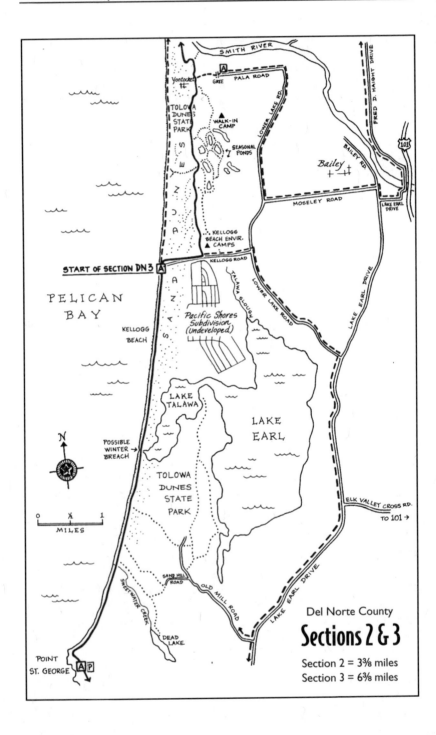

SMITH RIVER

FRED D. HAIGHT DRIVE

Yontocket

GATE  PALA ROAD

TOLOWA DUNES STATE PARK

▲ WALK-IN CAMP

LOWER LAKE RD.

SEASONAL PONDS

BAILEY RD

*Bailey*

MOSELEY ROAD

LAKE EARL DRIVE

101

▲ KELLOGG BEACH ENVIR. CAMPS

START OF SECTION DN3 Ⓐ

KELLOGG ROAD

PELICAN BAY

KELLOGG BEACH

TALAWA SLOUGH

LOWER LAKE ROAD

*Pacific Shores Subdivision (Undeveloped)*

LAKE TALAWA

LAKE EARL

N

POSSIBLE WINTER → BREACH

TOLOWA DUNES STATE PARK

ELK VALLEY CROSS RD.

TO 101 →

0 ½ 1
MILES

SAND HILL ROAD

OLD MILL ROAD

SWEETWATER CREEK

LAKE EARL DRIVE

Del Norte County

# Sections 2 & 3

Section 2 = 3⅜ miles
Section 3 = 6⅝ miles

DEAD LAKE

POINT ST. GEORGE  ⒶP

This hike explores an extensive system of ancient dunes deposited by the Smith River as it carved the Siskiyou Mountains. The vegetated dune complex has evolved into many different ecological communities supporting a vast array of plants and animals, with 250 bird species alone. Lake Earl and Lake Talawa, freshwater lagoons totaling more than 2000 acres, support a striking diversity of fish and aquatic vegetation. You'll find all this and more within the 10,000 acres of Tolowa Dunes State Park and Lake Earl Wildlife Area where up to half the acreage may be covered with water in the wet season. If you camp here in late spring/early summer, be prepared for the thriving mosquito population.

The native Tolowa people, who have lived in this area for at least 2300 years, consider the vegetated dunes around Yontocket to be the center of the world, the place where the First People created our world.

From Yontocket Trailhead, walk west on the gravel road behind the white gate for almost ½ mile to an intersection. The grassy double track running north-south is CCT. (To reach the Smith River mouth, turn right and head north between dunes for less than ¼ mile to another junction, then go left on the path west through the dunes, coming to the beach at 1⅛ miles. Turn right and walk the beach about 2 miles to the river mouth.)

Turn left on CCT and climb the short hill to the Yontocket Cemetery where a picnic table sits beside a trail junction. (The left fork leads ⅝ mile to a hike/bike/horse camp.) Take the right fork and descend into a grassy valley, then climb over a wooded ridge into another grassy swale. Ascend along a mossy slope, then follow a ridgetop where Sitka spruce grow.

At ½ mile from Yontocket your gravel road dips into a valley where common juniper grow between wooded dune ridges. Follow the valley to a junction at ⅞ mile where a side trail on the right heads through dune and marsh to reach the beach in ½ mile. CCT continues south past a trail on the left, ascending gently along the crest of a dune offering views of the coast to the west and a large pond to the east. Leave the dune crest at 1⅛ miles to drop through the dunes and over another sandy ridge.

Around 1⅜ miles as the gravel track veers left (it leads to Environmental Camps), the Coastal Trail veers right onto a grassy double track that descends south into a wooded valley. Climb through the forest to top a sandy ridge, then drop through grasslands with clumps of elderberry and huckleberry around 1⅝ miles. Contour past a stand of wind-shaped shore pines, then dip through a low area around 2 miles that may be wet in winter and spring. Continue through the grasslands, passing windswept dunes on your left around 2⅜ miles. Soon two side trails fork left toward the nearby camps. CCT stays on the double track until the parking area at 2⅝ miles.

CCT follows the parking loop to its end at Kellogg Road at 2¾ miles. Turn right and follow CCT west along the pavement to the end of Kellogg Road at 3⅜ miles where the beach stretches for miles up and down the coast. Del Norte Section 3 is on the left. The **Alternate Route**, which ends here, is on the right.

ALTERNATE ROUTE: If you prefer beach walking to exploring the mysterious vegetated dunes to the east, one long beach stretches from the south side of the Smith River mouth all the way to the end of Kellogg Road at 5¼ miles. In fact it might be easy to miss Kellogg Road since the beach continues all the way to Point St. George, a total distance of 10½ miles with a possible winter breach of the barrier beach at the mouth of Lake Talawa.

**SUGGESTED ROUND TRIPS & LOOPS:** If you're day hiking, you can loop back to Yontocket by several routes. Any of the trails east of CCT will lead to the network of trails in the eastern edge of the vegetated dunes where several seasonal ponds offer surprises. By heading north along the beach, you can turn east on either of two trails. The first, 1½ miles north of the end of Kellogg Road, may be wet in winter and spring. The second at 3 miles leads through the dunes, returning to CCT north of Yontocket.

## The Native Californians and the Center of the World

Before contact with white civilization, the abundant natural resources of California supported one of the highest population densities in North America. Most estimates place the California native population around 250,000, some argue two or three times that, about 10% of the native U.S. population. Like today's pattern, the highest concentration of people lived on or near the coast.

California in 1800 supported about 110 major tribes or language groups, with twenty-eight of those spread along the coast. Many other tribes made regular sojourns to the coast to harvest the ocean's bounty and to trade and visit with the residents. Of the twenty-eight coastal nations, Volume One traverses the territories of sixteen, while Volume Two visits a dozen.

We don't have space to discuss all these diverse cultures, so we recommend that you seek out the rich and varied literature on California's Native Americans. But let's take a quick overview.

Forget your stereotypes of Native Americans. No California natives lived in tipis. Rather they inhabited a diverse array of dwellings. None rode horses before white contact. California natives were among the most peace loving people on earth, though ritual war did occur. Elders of most tribes spoke several neighboring languages in response to the diverse tribal landscape.

Tribes near and far conducted trade along well established trails usually open to all. Intertribal gatherings were important social events in which the whole village interacted with visitors, feasting, dancing, storytelling and game-playing, often over several days.

The Tolowa people of Del Norte County provide a worthy example of one tribe and the tragedy they suffered upon white contact. The Tolowa nation inhabited eight or ten large villages of 100 to 300 people each, most of them on or near the coast between Smith River and Nickel Creek. Each village was its own tribe, sharing much language and culture with other Tolowa tribes.

The Tolowa and their neighbors considered the Tolowa village of Yontakit to be the center of the world. Every year Yurok from the south and Chetco and Tututnu from the north journeyed, as did other Tolowa villages, to Yontakit for a ten-day world renewal ceremony, believed essential for continuing the cycle of life.

At such a ceremony in 1853, white vigilantes from newly settled gold and timber towns nearby launched a sneak attack during the height of the ceremony. They set Yontakit village on fire and killed hundreds of residents. It was among the earliest and most violent incidents of unprovoked genocide marring the history of California.

# SECTION 3
# Kellogg Beach to Point St. George

**DISTANCE:** 6⅜ miles (10.3 kilometers).

**OPEN TO:** Hikers, equestrians.

**SURFACE:** Beach, short trail segment at south end.

**ACCESS POINT:** Kellogg Beach at end of Kellogg Road.

**HOW TO GET THERE:** Turn west off Highway 101 onto Elk Valley Cross Road .6 mile north of Highway 199 interchange. Turn right on Lake Earl Drive in .9 mile. At 2.9 miles from Highway 101, turn left on Lower Lake Road. At 5.5 miles go left on Kellogg Road and drive to its end, 6.9 miles from Highway 101.

**OTHER ACCESS:** Center portion south of Lake Talawa can be reached by three state park trails off Sand Hill Road.

**DIFFICULTY:** Easy.

**ELEVATION GAIN/LOSS:** 50 feet+.

**CAUTIONS:** In winter and spring this route may be impassable when Lake Talawa breaches the barrier beach, creating an impassable surge channel. In that case see Alternate Route. Watch for off-road vehicles on beach.

**FURTHER INFORMATION:** Kellogg Beach County Park (707)464-7230, Tolowa Dunes State Park 464-6101, ext. 5151, Lake Earl Wildlife Area (707)464-2523.

**FACILITIES:** None.

**CAMPGROUNDS:** Six Environmental Camps (short walk in) in state park north of Kellogg Road. You must call extension 5151 to make arrangements. Car camping at Keller County Park, Highway 101 and Elk Valley Cross Road, or at Jedediah Smith State Park.

**LODGING:** Many motels in Crescent City.

**MAP:** See page 28.

Nearly 12 miles of continuous beach form the shore of Pelican Bay from the Smith River mouth on the north to Point St. George on the south. Kellogg Road provides hikers access to the middle of this long, gently curving strand. Kellogg Road also allows off-road vehicles to reach the beach, but most of the year you won't see many ORVs on this CCT section. They prefer to drive north toward the Smith River. A more pressing worry is whether the Lake Talawa surge channel 3 miles down the beach is flowing when you visit. If it is, you will not be able to cross it, so you might call ahead to find out.

From the end of Kellogg Road, walk the long, virtually straight beach south-southwest. Your hike parallels a line of sand dunes along the top of the beach. On the clearest days, you'll see the often snow clad high peaks of the Siskiyou Mountains to the east. As you walk the tideline along this southern end of Pelican Bay, watch the surf for sneaker waves.

By 2½ miles the dunes east of the beach become lower, perhaps allowing a look at nearby Lake Talawa and Lake Earl to the east. You soon may notice several paths leading into the nearby Pacific Shores Subdivision, a maze of roads where development was halted by the Coastal Commission.

Around 3 miles you reach the low channel at the mouth of Lake Talawa which provides a seasonal outlet and more often a high-tide inlet for the brackish lake. If the surge channel has opened up allowing the lake to empty into the Pacific, you will need to turn back and take the **Alternate Route**.

Assuming you can cross the barrier beach at Lake Talawa's mouth, continue south along the tideline, soon entering Tolowa Dunes State Park. Several trails from Old Mill and Sand Hill roads end at the beach between 3¾ and 4⅝ miles, the last of which is the trail from Dead Lake. Just beyond Dead Lake Trail you come to a ford of Sweetwater Creek, an easy crossing except in winter. Continue along the sandy shoreline, crossing another seasonal creek around 5⅝ miles.

After the creek, the beach narrows as Point St. George rises ahead. You are soon walking a narrow beach at the base of vegetation-covered sandstone bluffs. Round the northern tip of Point St. George at 6¼ miles, promptly meeting a broad rocky path by which CCT ascends onto the grassy bluff of the point where wildflowers thrive in the moist habitat. As you climb onto the headland, the path quickly turns southeast, coming to the parking lot atop Point St. George at the end of Radio Road at 6⅜ miles.

**ALTERNATE ROUTE:** When Lake Talawa breaches the barrier beach and closes through access for CCT, the best route to follow is east on Kellogg Road to its end, then south on Lower Lake Road to Lake Earl Drive. Follow the latter south toward town. When you get to Old Mill Road around 8 miles, you have two choices. 1) Turn right and follow Old Mill Road to Sand Hill Road to its end, then follow one of two trails west and northwest to return to CCT south of Lake Talawa. 2) Continue south as Lake Earl Drive becomes Northcrest Drive, which ends at Highway 101, then follow the highway south to Washington Blvd. and turn right, following Washington until it rejoins CCT at Pebble Beach Drive in Del Norte Section 4.

**SUGGESTED ROUND TRIPS & LOOPS:** Walk Kellogg Beach from either the north or south access. To add variety, loop east through Tolowa Dunes State Park on one of the three side trails, returning to the beach by a different trail.

## SECTION 4
# Point St. George to Battery Point

DISTANCE: 4⅜ miles (7 kilometers).

OPEN TO: Hikers, road portions open to bicyclists.

SURFACE: Beach, city streets, paved trails.

ACCESS POINT: Point St. George.

HOW TO GET THERE: From the north end of Crescent City, take Washington Blvd. west from Highway 101. After the intersection with Pebble Beach Drive around 1.8 miles, Washington becomes Radio Road, which you follow to its end at 3 miles.

OTHER ACCESS: Anywhere along the route.

DIFFICULTY: Easy.

ELEVATION GAIN/LOSS: 110 feet+/130 feet-.

CAUTIONS: Some of the beaches along this section are impassable at medium to high tide.

FURTHER INFORMATION: Crescent City Public Works Department: (707)464-9506.

FACILITIES: None at access point. Restrooms, water, phone, picnic areas along route and at south end.

CAMPGROUNDS: Shoreline Campground in heart of town on Del Norte Section 5.

LODGING: Many motels in Crescent City.

This is the northernmost "city walk" along the California Coastal Trail. While Crescent City, population 4400, is tiny compared to the cities that CCT passes through farther south, in this vast wild land along California's north coast, the town may be a welcome respite of civilization for most hikers. Through-hikers on CCT will not encounter another true city until Eureka about 100 miles south, and that metropolis is only on CCT's Alternate Route.

This section of CCT, thanks to its virtually unlimited access, breaks nicely into smaller portions: the dramatic headlands of Point St. George, the pleasant beach/shoreline walk west of town, and the town/waterfront walk from Preston Island to Battery Point.

From the Point St. George parking lot at the end of Radio Road, CCT follows the road shoulder southeast over a dramatic unspoiled headland with views of near and far shores. Where the road turns southeast at ⅝ mile, take the path that climbs south over the grassy bluff. At ¾ mile you reach the top of the bluff where you look south to towering Castle Rock, an important seabird rookery, and west to St. George Reef Lighthouse seven miles out to sea. Descend south toward Castle Rock.

By ⅞ mile, about 200 feet before the end of the southernmost point, veer left on a single track trail descending east-southeast through grasslands to a rocky beach before one mile. Follow the beach northeast about ⅛ mile, observing the

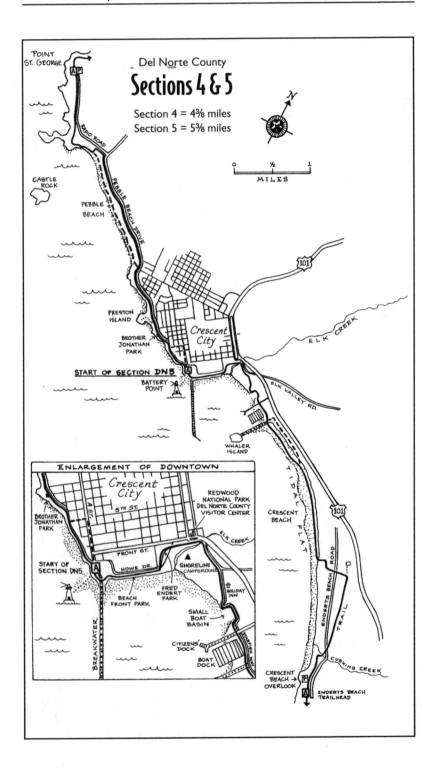

Del Norte County
# Sections 4 & 5

Section 4 = 4⅝ miles
Section 5 = 5⅝ miles

ENLARGEMENT OF DOWNTOWN

coast ahead. The beach narrows as it turns east then southeast. At a moderate to low tide you can continue southeast along the sometimes sandy, sometimes rocky Pebble Beach. When the tide is high you'll need to walk along Pebble Beach Drive which follows the blufftop above the beach. If you cannot walk the beach beyond 1⅛ miles, follow a faint path north just before a gully to return to Radio Road.

Our description assumes a high tide and follows Pebble Beach Drive, but at lower tides you can follow the beach. Follow Radio Road east to the Washington Blvd./Pebble Beach Drive intersection around 1⅜ miles, then turn right and walk the generally broad shoulder of Pebble Beach Drive. At a turnout at 1¾ miles a path offers the first chance to return to the beach. Beyond 2⅛ miles the beach is so narrow you can only walk it at low tide. As you continue along the now residential street, three stairways provide access between beach and bluff. They are located at 2½, 2⅞ and 3⅞ miles along your route.

Before Preston Island at 3½ miles, the rocky shore lacks any beach, forcing you onto the bluff where a pleasant paved path provides shoreline views and good footing out of the traffic. At Preston Island, which is actually a peninsula, a paved road serves as a short side trail to the pebble beach and tidepool area where there are picnic tables.

CCT continues along Pebble Beach Drive to Brother Jonathan Park at 3⅝

## California Lighthouses

CALIFORNIA'S RUGGED 1200-MILE COASTLINE has long been renowned for the fury of its hazardous waters and the deception of its offshore reefs and rocks. Only after California entered the United States in 1850 was any effort made to provide navigational aids. In 1854 Alcatraz Island Lighthouse in San Francisco Bay became the Golden State's first, soon followed by Fort Point inside the Golden Gate, Farallon Island 25 miles outside the Gate, and Point Loma near San Diego, four of the original eight west coast lighthouses. By 1900 48 lighthouses guided ships along the California shore.

Today 32 of these still stand, with 25 operational. The California Coastal Trail passes by or at least comes within view of most of them. In San Mateo County, CCT passes two lighthouses converted to hostels where you can spend the night.

One of the most remarkable lights was the St. George Reef Lighthouse, visible on clear days from most of the first 17 miles of the Coastal Trail. Seven miles offshore from Point St. George and guarding the western tip of a dangerous reef, the Light-

house Service built it in response to the disastrous wreck of the Brother Jonathan at Crescent City in 1865. California's northernmost lighthouse took ten years to build and was the most expensive in the state. Rising 150 feet from a treacherous seaswept rock, the St. George Light, the tallest on the west coast, was closed by the Coast Guard in 1975. Local citizens have since struggled to preserve the historic if precarious structure.

At the end of Del Norte Section 4, almost in the heart of Crescent City, the 1856 Crescent City Lighthouse at Battery Point lies only ⅛ mile off the Coastal Trail, reached by a walkway that's only passable at low to medium tides. When you can, walk out to the tidal island of Battery Point for a close look at the historic structure. Picnic tables there offer grand views of coast, harbor and town, but the real treat comes when the lighthouse, now a museum, opens for tours, Wednesday through Sunday, 10 to 4, tides permitting. Call (707)464-3089 to confirm hours.

miles. The small park memorializes the 213 people who lost their lives in the 1865 shipwreck of the *Brother Jonathan* off Point St. George. Restrooms are available and a picnic table sits on the point overlooking the shore. Follow Pebble Beach Drive east for its final two blocks, then walk Taylor Street to the end of Fifth Street where you can return to beach via a stairway unless it's high tide. In that case you'd need to follow Fifth Street to A Street, then turn right and walk A Street to its end at Battery Point at 4⅜ miles.

At Battery Point a side trail passable only at low tide leads ⅛ mile out to the 1856 Crescent City Lighthouse on a spectacular site on the rocky point. Tours are available in season and you can use the picnic tables anytime you can reach them, but don't get stranded by a rising tide.

**ALTERNATE ROUTE:** At low to medium tide you can follow the beach rather than Pebble Beach Drive for much of this section.

**SUGGESTED ROUND TRIPS & LOOPS:** You can take short to medium walks here. We recommend the trail at ⅝ mile that leads out onto the dramatic headland and down to the beach, the short side trips to Preston Island and Battery Point, or a brisk walk along the road shoulder and/or down one of the stairways and along the beach.

> **HOW TO IMPROVE CCT HERE:** Acquire more of Point St. George for public access. The state has been negotiating with the owners about a potential purchase.

# SECTION 5
# Battery Point to Enderts Beach Trailhead, Redwood National Park

**DISTANCE:** 5⅜ miles (8.6 kilometers).

**OPEN TO:** Hikers, town portions open to bicyclists, Crescent Beach open to equestrians.

**SURFACE:** Paved trail, city streets and parking lots, dirt trail, beach.

**ACCESS POINT:** Battery Point Overlook.

**HOW TO GET THERE:** From Highway 101 in Crescent City, turn west on Front Street, then turn left on A Street and drive to its end.

**OTHER ACCESS:** Various places along the Crescent City waterfront.

**DIFFICULTY:** Easy.

**ELEVATION GAIN/LOSS:** 220 feet+/ 20 feet-.

**CAUTIONS:** The north end of Crescent Beach may be impassable at high tide.

**FURTHER INFORMATION:** Redwood National and State Parks (707)464-6101.

**FACILITIES:** Restrooms and picnic area at Access Point. Grocery store, picnic tables, restrooms and more along the way.

**CAMPGROUNDS:** Shoreline Campground lies in the heart of town along the route. Walk-in primitive campground at Nickel Creek is ½ mile south of south end. You can car camp at nearby Jedediah Smith and Del Norte Coast Redwood State Parks.

**LODGING:** Many motels in town.

**MAP:** See page 34.

The city walk through Crescent City continues for the first two miles of this section, the real beauty here being that you walk right past the heart of downtown without getting bogged down in it. If you choose to leave CCT to shop or have a meal out or a capuccino, or even to check into the Holiday Inn for a night of R&R, it's all there in the first mile. The second mile explores the marine heart of town with seafood cafes, fishing boats and canneries along the route. Suddenly when you get to Crescent Beach, the city rapidly falls away and you approach the rugged wilderness coast of Redwood National Park.

The CCT follows the waterfront northeast over the breakwater. (A side trail follows the breakwater ¾ mile for a whale's eye view of town and sometimes a close-up look at migrating whales.) Descend the paved path from the breakwater to walk past the sewage treatment plant, quickly coming to Howe Drive at ⅛ mile.

A paved bike path parallels the length of Howe Drive on the bay side. Follow that path through Fred Endert Park, leaving the coast to follow Elk Creek upstream. The path passes the city indoor swimming pool at ½ mile. Continue along the creek until ⅝ mile where the Redwood National Park Information Center is across Front Street. Follow the paved service road upstream to a bridge across the creek beside Highway 101 at ¾ mile.

After you cross the bridge, the route of CCT becomes vague and tricky to follow. Basically you want to follow the waterfront southeast through the marina district. Beyond the Elk Creek bridge, veer right on a dirt trail and pass the entrance to Shoreline RV Park and Campground. Jog northeast briefly then follow a paved road east. Before one mile Sunset House Antiques is on your right. Turn right and walk along the edge of the parking lot, then walk southeast on a gravel track behind the Holiday Inn. Continue on a grassy track, following it as it turns southwest toward the waterfront.

You reach the waterfront at 1⅛ miles. Turn southeast and walk to the Small Boat Basin. Follow its perimeter east past a restroom, then south and west through the parking lot to 1½ miles. Turn left and walk through the vehicle entrance to the boat basin. The paved street straight ahead is called Starfish Way. Follow it past a couple of seafood restaurants and another RV park. When Starfish Way ends at 1¾ miles, turn right on the road signed "Marina." In 250 feet you have easy access to Crescent Beach on your left, stretching southeast. Another restroom is just beyond. (Another side trail heads seaward along the southern breakwater out to Whaler Island, a 1- to 1½-mile round trip.) At high tide you may have to veer east along the highway briefly before you are able to walk out onto the beach. But at medium to low tide, just scramble down the rocks of the breakwater and walk along the broad tidal flat of Crescent Beach.

CCT follows the beach for nearly 2 miles. (Crescent Beach continues south for about one mile beyond that point. You can use it as an alternate route, but it is

# Watch Out for That Wave!

The waves we see dashing against the coast start hundreds of miles offshore. As winds blow across the ocean's surface, they create waves of various sizes. A wave's size depends on wind velocity, duration and the distance the wind blows across the open ocean.

Waves break, showing a churning crest of foam along their leading edge when they become oversteep in deep water or when they enter shallow water. Waves break when they reach a water depth around 125% of their height. So we see endless sets of breakers as we explore the shore, each wave different than the wave preceding it, surf varying greatly from one day to the next, sometimes even within a day.

"Never turn your back on the ocean" is a cardinal rule of the coast because each wave can be so different from the last. The constant attack of waves upon the shore fascinates us with its constant and ever changing motion, but it also holds great danger. This danger increases the closer you get to the water and the larger the waves.

Two kinds of waves hold particular danger, sleeper waves and tsunamis. Sleeper waves, also known as rogue or killer waves, can occur any time although they're infrequent and unpredictable. They are most common on days of particularly big surf, when storms are active far at sea or in winter, but you never know when they'll strike. As the nickname killer implies, they present grave danger, sometimes being twice the size of the prevailing surf. They strike with powerful force, running far up the beach.

Large sleeper waves can sweep shoreline visitors into the sea. These rogues have claimed the lives of many an unwary seaside visitor. **When you walk the coast, you must be aware that sleeper waves can strike at any time.** Always be ready to retreat up the beach at the first hint of oversize waves. If you get swamped, be ready to abandon your gear or backpack. It's better to lose your possessions than your life.

The second dangerous wave, the tsunami or tidal wave, results from earthquakes, slides or volcanic eruptions at sea. Tsunamis offer extreme and widespread danger. You cannot outrun a tsunami. If you see one from the beach it's probably too late. Unlike sleeper waves, tsunamis are predicted by seismographic readings. Radio and TV stations broadcast tsunami warnings whenever seismological activity indicates they might occur. If you hear such a warning, get away from the coast.

Tsunamis 75 feet high have been seen. Tsunamis travel 400 miles an hour and are hardly visible on the open ocean. As they approach shore they rise up suddenly. The shallow depth of California 's continental shelf lessens the chance of 75-foot-high tsunamis.

However, smaller tsunamis can cause serious damage. The April 1964 Alaska quake launched tsunamis right at Crescent City. A series of 12-foot waves smashed ashore, running a third of a mile inland, destroying 29 blocks of the business district and causing $27 million in damage. Crescent City was rebuilt, its harbor today protected by 1600 25-ton concrete tetrapods shaped like children's jacks. While Crescent City is probably safe from tsunamis now, be aware of the dangers of oversize waves wherever you explore California's outer coast.

*The CCT turns wild as it approaches Enderts Beach.*

difficult to find the volunteer trail that climbs the bluff to join the main route.) Look for the trail east through the vegetation above the beach at 3⅜ miles. Follow the path past the Crescent Beach Picnic Area and restrooms and east across Enderts Beach Road, climbing to a terrace 80 feet above sea level where the path ends at a grassy trail running north-south.

Turn south and follow the CCT as it contours along the marine terrace. It descends to cross the paved road again at 4¾ miles. The path continues south on the west side of the road, dropping to cross a bridge across Cushing Creek in a beautiful wooded spot. A picnic table overlooks the verdant scene. The path climbs from the creek to parallel the paved road. At the top of the hill at 5⅜ miles you come to Crescent Beach Overlook, which has a deck from which you can survey the coast you just walked. Picnic tables are nearby. Del Norte Section 6 starts 300 feet south where Enderts Beach Road ends.

SUGGESTED ROUND TRIPS & LOOPS: From the Crescent Beach Picnic Area, you have a pleasant walk north or south along CCT. If you go north, you can stop for a seafood lunch.

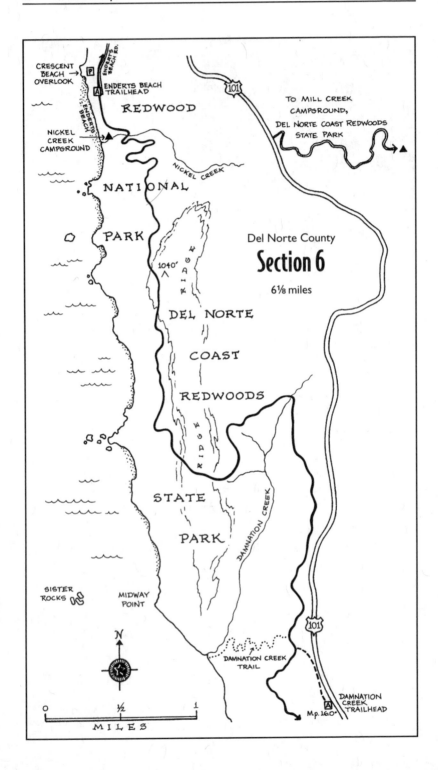

CRESCENT BEACH OVERLOOK

ENDERTS BEACH RD.

ENDERTS BEACH TRAILHEAD

REDWOOD

101

TO MILL CREEK CAMPGROUND, DEL NORTE COAST REDWOODS STATE PARK

NICKEL CREEK CAMPGROUND

ENDERTS BEACH

NICKEL CREEK

NATIONAL

PARK

1040'

RIDGE

Del Norte County

# Section 6

6⅛ miles

DEL NORTE

COAST

REDWOODS

RIDGE

STATE

PARK

DAMNATION CREEK

SISTER ROCKS

MIDWAY POINT

N

101

DAMNATION CREEK TRAIL

M.p. 16.0

DAMNATION CREEK TRAILHEAD

0    ½    1

MILES

## SECTION 6
# Enderts Beach Trailhead to Damnation Creek Trail, Redwood National Park

DISTANCE: 6⅛ miles (CCT) or 6¾ miles to Damnation Creek Trailhead (9.9 or 10.9 kilometers).

OPEN TO: Hikers, bicyclists.

SURFACE: Dirt trail, old road with some pavement.

ACCESS POINT: Enderts Beach Trailhead.

HOW TO GET THERE: Turn west off Highway 101 onto Enderts Beach Road 2 miles south of Crescent City. Drive 2.3 miles to end of road.

DIFFICULTY: Strenuous.

ELEVATION GAIN/LOSS: CCT Section, one way: 1330 feet+/ 560 feet-. To Damnation Creek Trailhead: add 140 feet+/40 feet-.

CAUTIONS: Trail beyond Nickel Creek is extremely steep.

FURTHER INFORMATION: Redwood National and State Parks (707)464-6101, ext. 5064.

FACILITIES: Chemical toilets at Nickel Creek.

CAMPGROUNDS: Nickel Creek Camp is a primitive trail camp ½ mile from start of section. Del Norte Coast Redwoods State Park has car camping east of Highway 101 not far south.

HOSTEL: DeMartin Redwood Hostel (707)482-8265 is near end of Del Norte Section 7.

LODGING: Motels in Crescent City.

The California Coastal Trail does its first serious climbing on this section, rising above a precipitous, impassable shoreline. Here CCT mostly follows the original Redwood Highway route over a steep grade offering sweeping views of the Del Norte coast. Part of the old road is on the National Register of Historic Places. What's remarkable about this section is its uncompromised wildness, even though you will see some of the old pavement.

Descend south along the now grassy old highway with views along the rugged shore. CCT descends through dense coastal scrub into Nickel Creek Canyon. Around ⅜ mile the side trail to the campground and Enderts Beach heads west. On the left, Creekside Trail heads east almost ¼ mile to a bench in a pretty spot. After CCT crosses the creek, you leave the old highway and begin a steep climb, gaining 900 feet in the next 1¼ miles.

CCT turns away from the canyon at ⅝ mile, ascending steeply through three long switchbacks. Rejoin the old highway at 1¼ miles, climbing south along a steep-sided ridgetop. Both the ridge and the worst of the ascent end beyond 1½ miles. Dip and rise gently to a second summit at 1⅞ miles where you might see

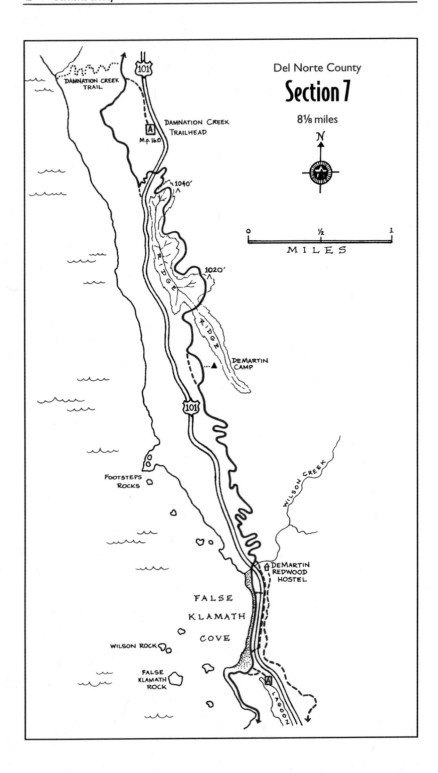

Del Norte County
# Section 7
8⅛ miles

N

0 ½ 1
M I L E S

DAMNATION CREEK TRAIL

101

DAMNATION CREEK TRAILHEAD

M.p. 16.0

1040'

RIDGE

1020'

RIDGE

DEMARTIN CAMP

101

FOOTSTEPS ROCKS

WILSON CREEK

DEMARTIN REDWOOD HOSTEL

FALSE KLAMATH COVE

WILSON ROCK

FALSE KLAMATH ROCK

LAGOON

the rugged coast far below.

A steady descent brings you into Del Norte Coast Redwoods State Park around 2⅛ miles where stately virgin redwoods line the route. Ascend gradually from 2½ miles, encountering fragments of the old highway pavement. Beyond 2⅞ miles a clear day offers a panoramic view north to Lake Earl.

CCT turns east toward the headwaters of Damnation Creek. Climb gradually into Anson Grove where redwood, fir and Sitka spruce grow ten feet in diameter. Contour then descend gently through primeval forest in Damnation Creek's headwaters. At the creek's main fork at 4½ miles, the trail jogs left across a sturdy bridge in a lush, beautiful spot.

Gentle ascents alternate with level stretches on the old road, while all around you the virgin forest remains a most inspiring sight. Pass a 14-foot-diameter redwood before 5¼ miles as the roar of traffic wafts through the forest.

After a short ascent, CCT meets the Damnation Creek Trail at 6⅛ miles. Here you have several choices. If you have time for the steep but beautiful Damnation Creek Trail, it descends 1½ miles from here to a wildflower-rich blufftop in a spectacular spot at the mouth of the creek. If you are day hiking, you can return the way you came, or, if you left a shuttle vehicle at the south end access, go 50 feet and turn left to climb the hill that leads ⅝ mile to Highway 101 at the Damnation Creek Trailhead. If you're continuing south on CCT today, see Del Norte Section 7 which continues south along the old roadbed from the Damnation Trail junction.

SUGGESTED ROUND TRIPS & LOOPS: Day hikers might take the easy one-mile round trip to Nickel Creek or Enderts Beach. If you climb the big hill, you'll at least want to continue to the Lake Earl view, 5⅞ miles round trip, or the crossing of Damnation Creek, 9 miles round trip.

## SECTION 7
# Damnation Creek Trail to Lagoon Creek, Redwood National Park

DISTANCE: 8⅛ miles (CCT) or 8¾ miles from Damnation Creek Trailhead (13.1 or 14.1 kilometers).

OPEN TO: Hikers.

SURFACE: Trail, beach.

ACCESS POINT: Damnation Creek Trailhead.

HOW TO GET THERE: On west side of Highway 101, 10 miles south of Crescent City (Milepost 16.0).

OTHER ACCESS: Wilson Creek Beach west of DeMartin Redwood Hostel.

DIFFICULTY: Strenuous.

ELEVATION GAIN/LOSS: 670 feet+/1530 feet-. If starting from Damnation Trailhead add 40 feet+/140 feet-.

CAUTIONS: Use caution crossing Highway 101.

FURTHER INFORMATION: Redwood National and State Parks (707)464-6101, ext. 5064.

**FACILITIES:** None at access point. Chemical toilets but no water at DeMartin Camp. Phone at Redwood Hostel. Picnic area, water, restrooms at Lagoon Creek.

**CAMPGROUNDS:** DeMartin Camp (walk-in) is near middle of section. Car camping at Del Norte Coast Redwoods State Park north of access point.

**HOSTEL:** DeMartin Redwood Hostel (707)482-8265 is near south end of section.

**LODGING:** Motel Trees is just south of south end of section. Other lodgings are in Crescent City to the north and Klamath to the south.

In this section CCT runs east of Highway 101 for its longest stretch in northern California, something the trail will not repeat until well into southern California. Even with this eastward jog, you're never more than a mile from the Pacific. The first half of this section provides CCT's most intimate exploration of a virgin redwood forest. While other sections visit virgin redwood groves, here you traverse virgin forest for 4 miles on a scenic new track that takes you through one giant tree and winds under and around many others in diverse terrain, allowing you a hand in glove experience of an ancient redwood forest. Consider a stay at DeMartin Camp, a walkers-only stopover where you can absorb the mysteries of the ancient forest round the clock. Or opt for beds, hot water and fellowship at Redwood Hostel in a 19th-century homestead farther along the route.

Day hikers follow the Damnation Creek Trail from Highway 101. It climbs over a ridge and drops through virgin forest to meet CCT in ⅝ mile. Turn left to follow CCT south. The mileage for this section starts counting from that junction.

CCT follows the pavement that was once Highway 101, winding south through a virgin forest of massive redwoods. After descending to a big bend at ⅜ mile, the road contours with glimpses of the rugged coast below.

Watch carefully on the left at 1⅛ miles for a narrow footpath. If you miss it, the old pavement merges with Highway 101 in 200 feet. CCT follows the footpath over a small ridge and down to the highway at 1¼ miles. Since there is no crosswalk across the busy road, use extreme caution crossing to the other side to find a "CT" sign marking the start of the DeMartin Section.

The trail descends by steps and switchbacks to a bridge at 1⅜ miles, then zigzags up through the forest to 2 miles. CCT reaches this section's summit and turns south to follow the lush coastal ridge where rhododendrons abound. Follow the winding ridge around a gulch at 2¼ miles.

After passing through a walk-through redwood, CCT leaves the ridge around 2⅜ miles, descending south by switchbacks on new tread completed in February 1998. Cross the head of a gulch, then contour southeast through more virgin forest, winding through two more gulches. Beyond 2¾ miles your trail climbs east to 3 miles. Contour south, winding through the heads of four more gorgeous gulches to 3½ miles. Then CCT climbs moderately east to a summit at 3¾ miles, a hill 1020 feet above sea level.

Descend steeply south, dip through a gully, then climb briefly through a pleasant grove to the coastal ridge at 4⅛ miles. As you descend south along the ridge, the forest thins to reveal the spectacular coast beyond giant Douglas firs with False Klamath Cove and False Klamath Rock in the foreground, Patrick's Point and Cape Mendocino stretching westward beyond. Continue a winding descent to a junction at 4⅝ miles.

The Coastal Trail turns left for a short climb to DeMartin Camp at 4¾ miles. The pleasant camp perches on the edge of deep forest overlooking DeMartin Prairie. Its ten sites offer tables, fire rings, and a composting toilet, but no drinking water. If you stay here, you need to stow your food in the metal bear boxes.

## The Struggle for Redwood National Park

The Redwood Highway, Highway 101 north from San Francisco to the Oregon border, represented a substantial engineering achievement when it opened in 1917, negotiating the twisting, slide-prone Eel River Canyon and the steep coastal cliffs south of Crescent City. The road's most significant accomplishment, however, was opening California's north coast to mass tourism.

Among the first visitors that summer were three prestigious conservationists. Madison Grant, founder of the New York Zoological Society, Henry Osborn, president of the American Museum of Natural History, and paleontologist John Merriam, later president of the Carnegie Institute. These men drove the new highway north to camp beneath the giant redwoods at Bull Creek in today's Humboldt Redwoods State Park. Awed by the giant forest and appalled by sounds of nearby logging, the three men returned home determined to preserve the tall trees.

They recruited other conservationists and civic leaders to their cause, founding Save-the-Redwoods League in 1918. Grant soon brought Stephen Mather, head of the National Park Service, to see the virgin groves. Grant was shocked at how many redwoods had been cut in only two years. Ironically the Redwood Highway allowed timber fallers and logging trucks to reach previously untouched groves.

Despite Mather's eloquent appeals,

Congress failed to protect any redwoods. So the League shifted tactics, convincing prominent citizens to donate money to buy the groves for California state parks. By 1922 they had protected 2200 acres of virgin forests along the Redwood Highway, creating Humboldt Redwoods State Park. Their ongoing efforts saved Dyerville Flats in 1925 and Bull Creek Flats in 1931, expanding the park to 12,000 acres. (It's 51,500 acres today.)

Save-the-Redwoods League continues their efficient work today, having saved 125,000 acres of redwoods. However, efforts to establish a Redwood National Park lay dormant for many years. After a National Geographic Society field team discovered the world's tallest redwoods on private timber lands along Redwood Creek in 1963, the struggle for a Redwood National Park resumed. Only after five years of bitter debate did Congress finally establish a 58,000-acre Redwood National Park encompassing the giant groves along Redwood Creek and three existing redwood state parks.

Over the next ten years, erosion from logging upstream threatened the Redwood Creek giants. Finally after more acrimonious debate between conservationists and timber corporations, Congress expanded Redwood National Park to 108,000 acres in 1978, protecting the Redwood Creek watershed above Tall Trees Grove.

provided to keep Yogi and BooBoo Bear out of trouble!

CCT ascends briefly through the spruce and alder forest before descending through the heart of DeMartin Prairie. From 5 miles your descending track drops alternately through forest and prairie. At 5¼ miles you dramatically approach the edge of deep Wilson Creek Canyon, the private lands of which have been logged.

Your descent continues, winding and switchbacking through charming forest. Beyond 5¾ miles the path levels briefly then ascends along a narrow ridgetop with views of the ocean through the forest, culminating in a grand vista of towering Footsteps Rocks along the rugged shore. Return once more to the edge of Wilson Creek Canyon, then climb to contour around a big rock outcrop beyond 6¼ miles.

Resume a winding descent to 6½ miles before CCT straightens out, then bends sharply right to follow an old road briefly. Fork right along a footpath through coastal scrub, soon bending left to descend along a power line. Open country provides views of False Klamath and Wilson Rocks offshore. After a series of long switchbacks, CCT drops into forest at 7 miles, making a winding descent that crosses eight small boardwalks.

Your trail levels at 7⅜ miles, coming to an overgrown stretch of old highway and a trail junction. In summer you'll want to take the footpath on the far side of the old road, descending to ford Wilson Creek below the highway bridge in ⅛ mile. At times of high water, however, turn right and follow the old pavement uphill 500 feet to Highway 101, then turn left to cautiously cross the highway bridge. At the south side of Wilson Creek, Redwood Hostel occupies the pioneer DeMartin House east of the highway. Wilson Creek Beach is west of the highway.

The main route of CCT heads south along Wilson Creek Beach for ⅝ mile to the mouth of Lagoon Creek and Del Norte Section 8. At high tide however, especially in winter, the center portion of the beach may not be passable. In that case you have two choices. 1) Walk the highway shoulder for about ½ mile to the mouth of Lagoon Creek where you can return to the beach. 2) Take the **Alternate Route** to meet Del Norte Section 8 one mile from the starting point, a route one mile longer.

**ALTERNATE ROUTE:** From the hostel south, you can also walk the Hostel/Trees of Mystery Trail east of Highway 101. Walk east 150 feet from the base of the hostel's front steps to find the trail's signed north end. The trail follows a gravel road, ascending then contouring through forest with occasional coastal views. The road becomes less traveled as you cross three forks of Lagoon Creek before 1⅛ miles. Then contour along a grassy track through lush undergrowth. At 1¾ miles it descends to the Trees of Mystery parking lot. Unless you crave pavement, veer left on the footpath above the lot which ends in ⅛ mile at the Trees Gift Shop. Here you'll find a great museum of Native American artifacts plus restrooms and a pay phone. Take the crosswalk to cross Highway 101, then turn right and walk in front of the motel to a clearly signed gravel path. Follow it west ½ mile to meet Del Norte Section 8 just south of Hidden Beach. Total distance is 2½ miles.

**SUGGESTED ROUND TRIPS & LOOPS:** It is a rewarding, spectacular hike to DeMartin Camp from either the north or south end with views more rewarding on the south part and the virgin forest the dominant feature on the north part.

## SECTION 8
# Lagoon Creek to Klamath River, Redwood National Park

DISTANCE: 5⅜ miles to Klamath Inn (8.6 kilometers). Without a boat shuttle it is 14¾ miles via Klamath Beach Road or 16½ miles via Flint Ridge Trail (23.7 or 26.6 kilometers).

OPEN TO: Hikers. Road portion open to bicyclists.

SURFACE: Trail, road shoulder.

ACCESS POINT: Lagoon Creek Parking Area.

HOW TO GET THERE: Turn west off Highway 101 into signed Lagoon Creek Parking Area (Milepost 11.8) one mile south of Wilson Creek, .9 mile north of Trees of Mystery.

SOUTH END ACCESS: Turn west off Highway 101 at Milepost 8.1 on to Requa Road. Go one mile to Klamath Inn or 2.5 miles to Klamath Overlook Parking Area (end of trail segment).

DIFFICULTY: Moderate.

ELEVATION GAIN/LOSS: 1020 feet+/1020 feet-.

CAUTIONS: To get from the end of this section to the start of the next one, you must either hire a boat to cross the Klamath River or make a 11- or 13-mile road detour. For a boat, contact Rivers West (707)482-5822 or (800)887-5387.

FURTHER INFORMATION: Redwood National and State Parks (707)464-6101, ext. 5265.

FACILITIES: Restrooms, water, phone, picnic area at access point.

CAMPGROUNDS: Several private campgrounds are around town of Klamath to south. State Park camping is available at Del Norte Coast Redwoods State Park to north or Prairie Creek Redwoods State Park to south.

HOSTEL: DeMartin Redwood Hostel (707)482-8265 is one mile north of access point.

LODGING: Motel Trees is .9 mile south on Highway 101. Klamath Inn is en route on north bank of Klamath River.

The Yurok tribe of the Klamath River country has always been one of the largest tribes of Native Americans in northern California. Yurok territory stretches from Wilson Creek on the north to Little River south of Trinidad on the south and up the Klamath River to its confluence with the Trinity River. When white settlers arrived in the 1850s, many Yuroks survived by retreating into the heart of their rugged country. In spite of conflicts, the Yurok tribe retains a viable culture and is currently growing in number.

CCT traverses traditional Yurok land for about 50 miles, along which you will see numerous signs of their culture, from traditional canoes and a reconstructed village site to modern tribal offices and vendors of smoked salmon. Please be especially careful to respect tribal lands and beliefs as you pass through. Most of this CCT section follows an ancient Yurok path through steep country above the sea's edge. You'll hike through contemporary Yurok land and cross the Klamath

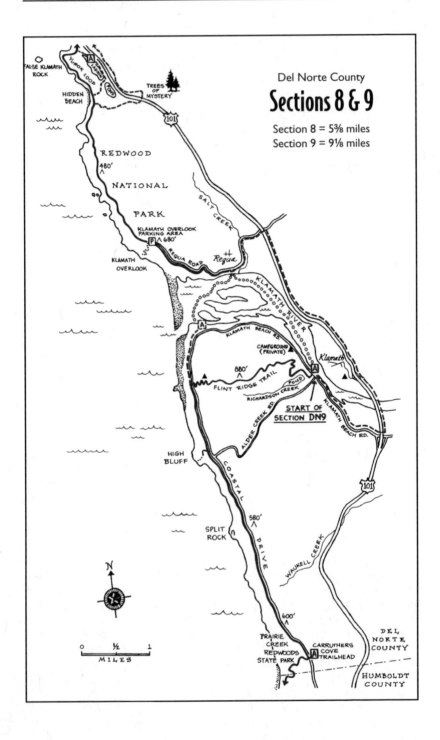

Del Norte County
# Sections 8 & 9

Section 8 = 5⅝ miles
Section 9 = 9⅛ miles

FALSE KLAMATH ROCK

YUROK LOOP

HIDDEN BEACH

TREES OF MYSTERY

101

REDWOOD

480'

NATIONAL

PARK

SALT CREEK

KLAMATH OVERLOOK PARKING AREA
680'

KLAMATH OVERLOOK

REQUA ROAD

Requa

KLAMATH RIVER

KLAMATH BEACH RD.

CAMPGROUND (PRIVATE)

Klamath

880'

FLINT RIDGE TRAIL

POND

RICHARDSON CREEK

START OF SECTION DN9

HIGH BLUFF

ALDER CREEK RD.

COASTAL DRIVE

KLAMATH BEACH RD.

101

580'

SPLIT ROCK

WAUKELL CREEK

N

½    1

MILES

0

600'

PRAIRIE CREEK REDWOODS STATE PARK

CARRUTHERS COVE TRAILHEAD

DEL NORTE COUNTY

HUMBOLDT COUNTY

River, lifeblood of their civilization.

From the Lagoon Creek Parking Area, walk northwest on the Yurok Loop/ Hidden Beach Section of the Coastal Trail. At a fork before ⅛ mile, the CCT north is on the right. Take the left fork across a bridge over Lagoon Creek, then climb west along the edge of the forest to overlook False Klamath Cove, the mouth of the creek, and several large offshore rocks.

CCT turns south along the spectacular shore, contouring through grasslands and scrub then through forest. After a short up and down, the Yurok Loop forks left to return to the parking lot. Continue along the shore, passing a side trail to Hidden Beach at one mile, then the Trees of Mystery Trail on the left (see Del Norte Section 7 Alternate Route).

The easy hiking ends as CCT climbs moderately then steeply through dense spruce/fir forest. Ascend sporadically beyond 1⅜ miles with superb views of the rocky coast. After dipping through a wooded gulch, the trail contours along a steep hillside where leather ferns sprout profusely from the trees.

Climb 22 steps to top the coastal ridge at 2⅛ miles. Contour along the verdant ridgetop to 2½ miles then descend to a saddle. Ascend steeply through

## The Vibrant and Resilient Yurok Culture

The Klamath River, California's second largest, and its abundant fisheries provide the central focus for Yurok civilization. In fact the river is so important to the Yuroks that their language traditionally expressed directions as upstream and downstream rather than the cardinal points used by most cultures. This was true even along the coast where settlements to the north were downstream for the Yurok, those south were upstream. The river has always brought the salmon essential to this water oriented culture.

The Yurok people carve canoes from redwood trees, short agile boats for the river, larger vessels with sails for the ocean. Each canoe has a small knob, the boat's heart, left near its stern. Without it a boat is dead and useless. Both neighboring tribes and tribes as far away as Shasta and Sinkyone traded for the excellent Yurok canoes.

Most Yuroks live along the 40 miles of the Klamath River from its mouth to its confluence with the Trinity River. Like their Athapascan Tolowa neighbors, the Algonquian Yurok culture is more closely linked to cultures of the northwest than to those of California. Traditionally Yuroks valued property and sought to accumulate wealth. Owning a good fishing ground insured survival. Wealth in the form of dentalium shells, woodpecker scalps, and white deerskins allowed one to hold status and marry a good wife.

Despite the importance of the aqueous world to Yurok culture, Yuroks traditionally also traveled over land on a well-developed trail system. Traditional Yurok belief considers trails to be living beings that could become resentful if travelers do not treat them with respect. A Yurok hiker would ask, "May I come this way again?" Along each major trail the tribe designated pleasant spots as special resting places. For travelers to pass such spots without resting showed disrespect for the trail. While you're visiting Yurok territory, please show respect for the people and their vibrant, durable culture as well as for their lands, both modern and traditional, as you walk through.

several twists in the trail to 2¾ miles.

Suddenly you leave the forest for grasslands and a marvelous view rewards your efforts. On a clear day you can see Patrick's Point, 30 air miles south. The nearby mouth of the Klamath River is hidden, but the rest of the rugged coast lies before you. CCT contours through grasslands and scrub. After regaining the ridgetop at the head of a stream, contour through alder forest and past a small pond.

Your trail ascends for ⅛ mile, then contours across steep open slopes. Climb briefly to 3¼ miles where the Redwood National Park maintenance center is on your left. Soon an overlook with a rest bench surveys the broad mouth of the Klamath.

Contour through the steep grasslands overlooking the river mouth until you enter a grove of spruce and cross a small creek around 3½ miles. Returning to grasslands, your trail ascends toward Klamath Overlook Parking Area. After another bench, a side trail forks right, winding ½ mile down to Klamath Overlook right above the sea stack guarding the river mouth. CCT climbs to the parking area where the dirt trail ends.

CCT descends east along the shoulder of Requa Road with grand views of the Klamath River and the rugged forests surrounding it until you leave the national park around 4⅜ miles. Continue down the road for another mile to the Klamath Inn, a stopover for coast travelers since 1885. The current building dates from 1914.

From there you must either find a boat to shuttle you to the south side of the river or detour 5½ more miles on road and highway to the start of the Flint Ridge Section of CCT.

**ALTERNATE ROUTE:** If you cannot find a boat, continue east on Requa Road until it ends at Highway 101 at 6⅞ miles. Turn right and cautiously walk the highway's left shoulder for 3⅜ miles. This last stretch, the long narrow bridge across the Klamath, is the most daunting part. Leave the highway at 10¼ miles to follow Klamath Beach Road west and northwest to Alder Camp Road at 12 miles.

Here you have a choice. You can either turn left and follow the beautiful Flint Ridge Section of CCT for 4½ miles to the Coastal Drive and the main CCT south, or you can continue west on Klamath Beach Road until it climbs above the river and becomes the Coastal Drive, a route less steep and 1¾ miles shorter, but much less rewarding.

**SUGGESTED ROUND TRIPS & LOOPS:** The Yurok Loop Trail is a pleasant one-mile trail. The side trip to Hidden Beach is worthwhile. You can make pleasant round trip hikes from either end of this section of CCT to the high point of the trail section. The hike is easier from the south end.

**HOW TO IMPROVE CCT HERE:** The National Park Service owns land south and southeast of Klamath Overlook. About ½ mile of trail could be developed to keep through-hikers off Requa Road until it leaves the park.

## SECTION 9
# Klamath River, South Bank, to Carruthers Cove Trailhead, Prairie Creek Redwoods State Park

DISTANCE: 9⅛ miles from Douglas Bridge Parking Area or 5½ miles from south bank of river near mouth (14.7 or 8.9 kilometers).

OPEN TO: Hikers. Bicyclists, equestrians allowed on road.

SURFACE: Trail, gravel road, paved road.

ACCESS POINT: Douglas Bridge Parking Area (or South Klamath Overlook).

HOW TO GET THERE: Unless you're taking a boat, turn west off Highway 101 just south of the Klamath River bridge and follow Klamath Beach Road 1.8 miles to Douglas Bridge Parking Area at Alder Camp Road.

OTHER ACCESS: Anywhere along Coastal Drive.

DIFFICULTY: Strenuous with Flint Ridge Trail, moderate without.

ELEVATION GAIN/LOSS: 1370 feet+/750 feet-. From river mouth: 850 feet+/290 feet-.

CAUTIONS: Coastal Drive is prone to slip outs and may be closed to vehicle traffic at times. During road closures may be the ideal time to walk this section, but inquire first.

FURTHER INFORMATION: Redwood National and State Parks (707)464-6101, ext. 5265. For boat shuttle, call Rivers West (707)482-5822 or (800)887-5387.

FACILITIES: None at access point. Chemical toilet, but no water at Flint Ridge Camp. Picnic area and wheelchair-accessible toilets at High Bluff.

CAMPGROUNDS: Flint Ridge Camp has walk-in camping. Car camping is available at Prairie Creek Redwoods State Park to the south. Riverwoods Campground, (707)482-5591, is near access point.

LODGING: Motels are in Klamath to the north and Orick to the south.

MAP: See page 48.

The verdant and pristine Flint Ridge Section of the Coastal Trail climbs to a wooded ridge above the mouth of the Klamath River, exploring some wind-gnarled virgin forest. Just before the west end of the trail descends to Coastal Drive, quiet Flint Ridge Camp offers pleasant walk-in camping.

The rest of the section follows lightly traveled Coastal Drive. Of course you CAN drive the road portion of this CCT section, barring closures for slip outs and other acts of nature, but walking it reveals breathtaking hidden vistas of a rugged and elusive coast that you're not likely to notice from your vehicle. Coastal Drive offers one of the great road walks along the Coastal Trail. I've driven the road many times, but walking it revealed unexpected treasures: abundant grouse calling from the alder forest between the road and the wild coast, changing vistas of the immense, elusive dome of Split Rock, even a Yurok brush dance pit hard by the banks of the churning Klamath River near its mouth.

If you take a boat across the Klamath River, ask the captain if he can drop you near the Douglas Bridge parking area or at Riverwoods Campground on the south bank. If not, he'll probably have to land around the old Dad's Camp near the river's mouth. If so, walk up the access road to meet Coastal Drive just south of South Klamath Overlook, missing the Flint Ridge portion of CCT and knocking 3⅝ miles from the total distance. Walk up Coastal Drive to the western Flint Ridge Trailhead around ½ mile.

If you're day hiking this section or if the shuttle boat drops you near the Douglas Bridge, cross Klamath Beach Road to the parking area and find the start of the Flint Ridge Trail just south. Flint Ridge Trail descends through dense alder forest to cross a bridge over Richardson Creek then heads upstream to Marshall Pond. After wrapping north and west around the pond, your trail switchbacks to the right around ¾ mile and ascends by many switchbacks through dense forest.

As you gain the ridge around 2 miles, you might glimpse the deep river canyon to the north. The trail climbs west with the ridgetop, passing redwoods to 12 feet in diameter, most with broken tops because of the harsh coastal winds. By 2½ miles it stays south of the ridgetop through several short ups and downs. From 2¾ miles you descend steadily for ½ mile, then climb to a second summit at 3¾ miles where alders start to mix with the giant redwoods. Soon alders dominate the forest as you descend by switchbacks toward the coast.

After a power line at 4¼ miles, watch for the side trail to Flint Ridge Camp on the right. Ten sites in a grassy clearing provide tables, metal food lockers (remember the bears), and a composting toilet, but no water. Flint Ridge Trail drops to Coastal Drive at 4½ miles.

CCT follows the road south, contouring across a steep slope with dense forest on the left. A side trail forks right at 4⅞ mile, descending ⅛ mile to a World-War-II-era radar station. Your road dips and climbs, passing another side trail on the right at 5⅝ miles. A road descends ⅛ mile to High Bluff Picnic Area where a short paved path offers a breathtaking view south.

The Coastal Drive climbs to a junction with Alder Camp Road. Turn right and follow the pavement as Coastal Drive contours above the shore weaving in and out of forest. From 6¾ miles you climb to a high point of nearly 600 feet, then make a roller-coaster descent with intermittent views toward the shore below.

After the descent bottoms out around 7½ miles, ascend to two more grand vista points at 8 and 8½ miles. At the second, Carruthers Cove Overlook, a stone wall turnout provides an eagle's view of the rugged coast 600 feet below with Carruthers Cove and Gold Bluffs Beach to the south and Split Rock to the north. Continue along Coastal Drive through forest to 9⅛ miles, where Carruthers Cove Trail, start of the next section, descends west from the road shoulder. The spot is easy to miss if the trailhead sign isn't in place. The Humboldt County line is ⅛ mile south. Coastal Drive turns inland, ending at Drury Parkway in one mile.

**SUGGESTED ROUND TRIPS & LOOPS:** Flint Ridge Trail offers the best hike. You might walk the least traveled part of Coastal Drive from South Klamath Overlook south to High Bluff Picnic Area and return, 3½ miles round trip. The best loop would be Flint Ridge Trail, returning via Klamath Beach Road, 7¾ miles.

# Humboldt County

HUMBOLDT COUNTY HARBORS about 12 percent of the California Coastal Trail, the largest chunk among the state's fifteen coastal counties. Humboldt not only has the longest coastline of California's counties, it also holds many of the state's most spectacular and remote sections of coast. From the rugged shoreline of southern Redwood National Park in the north, along the rocky convoluted coast around Trinidad, through the sandy beaches surrounding Humboldt Bay, on down to the wild, isolated shores of the Lost Coast, Humboldt 's Coastal Trail requires about two weeks to walk, even longer to fully explore.

Just as in Del Norte County, you'll find both some of the easiest and most strenuous sections of CCT in Humboldt. Also like Del Norte, you'll have abundant opportunities to commune with virgin forests and see wildlife. If you traverse the entire Coastal Trail through Humboldt County, you'll visit three state parks, two state beaches, seven county parks, two wildlife refuges, and an immense national conservation area on the Lost Coast as well as Redwood National Park. You'll want to arrange boat crossings of two major rivers, the Eel and the Mattole, and Humboldt Bay, California's second largest. You'll need to ford one lesser river and 28 creeks.

Of Humboldt's 143 miles on the Coastal Trail, 43 miles follow roads. Although that's 30 percent of the total, almost 20 of those road miles are on the remote and spectacular Mattole Road, where an impassably rugged coast forces hikers inland over high ridges. CCT hikers are forced onto a highway for only 1¼ miles in Humboldt County.

Our hats are off to the people in California's northernmost two coastal counties for their remarkable success in creating their parts of the California Coastal Trail.

Twenty of the creek fords occur along the Lost Coast from Cape Mendocino south to the county line, where CCT hikers will benefit from carrying a backpack to make their way through that remote, isolated country. The Lost Coast continues south about 30 miles into Mendocino County as well, where you'll have plenty more creeks to ford. While Humboldt's King Range Lost Coast is not yet a designated wilderness, we hope that soon it will finally be granted the official wilderness designation it has long deserved.

## SECTION I
# Carruthers Cove Trailhead to Gold Bluffs Beach Campground, Prairie Creek Redwoods State Park

DISTANCE: 6⅜ miles (10.3 kilometers).

OPEN TO: Hikers. Bicyclists from Ossagon Trail south.

SURFACE: Trail, beach, gravel road.

ACCESS POINT: Carruthers Cove Trailhead.

HOW TO GET THERE: Turn west off Highway 101 north of Orick and south of the Klamath River onto N. B. Drury Parkway at Milepost 137.45 (Humboldt County) from south, Milepost 0.3 (Del Norte County) from north. Go south .9 mile and turn right on Coastal Drive. Go 1.0 mile to trailhead on left marked by a sign "COASTAL TRAIL."

OTHER ACCESS: Via Ossagon Trail.

DIFFICULTY: Easy.

ELEVATION GAIN/LOSS: 40 feet+/580 feet-.

CAUTIONS: Stay away from wild elk. Mountain lions also frequent this area.

FURTHER INFORMATION: Prairie Creek State Park (707)464-6101, ext. 5300.

FACILITIES: None at access point. Chemical toilets at Ossagon Creek Camp and Gold Bluffs Beach Campground. Water at Gold Bluffs Beach Campground or purified from creeks. Toilets near Fern Canyon at end of Gold Bluffs Beach Road.

CAMPGROUNDS: Ossagon Creek Camp on the trail at 3 miles must be reserved in advance through Prairie Creek Redwoods State Park. Gold Bluffs Beach Campground has car camping with solar showers. Nearby Gold Bluffs Hike/Bike Camp has no auto access.

LODGING: Park Motel is on Highway 101 at Davison Road. Other motels are in Orick.

HOSTEL: DeMartin Redwood Hostel is 11 miles north.

As CCT leaves the Coastal Drive to descend Carruthers Cove Trail, it enters pristine 15,000-acre Prairie Creek Redwoods State Park, one of California's finest and earliest state parks, established in the 1920s. As you descend an old homestead road to the hidden shore, you enter Humboldt County. When you reach the sand-filled cove, immense rock outcrops towering overhead dwarf human scale, encouraging a feeling of awe for this rugged meeting of virgin-forested land and wild sea.

As recently as 1992, the beach south was passable only at low tide, but recent abundant sand deposits made it passable at any tide. That's the good news. The bad news is that the sand buildup now allows commercial fishermen to drive their vehicles along the beach of this recently wilderness coast. After 2½ miles you can leave the beach for the solid footing of CCT along the base of the Gold Bluffs, site of 19th century mining.

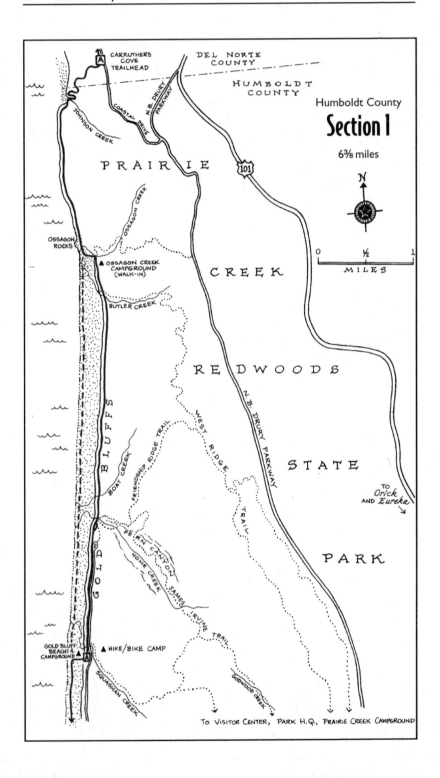

Humboldt County

## Section 1

6⅜ miles

Take the Carruthers Cove Trail as it drops to the old roadbed you descend to the beach. The overgrown road descends steadily, winding through forest of Sitka spruce and alder. Beyond ½ mile you may glimpse the coastline to the north, but mostly the shore remains hidden until ¾ mile where your trail passes a home-stead site and turns right for your first view of the massive rock outcrop at the mouth of Johnson Creek.

The trail descends moderately across the steep slope below the homestead. At the base of the slope, make your way through piles of driftwood to firm foot-ing on the beach sand by ⅞ mile. Walk south across the level sand of Carruthers Cove to the base of the rock outcrop at one mile. A seasonal lagoon may require you to veer west toward the nearby Pacific shore. The beach stretches north and south along the base of steep cliffs with the impressive dome of Split Rock rising 533 feet from the breakers two miles north.

CCT heads south along the broad beach. Between 1⅝ and 1¾ miles, several rock outcrops or sea stacks lie along the tideline. Continue along the broadening beach, coming to the Ossagon Rocks at 2¼ miles where the largest outcrop is up on the beach with more rocks at the surf line. You can see the canyon of Ossagon Creek not far to the southeast. Follow the beach to 2½ miles where you're directly west of the Ossagon Trail where it drops to the coastal plain.

CCT offers a choice of two routes south from here. You can choose to follow the tideline all the way to Gold Bluffs Beach Campground at 6⅛ miles. The more diverse and engaging route heads east or southeast to the Coastal Trail along the base of the bluffs. It's about ⅛ mile east across sometimes swampy ground to the trail at the mouth of Ossagon Creek Canyon. Ossagon Creek Camp there requires a reservation to stay overnight. In winter and early spring when the Coastal Trail from Butler Creek south may be wet or flooded, it's often better to stay on the beach for at least 1½ miles.

Our description heads east from 2½ miles, crossing sand to enter alder forest along Ossagon Creek. Near the creek crossing where the camp sits beside the trail, a sign points uphill for the Ossagon Trail to Drury Parkway. You want the trail south, which leaves the alder forest south of the ford to head south across flat coastal prairie. Keep your eyes open for the wild elk that favor this area; you may need to detour to stay out of their way.

CCT soon climbs along the hillside, contouring above the dunes for about ½ mile. Before your trail descends.to Butler Creek, West Ridge Trail heads east, following a ridge through virgin forest to the park's visitor center in 7⅜ miles. Descend to ford Butler Creek at 3 miles.

The Coastal Trail continues south, leaving alder forest to parallel the base of the Gold Bluffs through grasslands. In a wet winter or spring you may need to detour ¼ mile west through the dunes to avoid standing water on the next mile of trail. If it's not flooded, follow the trail past a large spruce snag and over a small rise. Pass a gravelly slide and veer to the right of some alders around 3½ miles. The roar of the surf echoes loudly from the cliff above as you skirt spruce forest along the base of the wooded bluffs.

Before 4 miles a short side trail forks left to an 80-foot waterfall hidden in the forest. CCT meets another short spur on the left in 300 feet. It leads to a rest bench beside Gold Dust Falls where a small stream plunges 100 feet to disappear into the sandy soil beneath the spruce forest. Not far beyond, a third waterfall dives off the cliff in wet season.

CCT rounds a small point at 4¼ miles from which you can look south to the alder thicket marking Boat Creek. Cross lupine-studded grasslands, then wind through the alders to ford Boat Creek where it emerges from its rugged canyon at 4¾ miles. Continue south through grasslands and into more alder forest. The James Irvine Trail forks left at 5⅛ miles, ending at the visitor center in 4¼ miles. It also leads to nearby Fern Canyon Loop, a fine ¾-mile loop through a narrow canyon with fern-draped vertical walls 60 feet high.

CCT fords Home Creek and continues south to meet the end of Gold Bluffs Beach Road at 5⅜ miles, where the new Fern Canyon parking area has restrooms. The Coastal Trail continues south along the dirt and gravel road, hugging the base of the Gold Bluffs. It's a pleasant, lightly traveled one mile along the road to section's end at 6⅜ miles at Gold Bluffs Beach Campground, in the dunes between road and beach just south of Squashan Creek. Another overnight choice is nearby Miner's Ridge Hike/Bike Camp which sits on a knoll east of the road. If you're still game for exploration, pleasant Miner's Ridge Trail follows Squashan Creek east before climbing over a ridge to the visitor center in about 4 miles.

**ALTERNATE ROUTE:** You can follow the tideline south of Ossagon Creek instead of walking east to the Coastal Trail.

**SUGGESTED ROUND TRIPS & LOOPS:** Carruthers Cove Trail to the beach offers a wonderful short round trip. You can continue south to Ossagon Creek and return from there, or loop back by ascending Ossagon Trail and return on Drury Parkway and Coastal Drive. Other pleasant choices start from Fern Canyon Trailhead. You can walk north on the Coastal Trail to Butler Creek and back, 5¼ miles, or Ossagon Creek, 6¼ miles, or make a 7½-mile loop by turning east on West Ridge Trail, then returning south along Friendship Ridge Trail. Also consider the short one-mile loop through amazing Fern Canyon.

## SECTION 2
# Gold Bluffs Beach Campground, Prairie Creek Redwoods State Park, to Redwood Information Center, Orick

DISTANCE: 11¾ miles or 11½ miles if walking highway at end (18.9 or 18.5 kilometers).

OPEN TO: Hikers. Road and levee open to bicyclists.

SURFACE: Beach, trail, highway shoulder, levee.

ACCESS POINT: Gold Bluffs Beach Campground.

HOW TO GET THERE: Turn west off Highway 101 north of Orick at Milepost 124.8 onto unpaved, steep and winding Davison Road. Go 7 miles to Gold Bluffs Beach Campground.

OTHER ACCESS: Espa Lagoon, Skunk Cabbage Creek Trailhead, or various points in Orick.

DIFFICULTY: Moderate.

ELEVATION GAIN/LOSS: 640 feet+/ 640 feet-.

CAUTIONS: Use extreme caution on Highway 101.

FURTHER INFORMATION: Prairie Creek Redwoods State Park (707)464-6101, ext. 5300. Redwood National Park (707)464-6101, ext. 5265.

FACILITIES: Chemical toilets and water at campground. Picnic area on Davison Road about ⅜ mile south of the campground.

CAMPGROUNDS: Gold Bluffs Beach Campground has primitive car camping with solar showers. Nearby Miner's Ridge Hike/Bike Camp has sites off the road. Orick RV Park, north end of town, is a private campground on this section.

LODGING: Park Motel is on Highway 101 at start of Davison Road. Several motels are in Orick.

This section, the longest since CCT left the Oregon border, divides nicely into two segments, the wild and verdant 7⅛ miles of beach and trail/forest walking, and the road-highway-levee walk through the tiny town of Orick. You start in the southwest corner of Prairie Creek Redwoods State Park, pass through enchanting forest in a little visited corner of Redwood National Park, then drop to Highway 101 before following the levee of Redwood Creek through town to finish at the park's southern visitor center.

Walk west from the campground to follow the tideline south along broad Gold Bluffs Beach. It is 1¾ miles to where Davison Road leaves the beach near Espa Lagoon, heading east to Highway 101. CCT continues south along the beach for another 1⅜ miles, crossing a small creek west of Espa Lagoon, then fording Major Creek, site of another 19th-century gold mine, around 2⅝ miles.

After you cross a small creek at 3 miles, watch on your left for an orange triangle and a sign marking the northern end of the Skunk Cabbage Creek Trail

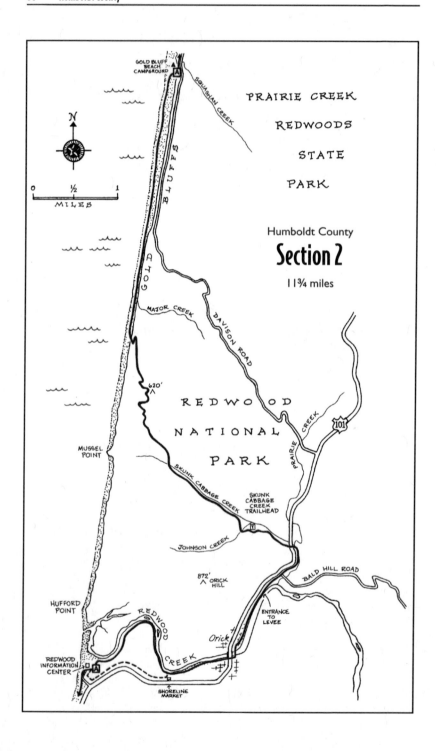

PRAIRIE CREEK
REDWOODS
STATE
PARK

Humboldt County
## Section 2
11¾ miles

GOLD BLUFF BEACH CAMPGROUND

SQUASHAN CREEK

GOLD BLUFFS

MAJOR CREEK

DAVISON ROAD

620'

REDWOOD

NATIONAL

PARK

MUSSEL POINT

PRAIRIE CREEK

101

SKUNK CABBAGE CREEK

SKUNK CABBAGE CREEK TRAILHEAD

JOHNSON CREEK

872'
ORICK HILL

BALD HILL ROAD

HUFFORD POINT

REDWOOD CREEK

ENTRANCE TO LEVEE

Orick

REDWOOD INFORMATION CENTER

SHORELINE MARKET

N

0    ½    1
MILES

before 3⅛ miles. Leave the beach here and take the trail ascending the steep bluff by steps and switchbacks. After passing through a tunnel of coastal scrub, you gain a ridgetop with views of the creek canyon to the east and the ocean to the west. Ascend south along the ridgetop above a magical stretch of fern-lined creek where osprey nests decorate twisted Sitka spruce.

Make a steep winding climb that soon turns away from the creek, crossing a boardwalk at 3⅞ miles. Continue along the ridgetop on a gradual ascent, passing an immense charred redwood stump around 4⅛ miles. You crest a ridge around 4⅜ miles and make a steep twisting descent through redwood forest east of the ridge.

Drop to a trail junction on the ridgetop beyond 4⅝ miles. The right fork leads quickly to an overlook and rest bench. Take the left fork heading east into dense spruce forest at the headwaters of Skunk Cabbage Creek. A winding descent crosses several small bridges, then crosses a bridge across Skunk Cabbage Creek around 5¼ miles. The descent eases through lichen-draped forest, crossing more tributaries. At 5⅞ miles, you cross Skunk Cabbage Creek again just below the confluence of its two main forks. Climb gently angling away from the creek.

Your trail joins an old road beyond 6⅛ miles, contouring above the creek across numerous side streams. On your left around 6⅜ miles, abundant skunk cabbage grow in the broad, marshy bed of the creek that bears their name.

After two more boardwalks, your trail descends a steep hill, dropping toward Johnson Creek. You pass several ancient redwoods spared when the surrounding forest was logged. Cross the creek on one more bridge and climb briefly to the parking area at Skunk Cabbage Creek Trail's southern trailhead at 7⅛ miles. CCT follows the gravel road out of the parking area, coming to a paved road at 7¾ miles. Descend the pavement to Highway 101 at 7⅞ miles.

CCT turns right to follow Highway 101 south into Orick. Cautiously cross the highway and follow its east shoulder above the placid waters of Prairie Creek. At 8¼ miles you cross Bald Hill Road. Prairie Creek empties into much larger Redwood Creek beyond 8½ miles.

Shortly after the confluence, veer left on a gated gravel road that follows the Redwood Creek levee south through the town of Orick. At 9⅜ miles creek and levee swing west to pass under Highway 101. At the highway crossing, follow the levee trail beneath the bridge. You want to cross the creek to follow the levee now on its south shore. It is easy to leave the levee near the bridge if you want to stop in town for supplies.

Follow the south levee west to the edge of town at 10¼ miles. Behind the Shoreline Market you have a choice. You can leave the levee and walk through the market parking lot to return to Highway 101, then follow the highway west to Redwood Information Center at 11½ miles, the route recommended in winter and spring. In summer and fall, continue along the levee as it winds north and south with the creek until 11⅝ miles, where you are just northeast of the Information Center, then head southwest to reach it at 11¾ miles.

**ALTERNATE ROUTE:** Generally only passable in summer at extremely low tides, the Beach Route continues south along the tideline around Mussel Point (the first questionable passage) and on down the beach to Hufford Point (second questionable passage) to the mouth of Redwood Creek (seasonal ford) where if you can ford you'll

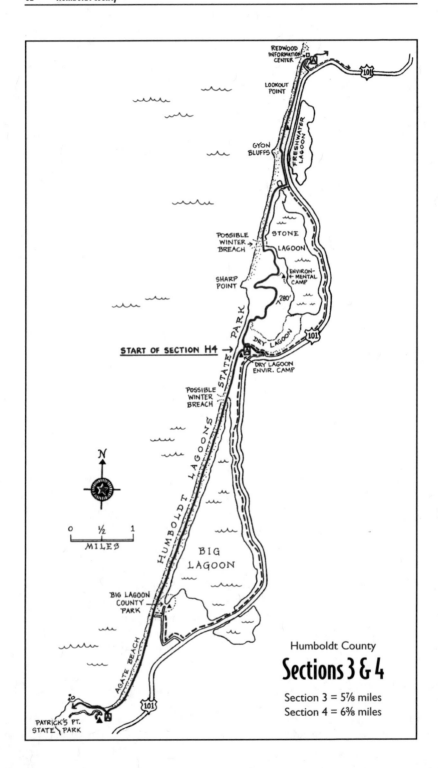

REDWOOD
INFORMATION
CENTER

LOOKOUT
POINT

FRESHWATER LAGOON

GYON
BLUFFS

STONE LAGOON

POSSIBLE
WINTER
BREACH

ENVIRON-
MENTAL
CAMP

SHARP
POINT

280'

DRY LAGOON

START OF SECTION H4 →

STATE PARK

DRY LAGOON
ENVIR. CAMP

POSSIBLE
WINTER
BREACH

HUMBOLDT LAGOONS

N

0   ½   1
MILES

BIG
LAGOON

BIG LAGOON
COUNTY PARK

AGATE BEACH

PATRICK'S PT.
STATE PARK

Humboldt County

## Sections 3 & 4

Section 3 = 5⅞ miles
Section 4 = 6⅜ miles

come to the Redwood Information Center in ⅜ mile. Total length: 6¾ miles.

**SUGGESTED ROUND TRIPS & LOOPS:** Follow the trail as described, either from Gold Bluffs Campground or Espa Lagoon. When you get to the southern trailhead for Skunk Cabbage Creek Trail, turn back and retrace your steps.

**HOW TO IMPROVE CCT HERE:** Designate the Levee Trail through Orick and west to Redwood Information Center as the CCT. Build a trail along Prairie Creek near Highway 101's east shoulder for the ¾ mile along the highway to the levee.

## SECTION 3
# Redwood Information Center, Orick, to Dry Lagoon, Humboldt Lagoons State Park

**DISTANCE:** 5⅞ miles (9.5 kilometers).

**OPEN TO:** Hikers.

**SURFACE:** Beach, trail, highway shoulder.

**ACCESS POINT:** Redwood Information Center.

**HOW TO GET THERE:** Turn west off Highway 101 one mile south of Orick. Day hikers park in Information Center parking lot, open 9 a.m. to 5 p.m. daily. If you need to leave your car overnight, either park in rest area lot south of Information Center or go to Information Center and make special arrangements.

**OTHER ACCESS:** Beach at Freshwater Lagoon or Stone Lagoon.

**DIFFICULTY:** Easy.

**ELEVATION GAIN/LOSS:** 320 feet+/320 feet-.

**CAUTIONS:** At Stone Lagoon an impassable surge channel breaches the lagoon's barrier beach during the rainy season and sometimes into early summer. In that case you must either find a boat shuttle across the lagoon east of the channel or make a long highway detour. Call ahead and ask if the beach is passable from Stone Lagoon Picnic Area to the trail around Sharp Point.

**FURTHER INFORMATION:** Humboldt Lagoons State Park (707)488-2041, Redwood Information Center (707)464-6101, ext.5265.

**FACILITIES:** Restrooms, water, phone and picnic area at access point. Stone Lagoon and Dry Lagoon have picnic areas and chemical toilets.

**CAMPGROUNDS:** Freshwater Lagoon has wayside camping between beach and highway. Inquire at Redwood Information Center. Stone Lagoon Environmental Camps are ⅛ mile off CCT on west shore of Stone Lagoon. Dry Lagoon Environmental Camps are a short walk from section's end. Several private campgrounds are in Orick and near Dry Lagoon.

**LODGING:** Several motels in Orick.

For the next eight miles three immense lagoons dominate the coastal terrain. The first, Freshwater Lagoon, is landlocked and east of Highway 101, presenting no challenge to your passage along the coast. You must make a short highway detour around the Gyon Bluffs south of Freshwater Lagoon. Both 521-acre Stone Lagoon and 1470-acre Big Lagoon breach their barrier beaches during the rainy season. When the lagoons breach, so does the Coastal Trail. In that case the powerful surge channels flowing into and out of the lagoons, depending on the tides, are impassable, requiring either a boat shuttle or a highway detour.

In summer, given the appropriate low tide at the bluffs south of Dry Lagoon, you generally can walk the next two CCT sections without other detours. This is one of the most marine segments of CCT, a salt-watery world where you'll seldom be far from the churning surf. One exception follows a pleasant, recently constructed trail over the wooded ridge between Stone Lagoon and Dry Lagoon for 2½ miles.

From the Redwood Information Center at Orick, walk south along the beach tideline. By ⅜ mile you pass the wooded hillside of Lookout Point which rises 693 feet one half mile east. By ½ mile CCT begins its crossing of the barrier beach of Freshwater Lagoon where recreational vehicles camp along Highway 101 just east of your route.

At 1½ miles the Gyon Bluffs rise from the beach. You can't get around the steep bluffs along the tideline. CCT detours east to follow the highway shoulder for ⅝ mile, then follows Stone Lagoon Road to the beach at 2⅛ miles where large Stone Lagoon looms to the south. When Stone Lagoon breaches its barrier beach at the south end of the sand spit (generally winter and spring, but inquire first), you'll have to detour farther along the highway by the Alternate Route unless you find a boat shuttle across the lagoon.

When Stone Lagoon isn't breaching, CCT simply continues along the beach, crossing the dry breach channel from about 2⅝ to 2¾ miles. The barrier beach ends at 2⅞ miles where the wooded hills around Sharp Point rise west of Stone Lagoon. Follow the lagoon shore east on a vague track through grasslands near the base of the bluff. (Sharp Point blocks through passage south along the beach.) By 3 miles you pass several large cypress in a draw on your right. After rounding a rocky point shrouded in dense coastal scrub, the path turns southeast. By 3⅛ miles the brushy hillside forces you along the lagoon's rocky shore.

At 3¼ miles, where the shore cuts east and gets brushy, look for a path west-southwest into the forest. It may be somewhat overgrown with twinberry, alders and willows. Follow the path, crossing a short boardwalk in 100 feet, then ascending gradually southeast and east. You top a wooded rise around 3½ miles.

Before 3⅝ miles CCT drops to meet a spur trail on the left which descends ⅛ mile to a pleasant boat-in/walk-in camp in the forest above a small cove on the lagoon shore. CCT takes the right fork, descending slightly, then contouring along a wooded canyon with bleeding heart and feral lilac. After crossing a gully at 4 miles, CCT ascends east. Pass a view of Stone Lagoon at 4¼ miles and cross a cantilever bridge, climbing to this section's summit at 4⅜ miles.

Your trail contours, passing a last glimpse down to Stone Lagoon's south end at 4½ miles. Descend gradually, winding through lush ferns and greenery. Beyond 4⅞ miles you descend near a ridge. CCT soon turns west, descending through dense spruce forest around 5⅛ miles. Soon a brushy clearing offers a view west to the Pacific and south over the marshes of Dry Lagoon.

A winding descent down a scrub-filled gully drops to the flats. Walk west to the beach's high tideline by 5½ miles. Follow it south for ⁵/16 mile, then walk east 300 feet, coming to the Dry Lagoon parking area at 5⅞ miles.

**ALTERNATE ROUTE:** From about December through April, Stone Lagoon's barrier beach is usually broken by a powerful surge channel which isn't fordable. Unless you can arrange a boat to carry you across the lagoon east of the channel, you must detour along Stone Lagoon Road, Highway 101, and Dry Lagoon Road, a distance of 5⅞ miles.

**SUGGESTED ROUND TRIPS & LOOPS:** The hike from Stone Lagoon to Dry Lagoon makes a worthwhile day trip. When Stone Lagoon breaches the barrier beach and you cannot reach the trail portion from there, you can start from Dry Lagoon and hike north as far as the surge channel.

**HOW TO IMPROVE CCT HERE:** Build an all-tide trail over Gyon Bluffs.

# SECTION 4
# Dry Lagoon, Humboldt Lagoons State Park, to Patrick's Point State Park

**DISTANCE:** 6⅜ miles (10.3 kilometers).

**OPEN TO:** Hikers.

**SURFACE:** Beach, trail.

**ACCESS POINT:** Dry Lagoon parking lot.

**HOW TO GET THERE:** Turn west off Highway 101 south of Orick at Milepost 114.4 onto Dry Lagoon access road. Go one mile to end of road.

**OTHER ACCESS:** Big Lagoon County Park.

**DIFFICULTY:** Easy.

**ELEVATION GAIN/LOSS:** None for first 6⅛ miles, then 180 feet+ to southern end.

**CAUTIONS:** Beach may be impassable at rocky point south of Dry Lagoon when tide is +2.0 feet or more. At north end of Big Lagoon when the lagoon breaches its barrier beach in winter and spring, beach route may not be passable. In these cases, see Alternate Route.

**FURTHER INFORMATION:** Humboldt Lagoons State Park (707)488-2041, Big Lagoon County Park (707)445-7652, Patrick's Point State Park (707)677-3570.

# The Teamwork of Preserving the Coast

Protecting and preserving the California coast, with its 1200-mile shore spanning fifteen counties, is a huge job. It requires ongoing efforts from many governments, agencies, private nonprofit groups, and individuals. Many of them have helped create the California Coastal Trail.

Redwood National and State Parks provide one excellent example of such efforts. The California State Parks Department holds more of California's coastal lands than any other agency. They've been saving the coast and building trails since the 1920s. Prairie Creek, among the first state parks, already sheltered half of today's 14,500 pristine acres by 1940, when Del Norte Coast and Jedediah Smith State Parks had begun as well. Protection of the north coast's natural environment accelerated after Redwood National Park was created in 1968. Today these state parks and the national park are managed co-operatively. These agencies created miles of the Coastal Trail here during the 1980s and 1990s. The National Park Service built some of the first Coastal Trail sections at Point Reyes National Seashore in the 1970s. NPS later created more CCT in Golden Gate National Recreation Area.

Three other federal agencies help preserve California's coast. The Bureau of Land Management operates the 60,000-acre King Range on the Lost Coast. The U.S. Fish and Wildlife Service operates the national wildlife refuges, with big holdings at Humboldt and San Francisco Bays, Moss Landing and elsewhere. More recently involved in coastal preservation is the National Oceanic and Atmospheric Adminsitration. NOAA manages California's four national marine sanctuaries, including the Monterey Bay National Marine Sanctuary, the nation's largest.

Other state agencies helping preserve the coast include Department of Fish and Game with 40 reserves and refuges in the coastal zone, and the University of California Reserve System with ten coastal reserves. The California Coastal Commission, created by the Coastal Act of 1976, plays a key role with its mission to protect, maintain, and enhance the coastal environment and maintain public access and recreational opportunities. The Coastal Conservancy preserves, improves, and restores coastal public access and natural resources by building trails and buying threatened land. County and city governments also help preserve the coast within their jurisdictions

The California Conservation Corps and the federal Americorps workers are unsung heros without whom many California trails would be in disrepair. These young workers do much of the hands-on physical labor required to build and maintain trails. On top of other important conservation work, CCC's and Americorps' trail work helps all the other government agencies get and keep trails open. Inmate crews and Division of Forestry crews also help with pressing trail work.

Many private groups help preserve the coast and provide land for the Coastal Trail. Foremost of these, Save-the-Redwoods League, has saved 125,000 acres for parks since 1918. The Nature Conservancy, with five coastal reserves in California, works for coastal preservation. The Planning and Conservation League, Trust for Public Land, and Coastwalk have all helped acquire coastal lands. Without the dozens of local land trusts involved in so many communities, far less coastline would be saved. When these groups team up, they accomplish even more work for coastal preservation.

You as an individual can also help preserve the coast. Be aware of coastal issues, write your elected representatives about them, and volunteer with a local or regional group or government agency to save our coast and complete the CCT.

**FACILITIES:** Chemical toilets, picnic areas at Dry Lagoon State Park and Big Lagoon County Park. Full facilities at Patrick's Point.

**CAMPGROUNDS:** Dry Lagoon Environmental Camps are near access point. Big Lagoon County Park and Patrick's Point State Park are en route.

**LODGING:** Motels are in Orick to the north or Trinidad to the south.

**MAP:** See page 62.

This section starts just south of the freshwater marsh known as Dry Lagoon. CCT follows the beach around a rocky, slide-prone point where you'll need a tide lower than 2.0 feet to get through. Then at ¾ mile CCT crosses the surge channel of Big Lagoon. When the channel flows in winter or spring, the long barrier beach of Big Lagoon cannot be reached from the north. See Alternate Route for the detour along Highway 101. When the surge channel is empty, you can follow CCT south along the lagoon's barrier beach. Beyond Big Lagoon County Park the long beach continues south along the base of bluffs into Patrick's Point State Park where the nature of the coast changes dramatically once again.

From the parking area, walk west to the high tideline, then turn left and walk south-southwest along the beach. Beyond ⅛ mile the strand narrows at the first of several large rocks along the tideline. Continue along the beach to ⅜ mile where a landslide from the bluff makes the beach very narrow. If the tide is higher than +2.0 feet, you may not be able to pass this point. (If you return this way later, you'll need a similar tide to get by.)

If you can continue, pass more big rocks along the tideline. If the surf is large when you pass through, watch for waves surging through gaps between the shoreline rocks. At ½ mile the beach broadens. Beyond another slide at ⅝ mile, you'll see Big Lagoon ahead.

You reach the north end of Big Lagoon at ¾ mile. At the surge channel here, Big Lagoon drains into the Pacific after heavy winter rains. At extreme high tides, waves may dump salt water into the lagoon here as well. If you cannot pass the channel, you must return to the access point and follow the Alternate Route.

When you can reach the barrier beach beyond the channel, you can follow the sandy shore all the way to Patrick's Point without interruption. (Be sure tides and weather are okay if you return this way!) The firmest footing is usually along the lagoon shore, but you may want to vary the long beach stroll by following the tideline or the crest of the barrier beach.

Around ⅞ mile you pass a large driftwood log atop the barrier beach, a good spot for a rest. As you continue south, the barrier beach broadens at 1⅛ miles, staying very broad until 1⅝ miles. Then the beach gradually narrows as Big Lagoon increases in width.

At 2⅛ miles you reach the first of several low spots in the beach where the breakers carry over the sand spit at extremely high tides. These low spots shouldn't be a problem since we warned you not to come out here at such tides. Continue past beach vegetation including dune tansy, sand verbena and beach

**Wooded Pewetole Island stands off Trinidad State Beach.**

strawberry. At 2⅞ miles a log atop the beach crest is posted "STATE PARK PROPERTY." Around 3 miles, Big Lagoon is more than a mile across. Several large driftwood logs provide seating and some shelter for a picnic and/or bird watching. This spot offers a good turn-around point for day hikers.

If you are continuing south on CCT, follow the sand spit another 1¼ miles. At 4¼ miles, you reach Big Lagoon County Park and the southern tip of Big Lagoon where restrooms, picnic tables, and a campground are a short walk east.

CCT continues along the sandy shore, with the previously watery views to the east replaced by golden cliffs that give the beach a sheltered feel. Cross the first of several seasonal creeks by 4½ miles where the cliffs rise as a low bluff. After a second seasonal stream, the cliffs rise 120 feet overhead.

Follow the beach as it curves southwest toward Patrick's Point, the dramatic wooded promontory ahead. Small agates are often found along this Agate Beach. After two more small creeks around 5⅛ miles, the dun cliffs rise dramatically, reaching their highest point around 5⅝ miles where they soar almost vertically 400 feet above you in tilted sandstone strata. Continue past a steep gully. Around 5⅞ miles abundant lupine covers the cliff face, providing a spectacular color display from April through June. Pass the cliff's steepest face beyond 6 miles.

Before 6⅛ miles you ford a creek flowing out of a deep gully. In another 75 feet you want to leave the beach (impassable in 300 feet) and take the Agate Beach Trail that ascends steps beside a gully through dense coastal scrub. By 6½ miles it gains a narrow ridge and climbs through forest with views back along the sweeping beach you just traversed. Reach the trailhead at Agate Beach parking area at 6⅜ miles where restrooms and water are available. Pleasant Agate Beach Campground is nearby.

**ALTERNATE ROUTE:** When the point south of Dry Lagoon is impassable at medium to high tide, or when Big Lagoon breaches the barrier beach at its north end, you can walk east on the park access road to Highway 101, then walk the highway shoulder south to Big Lagoon County Park and return to the beach there.

**SUGGESTED ROUND TRIPS & LOOPS:** There are no loops here, but you can turn back anywhere along this beach walk. When Big Lagoon breaches the barrier beach at its north end, you can get to the long sandbar from Big Lagoon County Park at the lagoon's southwest corner.

**HOW TO IMPROVE CCT HERE:** State Parks could build an all tide trail from the Environmental Camps over the point to the beach south of the low-tide-only point.

## SECTION 5
# Patrick's Point State Park to Trinidad

DISTANCE: 8⅛ miles (13.1 kilometers).

OPEN TO: Hikers. Bicyclists on road, horse trail open to equestrians.

SURFACE: Trail, road shoulder, beach.

ACCESS POINT: Agate Beach Trailhead.

HOW TO GET THERE: Exit Highway 101 north of Trinidad onto Patrick's Point Drive, Milepost 106.2 from north, Milepost 105.75 from south. Go .5 mile to park entrance and turn right to entrance kiosk. Follow signs one mile to Agate Beach parking lot.

OTHER ACCESS: Many places in Patrick's Point State Park. Anywhere on road segment. Trinidad State Beach, north and south lots. Beach parking lot at end of Edwards Street.

DIFFICULTY: Easy.

ELEVATION GAIN/LOSS: 750 feet+/790 feet-.

CAUTIONS: Use caution when walking or biking road.

FURTHER INFORMATION: Patrick's Point State Park (707)677-3570, Trinidad Chamber of Commerce (707)677-1610, City of Trinidad (707)677-0223.

FACILITIES: Restrooms, water, phone, picnic area.

CAMPGROUNDS: Patrick's Point State Park has 123 campsites in several campgrounds. Several private campgrounds are between the park and the town of Trinidad.

LODGING: Several motels and B&Bs are in and around Trinidad.

This section of CCT has three distinct parts. First, CCT follows the Rim Trail along the oceanside perimeter of beautiful, compact Patrick's Point State Park, passing six spur trails that explore the convoluted shoreline more closely. One spur leads to Wedding Rock where on a clear day you can see Cape Mendocino 50 miles south. Two other park attractions merit a visit. From 287-foot Ceremonial Rock, you might see the mouth of the Klamath River 30 miles north. At the reconstructed Yurok village of Sumeg on the park's east side, visit traditional dwellings like the ones local natives inhabited for millennia. The section's second and longest part is a pleasant road walk along not-too-busy Patrick's Point Drive and lightly traveled Stagecoach Road where you're almost always within hearing of the roaring surf with the Pacific often in view. It's a great bike ride if you prefer to follow the pavement on wheels. The section's third part traverses the length of 159-acre Trinidad State Beach, a little known but lovely stretch of coast.

Take the Rim Trail west, soon following a chain link fence that keeps foolish explorers off the dangerous steep bluffs to the north. You pass through berry thickets with views north over Agate Beach and northwest to Mussel Rocks. Enter

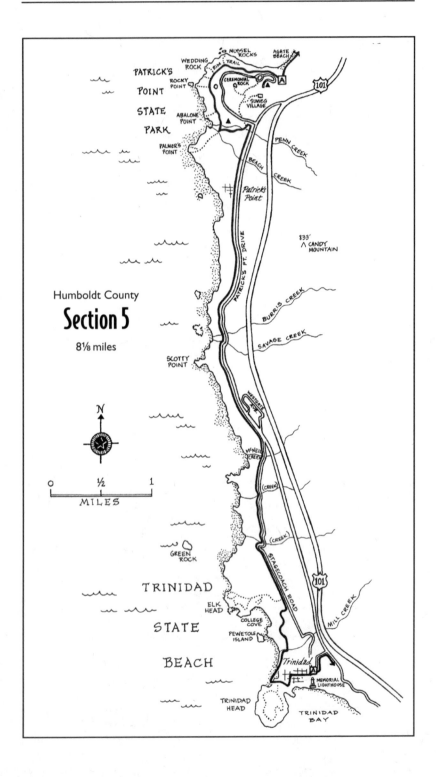

PATRICK'S
POINT
STATE
PARK

Humboldt County
## Section 5
8⅛ miles

N

MILES

MUSSEL ROCKS
AGATE BEACH
WEDDING ROCK
ELK TRAIL
ROCKY POINT
CEREMONIAL ROCK
SUMEG VILLAGE
ABALONE POINT
PALMER'S POINT
101
PENN CREEK
BEACH CREEK
Patrick's Point
833'
CANDY MOUNTAIN
PATRICK'S PT. DRIVE
BURRIS CREEK
SAVAGE CREEK
SCOTTY POINT
WESTGATE
McNEIL CREEK
(CREEK)
(CREEK)
GREEN ROCK
STAGECOACH ROAD
101
MILL CREEK
TRINIDAD
STATE
BEACH
ELK HEAD
COLLEGE COVE
PEWETOLE ISLAND
Trinidad
MEMORIAL LIGHTHOUSE
TRINIDAD HEAD
TRINIDAD BAY

dense forest around ¼ mile. Soon tiny Beaver Creek burbles on your left. Veer right to an overlook at bluff's edge, then wind left, crossing a bridge above a waterfall at ⅜ mile. After a tunnel of foliage, descend steps to Mussel Rocks spur trail (¼ mile round trip) on the right before ½ mile.

Rim Trail climbs steps, then turns south between two big rocks and descends to a picnic area. Head west past another coastal view to another picnic area at ⅝ mile. As you approach the Wedding Rock parking area, take the first right fork to avoid the congestion and descend to Wedding Rock spur trail. The spur drops then climbs to the top of Wedding Rock, a ¼-mile round trip.

CCT continues south on the Rim Trail, soon climbing steps to join a paved, wheelchair-accessible path and to meet the Patrick's Point spur at ¾ mile. The paved spur forks right, descending to postcard vistas, a ¼-mile round trip. Follow the Rim Trail as it wraps around the base of Lookout Rock on your left, quickly passing the Lookout Rock spur, a ⅛-mile round trip.

The Rim Trail descends through spruce forest to cross tiny Ickie Ughie Creek, then climbs to the Rocky Point side trail (a ⅛-mile round trip). Rim Trail climbs to a spur to the hike/bike camps, then turns south through alder forest with views seaward. Pass a large cypress at one mile and continue along the western edge of Abalone Campground. A spur forks right at 1⅛ miles, dropping to Abalone Point, ⅛-mile round trip.

Follow the Rim Trail southeast along the wooded bluff and across a small bridge. As the dirt track ends at a paved trail, turn right and cross a bridge over Penn Creek, coming to a junction of three trails. CCT leaves the Rim Trail here, turning left on the dirt path that heads east and north to the park entrance.

You can take one more side trip of a mile or more to Palmer's Point, the park's westernmost promontory. To do so, turn right and follow Rim Trail ⅜ mile until it joins the paved road to Palmer's Point, then walk the road shoulder ⅛ mile to its end, where the left fork leads to the tip of the point and the right fork descends to Cannonball Beach.

From the junction south of Penn Creek, CCT heads east along the creek, crossing a paved road. Cross Penn Creek by 1½ miles and fork left, climbing gradually through spruce forest and crossing several small bridges. Where you meet the park entrance road, the kiosk is about 300 feet west. CCT turns right to leave the park. You can easily loop back to your starting point by crossing the road to follow the trail north toward Ceremonial Rock — a great side trip — then follow signs to Agate Beach Campground.

CCT reaches the end of the park road at 1¾ miles. Turn right and walk the shoulder of Patrick's Point Drive south. The road dips across Penn Creek then Beach Creek at 2⅛ miles. Climb slightly as you pass through the community of Patrick's Point, coming back within view of the ocean. Continue along the road shoulder through forest with occasional glimpses of the shore. Top a rise before 3¼ miles. Descend across Burris Creek at 3⅞ miles, then Savage Creek. Climb over a rise above Scotty Point around 4¼ miles, then contour through forest into a clearing beyond Westgate Avenue at 4¾ miles.

Follow Patrick's Point Drive through the clearing until 5 miles where Stagecoach Road forks right. Turn right and walk the shoulder of Stagecoach Road as it dips across McNeil Creek before 5¼ miles. Ascend over a wooded headland, contour then dip across two unnamed creeks at 5⅝ and 6⅛ miles. After the latter

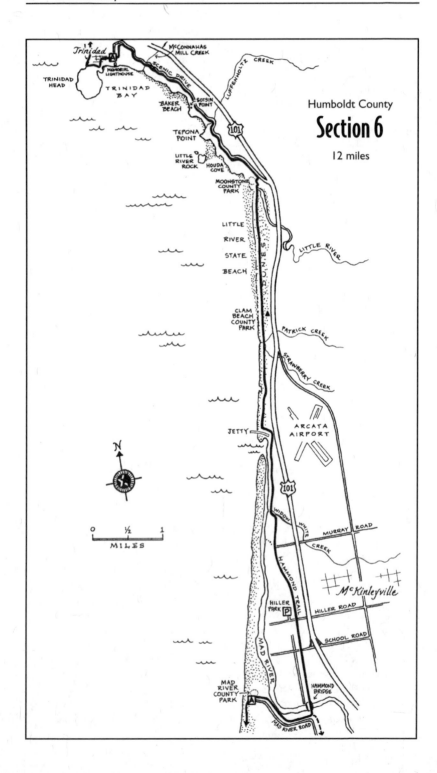

Humboldt County
# Section 6
12 miles

creek, follow the sleepy lane as it winds into a clearing and straightens out past numerous residences.

From 6⅝ miles, the parklands of Trinidad State Beach are on your right. At 6⅞ miles you pass the access road to Elk Head where a short, level and pleasant loop trail explores the head, also providing access to scenic College Cove Beach.

CCT continues almost ¼ mile along Stagecoach Road, then turns right to follow the trail behind a silver gate that winds south over wooded bluffs. It dips through one gully, then another at 7 miles. Crossing the wooded headland you might glimpse impressive Pewetole Island just offshore. Descend lush slopes to cross a bridge over Mill Creek at 7⅝ miles, then follow the path downstream to meet the Mill Creek Trail before 7¾ miles. Turn right, following the trail downstream to the beach at the creek's mouth. Turn left and walk the beach south to 7⅞ miles, then turn southeast and ascend the beach to a parking lot at the end of Edwards Street. An excellent side trail on your right makes a 1½-mile loop around rugged Trinidad Head.

CCT heads east along the base of the bluff through the boat trailer parking lot for almost ⅛ mile, then ascends the Galindo Street Trail. In 300 feet you come to the corner of Galindo and VanWycke. Continue up Galindo Street to Edwards Street, then turn right and follow Edwards along the top of the bluff overlooking spectacular Trinidad Bay. You reach this section's end at the Memorial Lighthouse at 8⅛ miles. Look left for Trinidad's tiny downtown.

SUGGESTED ROUND TRIPS & LOOPS: By staying within Patrick's Point State Park, make a wonderful, varied loop of 3½ to 5 miles depending on how many side trails you take. At Elk Head in Trinidad State Beach, you can choose loops of ⅝ or 1½ miles. At Trinidad Head, the Tsurai Loop is 1½ miles long.

> HOW TO IMPROVE CCT HERE: Build a trail along the road shoulder for the northern ¼ mile of Trinidad State Beach.

## SECTION 6
# Trinidad to Mad River County Park

DISTANCE: 12 miles (19.3 kilometers).

OPEN TO: Hikers. Bicyclists on Scenic Drive and Hammond Trail. Equestrians on latter.

SURFACE: Road shoulder, beach, trail.

ACCESS POINT: Downtown Trinidad.

HOW TO GET THERE: Exit Highway 101 north of Arcata at Trinidad, Milepost 100.9 from north, Milepost 100.6 from south. Go west on Main Street, then left on Trinity Street to its end at Edwards Street and park.

OTHER ACCESS: Scenic Drive, Moonstone County Park, Little River State Beach, Clam Beach County Park, Hammond Trail from Murray Road or School Road.

DIFFICULTY: Easy.

ELEVATION GAIN/LOSS: 325 feet+/490 feet-. To Clam Beach: 215 feet+/ 390 feet-.

**CAUTIONS:** Little River is fordable only at low tide. Mad River is nearly always too deep to ford.

**FURTHER INFORMATION:** Trinidad Chamber of Commerce (707)677-1610, City of Trinidad (707)677-0223, Hammond Trail, Humboldt County Parks (707)445-7652.

**FACILITIES:** Restrooms, water, phone, picnic area.

**CAMPGROUNDS:** Several private campgrounds are around Trinidad. Public campgrounds are at Patrick's Point State Park to the north, or overnight camping at Clam Beach County Park along this section.

**LODGING:** Several inns and motels are around Trinidad.

The longest section yet on CCT offers both great variety and a major transition in geography. While Trinidad is one of the smallest incorporated cities in California, as well as one of the oldest, it offers a supermarket and three good cafes. Trinidad must also have one of the highest concentrations of trails among America's small towns. You might take a side trip or two to further explore this dramatic meeting of land and sea.

Less than 4 miles south of town the rugged rock-studded shore suddenly yields to a 19-mile beach sprawling south-southwest to the mouth of Humboldt Bay. The inland terrain changes dramatically as well, with the mountainous landscape to the north yielding to low marine terraces and bayside bottomlands. Most of this section consists of easy walking along the beach and the firm treaded Hammond Trail, which follows an old railway along the Mad River. Here you'll see locals enjoying their shoreline access.

Before section's end, through-hikers need to make a decision. To follow Humboldt County Sections 7, 8 and 9 in sequence, you'll need to arrange a boat shuttle across the mouth of Humboldt Bay. Otherwise you must make a major 35-mile detour into and through Arcata and Eureka with no chance to rejoin CCT until 18¼ miles down the trail.

The Coastal Trail follows city streets out of tiny Trinidad. Walk Edwards Street east one block to its end, then walk north two blocks on Ocean Street to Main Street. Turn right and follow Main east two blocks to the Highway 101 interchange where CCT turns right to follow Scenic Drive south.

Walk the road shoulder through a wooded gully and over a bluff. After a glimpse of the ocean around ¾ mile, follow the road winding east and south, dipping across McConnahas Mill Creek at one mile, then winding through the Trinidad Indian Reservation. At 1⅜ miles you get your first sweeping vista of rock-studded Trinidad Bay.

The next part of Scenic Drive is prone to slip-outs. After a one-lane stretch of road, pass the Baker Beach side trail at 1⅞ miles. It descends 350 feet to secluded Baker Beach. Continue along Scenic Drive over Sotsin Point and to a turnout at 2 miles with a sweeping view from Trinidad Head to Samoa Peninsula . Descend to Luffenholtz Creek, then climb to Luffenholtz County Park around Tepona Point at 2½ miles. A side trail from the north end of the parking lot drops to a beach.

Another spur leads to the tip of the point. Follow Scenic Drive south over another slip-out at 2⅝ miles.

Scenic Drive tops cypress-shrouded Houda Point at 2⅞ miles where another spur descends stone steps to a beach beside towering Little River Rock. The beach is expansive at low tide, narrow or submerged when the tide is in. Continue south on Scenic Drive as it climbs steeply to a final vista at 3 miles. Then follow Scenic Drive as it winds east and descends to Moonstone Road at 3⅝ miles. Turn right and descend Moonstone Road to Moonstone County Park at 3¾ miles.

At Moonstone the coast changes dramatically. Instead of the rocky, convoluted coast that has made CCT spectacular but difficult to follow for the past dozen miles, one virtually continuous beach stretches south for 19 miles. The Coastal Trail drops to the beach at Moonstone County Park with only two watery obstacles to your progress in those 19 sandy miles. The first obstacle is immediate. In only 300 feet you reach the mouth of Little River, highly subject to change. Sometimes you can easily ford the river near its mouth at low tide except at flood. If the tide is high or the ford too deep, you may need to wait for low tide, or you might be able to ford at the top of the beach as far from the mouth as possible. The second obstacle lies 3½ miles down the beach. The mouth of the Mad River is virtually always too deep to ford, but CCT follows the pleasant Hammond Trail east of the river.

From the parking lot at Moonstone County Park, walk the beach south or southeast to ford Little River, then continue south along the tideline. You walk through Little River State Beach until 5¼ miles where you enter Clam Beach County Park. You probably won't notice the change in jurisdiction until you reach the ford of Patrick Creek and Strawberry Creek around 6 miles (their confluence is on the broad beach). Overnight camping is allowed near the highway frontage road not far to the east.

Follow the tideline to 6½ miles where the shoreline makes a significant indentation for ⅛ mile. Continue along the shoreline to 7⅛ miles where the trail turns inland. You may see a rock jetty that protects Highway 101 from the fickle currents of the Mad River in the shifting dunes near its mouth, or the jetty may be buried in sand. Follow the beach southeast, then walk south on the level shelf east of the Mad River. The Hammond Trail has not yet been completed this far north, but it's mostly easy walking on a two-lane track. Plans for the Hammond Trail include bridging Widow White Creek upstream from the current ford and extending the developed trail north to the jetty.

At 8⅜ miles you must ford Widow White Creek. The ford is passable except after major storms. Follow the river bank about 700 feet, then jog east up to the Hammond Trail. Follow the trail south along the east bank of the river, passing the Murray Road access at 8¾ miles, where a short spur descends to the river.

Then follow the Hammond Trail as it veers away from the river, passing residences. Cross Knox Cove Drive, then follow paved trail to Hiller Park at 9⅝ miles where you'll find restrooms, water and picnic tables. CCT crosses Hiller Road as the trail becomes more suburban. You soon follow a town street to School Street. Then follow a paved country lane down to the river's flood plain, coming to the Hammond Bridge across Mad River at 10⅞ miles.

Where the Hammond Trail meets Mad River Road south of the bridge at 11 miles, CCT turns west to follow Mad River Road to its end at 12 miles at Mad

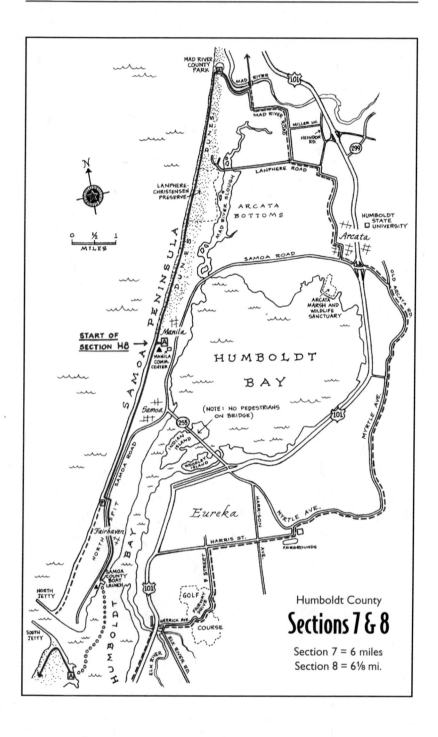

MAD RIVER
COUNTY
PARK

MAD RIVER

101

MAD RIVER

MILLER LN.

HEINDON
RD.

299

LANPHERE ROAD

N

LANPHERE-
CHRISTENSEN
PRESERVE

ARCATA
BOTTOMS

HUMBOLDT
STATE
UNIVERSITY

Arcata

0    ½    1
MILES

SAMOA ROAD

ARCATA
MARSH AND
WILDLIFE
SANCTUARY

OLD ARCATA RD.

S A M O A    P E N I N S U L A

D U N E S

M A D   R I V E R   S L O U G H

START OF
SECTION H8

Manila

A
P

MANILA
COMM.
CENTER

H U M B O L D T

B A Y

Samoa

(NOTE: NO PEDESTRIANS
ON BRIDGE)

255

INDIAN
ISLAND

WOODLEY
ISLAND

101

MYRTLE AVE.

Eureka

HARRISON

MYRTLE AVE.

SAMOA ROAD

NORTH SPIT

Fairhaven

HARRIS ST.

AVE.

FAIRGROUNDS

NORTH
JETTY

SAMOA
COUNTY
BOAT
LAUNCH

101

GOLF

FAIRWAY DRIVE

F STREET

H U M B O L D T   B A Y

SOUTH
JETTY

A

HERRICK AVE.

ELK RIVER

ELK RIVER RD.

COURSE

Humboldt County

# Sections 7 & 8

Section 7 = 6 miles
Section 8 = 6⅛ mi.

River County Park, where CCT returns to the beach. For another way into Arcata along the Hammond Trail, see **Alternate Route**.

**ALTERNATE ROUTE:** At the Hammond Bridge, instead of walking west to Mad River County Park, you can follow the Hammond Trail, now a bike lane, south on country roads into the town of Arcata, home of Humboldt State University. If you're through-hiking and can't arrange a boat shuttle between Sections 8 and 9, you must go via Arcata.

**SUGGESTED ROUND TRIPS & LOOPS:** Day hikers might consider following the Hammond Trail north from the south end of this section or from the Hammond Bridge, also an excellent bike ride. Or ford Little River at Moonstone County Park and walk the beach to the mouth of Mad River, 6¾ miles round trip.

**HOW TO IMPROVE CCT HERE:** Finish the Hammond Trail at north end.

## SECTION 7
# Mad River County Park to Manila

**DISTANCE:** 6 miles of CCT, 6⅝ miles to south end access (9.7 or 10.3 kilometers).

**OPEN TO:** Hikers, equestrians.

**SURFACE:** Beach.

**ACCESS POINT:** Mad River County Park.

**HOW TO GET THERE:** Exit Highway 101 north of Arcata onto Janes Road at Milepost 89.05 from north, Milepost 88.5 from south. Go west on Janes Road, then right on Heindon Road for .4 mile. Go left on Miller Lane for .7 mile. Then go right on Mad River Road, coming to Hammond Bridge in 1.7 miles. The road turns west following the CCT route (Section 6) to the parking area and access point in 1.1 miles (4 miles from Highway 101).

**OTHER ACCESS:** Lanphere-Christensen Dunes Preserve, call for permission (707)822-6378.

**DIFFICULTY:** Easy.

**ELEVATION GAIN/LOSS:** 10 feet- for CCT, 60 feet+/50 feet- to Community Center.

**CAUTIONS:** Watch for off-road vehicles on the beach.

**FURTHER INFORMATION:** Humboldt County Parks (707)445-7652. For boat shuttle call Humb Boats (707)443-5157.

**FACILITIES:** Chemical toilets, picnic area.

**CAMPGROUNDS:** Clam Beach County Park allows overnight stays. Several private campgrounds in Arcata area.

**LODGING:** Arcata has numerous motels.

While Mad River County Park consists of only 150 acres of dunes south of the Mad River mouth, it provides access to the 11 miles of continuous beach stretching south to the mouth of Humboldt Bay. If you have time, visit the Nature Conservancy's Lanphere-Christensen Dunes Preserve two miles south of Mad River County Park for a look at undisturbed dunes habitat.

From the parking area, follow a jeep track west-northwest through low dunes, coming to the tideline in about ⅛ mile. Head south along the firm sand just beyond the reach of the waves. By ½ mile the beach turns broader than at the start with high dunes to the east. Beyond one mile much large driftwood lies along the beach. At 1½ miles a pole stands atop the dune nearest the beach. A double track heads east into the dunes at 1⅝ miles where two large driftwood stumps lie at tideline. Continue along the unbroken beach.

Around 2 miles the dunes to the east stand about 70 feet tall. From 2¼ miles the protected habitat of the Lanphere-Christensen Dunes Preserve lies to your east. The preserve encloses the tallest dune, an 81-foot sandhill ⅜ mile east. Mad River Slough, an ancient outlet for the river when it flowed into Humboldt Bay, lies east of the preserve. The beach walk parallels the preserve until 3⅜ miles. The long beach walk continues with little notable change, low dunes rising on your left, breakers rolling in on your right.

By 5 miles you may notice a gap in the dunes to your east. You are now on the Samoa Peninsula, a half-mile wide sand spit between the Pacific Ocean and Humboldt Bay. Continue along the beach for another mile. You've left most of the agricultural lands behind. Now the small town of Manila lies to the east.

At 6 miles the CCT continues along the ocean beach. Although this section of the Coastal Trail ends, you have the option of turning east into the dunes to reach the section's south end access. To do so, look for a broad, sandy path east through a low point in the dunes. It's hard to spot on the long, straight beach.Follow it east ⅜ mile to the Manila Community Center in the old Manila School.

**ALTERNATE ROUTE:** For through-hikers, the pressing problem of Humboldt Section 8 to the south lies in the deep water crossing at the mouth of Humboldt Bay. To make the crossing you must arrange a boat before you arrive. If you are unable to arrange a boat, you'll need to leave the CCT at Mad River County Park or the Hammond Bridge. From the Hammond Bridge follow the Hammond Trail to Arcata, then walk east on 7th Street to head south on Bayside Road, Old Arcata Road and Myrtle Avenue to circle Humboldt Bay to Eureka. As you enter town, turn left on Hall Avenue, then follow Harris Street west to F Street. Walk south on F, which eventually becomes Fairway Drive. Follow it to its end, then walk Herrick Avenue west to Highway 101. Follow Highway 101, South Broadway and Humboldt Hill Road south to the Hookton Road exit which leaves Highway 101 6¾ miles south of Herrick. Then walk Hookton Road and Table Bluff Road 5½ miles to return to CCT at the base of Table Bluff in Humboldt Section 9. It's a long 30- to 35-mile detour, bypassing 18¼ miles of CCT. The town portion is not very pleasant compared to the CCT route and a boat crossing of the mouth of Humboldt Bay, but if you must walk through town you can compensate with a meal out and maybe an espresso drink or some other decadent town treat.

SUGGESTED ROUND TRIPS & LOOPS: Walk south along the beach from Mad River County Park for as long as you like, or walk north along the beach from the Manila Community Center at the south end.

## SECTION 8
# Manila to Mouth of Humboldt Bay, North Side

DISTANCE: 6⅛ miles to end of North Spit. For through-hikers or others taking a boat across Humboldt Bay, 5⅝ miles to the Samoa County Boat Launch (9.9 or 9.1 kilometers).

OPEN TO: Hikers, equestrians.

SURFACE: Beach, road shoulder if you're heading for boat launch.

ACCESS POINT: Manila Community Center.

HOW TO GET THERE: From the south, turn left off Highway 101 at the north end of Eureka onto Highway 255 at R Street. Go 2.6 miles, turn left onto Pacific Avenue, then left onto Peninsula Drive and go .2 mile to Community Center parking lot on right. From the north, exit Highway 101 at the south end of Arcata, Milepost 86.2, onto Highway 255/Samoa Boulevard. Go 5.5 miles, then turn right onto Pacific Avenue, then left onto Peninsula Drive and go .2 mile to Community Center parking lot on right.

OTHER ACCESS: Orange Drive, Bay Street, Samoa Dunes Recreation Area.

SOUTH END ACCESS: Coast Guard Station (May to Sept.) or Samoa County Boat Launch.

DIFFICULTY: Easy.

ELEVATION GAIN/LOSS: None for CCT Section; 30 feet+/40 feet- from Community Center.

CAUTIONS: This shore is particularly prone to rogue waves, especially near Humboldt Bay's mouth. Beware that off-road vehicles also use this area. Stay off the main part of the Coast Guard Reservation unless you know it is open to the public on the day you're hiking.

FURTHER INFORMATION: BLM for Samoa Dunes Recreation Area (707)825-2300. Manila Community Center (707)445-3309. For boat shuttle call Humb Boats (707)443-5157 .

FACILITIES: Restrooms and water when center is open.

CAMPGROUNDS: Samoa County Boat Launch (south end), Manila Beach and Dunes (north).

LODGING: None on peninsula but many in Arcata to north and Eureka to east.

MAP: See page 76.

The Manila Community Center occupies the old Manila School on the Manila Beach and Dunes Preserve, a reserve of 100 acres of coastal dunes. The preserve nestles among several parcels of private property, but also adjoins the long unbroken beach beyond the dunes along the Pacific shore of the Samoa Peninsula.

From the Manila Community Center walk west-northwest past the end of the old school building and continue on the path over the first dune. At the second dune crest, veer right to join a broader path. Continue west over another dune at ⅛ mile where you can see the ocean ahead. Dip through a vegetated valley in the dunes at ¼ mile, then climb over one more dune. You reach the tideline where CCT runs along the beach at ⅜ mile.

Turn left and follow the firm sand southwest with low dunes on your left and ocean breakers on your right. By 1½ miles a residential area at the north end of the town of Samoa is in the dunes to your east. By 2 miles you are paralleling New Navy Base Road, the main road along the south end of the north spit. The center of Samoa lies about ¼ mile east. After you pass the big industrial smokestacks of Louisiana-Pacific, the west end of Bay Street is one tenth of a mile east. New Navy Base Road curves away from the western shore only ¼ mile south, crossing to the eastern edge of the peninsula.

Continue along the beach paralleling the road to 3⅝ miles where you need to make a decision based upon whether you're day hiking or catching a boat shuttle across the bay. If you're day hiking to the end of the North Spit, continue along the beach at the tideline. You pass the north end of a drag strip near the old Eureka Airport around 4¼ miles. At 5⅝ miles you enter the Coast Guard Reservation on the tip of the North Spit. You have the right to continue along the beach below the mean high tideline. The North Spit ends at 6⅛ miles as you come to the sea wall and the North Jetty. Be especially careful of oversize rogue waves which may crest over the top of the sea wall. Return the way you came.

If you've arranged a boat shuttle from the Samoa County Boat Launch, you need to leave the beach at 3⅝ miles. Walk east to the parking area at the end of Bay Street, then walk the shoulder of New Navy Base Road for almost 2 miles. Around 5½ miles you'll see the County Boat Launch to the east. Another ⅛ mile brings you to the dock.

ALTERNATE ROUTE: Through-hikers see Alternate Route for Humboldt Section 7 if you cannot arrange a boat the take you across Humboldt Bay to the South Spit.

SUGGESTED ROUND TRIPS & LOOPS: Loop through the Manila Beach and Dunes Preserve on their trail system. From the Community Center it's ½ mile to the short Forest Loop. From there you can head northwest to the beach and CCT or return to your starting point.

## SECTION 9
# Mouth of Humboldt Bay, South Side, to Mouth of Eel River

DISTANCE: 7½ miles (12.1 kilometers).

OPEN TO: Hikers, equestrians.

SURFACE: Beach.

ACCESS POINT: North end of South Jetty.

HOW TO GET THERE: Take a boat across the bay or walk north from Table Bluff. If South Spit Road reopens to the public in summer 2002 as planned, you will once again be able to drive to the access point.

OTHER ACCESS: Table Bluff County Park.

HOW TO GET THERE: Exit Highway 101 south of Eureka at Milepost 68.0 from south, Milepost 68.15 from north onto Hookton Road and follow it west. In 3 miles it merges with Table Bluff Road. Continue 2 more miles to Table Bluff County Park. Where road is closed .2 mile farther, park near the gate. (If South Spit Road has reopened to the public, you can drive the 4.7 miles to northern access point.)

DIFFICULTY: Easy.

ELEVATION GAIN/LOSS: None for CCT. From Table Bluff: 170 feet+/170 feet-.

CAUTIONS: Watch for oversize waves when walking the beach. No camping on South Spit.

FURTHER INFORMATION: Humboldt County Parks (707)445-7652, Humboldt Bay National Wildlife Refuge (707)733-5406. For boat shuttle call Humb Boats (707)443-5157.

FACILITIES: None.

CAMPGROUNDS: KOA in Fortuna.

LODGING: Many are available in Eureka and Fortuna.

Unlike most CCT sections, this section and the next one have no vehicle access to their northern access points. (This section may change in summer 2002 if South Spit Road reopens.) This means you need to walk several miles to reach the northern access points unless you take a boat, across Humboldt Bay for this section, across the Eel River for the next. Humboldt County closed South Jetty Road to vehicle traffic at the end of 1997. Day hikers need to park at Table Bluff County Park and walk down the road .3 mile to the base of the bluff where the road turns northeast, running 4.4 miles to the end of the South Spit. The Coastal Trail follows the beach west of the road.

The most remarkable feature of the South Spit is the extensive tidal flats of Humboldt Bay along its eastern shore. At high tide the South Bay looks like a very large body of water, but when the tide drops below 0.0 feet, most of it becomes a giant mud flat where abundant shore birds gather and forage. To best observe the wildlife when you visit at low tide, consider walking along the western shore of

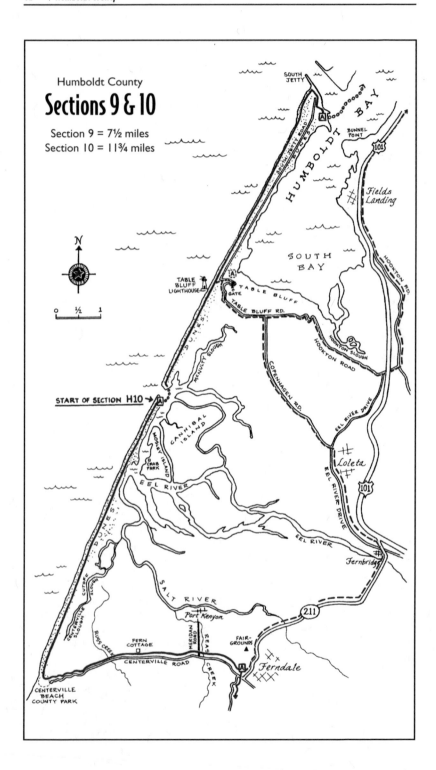

Humboldt County
# Sections 9 & 10

Section 9 = 7½ miles
Section 10 = 11¾ miles

Humboldt Bay east of the road. Much of the bay is in the Humboldt Bay National Wildlife Refuge.

At moderate to high tide it's better to follow CCT along the western shore. Most of the land on South Spit that was privately owned until 2000 is now held by the California Department of Fish and Game. The South Jetty Road is also public, and of course you always have the right to walk the beach below the mean high tideline.

If you crossed Humboldt Bay from the North Spit in a boat, the skipper probably dropped you on the eastern point at the tip of the South Spit. If so, walk west along the curving track for about ½ mile to South Jetty Road. Walk north ¼ mile to the end of the road, then walk northwest near the sea wall, coming to the base of the South Jetty before ¼ mile. The jetty extends ¾ mile out to sea but is extremely prone to rogue waves.

From the South Spit's northern tip, the Coastal Trail follows the western shore on another long beach walk. By ¾ mile you are west of the intersection of the

## The Discovery and Settlement of Humboldt Bay

The Algonkian Wiyot people were the original residents of the Humboldt Bay region, inhabiting Pacific and bay shores from lower Mad River on the north to lower Eel River on the south, thriving on the marine abundance of this rich and gentle coastal strip. Their mythology's depiction of abalone as the first people confirms the Wiyot are an ocean-oriented, coast-dwelling society.

Early European explorers overlooked Humboldt Bay because its narrow and shallow mouth was often hidden in fog. The notable exception to this came in 1806 when American sea captain Jonathan Winship discovered the bay when exploring for the Russian-American Fur Company. Winship's discovery was forgotten because he deemed the bay unnavigable.

After gold discoveries along the Trinity and Klamath Rivers in 1848, the search for a safe north coast harbor resumed, driven by the difficult inland route to the new mines. In late 1849 a party of eight men led by Dr. Josiah Gregg left the Trinity mines seeking the Trinidad Bay shown on Spanish maps. Though local natives told Gregg the journey to the coast would take eight days, his party lacked guides and lost

the native trail in a snowstorm. After a four and a half week ordeal, Gregg's starving party finally reached Trinidad Bay. They traded with the Yuroks for provisions, then followed the coast south.

They soon found Humboldt Bay, California's second largest. Christmas Day found Gregg's party camped beside the bay at the future location of Arcata, feasting on elk and clams provided by friendly Wiyots. The party headed south to tell booming California of their discoveries, but quickly found their ordeal had just begun. Gregg died of starvation en route. Their second leader, L. K. Wood, was mauled by grizzly bears in the Eel River canyon and crippled for life, but the survivors reached Sonoma eight grueling weeks after leaving Humboldt Bay.

Several ships immediately left San Francisco racing for Humboldt and Trinidad Bays. Settlement began at Trinidad in March 1850, at Humboldt Bay in April. By summer a trail was completed to the Klamath and Trinity mines, and by September Eureka had its first sawmill. By 1853 nine Humboldt Bay mills shipped 20 million board feet of lumber to San Francisco.

main road and east road. Continue along the firm sand at tideline. At 3¼ miles the sand spit narrows to barely one-tenth mile wide. As you continue along the beach, the spit broadens and the green rise of Table Bluff ahead grows prominent.

By 5 miles you draw even with Table Bluff as it rises 170 feet above the beach. South Jetty Road ends at the hairpin turn just east of the beach, becoming Table Bluff Road as it climbs by switchbacks to the top of the bluff.

CCT continues south from Table Bluff along the dark sand beach for about 2½ miles to the broad mouth of the Eel River. That mileage is approximate because the mouth of the Eel River moves irregularly as the powerful river shifts the unstable sands around its mouth. In a seven-year period from 1988 to 1995 the mouth of the river moved nearly two miles north. To continue south on CCT from the river mouth requires a boat. Even if you find someone with a boat who is willing to shuttle you across, winds and tides must also be in your favor. Call Humb Boats and see if they can arrange a shuttle. If not, through-hikers must follow the **Alternate Route** from Table Bluff.

To follow CCT south from Table Bluff, walk the tideline ⅛ mile to the base of the westernmost point of the bluff. Then continue south-southwest along the hard sand near the tideline. By 6½ miles McNulty Slough lies ⅜ mile east of the shore. By 6¾ miles a smaller slough is only ⅛ mile east. At 7 miles you begin to parallel North Bay Slough with large stacks of driftwood along the high tideline between you and the slough. Somewhere around 7½ miles you come to the mouth of the Eel River. You can't miss the only outlet for California's third largest river!

**ALTERNATE ROUTE:** If you're through-hiking and cannot arrange a boat shuttle across the Eel River near its mouth, take the following route south from Table Bluff. It will bypass the rest of Section 9 and all of Section 10. Walk Table Bluff Road south and east 2⅛ miles. Turn right on Copenhagen Road and walk it to its end at Eel River Drive at 5½ miles. Turn right and walk south on Eel River Drive through Loleta and into Fernbridge at 8⅛ miles. At Fernbridge turn right on Highway 211 and cautiously walk the busy highway shoulder southwest for 5 miles to Ferndale. At the south end of Main Street, turn right on Ocean Street and go one block. Humboldt Section 11 starts where the Mattole Road climbs from Ocean Street. The detour is about one mile shorter than the portion of CCT it bypasses, but not nearly as pleasant a hike.

**SUGGESTED ROUND TRIPS & LOOPS:** The nicest walk here starts at Table Bluff and follows the beach south to the mouth of the river, then returns along the high side of the beach with views over the sloughs, about 5 miles round trip, passing through the Eel River Wildlife Area.

## SECTION 10
# Mouth of Eel River to Centerville Beach to Ferndale

DISTANCE: 11¾ miles (18.9 kilometers).

OPEN TO: Hikers, equestrians.

SURFACE: Beach, paved road.

ACCESS POINT: Mouth of Eel River.

HOW TO GET THERE: Take a boat across the river or walk north from Centerville Beach.

OTHER ACCESS: Centerville Beach.

HOW TO GET THERE: Leave Highway 101 south of Eureka at Ferndale exit, Milepost 64.5 from north, Milepost 62.9 from south. Cross Fernbridge and go west 5 miles through Ferndale. At south end of Main Street, turn right and go 5 miles to Centerville Beach parking lot.

DIFFICULTY: Easy.

ELEVATION GAIN/LOSS: None for beach. Centerville to Ferndale: 225 feet+/145 feet-

CAUTIONS: Watch for off-road vehicles on beach.

FURTHER INFORMATION: Humboldt County Parks (707)445-7652.

FACILITIES: None except restroom, water, phone at Ferndale.

CAMPGROUNDS: County Fairgrounds north of Ferndale allows camping. Fortuna has a private campground.

LODGING: Ferndale has several.

MAP: See page 82.

If you took a boat shuttle across the Eel River near its mouth, this section offers a simple walk along the beach, followed by a road walk east to Ferndale where Humboldt Section 11 begins. Otherwise through-hikers will bypass this section altogether as they make the long road walk detour east through Loleta and Fernbridge (see Humboldt Section 9 Alternate Route).

If you're day hiking this section, start at Centerville Beach County Park and follow the beach north to the mouth of the Eel River. Whichever way you hike it, the beach distances are approximate due to the Eel River's tendency to move its mouth north or south from year to year. We based our report on the location of the river mouth in July 1997.

From the river's mouth walk west to the firm sand at the tideline, then follow it south-southwest along the sand spit between the Pacific Ocean and the Eel River. As you head south, Cannibal Island lies across the river to the east, then smaller Mosley Island appears across the river. By 1¼ miles you're opposite tiny Crab County Park on Mosley Island's west shore.

From 1½ to 1⅞ miles along the beach, the Eel River swings to the east. It's extremely broad at this spot. The tiny Salt River enters the Eel from the south just east of the barrier beach at this point. The sandbar you just crossed was the location of the Eel River mouth as recently as 1988.

As you continue down the beach, it soon turns from a barrier beach or sand spit to a long beach backed by low sand dunes which in turn are bordered by sloughs and canals. You might see the first large dune to the east around 2¾ miles. The dunes are taller again beyond 3⅝ miles. Around 3⅞ miles the westernmost dune is only 200 feet from the surf.

The tideline jogs westward between 3⅞ and 4⅝ miles. Watch for abundant sea birds over the surf, including cormorants, seagulls and pelicans. Shore birds abound including sandpipers and sanderlings. Beyond the low dunes to the east many migratory birds, the abundant Canada geese and tundra swans to name two, spend their winters sharing the area with the egrets and herons that reside here.

Around 4⅜ miles Cutoff Slough lies about ⅜ mile east of the tideline. The beach has a gradual slope here, but by 4¾ miles it steepens. Between 5 and 5¼ miles the beach is so steep you cannot see the dunes from the tideline. Narrow Centerville Slough lies just east of the dunes until around 5¾ miles.

Now it is less than a mile to the parking lot for Centerville Beach County Park. Watch for signs of the lot around 6⅝ miles where you want to turn east for ⅛ mile to meet Centerville Road. It would be easy to miss the parking lot in the fog and continue down the beach. If you see sandstone cliffs rising east of the beach, turn back, you've gone too far.

Where the parking lot meets Centerville Road at 6¾ miles, you want to turn left toward Ferndale and follow Centerville Road's shoulder east along the base of the hills at the edge of the river's flood plain. You pass Poole Road on the right before 7⅝ miles. Continue along Centerville Road, crossing Russ Creek and passing Fern Cottage before 9 miles. Pass Meridian Road on the left around 10½ miles, then cross Reas Creek. By 11 miles you approach Ferndale. The road jogs south briefly, following Ocean Drive into town and meeting the Mattole Road on the right at 11¾ miles, start of Section 11.

ALTERNATE ROUTE: See Humboldt Section 9 Alternate Route.

SUGGESTED ROUND TRIPS & LOOPS: It's an all day beach walk from Centerville Beach County Park to the mouth of the Eel River and back.

HOW TO IMPROVE CCT HERE: Since CCT turns inland to follow Mattole Road, develop a trail paralleling Centerville Road.

## SECTION 11
# Ferndale to Cape Mendocino

DISTANCE: 19½ miles (31.4 kilometers).

OPEN TO: Hikers, bicyclists.

SURFACE: Road shoulder.

ACCESS POINT: Town of Ferndale.

HOW TO GET THERE: Take Ferndale exit, Milepost 64.5 from north, Milepost 62.9 from south, from Highway 101 south of Eureka. Cross Fernbridge and go 5 miles to south end of Main Street. Turn right on Ocean Street and park near Mattole Road.

OTHER ACCESS: Anywhere along Mattole Road.

SOUTH END ACCESS: Unnamed creek one mile south of Singley Creek.

DIFFICULTY: Strenuous.

ELEVATION GAIN/LOSS: 2960 feet+/2940 feet-.

CAUTIONS: Watch for vehicle traffic on this steep winding road where drivers are not expecting to see anyone walking. Road is closed one day each May for the Tour of the Unknown Coast, a bicycle event. No services on route.

FURTHER INFORMATION: City of Ferndale (707)786-4224. Humboldt County Road Department (707)445-7421.

FACILITIES: Ferndale has restrooms, water, phone. Mattole Road has no facilities.

CAMPGROUNDS: Humboldt County Fairgrounds in Ferndale allows camping. Fortuna has a KOA campground.

LODGING: Ferndale has several.

South of Ferndale, rugged terrain along the coast forces the California Coastal Trail inland over high ridges of the Coast Range. CCT makes its longest passage away from the coast in northern California, following the paved Mattole Road until it returns to the coast south of Cape Mendocino.

This truly lost portion of the Lost Coast was not always so impassable. The original stagecoach road from Ferndale to Petrolia, completed in 1871, followed the tideline south from Centerville Beach past Bear Gulch before climbing steeply over Oil Creek Ridge to reach Capetown on the Bear River. In 1995 the author and ten other Coastwalkers hiked the 11 miles of this tricky and treacherous Lost Coast from Centerville Beach to Singley Creek. Preceded by several scouting trips, the trek took 2½ days to walk the 11 miles because no fewer than five points could be passed only at major minus tides. Even then we got very wet rounding one of the points and also had a precarious climb over a major mudslide only 1½ miles into our trek. The mudslide washed away in 1998-99 winter storm surf.

When the CCT Whole Hikers attempted the same feat the summer of 1996,

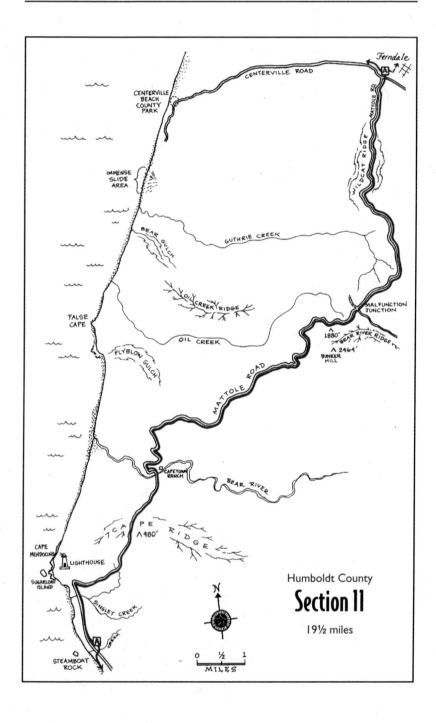

Humboldt County
## Section 11
19½ miles

they got drenched at one low-tide point and spent four soggy, chilled hours trapped at another. In short, walking this stretch of coast is **EXTREMELY HAZ-ARDOUS** and **NOT** recommended. The nature of the terrain often changes drastically from one year to another, and some years won't even have sufficiently low summer tides to make it through.

Walk the shoulder of Mattole Road south from town. The road climbs 800 feet in the first 1½ miles to gain Wildcat Ridge. Turn around for grand views over the verdant Eel River delta and the Victorian village of Ferndale visible for the first ½ mile. Your ascent eases as the road follows the ridge south, gaining another 200 feet by 2¼ miles. Before 3¼ miles you have climbed 1400 feet.

Mattole Road contours and descends slightly to 4 miles, then resumes climbing fitfully along the headwaters of Guthrie Creek. By 6⅛ miles you reach Malfunction Junction at 1818 feet, an intersection with Bear River Ridge Road on the left.

Continue along Mattole Road as it dips across the headwaters of Oil Creek at 6⅜ miles and turns west. Ascend to 1880 feet, the road's summit, at 7¼ miles where a clearing overlooks the Lost Coast around False Cape to the west and Eel River delta, Humboldt Bay and Trinidad Head to the north.

From 7⅜ miles your road offers the best views of the coast to the west as it descends around Bunker Hill until 8⅛ miles. The descent turns southwest to cross another fork of Oil Creek, then follows Bear River Ridge seaward. After a brief climb around 9 miles, begin a gradual but steady descent with occasional ocean vistas.

By 12⅜ miles you begin a steep winding descent into Bear River Valley. Arrive at Capetown Ranch only 50 feet above sea level at 14⅜ miles. You're only 1½ miles from the coast. Capetown was once a stagecoach stop, but only this private ranch remains today. Your road crosses the Bear River at 14½ miles and begins a steep ascent over Cape Ridge.

This last big climb continues for 1⅝ miles, passing an immense lily pond west of the road around 15⅝ miles, then topping Cape Ridge (980 feet) at 16⅛ miles. Descend briefly then contour to a seasonal fork of Singley Creek beyond 16¾ miles. Then descend steeply, paralleling Singley Creek's deep canyon toward the coast, with expanding views. The access road to the Cape Mendocino lighthouse is on the right at 17¾ miles.

A big bend to the left at 18 miles offers expansive views of the wild coast including towering Sugarloaf Island off Cape Mendocino, westernmost point in California. To the south Steamboat Rock sails on a brisk current. Follow the road as it straightens out to descend to the coast at Singley Creek at 18½ miles. Continue along the road shoulder for one more mile. At 19½ miles you come to a bridge across an unnamed creek just north of Steamboat Rock offshore. This is the start of Section 12.

**SUGGESTED ROUND TRIPS & LOOPS:** We DO NOT recommend you attempt to get around False Cape and nearby narrow points even at major minus tides. Well organized groups have done it during calm weather in summer at the very lowest tides of some years, minus 1.5 feet or better. You CAN day hike the coast south from Centerville Beach, 5 miles west of Ferndale. You need a minus tide even to get to

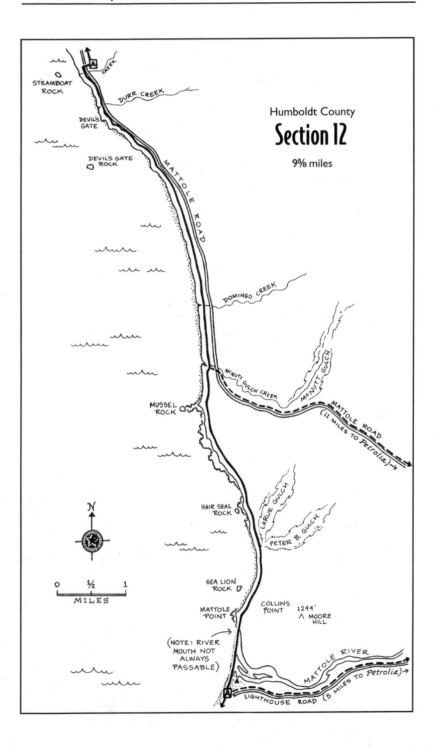

STEAMBOAT ROCK

DURR CREEK

CREEK

DEVIL'S GATE

DEVIL'S GATE ROCK

MATTOLE ROAD

Humboldt County

# Section 12

9⅝ miles

DOMINGO CREEK

McNUTT GULCH CREEK

McNUTT GULCH

MATTOLE ROAD (11 MILES TO Petrolia)

MUSSEL ROCK

HAIR SEAL ROCK

LARUE GULCH

PETER B. GULCH

N

0    ½    1
MILES

SEA LION ROCK

COLLINS POINT

1244'
∧ MOORE HILL

MATTOLE POINT

(NOTE: RIVER MOUTH NOT ALWAYS PASSABLE)

MATTOLE RIVER

LIGHTHOUSE ROAD (5 MILES TO Petrolia)

Guthrie Creek at 2⅜ miles. Another narrow spot impassable at tides above -1.0 foot is Bear Gulch at 2¾ miles where in 1996 the CCT Whole Hikers got trapped for 4 hours before beating a way through blackberry thickets. The beach south of there has at least three narrow passages which require even lower tides to pass, one at the base of Oil Creek Ridge, another at False Cape, and a third at Cape Mendocino.

> **HOW TO IMPROVE CCT HERE:** Acquire access at Singley Creek. Develop a path parallel to portions of Mattole Road, or develop a real trail along the coast.

## SECTION 12
# Creek at Steamboat Rock to Mattole River

**DISTANCE:** 9⅝ miles (15.5 kilometers).

**OPEN TO:** Hikers.

**SURFACE:** Beach.

**ACCESS POINT:** Creek at Steamboat Rock.

**HOW TO GET THERE:** From the north, follow directions to Section 11 access point, then drive Mattole Road (CCT) 19.5 miles to the second bridge after you reach the coast. From the south, follow directions for Section 13 to Lighthouse Road, then go 6.5 miles farther on Mattole Road to bridge at unnamed creek.

**OTHER ACCESS:** Devil's Gate, McNutt Gulch.

**DIFFICULTY:** Easy.

**ELEVATION GAIN/LOSS:** 40 feet+/40 feet-.

**CAUTIONS:** The Mattole River at the south end of this section may not be fordable in winter and spring or after rains. In that case you'd have to turn around and hike back to McNutt Gulch, then follow Alternate Route.

**FURTHER INFORMATION:** Bureau of Land Management (707)825-2300.

**FACILITIES:** None except chemical toilet and picnic area at south end. Phone in Petrolia.

**CAMPGROUNDS:** Mattole River Recreation Site at south end (no water), A.W. Way County Park 7 miles east of Petrolia on Mattole Road.

**LODGING:** Petrolia has Lost Inn and Ziganti's. Honeydew has Mattole River Resort.

Finally after nearly 25 miles of road walking away from the coast, CCT returns to the shore in dramatic fashion just south of Cape Mendocino, westernmost point in California. Although the Mattole Road stays within sight of the shore, you'll hardly notice the road as you walk the beach, your eyes diverted by the rugged grandeur of this wild meeting of land and sea. After a short jog up to the road before one mile, CCT returns to the beach where you can walk the tideline south all the way to the Mattole River mouth around 9 miles. However, through-hikers will want to confirm that they can ford the river when they get there, something not easy to do without sending someone to scout the ford. Try calling BLM to ask if the river's currently shallow enough to ford near its mouth, but there's no guarantee they'll have the answer. You're less likely to see other hikers on this CCT section than on the popular wilderness Lost Coast just ahead.

Walk from the north end of the highway bridge down the rocky banks of the unnamed creek. When you reach the mouth of the creek before ⅛ mile, turn south along the tideline. If you want to explore the coast north, given a moderately low tide you can walk north 1⅝ miles to Cape Mendocino where a large colony of sea lions lives. Give these immense marine mammals plenty of room. Beyond the sea lion colony you can easily walk the beach north to the mouth of Bear River at 4½ miles, but carefully time your trip so you don't get trapped by the rising tide on your return.

Heading southeast from the unnamed creek you walk a narrowing beach of fine dark sand with landmark Steamboat Rock about ⅜ mile offshore and many smaller rocks beyond the surf. The grandeur of this wild coast is breathtaking with a verdant ridge towering 1000 feet overhead to the east. When it's clear, you can see Punta Gorda 11 miles south with the most dramatic views north to looming Cape Ridge and towering Sugarloaf Island which rises 323 feet just offshore from Cape Mendocino.

You ford a seasonal creek around ½ mile. Continue southeast along the beach with the road to your east now shored up by rip-rap. At high tide you may be forced to leave the beach before Durr Creek around ¾ mile, but at moderate tides you can usually walk the beach to the big sea stacks at Devils Gate at ⅞ mile. There you must climb to the road on a path east of the rock outcrops with brief boulder hopping to reach the road. High bluffs rise steeply east of the road.

Walk the road shoulder briefly to a path that drops to the beach at a broad sandy flat bordered by tidepools, a good place to camp if you're through-hiking. You can again follow the beach south at least a mile. At a point around 2 miles where low Devils Gate Rock lies almost a mile offshore, the beach narrows to a thin strip inundated at tides higher than 3.0 feet. Walk the beach or the road until the beach again broadens beyond a seasonal creek at 2⅛ miles. Then it's an easy stroll on a broad beach, fording Davis Creek at 2⅞ miles, an unnamed creek at 3⅝ miles, then Domingo Creek at 4 miles.

Continue south to cross a small seasonal creek at 4⅛ miles. The next ford beyond 4¾ miles crosses McNutt Gulch Creek, the largest stream since Singley Creek. McNutt Gulch offers the last chance to return to Mattole Road before the questionable Mattole River ford. Mattole Road heads inland up McNutt Gulch to the small town of Petrolia, source of the only services for miles — store, cafe, phone, lodging. To reach the road just south of McNutt Gulch, look for two tall poles in the fence by the road. They mark the public path, with most of the remaining land up from the tideline private property.

To walk the beach south from McNutt Gulch, stay along the tideline, avoiding the private ranch property up from the beach. You also should be certain you can cross the Mattole River at its mouth, unless you are day hiking and plan to hike back north. The river is usually easy to ford from midsummer until the first big rainstorms of autumn. Sometimes a sand bar even closes off the Mattole's mouth during those months. Be forewarned that the river can rise rapidly after rainstorms of an inch or more.

The beach south of McNutt Gulch is extremely broad with low dunes to the east. By 5⅜ miles you come to Mussel Rock where a sandy point overlooks mussel beds along the low tideline. Several shell middens in the dunes indicate that this was a food gathering spot for the Mattole tribe that lived in this area.

Walk south from the point along the broad beach. At 6½ miles you pass a seasonal stream that only flows under the sand in the dry season. The beach narrows suddenly with dunes stacked against the bluffs. Continue south along

## The Cape Mendocino Triple Junction and the Amazing Uplift of 1992

At Cape Mendocino, California's Lost Coast thrusts westward against the driving California Current. The San Andreas Fault Zone trends west from its northernmost onshore extension at Shelter Cove to end as it joins the Mendocino Fracture Zone where the triple-plate junction of the North American, Pacific and Gorda Plates all meet. Directly offshore from the tiny Lost Coast hamlet of Petrolia, Gorda Ridge (flanked by the steep Mendocino Escarpment on the north), an undersea mountain range, sprawls westward for about 50 miles. South of this complex and still only partially understood geologic jumble, the California coast is uplifting from the Pacific. The coastline north of the Triple Junction currently seems to be sinking into the ocean.

Along the Lost Coast, radiocarbon dating shows that the land uplifted a remarkable 66 feet in the past 6000 years. If this still seems like a snail's pace, compare it to the more typical 80 or 100 feet of uplift occurring over 100,000 years elsewhere on the California coast. The Lost Coast apparently is rising from the Pacific Ocean 11 to 14 times faster than most of the California coast!

The rapid uplift along the Lost Coast seemed to be obscure academic information until April 25, 1992. Then the Ferndale earthquake, 6.9 on the Richter scale, shook up the Humboldt County coast. Lost Coast locals were not thinking about coastal uplift as they extinguished the quake-caused fire that destroyed Petrolia's only store, secured their homes against aftershocks, or surveyed the remaining edge of the quarter acre of land that dropped into the Pacific west of town.

About two weeks after the temblor, however, someone in Petrolia noticed a powerful stench wafting into town on the otherwise typical coastal breeze. When locals went to the shoreline to investigate, they found that nearly half of the biologically rich tidal zone sat high and dry above the surf with its once abundant tidal plants and animals rotting in the spring sun, creating an awful stink. After this news got around, dozens of scientists descended on the Lost Coast to study the disturbed tidal zone. Geologists measured the uplift near Devil's Gate south of Cape Mendocino at nearly three feet, all in the few seconds of the April 1992 quake. Marine biologists first surveyed the damage, then studied how long it would take various tidal critters to repopulate the tidal zone. Not only was the event a scientific gold mine, but it brought home just how quickly the Lost Coast is being created from the ocean floor.

the narrow beach unless a very high tide delays your progress. By 7⅛ miles you pass Hair Seal Rock directly offshore. Follow the narrow strand south to the mouth of Peter B. Gulch at 7⅜ miles. The beach becomes broad again at this pleasant spot where there might be room to camp just above the tideline with the high bluffs to the north providing shelter from the wind.

As you follow the beach south, it remains broad until an unnamed gully at 8 miles. Then the beach narrows along the base of high cliffs descending from Moore Hill and Collins Point. You pass Sea Lion Rock offshore. The beach broadens again as you approach Mattole Point at 8⅝ miles.

Continue along the tideline to the Mattole River mouth. While it is mapped as only ¼ mile south of Mattole Point, the position of the mouth may change from year to year. Be certain you can ford the river safely before proceeding. A local resident who had lived her entire life in the area was swept out to sea and drowned a few years ago when she underestimated the river's power.

After the ford it's a short stroll along the beach to the Mattole River Recreation Site at 9⅝ miles, starting point for the famous Lost Coast portion of the Coastal Trail.

**ALTERNATE ROUTE:** When the tides are too high to walk the beach, or the river is too deep and fast to ford, through-hikers can walk Mattole Road through Petrolia (11 miles from access point), then walk Lighthouse Road 5 miles to its end.

**SUGGESTED ROUND TRIPS & LOOPS:** You can take pleasant day hikes north or south along the beach from the access point, Devil's Gate or McNutt Gulch. In fact from McNutt Gulch, this section divides nicely into two nearly equal parts.

*Hiker approaches Cape Mendocino and Sugarloaf Island on the Lost Coast.*

# SECTION 13
# Mattole River to Smith-Etter Road, King Range National Conservation Area

**DISTANCE:** 12½ miles (20.1 kilometers).

**OPEN TO:** Hikers, equestrians.

**SURFACE:** Beach, trail.

**ACCESS POINT:** Mattole River Recreation Site.

**HOW TO GET THERE:** Leave Highway 101 at South Fork/Honeydew exit, Milepost 36.1 from north, Milepost 35.5 from south. Take Mattole Road west 23 miles to Honeydew, then turn right and follow Mattole Road 14 more miles to Lighthouse Road just before Petrolia. Go left on Lighthouse Road about 5 miles to its end at the beach.

**SOUTH END ACCESS:** Smith-Etter Road (steep 4-mile hike to CCT).

**DIFFICULTY:** Moderate.

**ELEVATION GAIN/LOSS:** Minimal, depending on route you take.

**CAUTIONS:** This isolated country is far from towns and services. Watch for the dwarf-sized timber rattlesnakes that live along the Lost Coast, especially in and around the creek canyons. Several points may be impassable at high tide.

**FURTHER INFORMATION:** Bureau of Land Management (707)825-2300 or 468-4000.

**FACILITIES:** Chemical toilet, campground, picnic area at access point. Phone in Petrolia.

**CAMPGROUNDS:** Mattole River Recreation Site is at start of section (no water). Primitive camping allowed along route. A.W. Way County Park is 7 miles east of Lighthouse Road on Mattole Road.

**LODGING:** Lost Inn and Ziganti's are in Petrolia. Mattole River Resort is near Honeydew.

The Lost Coast — even the name sounds dramatic and romantic, especially in a state as heavily populated as California. California's Lost Coast certainly qualifies as a dramatic landscape. It stretches roughly 80 miles along a rugged, lightly traveled coast, backed by a dozen peaks rising more than 2000 feet, crowned by the 4087-foot hulk of Kings Peak. Two dozen year-round streams cascade down deep, steep-walled canyons in a landscape so rugged the highway builders just shook their heads and went elsewhere. Of the four roads that reach this wild coast, two are one-lane dirt and all are twisting and steep. Yes, dramatic fits as does remote.

Whether the Lost Coast qualifies as romantic depends upon your point of view. Do you like to carry a backpack? Will you still like it when you're walking on miles of shifting sand or over high ridges? Can you forego the simple pleasures of civilization? Tables, chairs, hot showers and beds are all in very short supply along the Lost Coast. We find the Lost Coast romantic, but romance, like beauty, is in the eye of the beholder.

Now for the facts. CCT runs the entire length of the Lost Coast, roughly the next 64 miles of the trail. First it passes along 24½ miles of wilderness beach in

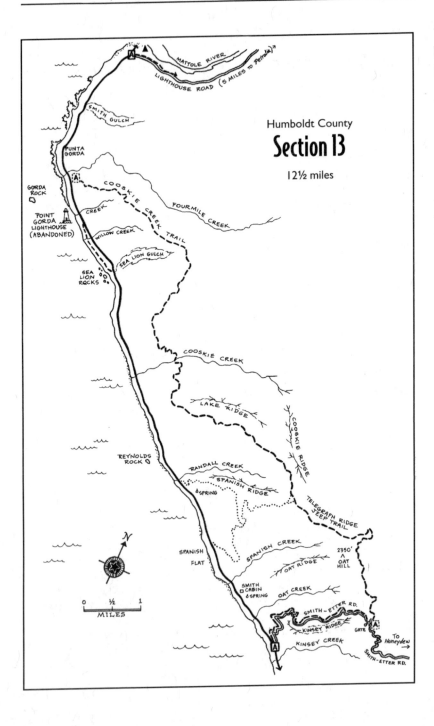

MATTOLE RIVER

LIGHTHOUSE ROAD (5 MILES TO Petrolia)

SMITH GULCH

PUNTA GORDA

GORDA ROCK

COOSKIE CREEK

CREEK

FOURMILE CREEK

POINT GORDA LIGHTHOUSE (ABANDONED)

WILLOW CREEK

TRAIL

SEA LION GULCH

SEA LION ROCKS

Humboldt County
## Section 13
12½ miles

COOSKIE CREEK

LAKE RIDGE

COOSKIE RIDGE

REYNOLDS ROCK

RANDALL CREEK

SPANISH RIDGE

SPRING

TELEGRAPH RIDGE JEEP TRAIL

SPANISH CREEK

SPANISH FLAT

OAT RIDGE

2350' OAT HILL

SMITH CABIN SPRING

OAT CREEK

SMITH-ETTER RD.

KINSEY RIDGE

GATE

To Honeydew

KINSEY CREEK

SMITH-ETTER RD.

N

0   ½   1
MILES

King Range National Conservation Area where in some places you have firm footing on dirt road or trail, in a few places you'll be scrambling over slippery rocks, but most of the way you walk on beach sand, firm in places and miserably soft in others. This section and the next cover this beach portion. The third Lost Coast section, Humboldt County Section 15, ironically follows a paved road 4½ miles over a 2000-foot high ridge — the Alternate Route is both steeper and harder. The fourth, sixth and seventh Lost Coast sections, Humboldt County Section 16 and Mendocino County Sections 2 and 3, take to the high country because no continuous route exists along the coast where cliffs rise as high as 1000 feet. Their cumulative elevation gain is 8000 feet with even more elevation loss. Fortunately you never climb more than 1450 feet before making a major descent. Slightly more than half way along the Lost Coast, the fifth section, Mendocino County Section 1, offers a respite, winding through gorgeous coastal terrain at the heart of Sinkyone Wilderness State Park for 2½ miles with only 500 feet of elevation change.

We most heartily recommend that hardy souls visit the Lost Coast, but being prepared and physically fit are essential for hiking the entire Lost Coast. So is having enough time. We suggest at least seven days to walk the entire 64 miles, although the Whole Hikers did it in 6¼ days. The other choice is hiking the Lost Coast in smaller pieces. Our trail sections provide ideas how to break it into more manageable chunks.

From the trailhead at the end of Lighthouse Road, you can either walk due west to the tideline and follow the dark sand beach south, or head south-south-west along an old jeep track near the base of the bluffs. The latter choice shortens the distance by about ⅛ mile, but offers less firm footing, important if you're carrying a backpack.

Pass a seasonal creek dropping from the steep bluffs at ¾ mile. Beyond 1⅛ miles you pass the more reliable creek of Smith Gulch usually jammed with wildflowers. Round a sandy point rimmed by tidepools at 1¼ miles. The bluffs protrude at Windy Point just beyond. The beach narrows and gets rockier as more seasonal streams drop to the beach.

At 2 miles you round the westernmost point of Punta Gorda where Conical Rock lies offshore. As you pass an old road descending from the bluffs at 2½ miles, the Punta Gorda lighthouse ruins come into view. For a break from beach walking you can follow a firm roadbed along the base of the bluffs.

Pass two cabins on the first of several private inholdings before Fourmile Creek at 2⅝ miles. Beyond the ford the Cooskie Creek Trail forks left, climbing east along a ridge. This Alternate Route is a CCT high route, the first of three CCT high routes on the trail. (The other two are in Big Sur and the Santa Monica Mountains. CCT continues down the coast on a firm track across grassy bluffs, passing crumbling ranch buildings. Gorda Rock lies offshore.

At 3 miles a path forks left to the lighthouse ruins. The light station, built after the wreck of the *Columbia* claimed 87 lives here in 1907, guided ships along this windswept, fogbound coast for 40 years. Today only the squat concrete tower remains. BLM razed the other buildings in 1970.

Continue down the coast on the old jeep road, crossing several more creeks. Beyond Willow Creek at 3½ miles you can return to the beach or climb a hill to

# California's Lost Coast: Worthy of Wilderness Protection

The rugged and remote Lost Coast offers North America's largest span of pristine beach and shoreline on the Pacific Coast outside of Alaska and Canada. Public lands here include 60,000-acre King Range National Conservation Area and 7400-acre Sinkyone Wilderness State Park, together stretching 40 miles along the coast. If you study the maps however, you'll see that the true geographic province of the Lost Coast extends another 24 miles north to Centerville Beach, held primarily in private ranch lands, and 16 miles farther south to Hardy Creek, mostly private timber lands. Altogether California's Lost Coast sprawls a phenomenal 80 miles along the shore of the nation's most populous state!

The federal government first recognized the area's remarkable scenic and biological values in 1929 when it withdrew public domain lands here from sale. Congress created the King Range Conservation Area in 1970. When I first visited the Lost Coast in the 1970s, plans were already afoot to protect much of the King Range as designated wilderness. Unfortunately, the King Range remains unprotected more than twenty years later.

Meanwhile during the 1970s, California State Parks began protecting the southern Lost Coast. In what was then called the Bear Harbor Project, the state acquired the remote Stewart Ranch in Mendocino County's northwesternmost corner. They changed the name to Sinkyone Wilderness State Park when the park was officially established in 1977, recognizing and striving to protect its essential wilderness values.

The park's southern neighbor, Georgia-Pacific Corporation, saw the Lost Coast in a different light. Several thousand acres of the company's coastal lands still held virgin forests of massive redwoods, firs and spruces in 1979. These forests had sur-vived because they were remote, even though sawmills had operated within 5 miles of them, at Usal around 1900 and Wheeler in the 1950s. G-P quietly began cutting these giants in 1980.

Not until autumn 1983 did word spread around the north coast of the last immense virgin trees around Usal falling to the chainsaws. Then about 200 action-oriented environmentalists moved to stop the cutting along Wheeler Road. They came to the Lost Coast under cover of darkness. When the loggers came to work at dawn, they found people blocking their way to the standing giants. After many showdowns and the death of many more giants, a court injunction halted logging. The last groves, most notably the Sally Bell Grove, were finally saved when the Trust for Public Land purchased the surrounding lands. Of the 7100 acres bought by TPL, Sinkyone State Park gained 3000, extending it south to Usal. In 1996 the other 4000 acres became Sinkyone Intertribal Park, where, in the nation's first intertribal park, major plant and watershed restoration are occurring.

While this controversy raged around the Lost Coast's southern end, the Bureau of Land Management, manager of the King Range, has slowly added to public lands there. Congress has already established 4000-acre Chemise Mountain Primitive Area just north of the Sinkyone. BLM proposes a 37,000-acre King Range Wilderness Area, while wilderness advocates support a larger one. One former stumbling block to wilderness designation was removed when BLM reversed their long-standing policy of allowing off-road vehicles on 3½ miles of beach at the King Range's southern end. Happily BLM closed that area to vehicles in 1998, bringing a big chunk of the Lost Coast closer to becoming the King Range Wilderness Area.

stay on the road. The road provides one more chance to return to the beach at 3¾ miles. Either route comes to steep Sea Lion Gulch at 4 miles. Its gully offers a water source and shelter from the wind. Sea lions, cormorants and pelicans inhabit Sea Lion Rocks offshore.

The beach narrows after the gulch. Around 4½ miles the beach may be impassable at high tide. When you pass through the narrow spot, slippery rocks of uneven sizes slow your progress. After you pass a barn and cabin above the beach at 4¾ miles, the walking becomes easier at the base of steep bluffs and cliffs.

At 6 miles you reach the broad deep canyon of Cooskie Creek. Sheltered camps lie within ¼ mile up the canyon. The Cooskie Creek Trail crosses the creek about ¾ mile upstream with private property not far beyond.

CCT continues along the Lost Coast, requiring a few hundred feet of boulder hopping before the footing improves as the beach widens at the base of cliffs draped with waterfalls. From 7¼ to 7¾ miles, massive landslides have jumbled the cliffs above the beach. Around 7½ miles walking gets rough with large, uneven rocks on a steeply slanting beach, then loose sand and gravel slow progress. After you pass Reynolds Rock offshore, the bluffs show greatly twisted rock strata created by geologic folding.

Come to the mouth of Randall Creek at 8⅛ miles. Narrower and more wooded than Cooskie Creek, Randall Creek also provides pleasant camps a short walk upstream. A road along the bluffs beyond the canyon provides firm footing down the coast. Just 250 feet from Randall Creek, the northern end of the Spanish Ridge Trail ascends from your road. Your path crosses rolling grasslands at the base of steep bluffs. Beyond 8⅜ miles you cross a small spring-fed stream where watercress grows.

The marine terrace along the shore broadens as you hike toward Spanish Flat. Beyond 9¼ miles a mostly level footpath crosses the lower bluff as the old road takes to higher ground. Pass two seasonal streams jammed with wildflowers, the second also with watercress and mint. The grassy headlands get broader and flatter as you reach the north end of Spanish Flat around 9¾ miles. Another spur trail forks left to ascend Spanish Ridge at 10 miles. Continue southeast along the broad flat.

Reach the broad flood plain of Spanish Creek canyon at 10⅞ miles with several campsites nearby. After dropping to the creek, climb to a mostly level grassland and follow it down the coast. After an old corral, you come to pioneer Paul Smith's cabin at 11½ miles above a broad beach. Continue along the sandy jeep track, passing Oat Creek at 11⅞ miles as it spills from a twisting rocky gorge. The jeep track meets the western end of the Smith-Etter Road at 12½ miles, halfway along the King Range Lost Coast.

**ALTERNATE ROUTE:** A CCT high route traverses the King Range south of Punta Gorda, but it is steep, longer than CCT, and hard to follow in places. From the south side of Fourmile Creek, follow the Cooskie Creek Trail inland. After 10 miles it joins the Telegraph Ridge Jeep Trail. In another mile you have the choice of continuing along the road to Smith-Etter Road to link with the Kings Crest Trail (see Humboldt County Section 14 Alternate Route) or descending the Spanish Ridge Trail to return to CCT at the beach.

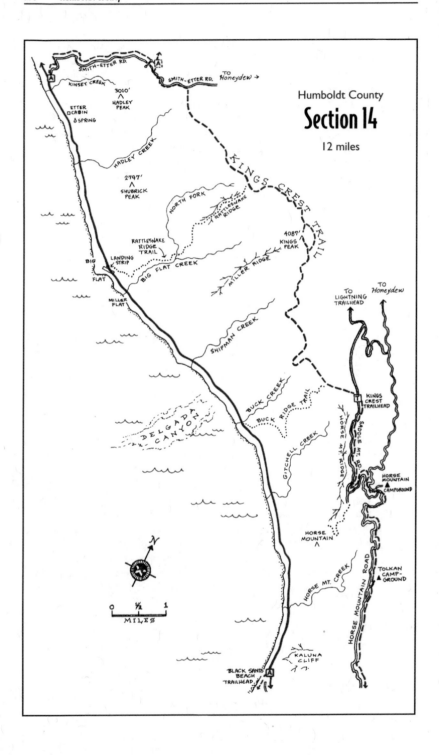

Humboldt County
# Section 14
12 miles

**SUGGESTED ROUND TRIPS & LOOPS:** The hike to Punta Gorda lighthouse and back makes a nice, if often windy, day hike. It takes a full day to get to Cooskie Creek and back. If you're game for some steep hiking, you might return on the Cooskie Creek Trail which offers rewarding views.

## SECTION 14
# Smith-Etter Road to Shelter Cove, King Range National Conservation Area

**DISTANCE:** 12 miles. Add 3¾ miles to reach CCT from access point.

**OPEN TO:** Hikers, equestrians.

**SURFACE:** Beach, dirt road, trail.

**ACCESS POINT:** Smith-Etter Road.

**HOW TO GET THERE:** Leave Highway 101 north of Weott at South Fork/Honeydew exit, Milepost 36.1 from north, Milepost 35.5 from south. Follow Mattole Road west 23 miles to Honeydew (store and gas). Go left 1.5 miles, then turn right on Smith-Etter Road. Drive 9 steep, winding, rough and unpaved miles to locked gate. From there it's a 3¾-mile hike down Smith-Etter Road to CCT.

**DIFFICULTY:** Moderate. Strenuous if you hike out to Smith-Etter Road trailhead.

**ELEVATION GAIN/LOSS:** Minimal for CCT. Depends on route you take. From Smith-Etter Road gate to CCT: 140 feet+/2460 feet-.

**CAUTIONS:** Smith-Etter Road may be closed from November to March, and anytime a landslide blocks it. Call BLM before you go. Watch for timber rattlesnakes, especially around canyons. Beach north of Shipman Creek may be impassable at high tide.

**FURTHER INFORMATION:** Bureau of Land Management (707)825-2300 or 468-4000.

**FACILITIES:** None.

**CAMPGROUNDS:** Primitive camping allowed along route. Honeydew Creek Tenting Area near start of Smith-Etter Road makes a good staging area. Private Shelter Cove Campground is near south end.

**LODGING:** Mattole River Resort is near Honeydew. Shelter Cove has several lodgings.

CCT continues along the King Range Lost Coast. Only fit hikers should access this section from the locked gate on Smith-Etter Road. To do so, hikers must descend nearly 2500 feet in elevation in only 3¾ miles. Most strenuous of all is climbing out the same way. The easiest way to experience this section is to hike north from Shelter Cove, retracing your steps at the end of your visit.

If you're starting from the Smith-Etter Road rather than walking the Lost Coast from the Mattole River, follow the jeep track northwest, climbing for ½ mile. After contouring atop Kinsey Ridge, descend steadily with grand coastal views. Descend the ridge's north face for ½ mile, then return to the ridge and descend steeply by long switchbacks. By 3 miles you reach the road's westernmost bend high above Oat Creek. Descend steeply as the wilderness coast stretches magnificently below. Switchback right at 3¼ miles and descend by five steep switchbacks to the coast to meet CCT. The mileage starts again from zero.

Where Smith-Etter Road meets CCT at the base of Kinsey Ridge, Lost Coast hikers follow a two-wheel track southeast. It crosses the broad, gravelly wash of Kinsey Creek in ¼ mile. Follow the track through grasslands below steep bluffs. At one mile your track passes west of the Etter cabin and a private inholding.

The road gradually fades to a sandy track as the headlands narrow at the base of steep grasslands rising to 3010-foot Hadley Peak, barely a mile from the Pacific. Come to Hadley Creek, also known as Big Creek, at 1⅝ miles. Dense forest in the deep, shady canyon shelters pleasant campsites within ⅝ mile of the beach.

CCT continues southeast in loose sand along a narrow beach. Around 1⅞ miles you pass high dunes backed against a steep grassy hill. A trail climbing the steep headlands just south provides better walking than continued slogging in sand. At 2 miles a slide covers the faint double track, but a narrow trail continues. Back on grasslands as the trail turns vague, stay high on the headlands below steep bluffs. After crossing a watercress-choked stream at 2⅛ miles, your trail descends to a gently rolling grassland, soon returning to an obvious dirt road.

After crossing a small creek at 2¾ miles, you reach Big Flat which stretches more than a mile along the coast. A firm road provides easy walking past numerous Indian shell middens. As Big Flat broadens to its widest point, the road draws away from the shore. At 3¼ miles your track meets a landing strip used by residents of the house ahead. Approaching the canyon of Big Flat Creek, watch for timber rattlesnakes that live on the flat and in the rocky wash of the creek.

After paralleling the runway, your trail forks. The road continues along the landing strip, then heads into the canyon where the most protected campsites lie among the trees alongside the broad gravelly wash. The rugged Rattlesnake Ridge Trail continues up the canyon, climbing 3400 feet in 4⅝ miles to the Kings Crest Trail west of Kings Peak.

CCT forks to the right at the junction, crossing the runway and following the edge of the willow and alder thicket near the beach. It passes two camps at 3¾ miles, the second with a driftwood shelter. From here you can look up Big Flat Creek Canyon to 4087-foot Kings Peak, the highest point along the coast north of Big Sur. The trail becomes vague crossing the broad wash of Big Flat Creek. Aim to the right of the trees on the far side and watch for rattlers.

Climb slightly to Miller Flat, broader and more wooded than Big Flat. Several campsites lie near the trail with more sheltered camps in the forest to the northeast. Your trail turns east, climbing gradually on the broad flat until a short descent at 4⅝ miles drops to the beach, now heading almost east.

Follow the beach along the base of steep bluffs. On your right lie many offshore rocks and tidepools. Beyond a small unmapped creek, the beach becomes very rocky. Round a small point at 5⅜ miles as the beach narrows.

Ahead lies a stretch of coast where passage may be blocked at tides above +4.0 feet. The rugged cliffs on your left have many small creeks, seeps and springs, supporting hanging wildflower gardens in spring and summer. The narrowest point lies just before Shipman Creek at 5¾ miles. Beautiful Shipman

Creek has camps in the driftwood above its mouth. At low tide you can visit tidepools to the west. You're 6¼ miles from Shelter Cove.

Continue down the broad beach. At 6½ miles you cross a small creek which plunges 1600 feet in its ¾-mile course. Offshore lies the deep submarine trench of Delgada Canyon, 450 feet deep only ½ mile from shore. Just around a point the beach turns rocky and narrow. Reach Buck Creek at 7 miles, passing the Buck Ridge Trail just beyond (ascends 3300 feet in 2½ miles to Kings Crest Trail). Many more creeks tumble down the cliffs on your way to Gitchell Creek at 8½ miles. A pleasant campsite sits beside its mouth. The off-road vehicle users once allowed this far north on the beach from Shelter Cove have now been excluded.

After a mile of sandy beach, you can follow a dirt road along the bluffs. At 10½ miles the road returns to the beach at the wooded canyon of Horse Mountain Creek. Big rocks lie along the beach at 10⅞ miles before another steep creek. The beach broadens and turns south, heading for Shelter Cove atop Point Delgada. Walk the beach below towering Kaluna Cliff which reaches its steepest pitch around the creek at 11½ miles. Cross Telegraph Creek at 12 miles and come to the Black Sands Beach parking area. The old parking area was destroyed by storm surf. It has now been replaced by a new lot up a gully above the beach at the end of Beach Road, just southeast of the former lot.

**ALTERNATE ROUTE:** The King Range high route follows the western end of Telegraph Ridge Jeep Trail and Smith-Etter Road to the north end of Kings Crest Trail. Some maps show it as North Slide Peak Trailhead, 1½ miles from the gate on Smith-Etter Road where it meets Telegraph Ridge Road, or 7½ miles from Smith-Etter Road's eastern end. From there the high route follows Kings Crest Trail south. You have two chances to return to the coast: the Rattlesnake Ridge Trail, 3 miles from the north trailhead, descends 4⅝ miles to Big Flat, or the Buck Ridge Trail at 10 miles descends 2½ miles to the mouth of Buck Creek. Otherwise, when Kings Crest Trail ends in 10⅞ miles at Saddle Mountain Road, follow the road 3⅝ miles, then go right on Horse Mountain Road (aka Kings Peak Road) for 6½ miles to paved Shelter Cove Road, part of Humboldt County Section 15.

**SUGGESTED ROUND TRIPS & LOOPS:** This steep, rugged country isn't particularly suitable for day hikes, but if you're ready for demanding overnight loops several possibilities exist. You can descend Smith-Etter Road, walk the coast north to ascend Spanish Ridge Trail, then return south by Telegraph Ridge Jeep Trail for the easiest 13-mile loop. More challenging possibilities include loops on Rattlesnake Ridge or Buck Ridge Trail to the south or Cooskie Creek Trail to the north. If you want to sample this part of CCT without a demanding trek, the best choice follows the beach north from Black Sands Beach. If you start early, you can make the all-day 12½-mile round trip hike to Shipman Creek.

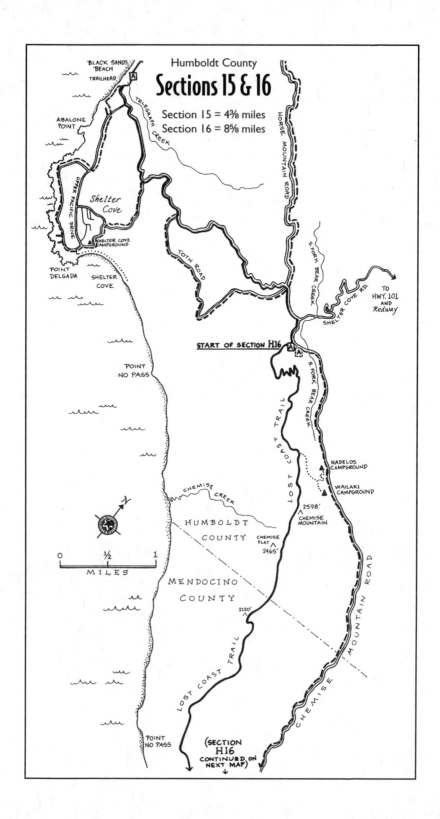

Humboldt County
## Sections 15 & 16

Section 15 = 4⅝ miles
Section 16 = 8⅝ miles

BLACK SANDS BEACH TRAILHEAD

ABALONE POINT

UPPER PACIFIC DRIVE

Shelter Cove

SHELTER COVE CAMPGROUND

POINT DELGADA

SHELTER COVE

POINT NO PASS

TELEGRAPH CREEK

TOTH ROAD

HORSE MOUNTAIN ROAD

S. FORK BEAR CREEK

SHELTER COVE RD.

TO HWY. 101 AND Redway

START OF SECTION H16

S. FORK BEAR CREEK

LOST COAST TRAIL

NADELOS CAMPGROUND

WAILAKI CAMPGROUND

2598' CHEMISE MOUNTAIN

CHEMISE CREEK

HUMBOLDT COUNTY

CHEMISE FLAT 2465'

N

0    ½    1
MILES

MENDOCINO COUNTY

2120'

POINT NO PASS

LOST COAST TRAIL

CHEMISE MOUNTAIN ROAD

(SECTION H16 CONTINUED ON NEXT MAP)

## SECTION 15
# Shelter Cove to Hidden Valley Trailhead, King Range National Conservation Area

DISTANCE: 4⅜ miles (7 kilometers).

OPEN TO: Hikers, bicyclists.

SURFACE: Road shoulder.

ACCESS POINT: Black Sands Beach.

HOW TO GET THERE: Leave Highway 101 at Garberville from the south (Milepost 10.8) or Redway from the north (Milepost 14.6). Take Redwood Drive to Redway, then Briceland Road/Shelter Cove Road west 21 miles. (From 17 miles you follow CCT which uses the road here.) As you descend to Shelter Cove, take the third right, Beach Road (signed "BLACK SANDS BEACH") and follow it 1.1 miles to trailhead.

OTHER ACCESS: Anywhere along route.

DIFFICULTY: Strenuous.

ELEVATION GAIN/LOSS: 2460 feet+/260 feet-.

CAUTIONS: Watch for traffic on the steep, winding Shelter Cove Road.

FURTHER INFORMATION: None.

FACILITIES: Chemical toilet at trailhead. Phone at Shelter Cove General Store at 2⅛ miles.

CAMPGROUNDS: Shelter Cove RV Park and Campground (707-986-7474) is 2 miles south of starting point. Nadelos (BLM) Campground is 1.4 miles south of south end.

LODGING: Shelter Cove has Beachcomber Inn and other lodgings.

The outpost town of Shelter Cove occupies a marine terrace at Point Delgada in the heart of the Lost Coast. This protruding promontory marks a dividing line between the two very different halves of California's Lost Coast. Most of the Lost Coast to the north offers long stretches of beach or headlands where one can follow the shore. To the south however, the Lost Coast becomes more precipitous with occasional pocket beaches separated by steep cliffs where one simply cannot walk along the shore because no level ground is available.

Both halves of the Lost Coast offer some of California's most spectacular coastal scenery. To reach the southern half of the Lost Coast from Shelter Cove however, CCT must turn inland to bypass the two places called Point No Pass on the coast south of Shelter Cove in order to find a canyon that penetrates this hidden coastal wonderland. So this section of the Coastal Trail follows paved roads inland for 4⅜ miles until it finds a canyon with a trail where CCT returns to a wilderness setting and follows the coast south. For information about Shelter Cove's convoluted coast, read the Alternate Route.

Wet your bandanna in the creek, put on your road walking shoes, and climb east along Beach Road for 1⅛ miles to its end at Shelter Cove Road, elevation 480 feet. Turn left and walk the shoulder of the steep, winding, busy road. At 1⅞ miles you meet Toth Road on your right, elevation 920 feet. For a route with almost no traffic, but one mile longer and a summit 80 feet higher, turn right and ascend Toth Road to its summit at 4⅛ miles, 2040 feet, then descend to Shelter Cove Road opposite Kings Peak Road at 4⅝ miles.

Shelter Cove Road climbs from its first junction with Toth Road, passing the Shelter Cove General Store on the right at 2⅛ miles, 1080 feet. Shelter Cove Road continues ascending, soon leaving views of the coast to the south. By 3 miles you've climbed to 1600 feet. Your ascent continues to 3⅝ miles where you meet unpaved Kings Peak Road on the left and paved Toth Road on the right, elevation 1960 feet. CCT's King Range high route rejoins CCT here.

Descend southeast on Shelter Cove Road for ½ mile to Chemise Mountain Road on the right before 4⅛ miles. Turn right and walk Chemise Mountain Road ¼ mile, then turn right to Hidden Valley Trailhead, start of Section 16.

**ALTERNATE ROUTE:** You can walk the beach south from Black Sands Beach Trailhead ⅝ mile to the first high rocky point. Walk east from there on a steep paved road that climbs to Upper Pacific Drive. To see the rest of the Shelter Cove coast, ascend Beach Road briefly, then go right on Humboldt Loop Road to Upper Pacific Drive at 1¼ mile. Go right on Upper Pacific, then right again on Albatross Road beyond 1⅜ mile. At 1⅝ miles go right on Lower Pacific Drive. At 2 miles Abalone Point coastal access is on the right. Around 2¼ miles you pass Sea Rock Picnic Area and coastal access. Lower Pacific Drive continues past the airport to Point Delgada at 2⅞ miles where a stairway from Mal Coombs Park provides coastal access to Point Delgada. The road continues to Shelter Cove Campground and Store on the left at 3 miles. On the right you can park and descend the boat launch road to the main cove at Shelter Cove where you can walk about 1½ miles east and south along the beach before you meet Point No Pass North, an impassable point.

**SUGGESTED ROUND TRIPS & LOOPS:** Consider the choices in **Alternate Route**.

**HOW TO IMPROVE CCT HERE:** Develop an off-road trail corridor that connects with the Hidden Valley-Chemise Mountain Trail. For example, a trail could start between the summit and the east end of Toth Road and contour east around the top of the McKee Creek watershed to meet the saddle west of Hidden Valley.

# SECTION 16
# Hidden Valley Trailhead, King Range National Conservation Area, to Needle Rock Visitor Center, Sinkyone Wilderness State Park

DISTANCE: 8⅝ miles (13.9 kilometers).

OPEN TO: Hikers. Equestrians and bicyclists on BLM land only.

SURFACE: Trail.

ACCESS POINT: Hidden Valley Trailhead.

HOW TO GET THERE: Exit Highway 101 from south at Garberville, Milepost 10.8, or from north at Redway, Milepost 14.6. Take Briceland Road from Redway (2.8 miles north of Garberville on Redwood Drive) for 17.7 miles. Go left on Chemise Mountain Road ¼ mile to trailhead on right.

OTHER ACCESS: Nadelos or Wailaki Campground.

DIFFICULTY: Strenuous.

ELEVATION GAIN/LOSS: 1450 feet+/2950 feet-.

CAUTIONS: Ford at Whale Gulch Creek may be impassable in rainy season. No water on trail until Whale Gulch. Watch for timber rattlesnakes and poison oak. Nearest year-round facilities at Shelter Cove.

FURTHER INFORMATION: Bureau of Land Management (707)825-2300 or 468-4000. Sinkyone Wilderness State Park (707)986-7711.

FACILITIES: None until south end.

CAMPGROUNDS: Nadelos and Wailaki Campgrounds are 1.4 and 1.7 miles south of access point.

LODGING: Garberville, Redway and Shelter Cove have several motels and inns.

MAPS: See pages 104 and 114 (Mendocino County Section 1).

This lightly traveled CCT section ascends a wooded ridge to the top of 2598-foot Chemise Mountain, the southernmost peak in the King Range. It then descends along the coastal ridge with magnificent views, entering Sinkyone Wilderness State Park and returning to the coast. While the middle portion requires a steep descent of 2800 feet, it reveals a wonderful transition from the hardwood and fir forests and dense chaparral of the King Range to the lush grasslands and redwood forests of the Sinkyone. If possible day hikers should arrange a shuttle or a pick-up at Needle Rock Visitor Center to avoid climbing back up the steep ridge from near sea level.

The trail heads southwest on an old road. Cross a tiny creek at ⅛ mile and enter the lush meadow of Hidden Valley from which you can see the ocean to the west and south. Go left at a fork at ¼ mile. The right fork leads to an old apple orchard, ending before ½ mile.

Come to a signed switchback overlooking Hidden Valley before ½ mile. Veer left and ascend north into forest, then climb steeply by a dozen switchbacks to a ridgetop saddle before one mile. Ascend steeply south past large firs along the ridgetop with the often snow-clad peaks of the North Yolla Bolly Mountains rising to the east.

Your trail follows the ridge as it contours then dips and rises repeatedly to 1⅝ miles. After climbing through a brush field with sweeping ocean views, return to forest and meet a junction at 1⅞ miles. The left fork descends to Wailaki and Nadelos Campgrounds on Chemise Mountain Road. Turn right and continue up the ridge through forest. The vegetation turns brushy again before the trail's summit at 2⅝ miles where a vague track on the left winds 150 feet to the very top of Chemise Mountain.

CCT continues along the ridgetop, descending briefly to contour then rise to another top at 2¾ miles. Dip and rise twice more before brushy Chemise Flat at 3⅛ miles. Descend steeply on rocky tread with short rises to two more ridgetop knobs by 3¾ miles. The steep descent turns shady before another brief ascent to the summit called Manzanita at 4 miles where an expansive view looks south over steep terrain to the Sinkyone Wilderness below.

CCT descends southeast by switchbacks, entering mature Douglas fir forest by 4¼ miles. After dropping steeply through a gully, contour to return to the ridge. After a steep descent, contour through a grassy clearing. Drop through mixed forest then climb to another ridgetop knob at 4¾ miles.The trail contours along a shady ridgetop to 5⅜ miles.

After a short steep descent, climb along the razor ridge crest around 5½ miles. CCT descends then climbs through a large grassy clearing with abundant native blackberry and sweeping views south. After dropping steeply through forest, descend gradually through grasslands with many wildflowers. You soon join a road and ascend to a flattop on the ridge at 6 miles where an unfinished hip-roofed building sits beside the trail.

As the trail descends along the ridgetop, it quickly enters Sinkyone Wilderness State Park, so equestrians and bicyclists should turn back here. CCT descends gradually through ridgetop grasslands until 6¼ miles where you return to forest and descend steeply. You soon see a private house below. Follow the trail down the razor ridge to avoid private property, the surf churning far below.

At 6⅜ miles your trail veers left and descends east through hardwood forest by switchbacks. After one more view down to the coast, the trail zigzags steeply east. At 6¾ miles CCT drops to a shady, slippery ford of Whale Gulch Creek. Across the creek the trail climbs uphill briefly, then winds south through small gullies to ascend to a summit overlooking the mouth of Whale Gulch.

Descend south above two small lakes at 7 miles, then climb southeast to cross a tiny creek. Leave the forest for grasslands, passing a side trail to Jones Beach on the right. Just beyond at 7⅝ miles, you pass Jones Beach Environmental Camp where three sites cluster around a eucalyptus grove beside a small creek, the only water source. To camp here you must register at Needle Rock Visitor Center one mile south.

CCT contours south on an old ranch road across the coastal prairie. Dip to cross a bridge over Low Gap Creek at 7⅞ miles, then contour through grasslands before climbing to the west end of the Low Gap Trail. Drop to a bridge across another creek at 8⅛ miles, then traverse the prairie. The trail rounds an eroding bluff edge to pass Streamside Camp and cross another creek at 8⅜ miles. Follow the bluff above the sea stack called Needle Rock, then climb east past Needle Rock Camp and a barn, coming to the unpaved park road and Needle Rock Visitor Center in the old ranch house at 8⅝ miles.

**ALTERNATE ROUTE:** The only other option follows Chemise Mountain Road south for 6¼ steep, dusty miles to Four Corners Junction. Then turn right and descend Briceland Road 3½ miles to Needle Rock Visitor Center.

**SUGGESTED ROUND TRIPS & LOOPS:** You can follow the trail to the top of Chemise Mountain or farther south to Manzanita, then return the way you came or loop back via Wailaki or Nadelos Campground and Chemise Mountain Road. A shorter day hike leaves from the south end and follows CCT north to the Whale Gulch ford, 3¾ miles round trip.

# Mendocino County

**W**ITH THE THIRD LONGEST COUNTY COASTLINE IN CALIFORNIA, Mendocino County offers some of the greatest existing trail mileage along the California Coastal Trail as well as some of the biggest challenges for the trail's completion. Of Mendocino County's 131-mile shore, about 52 miles, or 40 percent of it, can only be followed along Highway 1, a shocking amount of highway walking in a county renowned for one of the most beautiful and pristine coastlines in the state. When you consider that another 26 miles, or 20 percent, of Mendocino's CCT can be followed only along secondary roads, the paltry 50 miles of actual trail that CCT follows along the Mendocino coast clearly falls far short of the ideal.

The good news is that Mendocino County's portion of the Coastal Trail features an awe-inspiring 17- to 25-mile backpack through the rugged Sinkyone Wilderness State Park. This southern half of the Lost Coast presents one of the most dramatic coastal landscapes on earth. Other wonderful portions of CCT in Mendocino include the extensive dunes, beaches, forests and headlands of MacKerricher State Park, the wonderfully diverse and convoluted shore of Jughandle State Reserve, recently saved Point Cabrillo Preserve, expansive Manchester State Park, unique Schooner Gulch/Bowling Ball Beach, and the dramatic juxtaposition of historic town and jutting headlands at Mendocino itself. Even those portions of the CCT route that follow Highway 1, especially between the Navarro River and Manchester, offer some of the most breathtaking coastal views imaginable.

Nevertheless, Mendocino County calls out for and deserves so much more coastal preservation. If you walk the road miles of the Coastal Trail route through the county, you would be shocked at the miles of open and undeveloped shoreline just crying out to be saved. These areas include but are not limited to the wild coast from Usal Road south to Cape Vizcaino — the southern end of the Lost Coast — including Rockport Beach, the broad coastal shelf between Bruhel Point and Abalobadiah Creek, and the dramatic bluffs, coves and promontories of the shoreline from Albion south to Manchester.

In the four years since we published our first edition, some important improvements in public lands along the Mendocino coast have occurred, while others are pending. In a major breakthrough for the Coastal Trail, the Caspar Headlands have now been preserved for public access, becoming state park lands after Caspar residents organized to acquire 142 acres of their community for the public when most of their town's lands came up for sale. That acquisition provides a short but dramatic new headlands route overlooking the old doghole port at Caspar Cove. In the tiny north coast town of Westport, a chunk of the remaining undeveloped headlands have become a public space, providing another short but scenic off-highway route for CCT. The biggest public acquisiton on the Mendocino coast in years was completed in March 2002 after the Mendocino Land Trust teamed with federal and state agencies, nonprofit groups, and individuals to acquire 7334 acres of former timber land at Big River, including one of the largest estuaries on the west coast. Although the new state park at Big River won't change the CCT route there, it's gratifying to look up river from Big River bridge and know most everything in sight has been preserved for the public.

Pending acquisitions include the 1865-acre Stornetta Ranch astride Point Arena and an adjacent 500-acre parcel that could both be added to Manchester State Park, and a possible state park acquisition at Albion that would provide a wonderful link for the Coastal Trail there. Even with all these new acquisitions, much work remains to be done to complete Mendocino County's Coastal Trail.

## SECTION 1
# Needle Rock Visitor Center to Orchard Creek, Sinkyone Wilderness State Park

**DISTANCE:** 2½ miles (4 kilometers).

**OPEN TO:** Hikers, bicyclists, equestrians.

**SURFACE:** Dirt road.

**ACCESS POINT:** Needle Rock Visitor Center.

**HOW TO GET THERE:** Exit Highway 101 at Garberville (Milepost 10.8) from the south or Redway (Milepost 14.6) from the north. Take Briceland Road west from Redway 2.8 miles north of Garberville on Redwood Drive. In 12 miles go left through Whitethorn. In 4.5 miles (last part dirt), you come to the junction called Four Corners. Go straight, descending a steep, narrow, winding dirt road 3.6 miles to visitor center. This road is impassable to RVs or trailers and may even be closed after heavy rains.

**OTHER ACCESS:** You can park at various turnouts along the road south of the visitor center.

**DIFFICULTY:** Moderate.

**ELEVATION GAIN/LOSS:** 390 feet+/ 520 feet-.

**CAUTIONS:** This isolated country is far from phones, towns or services. Watch for vehicle traffic when you are walking road. Stay back from wild elk.

**FURTHER INFORMATION:** Sinkyone Wilderness State Park (707)986-7711.

**FACILITIES:** Filtered water, chemical toilet, camping self-registration, visitor center in historic building with nature and history exhibits.

**CAMPGROUNDS:** Needle Rock, Streamside and Jones Beach Environmental Camps are at the north end. Orchard Creek Environmental Camp is at the south end.

This area is the most "civilized" portion of 7567-acre Sinkyone Wilderness State Park, but don't expect to find the usual amenities. In the Sinkyone, civilization refers to historic development and perhaps a higher concentration of campsites, certainly not to commercial facilities.

The area was long the home of the Sinkyone tribe, southernmost of the Athapascan language tribes on the coast. European settlers came in the 1860s, developing cattle ranches, lumber mills and ship loading facilities. The heyday of such endeavors came at the dawning of the 20th century, but by 1960 most of the settlers had moved on. Nature quickly reasserted its control, obliterating most signs of human endeavor in short order. The visitor center has a wonderful album of historic photos showing the changes this wild coast has endured since 1860.

This CCT section follows the unimproved dirt road south to its end, with vistas of this enthralling coast and the coastal grasslands, forests and deep creek canyons all along the way. On the road you might encounter the herd of wild

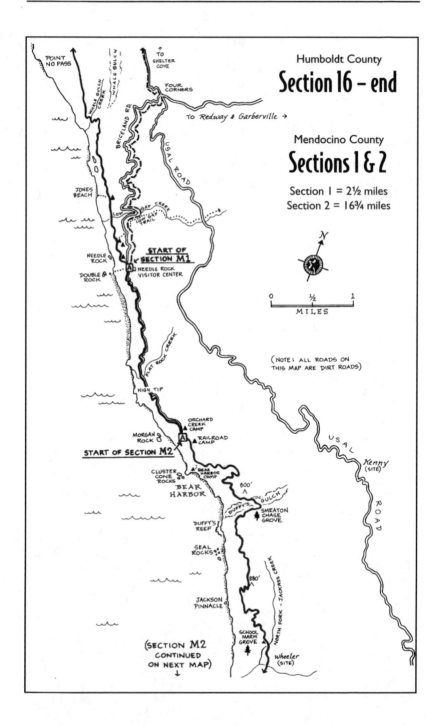

Roosevelt elk that roam the park. If you do, give them plenty of room, especially in mating season in September when the bulls sometimes charge without warning.

Follow the narrow dirt road south across coastal grasslands with superb ocean views. The road climbs and descends as it winds through several wooded canyons in the first mile. Descend to cross tiny Flat Rock Creek, then ascend over the flank of High Tip around 1½ miles. Descend steeply with grand views down the coast to cross another creek, then descend gently along a lush valley to road's end and Orchard Creek Camp at 2½ miles.

## SECTION 2
# Orchard Creek to Usal, Sinkyone Wilderness State Park

DISTANCE: 16¾ miles (27 kilometers).

OPEN TO: Hikers. Equestrians allowed on 4½ miles to Wheeler.

SURFACE: Trail.

ACCESS POINT: Orchard Creek.

HOW TO GET THERE: Follow directions to Needle Rock Visitor Center in previous section, then drive 2.5 miles to end of road.

DIFFICULTY: Strenuous.

ELEVATION GAIN/LOSS: 5300 feet+/5300 feet-.

CAUTIONS: Access road may be closed in rainy season. Permit required to stay overnight along trail; a fee is charged. Camping allowed only in designated areas. This isolated country is far from towns and traveled roads. Timber rattlesnakes, ticks, scorpions, poison oak and stinging nettles occur along trail. THIS IS THE MOST STRENUOUS SECTION OF THE ENTIRE CALIFORNIA COASTAL TRAIL.

FURTHER INFORMATION: Sinkyone Wilderness State Park (707)986-7711.

FACILITIES: Primitive camping, chemical toilets.

CAMPGROUNDS: Environmental Camps at Orchard Creek, Railroad Creek, Bear Harbor. Trail camps at Wheeler, Little Jackass Creek and Anderson Gulch. Car camping at Usal, the southern trailhead.

MAPS: See pages 114 and 116.

Heaven and hell go hand in hand on this most strenuous and most spectacular section of the Coastal Trail. Plan at least two days, preferably three or four, to hike the whole section. While the 17 miles may sound short, the elevation change is equivalent to hiking to the bottom of the Grand Canyon and back out. Fortunately you never exceed an elevation of 1200 feet. Still, it is a shame, and exhausting, to rush through such breathtaking country.

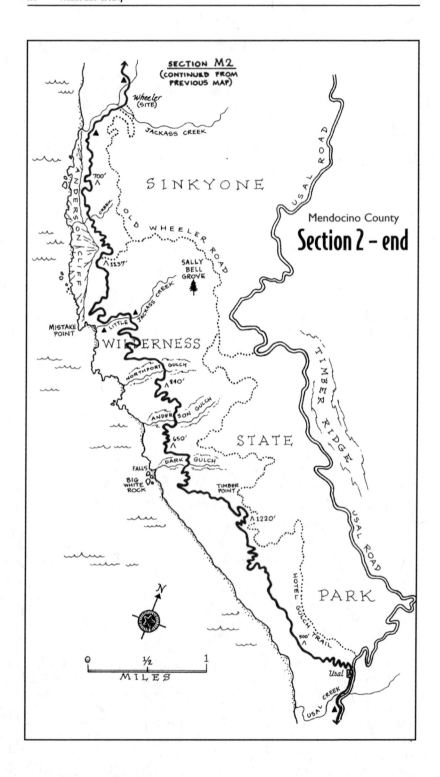

SECTION M2
(CONTINUED FROM PREVIOUS MAP)

Wheeler (SITE)

JACKASS CREEK

SINKYONE

Mendocino County
**Section 2 - end**

USAL ROAD

700'

OLD WHEELER ROAD

SALLY BELL GROVE

1137'

ANDERSON CLIFF

LITTLE JACKASS CREEK

MISTAKE POINT

WILDERNESS

NORTHPORT GULCH

840'

ANDERSON GULCH

TIMBER RIDGE

650'

STATE

FALLS
DARK GULCH

BIG WHITE ROCK

TIMBER POINT

1220'

USAL ROAD

N

HOTEL GULCH TRAIL

PARK

500'

0        ½        1
MILES

Usal

USAL CREEK

Sinkyone State Park was established in 1977, but the entire Lost Coast Trail opened only after the southern half of the park was acquired in 1987. As recently as 1980, vast virgin redwood forests still stood between Wheeler and Usal. After most of the big trees were logged out, the timber company agreed to sell. You will see serious scars from the timber operation, but the rugged grandeur of the land remains.

Follow the trail on a gentle descent past Railroad Creek Camp to Bear Harbor before ½ mile where more camps lie near the beach. The Lost Coast Trail heads east up a creek canyon. Cross the creek at ⅞ mile and ascend by switchbacks to views of the rugged coast. Top a ridge at 1½ miles, then descend into Duffy's Gulch on tread built in 1862. After crossing the stream beneath virgin forest at 2¼ miles, climb fitfully, patches of forest soon alternating with steep coastal grasslands. Follow the coast south, climbing steeply beyond 3¼ miles, then following a ridgetop as it dips and rises three times. Descend, then contour through forests and grasslands with coastal vistas.

At 4⅛ miles the trail switches to the east side of the ridge to descend long switchbacks into the virgin forest called Schoolmarm Grove. The descent ends at a grassy clearing beside the North Fork of Jackass Creek where the Wheeler School was located in the 1950s. Campsites and an outhouse are nearby. A spring lies in the gulch to the west.

The trail heads south across the creek and through the town site, coming to the mill site at the confluence of the North Fork and Jackass Creek at 4½ miles. Ford the creek and continue south, passing the cliff-edged beach at 4⅞ miles.

Follow the trail southeast up a gulch, soon climbing steeply through dense brush, then tall forest. Crest a ridge around 7 miles and descend into a hanging valley surrounded by the sheer Anderson Cliff along the shoreline. Cautiously cross an overgrown seasonal creek jammed with nettles at 7½ miles, then ascend steeply by a dozen switchbacks. The stiff climb ends at a grassy ridge at 8⅜ miles, elevation 1137 feet, offering the first glimpse of the coast south.

The trail descends gradually, then very steeply south, switchbacking nearly to sea level in Little Jackass Canyon by 9¼ miles. The trail levels at a junction where an outhouse serves the downstream camps. The side trip to the beach framed by the magnificent cliffs of Mistake Point is ¼ mile round trip.

CCT and the Lost Coast Trail go left at the fork, ascending the canyon and crossing the creek. Soon the trail passes two more campsites and another toilet beneath virgin redwoods near the creek. The trail south crosses the creek and ascends steadily by six switchbacks. At 10¼ miles the trail turns right and follows an old road south above Northport Gulch. Beyond 10⅞ miles, the road turns northeast at a broad landing, but the trail veers right to descend south. Drop steeply by nine switchbacks into Anderson Gulch. Reach the final trail camp with a view down Anderson Gulch to the ocean at 11¾ miles.

Descend two more switchbacks to a ford, then climb steeply to precipitous, grassy headlands above the rugged shore. Descend steeply to the edge of Dark Gulch, then follow it upstream to a crossing at 12⅞ miles.

The trail makes one last long ascent, climbing 900 feet in 1¼ miles to cross Timber Point. Descend south through forest, cross a seasonal creek, and drop into grasslands at 15¼ miles. Follow the grassy ridge southeast with great views over

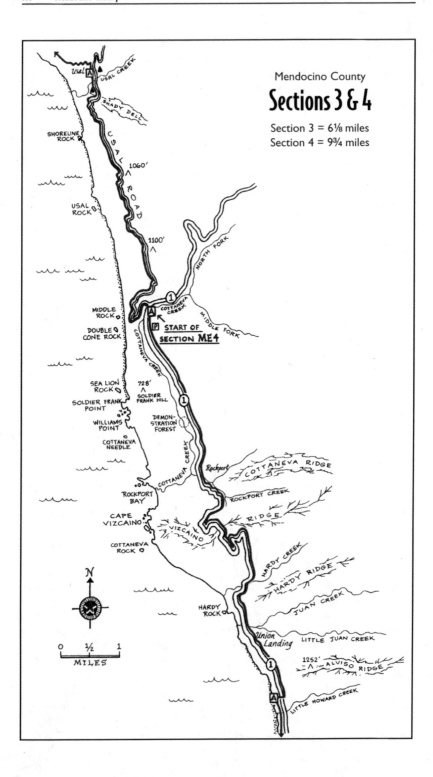

Mendocino County
# Sections 3 & 4

Section 3 = 6⅛ miles
Section 4 = 9¾ miles

Usal
USAL CREEK
SHADY DELL
SHORELINE ROCK
USAL ROAD
1060'
USAL ROCK
1100'
NORTH FORK
MIDDLE ROCK
COTTANEVA CREEK
MIDDLE FORK
DOUBLE CONE ROCK
START OF
SECTION ME4
SEA LION ROCK
728'
SOLDIER FRANK HILL
SOLDIER FRANK POINT
DEMON-STRATION FOREST
WILLIAMS POINT
COTTANEVA NEEDLE
COTTANEVA CREEK
Rockport
COTTANEVA RIDGE
ROCKPORT BAY
ROCKPORT CREEK
CAPE VIZCAINO
RIDGE
VIZCAINO
COTTANEVA ROCK
HARDY CREEK
HARDY RIDGE
HARDY ROCK
JUAN CREEK
Union Landing
LITTLE JUAN CREEK
1252'
ALVISO RIDGE
LITTLE HOWARD CREEK

N

0   ½   1
MILES

ocean and forest. After one more climb to the top of the ridge at 15⅞ miles, descend east by twenty switchbacks to Usal Road, 16¾ miles from Orchard Creek.

**ALTERNATE ROUTE:** If the elevation change for the section is simply too much, you can nearly halve it (and shorten your hike by 2¾ miles) by taking the following route, much less scenic. Follow the Lost Coast Trail to Wheeler. After the second creek crossing there, head east and south on the old Wheeler Road for 3½ miles, then turn right on the Hotel Gulch Horse Trail (Road 4500) and follow it 5¾ miles to Usal.

**SUGGESTED ROUND TRIPS & LOOPS:** For day hikers, a short walk to rugged Bear Harbor or a hike over the first ridge to the virgin redwood grove at Duffy's Gulch is quite manageable. The 10-mile round trip hike to Wheeler Beach is moderately strenuous, 2900 feet of up and down, so expect it to take all day. From its south end, the trail climbs more steeply, but the 5¼ miles round trip to Timber Point, or even the 1¾ miles round trip to the top of the first hill, provides inspiring views.

## SECTION 3
# Usal, Sinkyone Wilderness State Park, to Highway 1 at Usal Road

**DISTANCE:** 6⅛ miles (9.9 kilometers).

**OPEN TO:** Hikers, bicyclists.

**SURFACE:** Dirt county road.

**ACCESS POINT:** Usal Campground, Sinkyone Wilderness State Park.

**HOW TO GET THERE:** Turn west off Highway 1 at Milepost 90.88 (about 15 miles west of Leggett at Highway 101) onto unpaved, usually unmarked Usal Road. The narrow, winding road quickly climbs to 1000 feet, then drops by hairpin turns to sea level. At 6 miles, cross the narrow bridge over Usal Creek and continue .1 mile to Lost Coast Trailhead in Usal Campground.

**OTHER ACCESS:** Anywhere along route.

**DIFFICULTY:** Moderate.

**ELEVATION GAIN/LOSS:** 1320 feet+/1200 feet-.

**CAUTIONS:** Road may be impassable to vehicles in rainy season. Due to steep curves, it's never passable to RVs or trailers. Usal Campground has no water system — bring your own or purify creek water. This isolated country is far from services. Watch and listen for vehicles when walking this steep, twisting, narrow road.

**FURTHER INFORMATION:** Sinkyone Wilderness State Park (707)986-7711. Mendocino County Road Department (707)964-2596.

**FACILITIES:** Chemical toilets.

**CAMPGROUND:** Usal Campground at access point.

**LODGING:** Wonderful Howard Creek Ranch north of Westport is the nearest.

The section of Usal Road shared by the CCT is one of the most spectacular trail sections open to motorized traffic. The dramatic ascent from Usal and the high middle section before the summit provide vistas as stunning as those on the Lost Coast portion of CCT, even though they are not quite as pristine due to continued logging activity. Why walk this section when you can drive it? Because the views of the coast and the adjacent rugged terrain are continually inspiring, much more so than when you're enclosed in a vehicle.

From the Lost Coast Trailhead, follow level Usal Road south over the Usal Creek bridge and out of the campground. After passing the side canyon called Shady Dell at ⅜ mile, the road ascends steeply southwest, leaving the park at the first hairpin turn where a bird's-eye view of Usal and the rugged coast north to Big White Rock may steal your breath if the hill hasn't already. Continue the steep climb up the hairpins, watching and listening for traffic. The track skirts the edge of the forest with sheer grasslands to the west.

The ascent is unrelenting until 2 miles where you have gained an elevation of 1060 feet and left the grasslands for forest. Road and trail descend briefly, then contour with frequent views of the coast far below. Climb slightly around 2¾ miles, then descend into grasslands at the top of a steep slope plunging to the sea.

Climb moderately from 3¼ miles until you reach the section's 1100-foot summit in the forest around 3¾ miles. After a brief descent, your road contours through timber lands until 4¼ miles. Descend gradually to 4½ miles, then steeply down a winding, narrow stretch across a steep slope. Beyond 5¼ miles you return to coastal grasslands with the Pacific visible to the west. The steep winding descent continues.

At 5¾ miles Usal Road drops to a big bend overlooking a wild coastline with Middle Rock and Double Cone Rock offshore. If the weather is clear enough, you can look north back to Usal and the Sinkyone coast. If you look south, a rough path connects to a nearby ranch road that continues south along the high bluff above the wild shore. For now this path is across private property, but it would make an ideal route for the CCT. Until a better route is developed, you must descend ⅜ mile along Usal Road to the road's and section's end at Highway 1. CCT turns right to follow the highway shoulder south on the longest section of highway walking yet along CCT since the Oregon border.

**SUGGESTED ROUND TRIPS & LOOPS:** For a vigorous hill climb with spectacular views, walk the first mile or two up Usal Road from Usal Campground.

## SECTION 4
# Usal Road to Westport-Union Landing State Park Vista Point

**DISTANCE:** 9¾ miles (15.7 kilometers).

**OPEN TO:** Hikers, bicyclists.

**SURFACE:** Highway shoulder.

**ACCESS POINT:** Usal Road at Highway 1.

**HOW TO GET THERE:** On Highway 1 north of Rockport and south of Hales Grove at Milepost 90.88 where Usal Road heads north. Best parking available at Milepost 90.68.

**OTHER ACCESS:** Anywhere along highway.

**DIFFICULTY:** Moderate.

**ELEVATION GAIN/LOSS:** 920 feet+/1020 feet-.

**CAUTIONS:** Stay out of roadway and on shoulder. Use extreme caution when crossing road.

**FACILITIES:** None at access point. Chemical toilet and picnic area at Mendocino Redwood Company's Demonstration Forest. Chemical toilet, water, phone, picnic area at state park just south of south end.

**CAMPGROUNDS:** Westport-Union Landing State Park is just south of south end. Find more sheltered camping with showers at private Wages Creek Campground on next section.

**LODGING:** Howard Creek Ranch is a great bed and breakfast inn a mile south of vista point. Other lodgings in Westport.

**MAP:** See Page 118.

Suddenly the Coastal Trail hits the pavement for the first time since around Shelter Cove. Until we can get this section off the pavement, CCT hikers will need to follow Highway 1 on one of its steepest and most twisting segments for the next 9¾ miles. If you walk this stretch of highway be especially careful to stay out of the road. Though traffic isn't usually heavy, it does include plenty of logging trucks and RVs, many of which have trouble staying in their lane and even on the pavement. Read the feature *CCT Needs a Trail Corridor off Highway 1 around Rockport* and lobby your elected representatives to complete the CCT.

Follow the highway shoulder south on a gentle descent through the lush valley of Cottaneva Creek. Where you cross the creek around ¼ mile, abundant blackberry patches may offer a tasty snack in summer. Continue south past old ranch buildings and into the forest.

Beyond 2¼ miles, watch on the right for Mendocino Redwood Company's Demonstration Forest where the only outhouse and picnic area along this section offer a shady pleasant place to rest. A short side trail explores a scenic, wooded stretch of Cottaneva Creek.

Continue along Highway 1 through the ghost town of Rockport. At 3¼ miles you cross a bridge over the South Fork of Cottaneva Creek as the creek veers west down its canyon to the Pacific Ocean. Climb a big hill on the winding highway, gaining 710 feet in elevation in less than 2 miles. Just before the summit at 5¼ miles, a clearcut on your left offers a view north to the Lost Coast.

## The CCT Needs a Trail Corridor off Highway 1 Around Rockport

The south end of the Lost Coast doesn't just begin at Usal. You can already feel the Lost Coast (and see its King Range heart on a clear day) five miles north of Fort Bragg. When you get to Westport, you're already on the Lost Coast.

Magnificent Highway 1 follows California's coast for 711 miles, from Dana Point in Orange County until the highway turns inland north of Westport at Hardy Creek. Travelers stop on the blufftop above Hardy Creek to gaze north at steep, slide-torn hills plunging to the ocean. It looks like the end of the civilized world, and for most of the 80 miles of coastline to the north, the rugged terrain has thoroughly refuted efforts to tame it. The Lost Coast's precipitous, geologically active cliffs have certainly defeated highway builders. No highway follows the north coast again until Humboldt Bay.

Imagine the impact on travelers if we could post this sign at Hardy Creek:

---

← CALIFORNIA COASTAL TRAIL: OREGON BORDER VIA THE LOST COAST—233 MILES

---

THIS IS THE FINAL VIEW OF THE PACIFIC COAST FROM HIGHWAY 1

---

The California Coastal Trail stays off highways from the Oregon border south until Usal Road ends at Highway 1, with two exceptions of less than a mile. These 226 miles at CCT's northern end offer the trail's most complete portion to date.

Unfortunately, when CCT now reaches Highway 1 at the end of Usal Road, the trail's nature changes for the worse along the spectacular Mendocino coast. In the next 100 miles, CCT takes to Highway 1 for 52 miles, with another 26 miles on secondary roads, leaving only 22½ miles of trail walking in the rest of Mendocino County. The CCT's apparent Highway 1 obsession starts with 9¾ miles along one of the most crooked, narrow, and dangerous portions of the highway.

A great opportunity exists to get the Coastal Trail off Highway 1 for some of the seven miles south of Usal Road. Mendocino Redwood Company now owns about 1000 acres along the dramatic, rugged coast from Soldier Frank Point south to Hardy Creek. Another timber company, Soper-Wheeler, owns adjoining headlands north to Usal Road, and though their land isn't for sale, they already lease access to that property to a hunting club and might be convinced to lease an easement for CCT.

Coastwalk has talked with Mendocino Redwood Company about allowing the CCT to cross their land around spectacular Rockport Beach. The company's representatives expressed interest in allowing an off-highway route for the CCT on their property around Rockport. If the idea becomes reality, hikers would have access to a new CCT route there by getting a permit that would be available from Coastwalk. With a trail over Cape Vizcaino to Hardy Creek, public access along the Lost Coast would be expanded, and CCT's highway mileage in Mendocino would fall by 10 percent. This would make dramatic steps toward completing California's Coastal Trail.

Highway 1 descends gradually then steeply by sweeping curves. After a grand view of the coast south all the way to Mendocino at 5½ miles, follow the highway shoulder as it drops through the wooded canyon of a fork of Hardy Creek. At 7⅛ miles you round a bend to the right, and the Pacific comes into view. Cross Hardy Creek at 7¼ miles and climb along the shoulder up to the ocean bluff where a broad shoulder on the right provides stunning views north to razor-edge Cape Vizcaino and south past Hardy Rock to the northern Mendocino coast.

Follow the highway south as it climbs and descends with ocean vistas, crossing Juan Creek at 8⅛ miles. Around 8⅜ miles you pass another ghost logging settlement at Union Landing where nothing remains of a small lumber town that lasted into the 1920s. As you continue along Highway 1, state park lands begin west of the road at 8½ miles, but no trail provides relief for your road-weary soles until you come to section's end at the vista point on the right at 9¾ miles.

# SECTION 5
# Westport-Union Landing State Park Vista Point to Bruhel Point North Access

DISTANCE: 5⅞ miles (9.5 kilometers).

OPEN TO: Hikers. Bicyclists on roads, wheelchairs on most of first 1⅞ miles.

SURFACE: Road shoulder, beach, trail, highway shoulder.

ACCESS POINT: Vista Point at north end of Westport-Union Landing State Beach.

FACILITIES: Chemical toilets, picnic area, phone, water available must be purified.

DIRECTIONS TO ACCESS POINT: On Highway 1 1.8 miles north of Westport and 17 miles north of Fort Bragg, turn west into vista point and park at the north end of the lot.

OTHER ACCESS: Pete's Beach on west side of Highway 1 at Milepost 77.78, Westport Headlands in town, or anywhere south along highway.

DIFFICULTY: Easy for first half, moderate for second half.

ELEVATION GAIN/LOSS: 520 feet+/400 feet-. To Westport Store: 160 feet+/120 feet-.

CAUTIONS: Beach south of DeHaven Creek is passable only at a tide of 2.0 feet or lower.

FURTHER INFORMATION: Mendocino Area State Parks (707)937-5804.

CAMPGROUND: Westport-Union Landing State Beach offers primitive camping year round. Wages Creek Campground (private) offers showers, flush toilets and more sheltered camping.

LODGING: Howard Creek Ranch is near start of section. Several in Westport area.

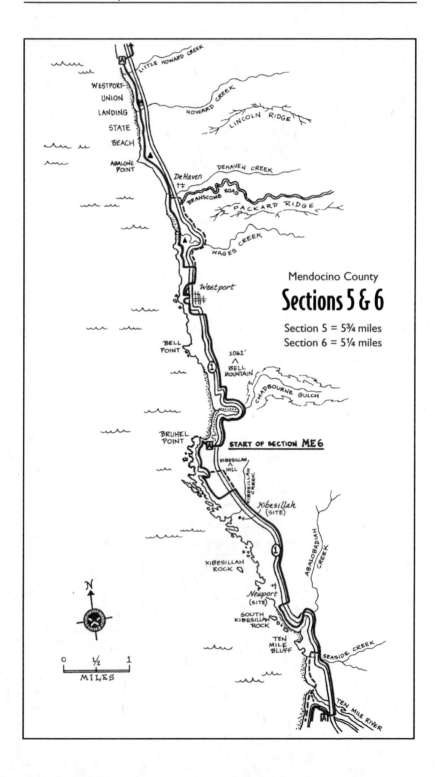

LITTLE HOWARD CREEK

WESTPORT-
UNION
LANDING
STATE
BEACH

HOWARD CREEK

LINCOLN RIDGE

ABALONE
POINT

DeHaven

DEHAVEN CREEK

BRANSCOMB ROAD

PACKARD RIDGE

WAGES CREEK

Westport

Mendocino County

# Sections 5 & 6

Section 5 = 5¾ miles
Section 6 = 5¼ miles

BELL
POINT

1062'
∧
BELL
MOUNTAIN

CHADBOURNE GULCH

BRUHEL
POINT

**START OF SECTION ME 6**

KIBESILLAH
∧
HILL

KIBESILLAH CREEK

Kibesillah
(SITE)

KIBESILLAH
ROCK

ABALOBADIAH CREEK

N

Newport
(SITE)

SOUTH
KIBESILLAH
ROCK

TEN
MILE
BLUFF

SEASIDE CREEK

0      ½      1
MILES

TEN MILE RIVER

Westport-Union Landing State Park officially comprises only 60 acres in a long narrow strip west of Highway 1, but its spacious pastoral setting and rocky tide zone make it seem much larger. Paved portions of the Coastal Trail follow old Highway 1, but plan to visit during a low tide to enjoy the rich intertidal zone. CCT follows the bluffs or tidal zone of the state park and tidal beaches to the south for the section's first 3 miles. Then CCT visits Westport's fine new 8-acre public access headlands and follows residential streets before the provisional route follows Highway 1 to section's end.

The settlement called Union Landing perched on the windy bluff a mile north of the vista point from 1899 until the 1920s. Lumber and other goods slid down a loading chute to waiting ships. The town of Westport has had a much longer life, although it's been rather boom and bust as well. Founded as Beall's Landing in 1864, the town began to boom in the late 1870s when it acquired its current name. Westport soon had two wharves, 380 and 610 feet long on either end of Omega Street. Its two sawmills supported 400 people and two dozen businesses before 1900, but economics then fire took their toll, and little was left by 1950.

From the north end of the vista point, follow the western edge of the pavement south for the best vistas of the rocky intertidal and offshore zones. Leave the vista point behind after ⅛ mile, passing a silver gate and continuing south along the pavement through the northern end of the state park campground.

Come to the end of the road at ⅝ mile and descend the wooden stairway to ford tiny Howard Creek, then cross the small pocket beach, the sands of which are often streaked with pink grains.

For the quickest route, climb the stairway at the south end of the beach to return to pavement and the southern part of the campground. For a more scenic route when the tide is 2.0 feet or less, instead of ascending the stairway, veer west and follow the sandy then rocky beach south around Abalone Point. The beach route is about ⅛ mile longer than the pavement, and tricky footing on slippery rocks makes it more difficult and slower.

Continue south past Abalone Point and several camp and picnic areas, coming to the park's southern end at ⅞ miles. Take the trail dropping to sandy DeHaven Creek Beach, soon coming to the little creek, an easy ford in summer, usually a wet one in winter. Just beyond 2 miles, you reach a rocky point where you can gauge whether the tide is low enough to continue. If the tide is rising and the surf comes over the tidal rocks onto the beach, turn back or detour south along Highway 1.

Assuming you passed the test, the beach widens beyond the rocky point. Walk the beach south and round a second rocky point at 2⅛ miles. The beach widens by 2¼ miles with lower cliffs on your left. Beyond 2⅜ miles, the cliffs end at broad Wages Creek Beach. Just up canyon is private Wages Creek Campground. Please don't enter the campground unless you'll be staying there.

Walk the tidal zone to the south end of the beach at 2⅝ miles where you ford Wages Creek if the tide is low enough to continue. The beach turns very narrow with a sea stack dissected by a wave tunnel on your right, then Pete's Beach offers easy walking to 2⅞ miles. Just 200 feet before the south end of the beach, the Coastal Trail veers left on a path that ascends 87 steps to the blufftop beside Highway 1. If you're day hiking and the tide is still low enough, return the way you came.

The Coastal Trail follows Highway 1 into the nearby village of Westport. Cautiously follow the highway shoulder until you see Omega Drive on the right. Take Omega to stay as close as possible to the shore. It soon veers east and ends at Highway 1 in downtown Westport opposite the Community Store at 3⅜ miles.

To follow CCT, walk the highway shoulder south for 200 feet to the new Westport Headlands access on your right. Turn right and walk the path west onto the new 8-acre public access. In 150 feet the path splits in three. Turn left (south) and follow the path across a seasonal creek. CCT, following the main path here at the fine new community open space, wanders west to overlook a dark sand beach and Westport's rock-studded shoreline. A steep, rough path descends to the beach. CCT heads south, quickly coming to another junction. While the main fork veers left, stay to the right and follow the bluff's edge to another junction at a point at 3½ miles. Here CCT turns left and heads east to return to the highway shoulder. Before you go, consider a short side trail that heads 150 feet west onto the narrow point for the most spectacular view of Westport's steep and rugged rocky shoreline.

Walk east to reach Highway 1 before 3¾ miles, then follow the highway's right shoulder 330 feet to Pacific Avenue. Veer right onto Pacific Avenue and walk it south, then east to Highway 1 around 3⅞ miles. For now the only route south for CCT follows Highway 1, so cautiously walk the shoulder south, climbing gradually over the flank of Bell Mountain. You crest the hill just south of Bell Point at 4¼ miles. Follow the highway for ½ mile as it descends along the top of a high cliff.

From the hairpin turn around 4⅞ miles, follow the highway cautiously as it corkscrews to sea level. A dirt road on the right at 5 miles leads quickly to the beach at the mouth of Chadbourne Gulch. When you pass through here at a minus tide, you might follow an undeveloped route of CCT south along the beach. The crucial point for the low tide is the rocky point .3 mile south of the gulch. If you can get around the point, subject to wave action as well as the tide, you must ascend a steep bluff to reach to Bruhel Point.

Until that route is improved, CCT continues along the highway, ascending from Chadbourne Gulch and following the steep bluffs south to 5⅞ miles and Milepost 74.6, where this section ends at a broad dirt turnout west of the highway.

**ALTERNATE ROUTE:** If the tide is in and you cannot get around the points at 2 or 2⅝ miles, you must follow the highway shoulder south.

**SUGGESTED ROUND TRIPS & LOOPS:** The pleasant walk south from the Access Point along the tideline or the bluffs makes an easy day hike. Following the tideline south from 2 miles at medium to low tide offers a rich tidal area and secluded beaches. The new 8-acre Westport Village Headlands Access offers a short but pleasant walk. Chadbourne Beach offers a pleasant walk at medium to low tide.

**HOW TO IMPROVE CCT HERE:** Since state parks ownership extends north almost one mile from the vista point, develop a trail north to the end of state park property. Build an improved trail at Bruhel Point that avoids the steep decent to the beach. Build a trail between Chadbourne Beach and Bruhel Point and find other ways to get CCT off the highway shoulder south of Westport.

## SECTION 6
# Bruhel Point to Ten Mile River, MacKerricher State Park

**DISTANCE:** 5⅝ miles (9.1 kilometers).

**OPEN TO:** Hikers. Bicyclists on highway.

**SURFACE:** Trail, highway shoulder.

**ACCESS POINT:** Northern end of Bruhel Point.

**HOW TO GET THERE:** South of Westport and north of Fort Bragg, turn west off Highway 1 at Milepost 74.6 into unmarked broad dirt turnout.

**OTHER ACCESS:** Vista Point at Milepost 74.09 or anywhere along highway portion.

**DIFFICULTY:** Easy.

**ELEVATION GAIN/LOSS:** 460 feet+/560 feet-. For Bruhel trail: 130 feet+/160 feet-.

**CAUTIONS:** If you attempt to ford Ten Mile River, use extreme caution and don't be afraid to turn back. Always stay off road and use caution when walking highway shoulder.

**FURTHER INFORMATION:** CalTrans (707)445-6444.

**FACILITIES:** None at access point. Picnic tables at South Kibesillah View Area.

**CAMPGROUNDS:** MacKerricher State Park is on next section. Westport-Union Landing State Beach was on previous section.

**LODGING:** Several in Westport to north or Cleone and Fort Bragg to south.

**MAP:** See page 124.

After a pleasant respite from the pavement at the dramatic headlands overlooking Bruhel Point's tidepools, the Coastal Trail returns to highway shoulder until it reaches MacKerricher State Park at the Ten Mile River. Once again most of the road portion looks out over mostly open headlands and marine terraces where a suitable route could be found for the CCT.

Once upon a time an earlier coastal trail traversed all these bluffs and headlands. By 1868 the Humboldt Trail traversed this coastline, more or less, from Fort Bragg to Eureka. It was established so that Mendocino coast settlers could ride a horse or walk to the State Land Office branch in Eureka to register their land claims. The modern CCT follows the route of the Humboldt Trail in several places, notably along the coastline of today's MacKerricher State Park, along Usal Road, at Duffy's Gulch in Sinkyone State Park, and at Bruhel Point and north of Seaside Beach on this section. Most of the Humboldt Trail fell into disuse by the 1920s, when steamships and better roads provided easier links between the two north coast cities.

Of course even before the Humboldt Trail, many native tribes developed and used trails along the coast. What we today call Bruhel Point was an important hub and destination for native trails of several tribes. The Coast Yuki people, who resided here and from Rockport to Ten Mile River, called this placed Lilim. Kato and Huchnom people came from the east, Sinkyone and Wailaki from the north, and Northern Pomo from the south to camp at Lilim to harvest shellfish and net and spear salmon and surf fish for drying at this bountiful spot. The marine waters at Bruhel Point were so abundant that all these tribes, several of them not otherwise on friendly terms, agreed to use Lilim as a neutral place where the harvest would be shared by all. Remarkably the tidal zone here still yields an abundant harvest to fishers, tidepoolers and divers who visit.

From the break in the fence, descend west across sloping headlands, heading toward the tip of Bruhel Point. Around ⅛ mile, as you approach the tip of the

## Thar She Blows! Whale Watching

The California Coastal Trail provides some of the best whale watching in the state. If you hike the coast between December and May, you'll have excellent chances to see some of the 18,000 California gray whales that swim the west coast each year. If you hike CCT in summer or autumn, you might get lucky and spot humpback whales or harbor porpoises swimming or breeding offshore.

Unlike other whales, grays migrate in sight of land, giving you a great chance to observe their 12,000-mile round trip between Alaska's Bering Sea and Baja California. The gray whales, led by pregnant mothers, first appear off northern California in mid-December, continuing their trek south to Baja into February. They travel about five miles an hour up to twenty hours a day, cruising a mile or two offshore.

Grays return north in March and April. Mothers with young calves (1500 pounds at birth!) dawdle along as late as July. The northern trekkers minimize current drag by swimming just beyond the forming breakers.

California's official marine mammals usually travel in pods of three to eight, although some prefer to cruise solo. An average gray weighs 30 tons and is 40 feet long, with a life span similar to ours. They've been making their annual trek for around five million years. Their ancestors once lived on land, turning to the sea around 30 million years ago.

Humpback whales also migrate off California's coast, but mostly stay far from shore. While spotting humpbacks from land is unpredictable, they come closest to local shores during summer or autumn feeding. Sometimes humpbacks breed along the north coast, a rare sight to see from land. Harbor porpoises, much smaller cetaceans, sometimes visit the California coast in summer.

You're most likely to spot the whale by its spout or blow, the misty exhalation from the blowhole atop its head. Grays and humpbacks blow steam six to 15 feet high. You might hear the "whoosh" of exhalation from a half mile away.

Whales typically blow three to eight times at 10- to 30-second intervals, then take a deep dive, or sound, flipping the fluke (tail) on the way down. A normal dive lasts about four minutes, reaching depths of 120 feet.

Your best whale watching occurs when the ocean is calm before winds and waves pick up, often in the morning. Binoculars enhance viewing, but when whales are there you can see them with the naked eye. For the best viewing from shore, find a point jutting out to sea. If you are visiting the coast during prime whale season, consider taking a whale watching cruise from the nearest harbor.

grassy bluff above the rocky point, look for a path that drops steeply south to a tiny beach. Use caution descending the rough trail down the steep slope, then scramble across the rock shelf to the beach. Cross the beach and ascend the rough trail that climbs east to the headlands around ¼ mile.

Locate the vague path that follows the edge of the grassy bluff and follow it south. The trail winds along the blufftop overlooking a large rocky tidal zone. CCT stays on the bluff edge past several steep side trails that descend to the tidal flats.

Around ⅝ mile, your trail forks. You can take the side trail on the right for a longer exploration along the bluff's edge. The Coastal Trail follows the left fork, veering southeast then south toward a stand of Monterey pines. Past the pines at ⅞ mile, it comes to a "T" intersection with an east-west trail. You have a choice here. With a left turn you'd quickly climb to a paved vista point, from which you would need to follow the highway shoulder south. The CCT's new slightly longer but more pleasant route turns right to descend west to the bluff's edge at one mile, then turns left to head south across the headlands near the bluff's edge. Around 1¼ miles the path splits, but both forks soon rejoin. At the next fork in 300 feet, the right fork leads 150 feet to approach a deep rocky cove, a good fishing spot. CCT follows the left fork southeast near the bluff's edge, passing through a broken down fence, then climbing to top a hill at 1½ miles at a fence marking the private property of Pacific Star Winery. Turn left and climb along the fenceline on a vague path. When you near Highway 1 at 1¾ miles, angle northeast toward a big clump of cypress. Find a vague path just to the right of the cypress clump and left of two smaller cypresses and follow it to a two-wheel track along a phone line right of way. CCT turns right and follows the track briefly, returning to the highway shoulder at Milepost 73.64.

From there you must follow the highway shoulder south. Dip across tiny Kibesillah Creek at 2 miles, then ascend past a cluster of old buildings to the west. These weather-beaten structures are the remains of the lumber ghost town of Kibesillah which thrived here from 1867 until 1885 when the sawmill's new owner moved his lumber operation to the abandoned military post at Fort Bragg. Most of Kibesillah's residents followed, and Fort Bragg soon became an important commercial center.

CCT continues along the highway shoulder, climbing until almost 2⅝ miles, then descending south with Kibesillah Rock the largest of the many picturesque sea stacks offshore. As the road levels around 3⅛ miles, you pass the remains of another ghost town west of the road. Newport was a busy shipping point from 1875 until 1900. Follow the highway over a bluff and across a gully at 3½ miles.

You come to South Kibesillah View Area on the west side of the highway. CCT leaves the road shoulder at a paved road leading to blufftop picnic tables with views south along the coast. But unless you're staying to enjoy the great view, walk south to find a rough two-wheel track west of the highway. Follow its right fork south for 1600 feet until it returns to the highway around 3⅞ miles, where you once again are forced along the highway shoulder.

Use caution as the road narrows and winds down to cross Abalobadiah Creek at 4⅛ miles, then winds back up to the blufftop with the ocean obscured by private residences. You soon drop along a cypress windbreak to cross tiny Seaside Creek at 4¾ miles. Just before the windbreak ends, look east of the roadway for the remains of the tread of an earlier coastal trail. Named the Humboldt Trail, it was built in the 1860s to allow Mendocino coast settlers to get to Eureka to file land claims at the state land office there.

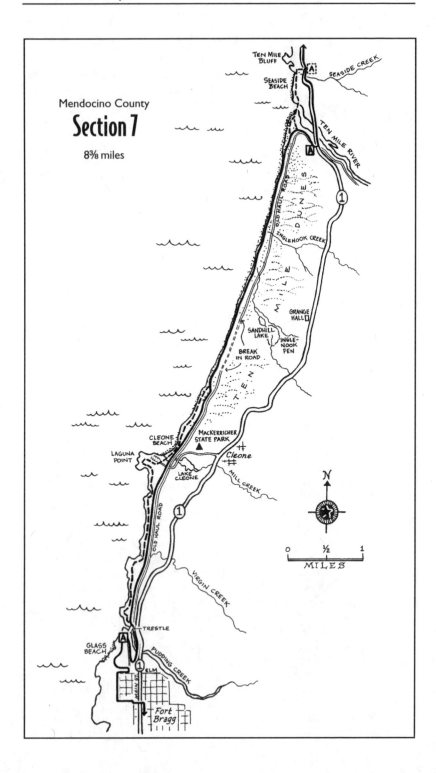

Mendocino County
# Section 7
8⅜ miles

At Seaside Creek you have access to Seaside Beach which stretches south ⅜ mile to Ten Mile River. See **Alternate Route**. Due to the uncertainty of the river ford, the CCT continues along the highway shoulder, winding east up to a bluff, then contouring south. Cross the long, narrow Ten Mile River bridge and reach the section's end at 5⅝ miles. Happily the CCT stays off Highway 1 for most of the next 32 miles.

**ALTERNATE ROUTE:** In summer and early fall you can leave Highway 1 at Seaside Beach and walk the beach south to ford the Ten Mile River at its mouth. During those times the river usually ranges from knee-deep to waist-deep, depending on tides and recent rains. Do not attempt to ford the river when it is deeper, especially during the rainy season.

**SUGGESTED ROUND TRIPS & LOOPS:** Explore Bruhel Point from either the north or south end. North of the vista point you can loop back on the upper path after walking the blufftop route. Walk Seaside Beach to the mouth of Ten Mile River.

**HOW TO IMPROVE CCT HERE:** Acquire route across ranch lands west or east of the highway.

## SECTION 7
# Ten Mile River to Fort Bragg, MacKerricher State Park

**DISTANCE:** 8⅜ miles until trestle opens, 7½ miles with trestle open (13.4 or 12.1 km).

**OPEN TO:** Hikers. Bicyclists on part, equestrians on alternate routes, wheelchairs on part.

**SURFACE:** Paved road closed to motor vehicles, beach, trail, highway shoulder.

**ACCESS POINT:** South end of Ten Mile River bridge.

**HOW TO GET THERE:** Turn west off Highway 1 north of Cleone and Fort Bragg, south of Westport at Milepost 69.67 into small dirt parking lot.

**OTHER ACCESS:** Main park entrance at south end of Cleone at Milepost 64.87, parking lot west of Highway 1 at Milepost 62.7, north end of Fort Bragg.

**DIFFICULTY:** Easy.

**ELEVATION GAIN/LOSS:** 160 feet+/150 feet-; once trestle opens: 110 feet+/110 feet-.

**CAUTIONS:** Blowing sand can make this walk miserable in high winds, especially north half.

**FURTHER INFORMATION:** Mendocino area State Parks (707)937-5804.

**FACILITIES:** None at access point, but MacKerricher State Park has restrooms, water, phones, picnic areas, campgrounds.

**CAMPGROUNDS:** MacKerricher State Park has 143 sites and 11 walk-in sites adjacent to trail.

**LODGING:** Cleone Lodge nearby, many choices in Fort Bragg.

The Old Haul Road, the seaside portion of a former private logging road between the lumber mill at Fort Bragg and the forests of Ten Mile River, has become a community institution. People of all ages come here from morning until night to walk, bike or jog. Generally the crowds stay along the southern half. The northern end sees scant traffic once it leaves the beautiful Ten Mile River estuary. If you prefer to stay off the pavement, you can walk the beach south from Ten Mile River for about 4 miles (**Alternate Route A**), jog east to follow the Haul Road about a mile, then follow longer, meandering **Alternate Route C** along the blufftop to Pudding Creek.

Before the road was laid in 1949, a logging railway built in 1916 followed the same route. When storm surf destroyed a mile of the road in 1982, log trucks switched to the nearby highway. State Parks bought the road in 1994, saving it from development after the timber corporation that owned it threatened to sell to the highest bidder. Coastwalk and many individuals who use the Haul Road protested the attempt to sell the road to anyone other than state parks. Recently, the MacKerricher Park General Plan abandoned the plan to build a boardwalk or paved path to bridge the gap in the Haul Road around 3 miles. It would've had a big impact on the sensitive environment of Ten Mile Dunes. Plans still include restoring the old railroad trestle at section's end and opening it to pedestrian traffic.

From the parking area, take the path that descends north toward the river, dropping over sand dunes to the paved Old Haul Road. Follow the pavement toward the river mouth, guarded on the north by the sea stacks of Seaside Beach. By ½ mile the Haul Road starts a big bend left to head south paralleling the shore. You meet the Alternate Route from Seaside Beach here, coming south from the seasonal ford at the river mouth. See **Section 6 Alternate Route**. You can take a side trip north about ¼ mile to the river's mouth, and/or you can veer west here and walk the beach south. See **Alternate Route A**.

The Haul Road angles south-southwest through the extensive Ten Mile Dunes. This was the site of the Mendocino Indian Reservation from 1856 to 1866, the fourth reservation in the nation. Traverse the broadest section of the dunes at 1½ miles, then cross Inglenook Creek around 1⅞ miles. The level, nearly straight road continues along the shore. Cross the small creek that flows from nearby Sandhill Lake and its adjacent Inglenook Fen at 2⅜ miles, then pass an old farm gate on the left. The next ¼ mile of pavement is often covered with sand and some of it has been damaged by the surf.

Around 2⅝ miles the Haul Road ends abruptly where powerful winter storm surf destroyed a mile of road. While you can continue straight across the soft dunes, the best walking follows the tideline 200 feet west. Watch for sneaker waves as you follow the wet sand south for about a mile.

By 3⅝ miles you'll again see the Haul Road on your left at the top of a 30-foot bluff. You can return to the pavement via a horse trail here or walk the beach up to another ½ mile if the tide isn't too high. Back on the pavement, you quickly see signs of civilization. Before 3⅞ miles you pass the Ward Avenue access and continue along the pavement above tiny pocket beaches sandwiched between rocky headlands.

By 4⅜ miles the state park campground lies to the east. After a side trail west to the beach, a second spur forks east to the wooded campground. After a horse trail forks east at 4¾ miles, dark-sand Cleone Beach (**Alternate Route B**) is on your right. You quickly reach a spot where storm surf reduced the elevated Haul Road to a narrow dirt track for 500 feet. Freshwater Lake Cleone lies to the east. After the pavement resumes, it soon crosses a wooden overpass then at 5⅛ miles passes a gravel track on the right that leads to the Laguna Point parking lot and **Alternate Route C.**

The Haul Road route immediately comes to a silver gate where a side trail heads east to the nearby campground which includes pleasant walk-in sites very close to the CCT. Haul Road and CCT continue south through a corridor lined with shore pines and wax myrtles. From 5½ miles, the Haul Road mostly has state park lands only to its west with the rocky shore nearby. At 6⅜ miles your route dips across Virgin Creek on a wooden bridge. Soon an industrial zone lines the east side of the road, followed by several motels. It must be time to welcome through-hikers back to civilization for what it's worth!

A second silver gate marks another access point to the Haul Road at 7⅛ miles. If you are walking into Fort Bragg, the Haul Road continues to the north end of the old Pudding Creek Trestle, the original railroad bridge dating from 1916, at 7⅜ miles. Until the trestle is restored for foot traffic, you must take the narrow dirt path on the left that descends to the parking area for Pudding Creek Beach. Then walk south along the parking area to the Pudding Creek highway bridge and cautiously walk the shoulder up the hill. At the stoplight, turn right on Elm Street and go two blocks west, then north to the end of the street and the south end of the trestle and section's end.

Once the trestle opens to pedestrian traffic, CCT will simply follow the Haul Road over the trestle to its south end at 7½ miles.

**SUGGESTED ROUND TRIPS & LOOPS:** In late summer and autumn when Ten Mile River is low enought to ford, cross it and walk north to Seaside, about 2 miles round trip from access point. Walk the Old Haul Road to the break and return on the beach, 5¼ miles round trip. From Laguna Point lot, walk west to the point and follow the bluff trail south to Virgin Creek Beach, returning by the Haul Road if you'd like, about 3 miles total. At Lake Cleone, a pleasant 1⅜-loop circles the lake. The first portions of the latter two choices follow raised boardwalks passable to wheelchairs.

**ALTERNATE ROUTES:** A) From the mouth of Ten Mile River or the side trail to it, you can walk the beach rather than the pavement for about 3 miles, requiring two creek fords in winter and spring. Then rocky headlands make the Haul Road the best choice. B) At Cleone Beach the tideline is again easy to follow to the Laguna Point parking lot. C) At Laguna Point you can follow a boardwalk west, then a bluff edge trail south along the shore to Virgin Creek Beach, then a dirt path again to Pudding Creek, adding ½ mile to one mile to total.

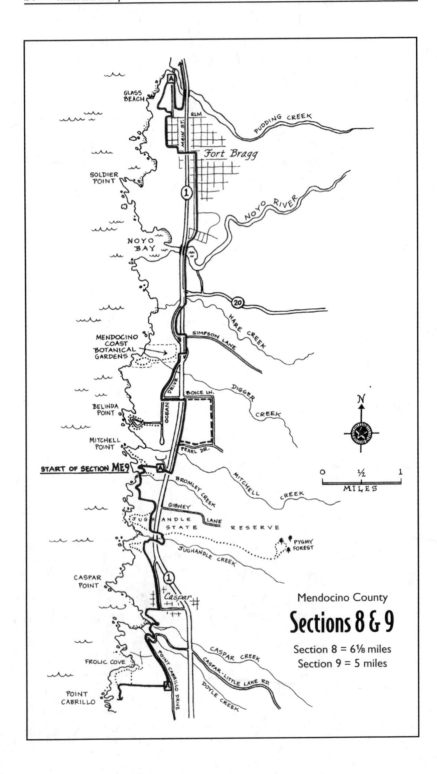

GLASS
BEACH

ELM

MAIN ST.

PUDDING CREEK

*Fort Bragg*

SOLDIER
POINT

NOYO RIVER

① 1

NOYO
BAY

② 20

HARE CREEK

SIMPSON LANE

MENDOCINO
COAST
BOTANICAL
GARDENS

OCEAN DRIVE

BOICE LN.

DIGGER CREEK

BELINDA
POINT

MITCHELL
POINT

PEARL DR.

**START OF SECTION ME9**

BROMLEY CREEK

MITCHELL CREEK

GIBNEY

JUGHANDLE  LANE
STATE   RESERVE

PYGMY
FOREST

JUGHANDLE CREEK

CASPAR
POINT

① 1

*Caspar*

FROLIC COVE

CASPAR CREEK

CASPAR-LITTLE LAKE RD.

POINT
CABRILLO

POINT CABRILLO DRIVE

DOYLE CREEK

N

0    ½    1
MILES

Mendocino County
## Sections 8 & 9
Section 8 = 6⅛ miles
Section 9 = 5 miles

## SECTION 8
# Pudding Creek Trestle, South End, Fort Bragg to Pine Beach Inn

DISTANCE: 6⅛ miles (9.9 kilometers).

OPEN TO: Hikers, bicyclists.

SURFACE: Trail, sidewalk, highway shoulder.

ACCESS POINT: South end of Pudding Creek Trestle.

HOW TO GET THERE: In Fort Bragg the northernmost street west of Highway 1 is Elm Street. Go west on Elm two blocks, then turn right on Old Haul Road and go .4 mile to parking area at north end of street.

DIFFICULTY: Easy.

ELEVATION GAIN/LOSS: 200 feet+/160 feet-.

CAUTIONS: Use crosswalks and watch for traffic when crossing streets.

FURTHER INFORMATION: Mendocino Coast Chamber of Commerce (707)961-6300.

FACILITIES: None at start. Restrooms, water, phones, campgrounds along the route.

CAMPGROUND: Harbor RV Park, Pomo Campground and Woodside Trailer Park are private campgrounds along section. MacKerricher State Park has camping 3 miles north.

LODGING: Fort Bragg has more than two dozen choices, from the budget Chelsea Inn and Shoreline Cottages to the deluxe Grey Whale Inn and Avalon House B&B.

You can walk many routes through Fort Bragg, but this one keeps you as close to the ocean and out of traffic as possible while still exploring the heart of the downtown area. The civilized amenities will likely be a welcome sight to anyone who has just walked the Coastal Trail through the Lost Coast.

Take the dirt path west across the grassy headlands above the mouth of Pudding Creek. The trail soon turns south along the rocky Pacific shore, passing through an area with abundant wildflowers, including several rare and endangered species. Beyond ¼ mile dip through a gully shaded with cypress, then follow the bluff's edge southwest. You soon overlook Glass Beach, a tideland that was once the city dump where one can find wave-polished glass, pottery and other trinkets. Several side trails descend to the popular beachcombing area.

By ½ mile the fenced lumber yards of Georgia-Pacific block coastal access to the south. Turn left and walk the pavement east to Elm Street at ⅞ mile. Walk the sidewalks of Elm Street one block east, then turn right and walk Stewart Street one block. Turn right and walk Spruce Street one block to its end, then head south on West Street. In this residential neighborhood, you can see the blue Pacific beyond the single row of houses.

After three blocks, West Street ends within sight of the big lumber mill. Turn left on Pine Street and parallel the railroad yard of the Skunk Train, California Western Railroad. Beyond Stewart Street, turn right and walk through the excursion train's parking lot to its depot where trains depart daily (except in winter) for the twisting 40-mile trip east to Willits on Highway 101. When the Skunk Depot or the adjacent Depot Shopping Mall is open, you'll find public restrooms inside.

Turn east on Laurel Street, crossing Main Street/Highway 1 in one block. (One block left is the North Coast Brewing Company, one of California's finest microbreweries.) Continue east on Laurel Street past Headlands Coffeehouse, the "Mount Rushmore of coffee heads." At the next corner, turn right and follow Franklin Street south through downtown. In two blocks you pass a supermarket and the post office around 2 miles. Continue south on Franklin to its end at North Harbor Drive at 2⅞ miles. Turn right and follow the left side of the street to Highway 1, which has the only bridge across the Noyo River.

Follow Highway 1 south over the Noyo Bridge and past McDonald's to the traffic signal at Ocean View Drive where you want to cross the highway. Follow its west side south past the traffic light at Highway 20 and over the Hare Creek bridge at 3¾ miles. Get off the busy highway at the first opportunity on its west side, namely Old Coast Highway, a quiet side street that keeps you off the highway until 4¼ miles.

From Simpson Lane to the Mendocino Coast Botanical Gardens, you must cautiously follow the Highway 1 shoulder. At the Botanical Gardens entrance, walk through their lovely landscaped parking lot. For a small fee, the side trail through the Gardens to coastal access is well worth the time. From the gift shop at the Gardens entrance, walk south through a grassy parking lot and turn right on Ocean Drive, an old section of Highway 1 that keeps you out of heavy traffic for ½ mile. Then turn left and walk east on Boice Lane to 5¼ miles where CCT currently follows Highway 1 south for nearly a mile. To stay off the highway as much as possible, try **Alternate Route B**.

Assuming you walk the highway, stay as far from traffic as possible on the left shoulder. People drive very fast on this stretch. You will see the sign for the Pine Beach Inn before you notice the road it's on, Ocean Drive. Turn right on Ocean and walk 150 feet to the trailhead on your left at 6⅛ miles, start of the next section.

**ALTERNATE ROUTES:** A) Noyo River Route: If you turn left instead of right on North Harbor Drive, you descend to the Noyo River. There hasn't been a bridge from here to the south side in many years, but Noyo fishing village has many boats on which you might catch a shuttle. You can also call or stop by Noyo Pacific Outfitters, 32450 North Harbor Drive, (707)961-0559, if you need a shuttle across the river, and ask them the cost. Walk South Harbor Drive up to Highway 20, then walk the highway's broad south shoulder to Highway 1 near the Hare Creek Bridge. This adds about ⅜ mile to total. B) Following Boice Lane east and south and Pearl Drive west to highway avoids ¾ mile of highway walking but adds ⅞ mile to total.

**SUGGESTED ROUND TRIPS & LOOPS:** Walk CCT from access point to Glass Beach and loop back on a different trail, a one-mile circuit. Take a loop to the bluffs at the Mendocino Coast Botanical Gardens, 1¼ miles or more.

**HOW TO IMPROVE CCT HERE:** If Georgia-Pacific ever abandons its industrial hold on the headlands west of Fort Bragg, CCT could follow its rugged, convoluted shore for 2 miles, avoiding all of town north of the Noyo Bridge.

Ocean Drive continues south from Boice Lane about ⅝ mile before ending at Mitchell Creek. If only 300 feet of CCT easement could be acquired there, CCT could stay off the highway all the way from Mendocino Coast Botanical Gardens to Jack Peters Creek just before Mendocino. This would shorten the route by about ⅞ mile.

## SECTION 9
# Pine Beach Inn to Point Cabrillo Preserve

DISTANCE: 5⅜ miles (8.6 kilometers).

OPEN TO: Hikers. Bicyclists on road portion.

SURFACE: Trail, beach, gravel road, paved road.

ACCESS POINT: Trailhead near Pine Beach Inn.

HOW TO GET THERE: Turn west off Highway 1 at Milepost 57.6 south of Fort Bragg, north of Caspar onto Ocean Drive at Pine Beach Inn. Turn left into dirt trailhead parking just after Pine Beach Inn sign.

DIFFICULTY: Easy with one steep ascent.

ELEVATION GAIN/LOSS: 360 feet+/290 feet-. To Jughandle parking lot: 110 feet+/150 feet-.

CAUTIONS: Don't trespass on adjacent private property. Use caution at Caspar Creek ford and don't interfere with fish migrating upstream in wet season or migrating birds in spring and fall. Dogs must be leashed on Caspar Beach.

FURTHER INFORMATION: Mendocino area State Parks (707)937-5804.

FACILITIES: None at access point. Chemical toilet, water, phone, picnic area at Jughandle parking lot. Chemical toilet at Caspar State Beach.

CAMPGROUND: Pomo Campground and Woodside Trailer Park are one mile north. Caspar Beach RV Park and Campground is on route near section's south end.

HOSTEL: Jughandle Creek Farm & Nature Center, (707)964-4630, has hostel-style lodging in seven rooms of their 100-year-old farmhouse near Jughandle Creek.

LODGING: Pine Beach Inn is at trailhead, Annie's Jughandle Beach Inn is on highway .25 mile south of access point. Other lodging in Fort Bragg.

MAP: See page 134.

The big news in Mendocino Section 9 is that the Caspar headlands have been preserved and that the CCT follows a fine and historic new route there. See below for details. This section starts on an old portion of Highway 1 that the state abandoned around 1960. After CalTrans opened the new highway to the east, they sold the old right-of-way where it crossed Mitchell Creek just north of this access point. You can still walk north on Ocean

Drive past the Pine Beach Inn to find the road's current terminus at Pine Beach at the mouth of Mitchell Creek. The private property sold off by the state precludes continuing north to the rest of the old highway, called Ocean Drive, only 300 feet north.

State Parks acquired the headlands north of Jughandle Creek just in time to keep the right-of-way for the CCT. The surrounding subdivisions attest that the park acquisition was none too soon. If you stay nearby or have extra time, you'll want to explore sheltered Jughandle Cove, a short walk from the Jughandle parking lot, or take the famous Jughandle Ecological Staircase Trail. This 4½- or 5-mile round trip, depending on whether you take the ½-mile headlands loop, explores the uplifted marine terraces that have

## Marine Terrace Geology and the Pygmy Forest

From Mendocino County south to San Diego, an irregular series of marine terraces, or wave-cut benches, occur between the shoreline and the coastal foothills. Carved by waves and wind-driven water at sea level, these terraces feature a vertical, or steeply rising, cliff face at their seaward edge (bluffs) backed by a level or gently sloping bench. Where harder rocks occur within a forming terrace, these erosion-resistant rocks eventually rise above the surrounding terrace as offshore rocks or sea stacks. Where the coastline is being pushed upward over time by the collision of two tectonic plates, a series of terraces exists, each one backed by another terrace around 100,000 years older and 100 feet higher than the one closer to the coast.

Well developed marine terraces along the Mendocino coast dramatically demonstrate the process of coastal uplifting and terrace formation. Stand on the bluff's edge at the Jughandle or Mendocino Headlands and look seaward over the new terrace forming at sea level. It's most apparent at low tide when you can see the smoothed rocky bottom that will become the next terrace. Look eastward from the coast to see the level or gently sloping first terrace that was the ocean floor at sea level roughly 100 millennia ago. Look farther east beyond that first terrace and you may see the distinct rise of the seaward edge of the next, or second terrace, about 100 feet above your blufftop elevation. You can typically locate five succeeding wave-cut

terraces in a two- to three-mile strip along the Mendocino coast.

Marine terraces occur in many places along the world's coasts. In California you can also see them above Bodega Bay in Sonoma County, at Duxbury Reef in Marin County, along the Santa Cruz coast, and at Dana Point in Orange County. In the Palos Verdes Hills near Los Angeles, a series of 13 terraces rises to 1300 feet above sea level.

Marine terraces generally feature distinct plant populations corresponding to the climate since the terrace rose above sea level, and to the terrace's rocks and soils. Only on the Mendocino and Sonoma coasts, however, do the upper terraces feature the unique botanical habitat called Pygmy Forest. These dwarfed forests occur in pockets on the upper ends of the third, fourth and fifth terraces, where a combination of flat terrain and sandy soils undergoes a complex transformation that creates impoverished acidic soils with poor drainage caused by underlying hardpan, leading to mature pockets of stunted vegetation. In the Pygmy Forest habitat, mature Mendocino cypress, Bolander and Bishop pines, and even redwood may grow only ten, five, or even three feet tall over 100 years. Other plants thriving in this harsh habitat include Fort Bragg manzanita, Labrador tea, rhododendron, huckleberry, reindeer moss, and the tiny sundew, an insect-eating plant.

formed the gentle landscape along this part of the Mendocino coast. The Staircase Trail ends in the amazing Pygmy Forest Reserve where century old trees stand only waist high. If you go, the brochure available at the Jughandle parking lot is recommended.

South of Jughandle State Reserve, CCT passes through the former lumber town of Caspar, where residents have been organizing since 1998 to acquire large portions of the quiet town and its surroundings that were for sale. Happily they succeeded in acquiring 142 acres for public access, including the dramatic south headlands.You can now walk those headlands, recently deeded to state parks, on a scenic hike that follows an historic route and adds a fine ⅜ mile to this section. After fording Caspar Creek and crossing Caspar Beach, the section follows the old highway again to Point Cabrillo Preserve.

The CCT heads west through grasslands and shore pine forest with private property immediately to the north. Beyond ¼ mile, two side trails fork right to cross a seasonal creek and head northwest to Mitchell Point. Continue west as the trees soon part to reveal a convoluted, rocky shore.

By ⅜ mile you reach a narrow promontory with pocket beaches on both sides. CCT turns southeast along the bluff's edge and soon comes to a fork above tiny Bromley Creek. Turn right and descend beside the creek to secluded Bromley Beach. Cross the creek and walk south across the beach to its southern end at ½ mile. A steep, sometimes slippery footpath there requires scrambling up the bluff face to the level headland on top. Walk east briefly, then turn south and descend across another seasonal creek and climb up the other side. Veer right at a fork and follow the bluff's edge out to another point, then southeast to another junction.

Since private property lies to the south, you want the trail on the left that heads east, coming almost back to Highway 1 at 1¼ miles, directly opposite Gibney Lane and Annie's Jughandle Beach Inn. When you come to a gravel road, turn right and follow it south, paralleling the highway.

Shortly after the driveway turns right, you come to a private property sign. This is your cue to leave the road and head south, again paralleling Highway 1, this time through a grassy field which often has no obvious path. Watch for uneven footing on this lightly traveled leg. Pick your way south until you find a broad track around 1⅝ miles, the Jughandle North Headlands Trail. You can use it as a side trail to head west to the bluffs north of Jughandle Cove, but CCT only veers west briefly, about 50 feet on the North Headlands Trail. Then pick your way south on one of the vague tracks parallel the highway for 500 feet before turning east on a path that quickly dips under the north end of the Jughandle Creek highway bridge.

On the east side of the highway you meet the Jughandle Ecological Staircase Trail. A left turn leads to a great 1⅜-mile side trip to the otherworldly Pygmy Forest Reserve. The CCT turns right and descends into Jughandle Creek canyon, crossing a bridge over the creek around 1⅞ miles. Turn right and climb the stairway past some of the southernmost specimens of Sitka spruce in North America. At the top, turn right and follow the path under the highway at the south end of the bridge, then turn south through lush vegetation above Jughandle Cove. Stay to the left at the next junction and you'll come to the Jughandle State Reserve parking lot at 2⅛ miles where you'll find privies, a water faucet and a picnic area.

CCT follows the Ecological Staircase Trail west onto the Jughandle Headlands south of the cove. In less than ⅛ mile, take the trail that forks left to head south. It angles toward the southeastern corner of state park land, where it meets Caspar Road at 2½ miles.

*Members of the CCT Whole Hike of 1996 explore the narrow promontory above Bromley Beach at Jughandle State Reserve.*

Follow the new gravel path south along the west shoulder of this old Highway 1 leg through sleepy Caspar, once a booming lumber town. By 3 miles you pass the new Caspar Community Center behind the Mendocino Coast Jewish Center on your left. Continue on the gravel shoulder path. Once you pass Caspar Street on the left, state park's new Caspar Headlands parcel is to the west. Eventually a gate here will allow CCT to head west to explore more of Caspar Headlands. (If the gate is there, by all means go that way.) For now CCT continues on the gravel path to the end of Caspar Road at 3⅛ miles.

From road's end, the new CCT link heads west from the southernmost of the two gates onto the Caspar Headlands. By 300 feet you encounter remnant pavement from Caspar's old railroad and lumber drying yards, which once occupied these bluffs. Follow the two-wheel track winding west. Before 3¼ miles the track splits in two. While you can take the right fork to explore more of Caspar's headlands, CCT takes the left fork, winding west to near the bluff's edge at 3⅜ miles, where a loading chute once supplied lumber ships anchored in Caspar Cove below.

CCT turns left, following a path south that soon veers left toward Caspar Beach. At 3½ miles CCT veers to the right on a path that descends gradually east-southeast to the right of a cypress windrow, following the old tramway incline down toward the mill site. Pass through a gate and descend the path, passing through a brushy area around 3⅝ miles. As you approach a grove of eucalyptus, take the second of two rough paths on your right and descend to Caspar Creek. A pedestrian bridge may eventually be built here. For now, if the creek is low, turn right and walk to its mouth and ford (you can usually rock hop across) to reach Caspar Beach. When the water is higher, you'll likely need to wade.

Either way you come to little Caspar Beach south of the creek at 3¾ miles. Walk the tideline south to ford even smaller Doyle Creek, then angle southeast to Point Cabrillo Drive, another former stretch of Highway 1, at 4⅛ miles. Walk the road shoulder south, climbing by two tight hairpin turns.

At the top of the hairpins, follow Point Cabrillo Drive as it climbs south. The road contours from 4¾ miles with ocean views over the pristine Point Cabrillo Light Station and Preserve. This section ends at 5 miles at the Preserve's main entrance. CCT heads west on a semi-paved road north of the new parking area. (The gate marked "13800" has been removed.)

**SUGGESTED ROUND TRIPS & LOOPS:** Walk the first 1⅝ miles of this section and return, 3¼ miles round trip, or you can add side trips to Mitchell Point or Jughandle North dle headlands. Take the great Jughandle Ecological Staircase Trail to the Pygmy Forest, 4½ miles round trip with a short loop at the end.

> **HOW TO IMPROVE CCT HERE:** Encourage State Parks or Coastal Conservancy to buy a trail corridor across the 300 feet of private property to Ocean Drive. Then Ocean Drive would become the CCT route south from the Botanical Gardens, with a side trail to Belinda Point.
> Build and maintain a trail across entire Jughandle north headlands.

# SECTION 10
# Point Cabrillo Preserve to North Mendocino Headlands

**DISTANCE:** 5¼ miles (8.4 kilometers).

**OPEN TO:** Hikers. Bicyclists on road.

**SURFACE:** Trail, road shoulder, very short highway shoulder leg.

**ACCESS POINT:** Point Cabrillo Light Station and Preserve.

**HOW TO GET THERE:** Turn west off Highway 1 south of Caspar and north of Mendocino at Milepost 54.66 onto Point Cabrillo Drive. Go 1.7 miles to Point Cabrillo Preserve. This section starts by heading west on the semi-paved road north of the new parking area.

**OTHER ACCESS:** Point Cabrillo Drive south of Indian Shoals, Russian Gulch State Park, Road 500D south of Russian Gulch, Lansing Street north of Heeser Drive.

**DIFFICULTY:** Easy.

**ELEVATION GAIN/LOSS:** 370 feet+/470 feet-; 170 feet+/160 feet- for Point Cabrillo portion.

**CAUTIONS:** Some uneven footing requires caution beyond the lighthouse. Please observe marked closed areas. Dogs must be leashed while in Preserve.

**FURTHER INFORMATION:** Point Cabrillo Light Station and Preserve (707)937-0816, Mendocino area State Parks (707)937-5804.

**FACILITIES:** Point Cabrillo Preserve has chemical toilet near caretaker's house, flush toilet and water only when the lighthouse is open, picnic tables near the lighthouse. Russian Gulch has restrooms, water, picnic area, phone.

**CAMPGROUNDS:** Russian Gulch State Park campground open April through October. Other times, or when that campground is full, try Caspar Beach RV Park, opposite

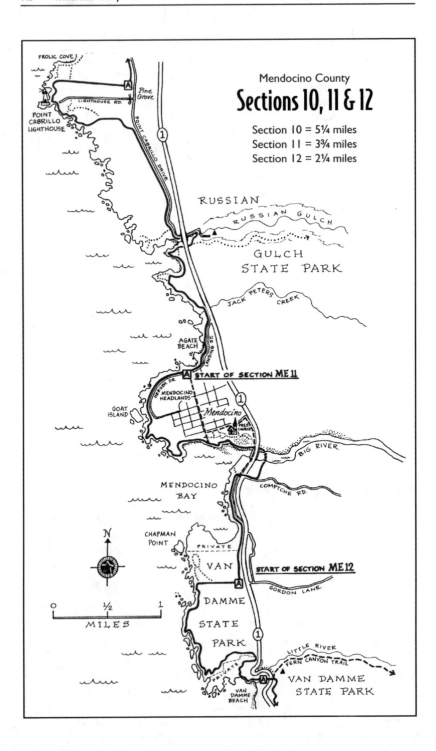

Mendocino County
# Sections 10, 11 & 12

Section 10 = 5¼ miles
Section 11 = 3¾ miles
Section 12 = 2¼ miles

FROLIC COVE

LIGHTHOUSE RD.

Pine Grove

POINT CABRILLO LIGHTHOUSE

POINT CABRILLO DRIVE

1

RUSSIAN

RUSSIAN GULCH

GULCH STATE PARK

JACK PETERS CREEK

AGATE BEACH

LANSING ST.

START OF SECTION ME 11

HESSER DR.

MENDOCINO HEADLANDS

GOAT ISLAND

Mendocino

1

BIG RIVER

MENDOCINO BAY

COMPTCHE RD.

N

CHAPMAN POINT

PRIVATE

VAN

START OF SECTION ME 12

GORDON LANE

DAMME

0      ½      1
MILES

STATE

1

PARK

LITTLE RIVER

FERN CANYON TRAIL

PRIVATE

VAN DAMME BEACH

VAN DAMME STATE PARK

Caspar Beach on Point Cabrillo Drive.

**LODGING:** Many lodgings in Mendocino 3 miles south.

Point Cabrillo Preserve was snatched from the hungry jaws of land speculators when the Coastal Conservancy completed its acquisition in 1992. The preserve's 300 acres offer a prime example of the abundance of the northern California coast's rich biological diversity. You may see whales, seals and sea lions offshore, and a rich selection of raptors and other birds, deer and wildflowers within the preserve boundaries. Human history is abundant too. The farming community of Pine Grove sprang up here around 1860 and the lighthouse service established the still operating light in 1909.

This route explores the gorgeous headlands around the lighthouse. You can also follow a side trail or loop north to the preserve's northern boundary, or take a ⅛-mile detour to the lighthouse, from which you can continue to the very tip of Point Cabrillo.

The short segment of CCT through Russian Gulch State Park barely touches on the diverse spectacular scenery there. Two short side trails seaward are highly recommended, and the longer Waterfall Trail is also worth a trip if time allows. The park's name originated in tales the local Pomo people told of seeing Russian fur hunters there, probably in the late 18th century.

Follow the narrow, semi-paved north road (just north of the new parking lot) through a cypress grove and down the hill, enjoying expanding ocean vistas. The pavement ends around ⅜ mile as the path forks. The side trail on the right heads north to overlook Frolic Cove at the preserve's northwest corner. If you take the right fork, you can loop back along the bluffs to rejoin CCT ahead, adding about ½ mile to your hike. The Coastal Trail continues west to the bluff's edge at ⅝ mile where you meet the bluff trail. To the north you can see Caspar Point with the Lost Coast visible beyond on the clearest days.

A right turn follows a side trail north to Frolic Cove, but the Coastal Trail turns left, heading south toward the lighthouse. After dipping across a wooden bridge, you pass through a fence line at ¾ mile and come to the paved lighthouse road. You can take a short detour west along the pavement for a closer look at the recently restored vintage lighthouse, to use the picnic tables, or to explore the eroded tip of Point Cabrillo northwest of the lighthouse.

The Coastal Trail turns east, following the pavement briefly. Before ⅞ mile opposite the second house, the Coastal Trail turns right to follow a semi-paved track angling southwest over the grassy headlands. (An outhouse is 250 feet east along the paved road.) When the semi-paved track ends, veer west then south on a grassy track. By one mile it follows the bluff's edge where offshore rocks beyond a small cove often have harbor seals resting. Follow the grassy track south along the blufftop, then across a sturdy bridge over a small creek. Pass through a fence line and follow the track south toward a rocky point. As you reach the point at 1⅛ miles, the trail dips, then veers left up a short hill into lush growth. A short spur on the right leads to the rocky shelf and views of a cove with surge tunnels and a small waterfall. To the south you can see the Mendocino headlands with the round swell of Stillwell Point rising beyond Little River.

The CCT veers left to cross a bridge over a verdant creek just above where the creek plunges over a cliff into the sea with a surge tunnel invisible below. Follow the bluff trail past a razor-thin promontory as CCT turns northeast, passing a healthy patch of kinnikinnick and circumventing a deep cove on your right. At the head of the cove, the trail turns east and south.

Before 1¼ miles as the path becomes vague, you meet a track climbing northeast. Turn left and follow it east for 300 feet until it merges with a track climbing northeast through the grasslands toward a broad pine up the hill. Follow it ⅛ mile until you pass to the left of the pine and through a fence line. Continue climbing northeast then east.

Near the top of the hill you pass the blank side of a sign. On the front of it are posted the preserve regulations. The main path heads east onto the private property of a trailer park. You want to turn southeast climbing on a vague track along

## We Want a Marine Sanctuary, not Offshore Oil!

Imagine, as you walk along the north coast on the Coastal Trail, looking out over the Pacific and seeing ten oil drilling platforms. That's what Big Oil wants and the U.S. Department of Interior has proposed in Lease Sale #53, currently on hold thanks to intense public opposition. As long as our society is dependent on oil or until a permanent marine sanctuary is established along the north coast, however, the danger of oil development on the pristine Mendocino, Humboldt and Del Norte coasts remains a threat.

If you think offshore oil isn't a bad trade off for unlimited use of the family car, imagine further, as you pass scenic north coast hamlets, onshore service bases with 30 acres of tanks, pipes, towers, buildings and pavement blotching the landscape. Consider the visual effect of pipeline right-of-ways paralleling the trail or Highway 1 and spanning the canyons, walls of concrete rip-rap disrupting sweeping sets of surf.

Ponder dozens of helicopter flights daily shuttling supplies and crews between land and platforms. Worst of all, imagine a major oil spill devastating abundant coastal marine life, clogging estuaries and beaches with tarry goo, reducing bird populations and wreaking mayhem on this enthralling shoreline.

In 1988 thousands of coast residents testified for two days before a Department of Interior panel in Fort Bragg, voicing their opposition to oil development through anger, tears, humor, song, poetry and dance, bringing the attention of national media and politicians to this quiet area. Rachel Binah, owner of Rachel's Inn at Little River, who spearheaded the opposition, proposed a National Ocean Sanctuary to protect the unspoiled coast from oil and other heavy industrial threats.

In 1989 Congress established the permanent Cordell Bank National Marine Sanctuary off the Sonoma/Marin coast. In 1992 protection was won for California's central coast in the Monterey Bay National Marine Sanctuary, but Congress has failed as of this writing to provide permanent protection for the Mendocino, Humboldt and Del Norte County coasts.

Now with George W. Bush as president, Big Oil wants the north coast more than ever. If, after doing some hiking here, you'd prefer we all owned the north coast and kept it safe, get an Ocean Sanctuary or No Offshore Oil! bumper sticker for your car. And when you get home, tell your elected representatives how you feel about oil development on California's north coast.

the property line. In 200 feet as you pass a row of pines, look southeast for a utility pole on Point Cabrillo Drive. Make your way to the pole which is easily visible as you top a rise south of the trailer park before 1¾ miles. You reach the pole and a break in the fence leading to Point Cabrillo Drive around 1¹³⁄₁₆ miles.

Turn right and walk the shoulder of Point Cabrillo Drive south to the entrance to Russian Gulch State Park at 2¾ miles. From the entrance kiosk, descend south along the shoulder of the main park road. By 2⅞ miles, a side road on the right heads west to the park's spectacular north headlands. It's ⅜ mile to the Devil's Punchbowl, about ½ mile to land's end. CCT continues on the main park road, descending under the highway bridge. At 3⅛ mile, CCT turns right on the road signed "BEACH." The park's pleasant campground is to the east as is a popular 3-mile side trail to the Russian Gulch Waterfall.

Follow the beach road briefly to the Group Campground on the right. Across the road, ascend the South Trail through a lush understory in tall forest. When the path forks, turn right and walk under the highway bridge to a junction. Either fork leads to the CCT. The right fork is recommended, although it's slightly longer. It descends around a wooded high headland with stunning views of rugged Russian Gulch Cove on your right, then rounds a wooded point and ascends southeast to meet the other fork. Turn right and follow the trail south around another cove.

By 3⅞ miles you come to a paved cul-de-sac. Follow the pavement for 400 feet, then descend along the dirt path on the right through a stand of Monterey pines. When you pass the last of the trees and come to open grasslands, the CCT veers left on a path south. A pleasant short side trail continues west ⅛ mile to the tip of the point. The CCT soon reaches the convoluted south shore of the promontory where a blowhole hides among the trees. Turn left and return to the pavement at 4⅛ miles, then turn right and follow this old stretch of the coast road (Road 500D) to Highway 1.

The only way to cross the chasm of Jack Peters Gulch is on the highway bridge, so cautiously walk the highway shoulder south over the bridge. You immediately turn right and follow Lansing Street south above Agate Cove. At 5 miles, turn right onto Heeser Drive and descend the road shoulder to a parking lot and restrooms, start of Section 11.

**ALTERNATE ROUTE:** You can save 1½ miles by staying on the shoulder of Point Cabrillo Drive, but you'd miss much of this section's beauty.

**SUGGESTED ROUND TRIPS & LOOPS:** At Point Cabrillo, take the short walk to the lighthouse and back, or loop all around the headlands of the preserve. At Russian Gulch State Park, walk the splendid short side trail west to the Devil's Punchbowl and the point beyond, or hike the longer side trail east to the waterfall up the canyon. Either of these choices has a short loop option near its end.

> **HOW TO IMPROVE CCT HERE:** Develop a trail from the northeast corner of Point Cabrillo Preserve to the lighthouse road parking area or to Frolic Cove. Develop a trail along the entire length of Point Cabrillo Drive that keeps hikers and perhaps bicyclists off the roadway, especially important between the preserve and Russian Gulch State Park.

## SECTION 11
# North Mendocino Headlands to Chapman Point Trailhead

**DISTANCE:** 3¾ miles (6 kilometers).

**OPEN TO:** Hikers on whole section, bicyclists on road sections.

**SURFACE:** Trail, beach, road shoulder, highway shoulder.

**ACCESS POINT:** North Mendocino Headlands.

**HOW TO GET THERE:** Turn west off Highway 1 at Mendocino's only traffic signal at Milepost 50.85 onto Little Lake Road. At the stop sign, turn right on Lansing Street and go .3 mile. Turn left on Heeser Drive and go .2 mile to parking lot on right.

**OTHER ACCESS:** Anywhere along the route.

**DIFFICULTY:** Easy.

**ELEVATION GAIN/LOSS:** 280 feet+/200 feet-.

**CAUTIONS:** Stay back from steep crumbly bluff edge. Don't try to ford Big River.

**FURTHER INFORMATION:** Mendocino area State Parks (707)937-5804. For boat shuttle, call Catch-a-Canoe (707)937-0273.

**FACILITIES:** Restrooms, water, picnic area at access point. Phones in town.

**CAMPGROUNDS:** Mendocino Campground (private) at corner of Highway 1 and Comptche-Ukiah Road is open April to October.

**LODGING:** Many choices in Mendocino.

**MAP:** See page 142.

At Mendocino Headlands the trail meanders along the edge of a convoluted bluff with numerous choices for shorter or longer routes. While you may not want to walk out to every point, you won't want to rush by this spectacularly twisting shoreline either. If you were to walk every twist of this serpentine shore, you would walk about 3 miles just from the north parking lot to Big River Beach, a north-to-south distance of only ¾ mile.

Immediately south of Mendocino, since Big River is too deep to ford, you need to arrange a boat shuttle or detour across the highway bridge. Call Catch-a-Canoe on the river's south shore and ask if they can provide a shuttle, when, and how much it costs. The first mile of shoreline south of Big River is privately owned, but a quiet stretch of old highway and two broad turnouts allow you to keep off the highway for all but a few hundred feet.

Walk north behind the restrooms through the cypress grove to find the trail along the edge of the bluff. Turn left and follow the trail west, not the well-beaten side trail that heads north to a point. By ⅛ mile CCT leads back toward Heeser Drive, drawing beside it briefly before meandering along the bluff edge. Descend to a north-facing promontory with views of several islets to the west and Point

Cabrillo up the coast.

Before ⅜ mile the trail turns south, passing another parking lot, then a side trail out to a narrow peninsula. CCT draws alongside the road briefly before turning west to round Mendocino headland's westernmost point around ⅝ mile where a side trail heads west to the point's rocky tip. Follow the path along the bluff's edge which leads back beside Heeser Drive at ¾ mile, then out to the bluff overlooking an inlet between you and Goat Island offshore. After passing the first trees since the start of the section, look west to see a natural bridge on the headland just south of Goat Island.

The CCT turns vague as it comes to a large parking lot at ⅞ mile. Circle the west end of the lot, then head south to a point at one mile. The trail twists east, north and south to round two stunning coves, then wanders farther south along the shore of the southernmost peninsula which juts out into Mendocino Bay.

The southern tip of the point is marked by a wooden carving. These old virgin redwood posts were first used to tie down ships that anchored in the bay, much later carved into the fanciful shapes you see today. The southeastern tip of the point holds the ruins of the loading chute. CCT turns north to pass the blowhole and continue toward the town's picturesque Main Street. Soon the trail broadens and turns east, passing benches and a stairway to tiny, south-facing Portuguese Beach around 1¾ miles. A nearby plaque commemorates artist Emmy Lou Packard who led the fight to save these headlands from development.

CCT continues east along the bluff's edge, heading for the mouth of Big River. Around 1⅞ miles after dipping through a small gully, you meet a trail forking left into town. CCT continues along the bluff with several choices for shorter or longer routes.

As you pass the town's landmark white Presbyterian Church, the trail descends to the stairway to Big River Beach at 2⅛ miles. If you have arranged a boat shuttle across Big River, descend to the beach and meet your shuttle near the highway bridge around 2⅜ miles. Otherwise you want to detour on **Alternate Route B**.

CCT heads east along Big River Beach, then catches a shuttle across Big River. Walk up the road from Catch-a-Canoe, then turn right and walk the shoulder of Comptche-Ukiah Road briefly to Highway 1 at 2⅝ miles. Cautiously cross the highway to pick up Brewery Gulch Road on the west side.

Brewery Gulch Road serves as the CCT for the next stretch. This old piece of the coast highway hugs the shore of Mendocino Bay while offering fine views. Just 200 feet from Highway 1, a short side trail on the right leads right to the bay's edge. CCT continues uphill to the end of the road, then turns right and follows the edge of the vista point which overlooks Brewery Gulch Cove and Chapman Point south of Mendocino Bay.

From the vista point, CCT follows Highway 1 briefly to cross Brewery Gulch, then comes to private Chapman Point Road at 3⅜ miles. It's state park land south of the southernmost driveway. While there is no developed trail at press time, cross the fence and walk south, paralleling the highway on state land. Ascend to the top of a rise at 3¾ miles and meet a well traveled path heading west along a fence. The grassy parking area directly to the east is the starting point for the next CCT section.

**ALTERNATE ROUTES:** A) Here's a shortcut if you don't have time to walk the whole head-lands. Take the trail 50 feet west of the driveway across the street from the access point. Walk south through the Mendocino High School grounds, then descend Kasten Street to Main and walk the path south to CCT. **B)** From the top of the stairway to Big River Beach, go north past the church to Main Street. Turn right and head east to Highway 1. Go right again and cross Big River bridge, then take the first right onto Brewery Gulch Road.

**SUGGESTED ROUND TRIPS & LOOPS:** Walk the headlands loop to 1⅞ miles and return via the high school, a 3-mile loop. Extend that loop with a side trip to Big River Beach.

## SECTION 12
# Chapman Point Trailhead to Van Damme Beach, Van Damme State Park

**DISTANCE:** 2¼ miles (3.6 kilometers).

**OPEN TO:** Hikers.

**SURFACE:** Trail, highway shoulder, beach.

**ACCESS POINT:** Chapman Point Trailhead.

**HOW TO GET THERE:** Turn west off Highway 1 at Milepost 48.94, south of Mendocino, north of Little River, into grassy parking area opposite Gordon Lane.

**OTHER ACCESS:** Peterson Lane.

**DIFFICULTY:** Easy.

**ELEVATION GAIN/LOSS:** 100 feet+/250 feet-.

**CAUTIONS:** Stay off adjacent private property.

**FURTHER INFORMATION:** Mendocino area State Parks (707)937-5804.

**FACILITIES:** Only at south end, chemical toilets, picnic area, phone across highway at entrance kiosk.

**CAMPGROUNDS:** Van Damme State Park at south end, Mendocino Campground on previous section open April to October.

**LODGING:** Several in Little River, many in Mendocino.

**MAP:** See page 142.

Of Van Damme State Park's nearly 2400 acres, more than 300 acres west of Highway 1 acquired since 1974 provide an ideal, gorgeous setting for this CCT section. Three separate acquisitions puzzled together the first two miles of trail. While the northern and southern chunks became state park lands in 1975, only in 1996 did state parks acquire the centerpiece 162 acres offered to the state by the Spring family. All three parcels formed part of the original Beall ranch settled in the 1850s. The Bealls sold to the Kents in 1857, who later sold to the Springs. The Coastal Trail here enjoys solitude and a remote feeling despite being close to the historic towns of Mendocino and Little River. The headlands offer great whale watching in season and access to choice tidepools at low tide.

The Coastal Trail heads west from the parking area along a path bordered by a fence on the left and Monterey pines on the right. You soon descend gradually toward the shore with glimpses of Mendocino to the north. After climbing a small rise, the path descends to the first marine terrace. As the descent eases beyond ¼ mile, CCT takes the left fork to continue west. You can take the side trail on the right to explore the north end of this state park property. The left fork quickly comes to level open headlands.

At ⅜ mile just before you reach the bluff's edge, the fence jogs south and so does the Coastal Trail. You quickly meet a break in the fence. Walk east through the break, then south onto the recently acquired Spring Ranch headlands. Although the trail is vague, you simply follow the bluff's edge as it winds east and south.

At ⅝ mile CCT jogs west with the bluff edge, passing above a pretty pocket beach. After heading south through a fence, you veer west again across a tiny stream where watercress grows. Then follow the western edge of the headlands south. After a jog east before one mile, your bluff-edge path again angles south.

You quickly pass through a fence line, leaving the Spring Ranch portion of Van Damme State Park for land acquired in 1975. CCT fords a tiny stream and meanders generally south near the bluff's edge, passing clusters of cypresses. On your left you might notice two side trails that explore the pine-spattered grasslands to the east.

Around 1¼ miles, the Coastal Trail turns east past a short side trail heading south to the tip of a small promontory. Follow the main trail east past the head of a deep rocky cove. Before 1⅜ miles the path turns northeast across a grassy field. You soon start climbing up to the second terrace. Around 1½ miles you merge with a side trail from the west. (Turn west for a loop back to the trailhead.) Walk east 150 feet. When the main trail veers right toward houses, take the narrow track forking left to ascend through grasslands with scattered pines. After heading east over a hill, you draw near Highway 1 around 1¾ miles. Veer right at a fork and head south paralleling the highway, descending toward Rachel's Inn.

Just before you get to the inn at 1⅞ miles, turn left through the break in the fence and walk the highway shoulder south briefly to paved Peterson Lane. Turn right and walk ⅛ mile west on Peterson Lane, then take the signed path that descends south. It winds down through a gully filled with wildflowers and escaped domestic fuchsias, coming to the northern end of the long crescent of Van Damme Beach. Turn left and walk the beach east and south to a ford of Little River. After you cross the small stream, walk east to the parking lot, start of the next CCT section.

**ALTERNATE ROUTE:** At high tide, especially in winter, you may not be able to get around a rocky point just west of the Little River ford. In that case retrace your steps to Peterson Lane, walk east to Highway 1, then turn right and walk the highway shoulder to the Van Damme Beach parking lot.

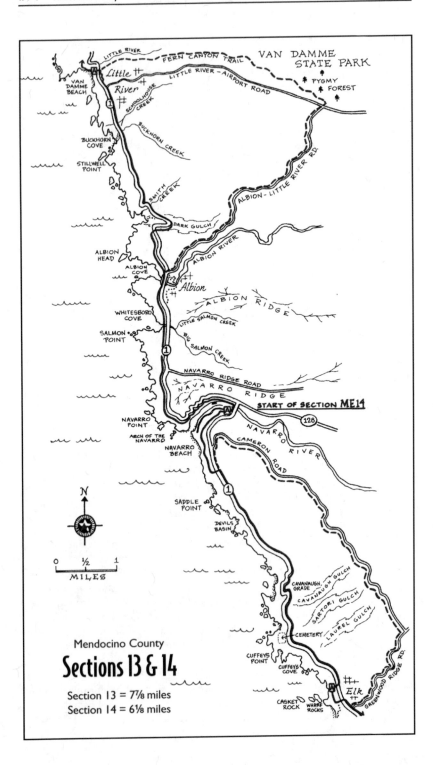

LITTLE RIVER
FERN CANYON TRAIL
VAN DAMME STATE PARK
Little River
LITTLE RIVER – AIRPORT ROAD
PYGMY FOREST
VAN DAMME BEACH
SCHOOLHOUSE CREEK
BUCKHORN CREEK
BUCKHORN COVE
STILLWELL POINT
ALBION – LITTLE RIVER RD.
SMITH CREEK
DARK GULCH
ALBION HEAD
ALBION COVE
ALBION RIVER
Albion
ALBION RIDGE
WHITESBORO COVE
LITTLE SALMON CREEK
SALMON POINT
BIG SALMON CREEK
NAVARRO RIDGE ROAD
NAVARRO RIDGE
START OF SECTION ME14
NAVARRO POINT
128
ARCH OF THE NAVARRO
NAVARRO RIVER
CAMERON ROAD
NAVARRO BEACH
SADDLE POINT
DEVILS BASIN
N
CAVANAUGH GRADE
CAVANAUGH GULCH
SARTORI GULCH
LAUREL GULCH
0  ½  1
MILES
CEMETERY
CUFFEYS POINT
CUFFEYS COVE
GREENWOOD RIDGE RD.
Elk
CASKET ROCK
WHARF ROCKS

Mendocino County
**Sections 13 & 14**

Section 13 = 7⅞ miles
Section 14 = 6⅛ miles

SUGGESTED ROUND TRIPS & LOOPS: You can make a 1¼-mile loop around the northern headlands from the access point. The southern headlands offer a small loop around its southwest quadrant and several other side trails.

<h1 style="text-align:center">SECTION 13<br/>Little River to Navarro River</h1>

DISTANCE: 7⅞ miles (12.7 kilometers).

OPEN TO: Hikers, bicyclists.

SURFACE: Trail, highway shoulder.

ACCESS POINT: Van Damme Beach parking lot, Little River.

HOW TO GET THERE: Turn west off Highway 1 south of Mendocino at Van Damme State Park, Milepost 48.05, into paved parking lot.

OTHER ACCESS: Anywhere along section.

DIFFICULTY: Easy.

ELEVATION GAIN/LOSS: 710 feet+/690 feet-.

CAUTIONS: Stay on shoulder, out of road, and watch for traffic. Use extreme caution crossing highway.

FURTHER INFORMATION: Mendocino area State Parks (707)937-5804.

FACILITIES: Chemical toilets, picnic area, phone, water at access point.

CAMPGROUNDS: Van Damme State Park at the north end has 85 units. Navarro Beach unit of Navarro River Redwoods State Park at the south end has primitive sites, no water. In Albion private Albion River Campground has sites on the river.

LODGING: Several in Little River and Albion.

Such a beautiful stretch of coast deserves public access, but so far almost all of the next 8 miles of CCT are forced along the shoulder of busy Highway 1. As if that weren't bad enough, several of these miles follow narrow, twisting highway where drivers are either frightened or driving faster than safety allows or both. If you walk this stretch, use extreme caution, hike in a group and wear bright clothing. Symbolically, the first sixteenth mile offers a safe trail off the highway, but most of the section offers hazardous walking on the highway shoulder.

From the beach parking lot walk east using extreme caution as you cross Highway 1. Continue to the Van Damme State Park entrance kiosk. A pleasant side trail that also serves as a CCT Alternate Route follows the park road ¾ mile to its end, then continues 2½ miles up Fern Canyon along Little River with a 3½-mile loop at its end climbing to the Pygmy Forest. From the kiosk CCT takes the shady trail on the right that climbs south paralleling the highway. In about 300 feet it ends at the driveway for Little River Inn. Turn right and descend to the highway.

Head south along the highway shoulder, climbing a hill out of the "downtown" of the tiny town of Little River. Top a hill around ⅜ mile and descend past the cemetery, then climb over a second hill at ⅝ mile. The highway descends until one mile where it crosses Buckhorn Creek as the road narrows. Ascend moderately to crest Stillwell Point at 1⅝ miles, then contour through tight winding turns with lousy visibility. Descend past Heritage House Inn and across tiny Smith Creek.

Around 2⅝ miles an unmarked side trail on the right descends to a deep cove at the mouth of Dark Gulch. Descend the highway east across Dark Gulch at 2⅞ miles, then ascend it west, rounding a big bend to return to the coastal terrace around 3⅛ miles.

Ascend gently south, then descend toward the town of Albion. A short dip and climb leads to the north end of the Albion River bridge around 4 miles. Just before the bridge, on the left Albion River North Side Road descends to a private campground along the lower river. If you camp there, you might find someone with a boat to shuttle you across the river, then ascend Albion South Side Road through the heart of the little town to rejoin the highway.

CCT crosses the high Albion River bridge and follows Highway 1 past the heart of town (just up Albion Ridge Road) at 4½ miles. Residents, the Coastal Conservancy and some state legislators are working to acquire 502 acres in coastal Albion for a state park that would provide several miles of a fine CCT route. Around 4¾ miles follow the highway as it dips across Salmon Creek's canyon with Whitesboro Cove to the west, then climb a long straight hill to its top at 5⅜ miles. Enjoy the wide highway right-of-way as you contour to Navarro Ridge Road at 5¾ miles.

The highway narrows, then climbs as it winds over Navarro Head, where Mendocino Land Trust acquired 55 acres west of the highway including rugged Navarro Point in late 1999. It will eventually provide a short off-highway link for the CCT. Begin a gradual descent, but be prepared for narrow blind curves ahead.

At 6⅝ miles the highway bends sharply left to make a wiggling descent northeast. If you can find a safe place to stand off the road, enjoy the stunning views south along the coast all the way to Point Arena, then down over the estuary of the Navarro River.

By 7⅜ miles the worst of the curves are over and you have descended nearly to sea level, overlooking an island in the nearby broad Navarro River. Walk the shoulder to the Highway 1 bridge across the Navarro at 7¾ miles. Turn right and cross the bridge, coming to Navarro Beach Road at 7⅞ miles, start of Mendocino County Section 14.

**ALTERNATE ROUTE:** Through-hikers can hike to the Pygmy Forest, then follow Albion-Little River Road south to Albion. It's steeper and twice the length of highway route to Albion, but more enjoyable with little traffic.

**SUGGESTED ROUND TRIPS & LOOPS:** The best choice is the trail up Fern Canyon and the Pygmy Forest loop, 8½ miles round trip from the Van Damme kiosk.

**HOW TO IMPROVE CCT HERE:** Acquire the 502 acres for Albion State Park and route CCT across it. Open a headlands CCT route north of Albion on OTD trails there. Find other options to route CCT off highway on this section. One would be to route CCT up Navarro Ridge Road a ways if a CCT easement could be acquired across the steep slope between there and Highway 1 near Navarro River bridge.

## SECTION 14
# Navarro River to Elk

DISTANCE: 6⅛ miles (9.9 kilometers).

OPEN TO: Hikers. Beach road and highway open to bicyclists.

SURFACE:

ACCESS POINT: Navarro Beach Road at Highway 1.

HOW TO GET THERE: From Highway 1 just south of the Highway 128 junction and the Navarro River bridge, turn west at Milepost 40.15 and park. You can also drive .4 mile to trailhead parking.

OTHER ACCESS: Anywhere along highway segment.

DIFFICULTY: Easy.

ELEVATION GAIN/LOSS: 550 feet+/430 feet-.

CAUTIONS: Watch for poison oak on the old highway.

FURTHER INFORMATION: Mendocino area State Parks (707)937-5804.

FACILITIES: Chemical toilets, picnic area.

CAMPGROUNDS: Primitive camping (no water) at Navarro Beach, .75 mile from access point. Also, Dimmick Campground 8 miles up Highway 128.

LODGING: Elk Guest House is on this section, plus several inns in Elk.

MAP: See page 150.

Towering cliffs plunge to a rocky, convoluted shoreline punctuated by tall sea stacks. Numerous steep canyons and pioneer cypress windbreaks dissect a high marine terrace with historic town sites. This may well be the most spectacular section of highway walking on the CCT, certainly one of the great photogenic legs of Highway 1. The bad news is that the sparsely settled headlands have ample space for a world class trail that does not yet exist. The good news is that the 1¼-mile span of trail at the section's beginning allows an undistracted look at some of this marvelous shore.

Follow the paved beach access road toward the river mouth. At ⅜ mile, just before an old house on the left, the pre-1960 roadbed of Highway 1 climbs behind the house. At press time the old road was signed, "CLOSED TO ALL VEHICLES AND PEDESTRIAN TRAFFIC . . .," but since that pavement now runs across county and state property and since the old access trail from the beach is no longer maintained, CCT veers left past the sign to follow the old pavement climbing south-southwest. (The beach road continues to Navarro Beach Campground, ¾ mile from Highway 1.) Ascend the old highway, overgrown in spots and wet in winter, but otherwise easy walking. After passing behind the old house, cross two seasonal creeks around ½ mile, then walk a stretch of road overgrown with alder and elderberry. You soon reach open pavement, then a grand view of the river mouth and the dramatic (especially from here) Arch of the Navarro.

At ⅝ mile you look down on the beach and campground, passing the old, now very overgrown access trail. Walk south on the crumbling pavement, ascending gradually along the face of a rocky cliff with grand views of river, mouth and spacious beach. Beyond ¾ mile a mudslide covers the pavement, but you can easily get around it. Climb past another mudslide, then a rockslide. Traverse skinny pavement along the base of the rock cliffs at one mile. Around 1⅛ miles the old highway has recently slipped out. Follow a volunteer path that veers left through a broken fence to cross grasslands briefly, then quickly cross the fallen fence to return to the roadbed beyond the slide.

Before 1¼ miles the road/trail reaches still maintained pavement. Continue past a cluster of homes up to a spur of pavement at 1⅜ miles that connects to Highway 1. The CCT follows the highway south to Elk. The only alternative is to go north ⅜ mile and follow Cameron Road as described in the Alternate Route.

The highway rises over Saddle Point, passes the Elk Guest House, then dips across a gulch before passing Devil's Basin on the right at 2⅜ miles. This amazing 200-foot-deep sinkhole has churning surf at its bottom, but you get only a glimpse from the road.

Overlook a dizzyingly rugged coast as the highway contours to 3¼ miles, then rises and dips three times, the last dip leading to the twisting descent of Cavanaugh Grade. Before the bottom of the grade at 4¼ miles, look south to the big field east of the highway. The town of Cuffey's Cove occupied the site in the late 1800s. The beautiful headlands of the Roth Ranch look inviting, but the area is patrolled lest you consider trespassing.

Highway 1 dips across Sartori Gulch, then rises to the Cuffey's Cove Cemetery at 4⅞ miles, a nice place to take a break. The highway descends fitfully with grand coastal vistas evolving with each step. After you enter the town of Elk at a big bend at 5⅝ miles, continue along the highway shoulder until you see the Greenwood State Beach Visitor Center on your right. For a break from the pavement, veer right and take the short trail south from the visitor center across the headlands to the Greenwood State Beach parking lot in the center of town around 6⅛ miles.

**ALTERNATE ROUTE:** To really stay off the highway for most of this section, you can follow a steeper, longer route up Cameron Road and down Greenwood Ridge Road to Elk. Only 3¼ miles longer than the highway route, its main disadvantages are the elevation change (an additional 800 feet+/920 feet-), limited coastal vistas, and the narrow, winding descent 2⅜ miles on moderately busy road at the end. Most of the route offers good views and very little traffic.

**SUGGESTED ROUND TRIPS & LOOPS:** Explore Navarro Beach and Bluffs at the start of this section. If you're adventuresome you might walk the first mile along the highway for some more grand views. Stay at the Elk Guest House and hike their headlands trails. Take the excellent, if demanding, bicycle loop up the Cameron Road **Alternate Route**, returning north on the highway.

**HOW TO IMPROVE CCT HERE:** Most of the land from Saddle Point to Elk is held in three large parcels. The largest of these, the Roth Ranch, already protected from development by a conservation easement, might someday allow a CCT corridor. Other owners might be approached. While rugged terrain precludes a trail west of the highway in a few spots, most of the land would allow an excellent trail.

## SECTION 15
# Elk to Alder Creek, Manchester State Park

DISTANCE: 10¼ miles (16.5 kilometers).

OPEN TO: Hikers. Bicyclists on road segment.

SURFACE: Highway shoulder, beach.

ACCESS POINT: Greenwood State Beach parking lot, Elk.

HOW TO GET THERE: Turn west off Highway 1 in the town of Elk, 16 miles south of Mendocino, at Milepost 34.05 into Greenwood State Beach parking lot.

OTHER ACCESS: Anywhere along the highway portion.

DIFFICULTY: Easy.

ELEVATION GAIN/LOSS: 850 feet+/990 feet-.

CAUTIONS: Stay on shoulder, off roadway and watch for traffic. Use extreme caution when crossing highway. No parking or vehicle access at Irish Beach.

FURTHER INFORMATION: Mendocino area State Parks (707)937-5804.

FACILITIES: Chemical toilets, picnic area, phone.

CAMPGROUNDS: Nearest campgrounds are Navarro Beach (primitive) at start of previous section, Manchester State Beach and Manchester KOA on next section.

LODGING: Many in Elk.

Here's another section that follows Highway 1 for nearly its entire length. Fortunately traffic is usually light between the tiny towns of Elk and Manchester. Still, road walkers will find plenty of dangerous curves and blind spots as the highway dips through canyons and crosses high marine terraces with stunning coastal vistas. The frustrations of seeing vast open space as you walk the highway shoulder mount for through-hikers who, by section's end, have literally been "on the road" for all but two of the last twenty-four miles.

Happily through hikers can finish this section with a marvelous walk along attractive, secluded Irish Beach. Day hikers must note that they can only reach Irish Beach from its south end, namely the mouth of Alder Creek at the start of the next section, since there is no parking or public vehicle access to the north end of Irish Beach.

A pleasant side trail at the access point could potentially become a link in CCT. The ⅜-mile trail that descends to Greenwood Beach and Cove allows a closer look at this enthralling coast. Ten years ago a trail followed Greenwood Creek upstream to the highway bridge, but several years of harsh winters with high water and fallen trees obliterated the old path. Still, if you have time, we recommend visiting the beach.

Follow the shoulder of Highway 1 south out of town, descending across

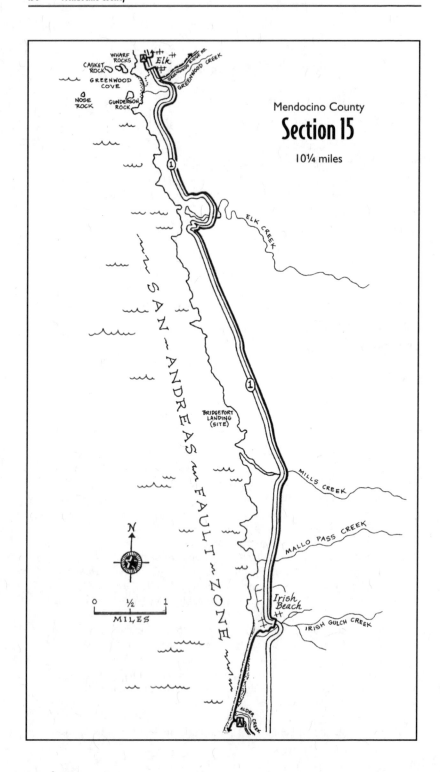

Mendocino County
## Section 15
10¼ miles

Greenwood Creek before ¼ mile, then climbing to a high grassy terrace at ⅝ mile. The highway contours across this terrace, staying close to the bluff's edge where cliffs plunge 200 feet to the breakers.

Around 2 miles you begin a winding descent into the deep, broad canyon of Elk Creek. After crossing the creek at 2½ miles, begin a corkscrew climb out of the canyon, ascending tight curves featured on local scenic postcards as "Dramamine Drive."

Take a minute to catch your breath at the last sweeping turn around 3 miles where a spectacular view surveys canyon, cove and coast. The highway straightens out for a long, undulating crossing of a heavily farmed marine terrace, this one even higher than the last. Visibility is good here except at a set of curves bracketing the crossing of a seasonal creek around 5 miles. The long straightaway ascends one more hill then descends past Bridgeport Ranch at 6 miles, the center of a thriving agricultural community in the late 1800s. Then it's up and down to a winding crossing of Mills Creek around 6⅝ miles before the road straightens out again to contour south.

At 7½ miles you begin a descent that crosses Mallo Pass Creek at 7¾ miles. Today's landfill crossing of the creek's 200-foot deep canyon gives no indication what a barrier the canyon was to early travel along the coast. As you cross the deep canyon hidden in dense vegetation, look west to see the jagged rock pinnacles guarding the northern entrance of the cove to the west. As you ascend south you might take a break at the vista point around 8 miles that gives another view of this rugged hidden coast.

Continue along the highway shoulder as it tops a hill, then descends through the Irish Beach subdivision. Descend past the subdivision office (vacation rentals available, 707-882-2467) at 8⅝ miles, round a bend to the left and descend east to a one-way road on the right at 8¾ miles signed "DO NOT ENTER." The sign pertains to vehicle traffic. You want to turn right and descend the one-way narrow road yielding to vehicle traffic as you descend the canyon to the beach at 9⅛ miles.

To the north the beach ends at abrupt cliffs about ⅝ mile from Irish Gulch Creek, but to the south one long wave-swept beach stretches all the way to the mouth of the Garcia River 5 miles south just short of Point Arena. Walk to the tideline and follow it south to the mouth of Alder Creek at 10¼ miles. A roughly triangular lagoon marks the mouth of the creek. Its canyon is also the first big gap in the high cliffs and bluffs that back the beach north of Alder Creek.

Three notable facts mark Alder Creek. The San Andreas fault goes out to sea here. The 5272-acre Manchester State Park stretches south and southeast. The access road just south of the creek is this section's end and the start of Mendocino County Section 16.

**ALTERNATE ROUTE:** If you don't descend to Irish Beach, continue along Highway 1 to Alder Creek Road and the north end of Manchester State Park.

**SUGGESTED ROUND TRIPS & LOOPS:** Walk north along the tideline from the end of Alder Creek Road for about 1¾ miles. The walk south is covered in the next section.

**HOW TO IMPROVE CCT HERE:** Get the CCT off the highway! Develop a trail from Greenwood Beach up the south slope to meet the highway.

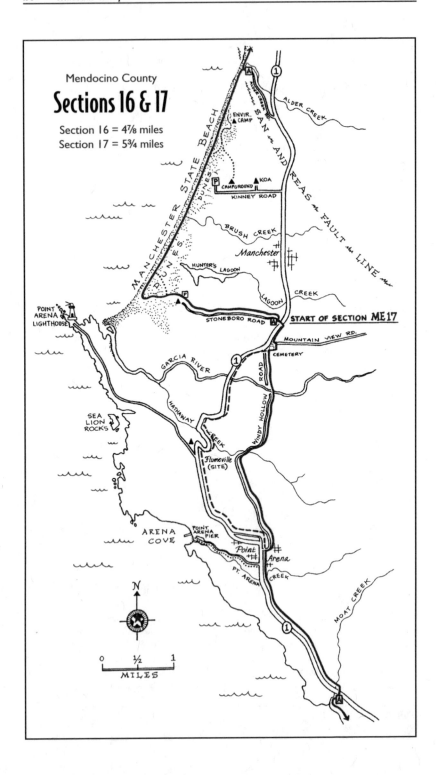

Mendocino County
# Sections 16 & 17
Section 16 = 4⅞ miles
Section 17 = 5¾ miles

## SECTION 16
# Alder Creek to Stoneboro Road at Highway 1, Manchester State Park

**DISTANCE:** 4⅞ miles (7.8 kilometers).

**OPEN TO:** Hikers. Bicyclists on road.

**SURFACE:** Beach, trail, road shoulder.

**ACCESS POINT:** Mouth of Alder Creek, Manchester State Park.

**HOW TO GET THERE:** Turn west off Highway 1 at Milepost 22.48 north of Manchester onto Alder Creek Road. Go .7 mile to end of road.

**OTHER ACCESS:** Kinney Road, Stoneboro Road.

**DIFFICULTY:** Easy.

**ELEVATION GAIN/LOSS:** 190 feet+/120 feet-.

**CAUTIONS:** Watch for sneaker waves on beach.

**FURTHER INFORMATION:** Mendocino area State Parks (707)937-5804.

**FACILITIES:** None at access point. Chemical toilets and picnic area at end of Kinney Road, ⅛ mile east of trail. Phone and water on Kinney Road at campground ½ mile east.

**CAMPGROUNDS:** Manchester State Park Campground on Kinney Road offers primitive camping. The park also has walk-in camping about ½ mile south and ¼ mile east of the access point, but you must register with state parks before your arrival. For more amenities try Manchester KOA east of state campground or Rollerville Junction on Highway 1 at Point Arena Lighthouse Road south of this section.

**LODGING:** Several in Point Arena to south.

This pleasant walk along an expansive wave- and windswept beach currently offers the longest off-road section of CCT between Little River and Sea Ranch. We're working to encourage state legislators and administrators to improve the CCT in southern Mendocino County where extensive agricultural lands still offer an opportunity to acquire a trail corridor for much of the distance that requires road walking as this book goes to press.

Manchester State Park comprises 5272 acres of recreational land and prime bird habitat. It offers one of the most lightly used of Mendocino's state parks, especially considering its size. The beach cuts across prevailing ocean currents, offering a beachcomber's paradise. Incidentally, the westward sweeping promontory of Point Arena so visible to the south is the closest place to Hawaii on the North American continent.

From the end of the road, walk west at the base of low cliffs covered with wildflowers. In 300 feet where a garden of succulents grows on the cliff of fractured rocks, you cross the San Andreas fault which runs offshore paralleling the coast to the north and angles southeast along Alder Creek and the Garcia River inland from this section.

Veer west to follow the tideline, which offers the best walking south. By ¼ mile beach grass covers the cliffs east of the driftwood-strewn beach. As you follow the tideline toward the Point Arena Lighthouse, sand dunes have replaced the cliffs east of the beach by ½ mile. In 300 feet a small gully makes a gap in the dunes. If you walk east up the gully, you'll reach the walk-in camps in about ¼ mile. CCT continues along the tideline, passing the broad outflow from seasonal Davis Lake at ⅝ mile. The dunes become higher as you walk south, reaching their highest peaks around one mile.

At 1⅛ miles you pass a path leading out of the dunes. It leads to the end of Kinney Road and the park's main campground. The beach becomes more broad as you head south, and low wildflower-covered bluffs replace the dunes. A bright yellow sign proclaims "CABLE LANDING," the spot where the trans-Pacific cable heads west to Hawaii. Pass the mouth of Brush Creek around 1⅝ miles. At 1¾ miles a lagoon strewn with large driftwood lies east of the beach. It marks the northern end of a broad wildlife area used by abundant bird populations, including flocks

## The San Andreas Fault System

The California coast as we know it has been and continues to be created by the collision of two immense tectonic plates, the North American continental plate and the Pacific oceanic plate. The head-on collision of the two plates about 150 million years ago created the Sierra Nevada Range. Approximately 20 million years ago, the Pacific plate stopped moving east and began sliding northwest along the North American plate's edge. The meeting of the plates became a sideswipe collision, replacing the Sierra-building head-on crash. The San Andreas Fault System formed to accommodate this movement.

The San Andreas fault and the smaller affiliated faults comprising the system have, more than any other factor, created the California coast we know today. The San Andreas stretches 750 miles northwest from Mexico's Gulf of California to Cape Mendocino near Eureka. The northern half of the San Andreas fault runs on or near the coast. South of Monterey the Fault Zone runs from 30 to 90 miles inland. California is slowly being torn apart along the San Andreas fault. The parts of California west of the fault, including San Diego, Los Angeles, Monterey, Point Reyes and Point Arena, are moving north at a rate of one to two inches a year. In effect these movements constantly re-create the California coast as we know it. Fortunately the shift is slow enough to allow us time to enjoy the spectacular beauty of this leading edge of the North American continent.

Most of the movement along the San Andreas fault is slow and constant, not discernable without scientific instruments. Only after pressure builds as the sliding motion gets caught in a particular area do we have earthquakes. Then the movement becomes violent, jumping as much as 20 feet in seconds. California's best hope is that movements along the fault continue at a steady, incremental pace, avoiding the resistance that causes earthquakes.

The San Andreas fault first comes ashore at Alder Creek north of Point Arena, the Coastal Trail crossing it near the start of this section. The Fault Zone follows the canyons of the Garcia and Gualala Rivers southeast before angling back offshore south of Fort Ross. It returns to land briefly near Bodega Bay then again through western Marin County before running offshore again from Bolinas to Pacifica where the Fault Zone comes ashore to stay.

of tundra swans that winter in the area.

Continue southwest along the beach as the lighthouse looms ever larger. At 2 miles large Hunter's Lagoon hides in the dunes ¼ mile east. Dunes soon back the beach as you head south.

Around 2¾ miles the Coastal Trail heads east on either of two trails that leave the beach to head through the low dunes. To the southwest the beach continues one more mile to the mouth of the Garcia River, a beautiful peaceful spot with much bird life. The tidal river is most often too deep to ford. Even if you could get across, about ¼ mile of private property stands between the river and the Point Arena Lighthouse. If those two obstacles could ever be overcome, CCT could continue south right along the coast. See HOW TO IMPROVE CCT below.

The two trails east soon merge into one. Around 3¼ miles you reach the end of Stoneboro Road. The river and private property to the south force the Coastal Trail to follow sleepy Stoneboro Road as it winds east to Highway 1 at 4⅞ miles, the end of this section and start of another road walking section of CCT. If you need supplies, the tiny town of Manchester about a mile north has a market and post office. The town of Point Arena on the next section has shopping and eating places.

**ALTERNATE ROUTE:** None, unless you prefer walking the highway shoulder.

**SUGGESTED ROUND TRIPS & LOOPS:** The large natural area of Manchester State Park offers ample room to explore. In addition to the CCT route, you can take the side hike southwest to the Garcia River mouth, about 3 miles round trip from the end of Stoneboro Road. A one-mile trail between the main park campground and the walk-in camps offers loop possibilities with the beach route. You can also walk the beach north from the access point for 1½ miles until it ends north of Irish Gulch at steep cliffs (see previous section).

**HOW TO IMPROVE CCT HERE:** Proposition 40, approved by voters in March 2002, may provide funds for the state to acquire the 1860-acre Stornetta ranch south of the river. With a safe ford or footbridge across the Garcia River, this would provide an appropriately dramatic coastal route for the CCT south of this section.

## SECTION 17
# Stoneboro Road at Highway 1 to Moat Creek

**DISTANCE:** 5¾ miles (9.3 kilometers).

**OPEN TO:** Hikers, bicyclists.

**SURFACE:** Road shoulder, highway shoulder.

**ACCESS POINT:** Highway 1 at Stoneboro Road.

**HOW TO GET THERE:** Turn west off Highway 1 at Milepost 19.65 south end of Manchester onto Stoneboro Road and park.

**OTHER ACCESS:** Downtown Point Arena or anywhere along this road section.

**DIFFICULTY:** Easy.

**ELEVATION GAIN/LOSS:** 570 feet+/600 feet-. To Point Arena: 450 feet+/320 feet-.

**CAUTIONS:** Garcia River ford is not safe at high water in winter and spring. See Alternate Route. Bicyclists may not be able to ford river even in summer.

**FURTHER INFORMATION:** Mendocino County Road Department (707)463-4363.

**FACILITIES:** None at start. Restrooms, water, phone in Point Arena.

**CAMPGROUNDS:** None on route but Rollerville Junction is on Highway 1 2.6 miles south of Stoneboro Road. Also see previous section.

**LODGING:** Several in Point Arena.

**MAP:** See page 158.

Most of the first two-thirds of this section offers a pleasant road walk, assuming the Garcia River is shallow enough to ford when you get to it. However, the final leg south from the town of Point Arena along Highway 1 until you reach Moat Creek leaves much to be desired. Worst of all, you overlook lightly populated, mostly pastoral coastal bluffs that would be an ideal place for the Coastal Trail. You might plan time to enjoy a meal out in Point Arena, the largest coastal town between Mendocino and Gualala at the Sonoma County line. After Gualala you won't see another town of notable size until Bodega Bay 40 miles south.

For lack of continuous public access along the coast, the current route of CCT turns inland. From Stoneboro Road walk the highway shoulder south for ¼ mile to Mountain View Road where you must make a decision. At times of high water, generally October to May, you may not be able to ford the Garcia River on the main CCT route along Windy Hollow Road. In that case, follow the Alternate Route. When the ford is safe, go left on Mountain View Road, then immediately right, following a dirt road through the pioneer Manchester Cemetery to its southwest corner. There you pick up Windy Hollow Road, a sleepy lane that descends a cypress-lined ridge to the Garcia River at one mile.

At press time, there was no bridge across the river, requiring a ford that is

*Hikers examine large concretions embedded in the cliff at Bowling Ball Beach.*

usually easy from about June through September, but should never be attempted at high water. Beyond the gravel riverbed surrounding the ford, you again pick up Windy Hollow Road to climb over a ridge with views west to the Point Arena Lighthouse around 1⅜ miles. Your road descends to Hathaway Creek at 2 miles, then rises gently along its south fork to 3 miles. Ascend moderately to Windy Hollow Road's end at Riverside Drive. Turn right for a brief block and come to Main Street/Highway 1 in Point Arena at 3½ miles.

The CCT turns left and descends on the sidewalk through the compact town's commercial district. Just before the bottom of the hill, Port Street on the right heads west to Arena Cove, coastal access, and the rightful route of CCT.

However, due to private property south of the cove, for now the CCT continues south on Highway 1, climbing a canyon out of town and quickly gaining a ridge with expansive views around 4¼ miles. The rolling headlands to the west are where the CCT should be. For now be grateful the stint on the highway is short. At 5 miles the highway descends, coming to Moat Creek at 5¾ miles where the next section of CCT begins at the parking lot west of the highway.

ALTERNATE ROUTE: When the Garcia River is too high to ford, you must walk Highway 1 all the way from Stoneboro Road to Point Arena. When you get to town, follow Lake Street to town center.

SUGGESTED ROUND TRIPS & LOOPS: Windy Hollow Road offers a pleasant walk or bike ride as does the side trip to Arena Cove. A seafood cafe and pizza parlor are near the pier there.

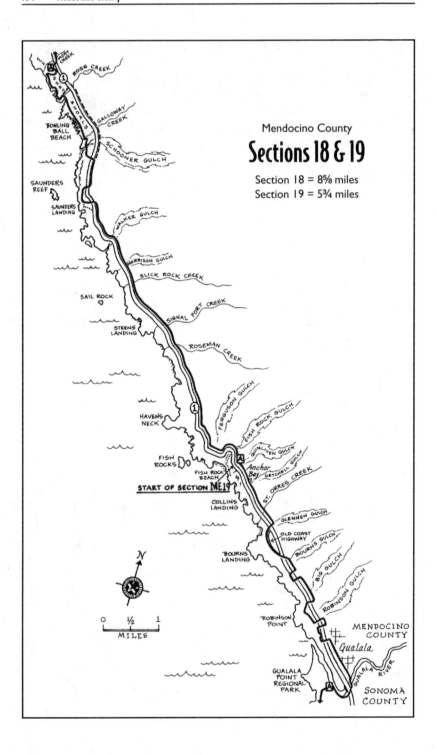

Mendocino County

# Sections 18 & 19

Section 18 = 8⅝ miles
Section 19 = 5¾ miles

**HOW TO IMPROVE CCT HERE:** Only two hurdles block CCT's rightful route south along the coast. 1) The Garcia River is usually difficult to ford near its mouth at the south end of Manchester State Park. 2) If you can ford the river near its mouth, the Stornetta Ranch owns about ¼ mile of the ideal route between the river mouth and the Point Arena Lighthouse property. Proposition 40, approved by voters in March 2002, may provide funds for state acquisition of the 1860-acre ranch. If that occurs and a safe ford or footbridge established, CCT could then head south to follow Lighthouse Road 2¾ miles to Highway 1 at Flumeville. An even better route would follow Lighthouse Road for ⅞ mile, then take to the bluffs now held by the ranch and the Coast Guard Loran Station, paralleling the jagged shore south for 1⅝ miles, then east for another mile to Arena Cove.

## SECTION 18
# Moat Creek to Anchor Bay

**DISTANCE:** 8⅝ miles (13.9 kilometers).

**OPEN TO:** Hikers. Bicyclists on road.

**SURFACE:** Trail, beach, highway shoulder.

**ACCESS POINT:** Moat Creek Access.

**HOW TO GET THERE:** Turn west off Highway 1 south of Point Arena at Milepost 12.9 into dirt parking lot.

**OTHER ACCESS:** Ross Creek Trail, Schooner Gulch/Bowling Ball Beach, or anywhere south along Highway 1.

**DIFFICULTY:** Easy.

**ELEVATION GAIN/LOSS:** 650 feet+/600 feet-. Moat Creek to Schooner Gulch trailhead: 230 feet+/190 feet-.

**CAUTIONS:** Use caution on trail along blufftop. Stay back from bluff's edge. Along highway, stay on road shoulder. Watch for traffic and use caution crossing highway.

**FURTHER INFORMATION:** Mendocino area State Parks (707)937-5804.

**FACILITIES:** None at start. Chemical toilets at Schooner Gulch. Restrooms, phone in Anchor Bay.

**CAMPGROUNDS:** Private Anchor Bay Campground is just before end of section.

**LODGING:** Four are along route just north of Anchor Bay, plus several in Point Arena.

Happily the Coastal Trail returns to the shoreline for the next two miles, first along remnants of another subdivision shut down by California voters supporting coastal access, then along a tidal beach with intriguing geologic anomalies. Plan your hike for a tide less than 2.0 feet, especially in winter when storm surf erodes

Bowling Ball Beach sand. Lack of public access again forces the second portion of this CCT section along the highway.

Moat Creek Access, one of the hundreds of "Offer to Dedicate" (OTD) coastal access ways generated by 1972's successful voter initiative for the Coastal Protection Act, was the first OTD sponsored by a private group. Whiskey Shoals was a pre-Coastal Initiative subdivision north and south of Moat Creek. When California voters passed the initiative, the unfinished subdivision was shut down for not complying with the new laws, then acquired by the state when the developer defaulted on commitments to upgrade it. The Coastal Conservancy held the land for several years, then sold most of it to individuals, retaining a blufftop trail from Moat Creek to Ross Creek. The name Whiskey Shoals harks back to the days of Prohibition when rum runners used these fog-shrouded cliffs to land their illegal cargoes.

From the Moat Creek parking lot, the CCT now follow a new trail that heads east briefly from the top of the lot, then turns right (south) at a junction to climb to the blufftop. There the Coastal Trail veers right to circle the bluff's edge counterclockwise. At ⅛ mile you meet the top of the rough former trail, now abandoned, that climbed steeply from the mouth of Moat Creek. Stay on the path that follows the bluff edge down the coast, overlooking the magnificent golden striated cliffs that are a striking feature of the shoreline south of Point Arena. Heed the bright red and yellow signs that warn, "DANGER, BLUFFS CRUMBLE," and stay back from the edge. Around ½ mile the CCT veers left around a horseshoe cove.

By ⅝ mile you reach the south end of the Whiskey Shoals bluff. The CCT makes a dramatic, now well graded descent south toward Bowling Ball Beach, assisted by 33 steps on the steepest portion. At the bottom of the hill, the Coastal Trail veers left along the base of the grassy bluff to meet the Ross Creek Trail. Turn right and descend to the mouth of Ross Creek and tideline at ¾ mile. A small sea stack stands in the tidal zone beside the creek.

If you hike through here at a tide higher than 2.0 feet, especially in winter, you may not be able to get around the point ¼ mile south. In that case you must detour via the **Alternate Route**. Otherwise continue southeast along the beach from Ross Creek. The beach narrows and turns rocky around ⅞ mile, then broadens and becomes sandy as you approach the point at one mile. Around the point you can see the strata of the cliff face as they cross the tidal zone and run out to sea. These are the bowling lanes of Bowling Ball Beach, which runs southeast from the point.

Walk down Bowling Ball Beach, passing fissures in the striated cliffs beyond 1⅛ miles. You soon pass large circular disks of yellow sandstone protruding from the cliffs of gray sandstone. These weathered concretions, which look like giant chariot wheels, formed deep below the ocean and were deposited under great pressure in concentric layers.

Continue along the beach past another narrow point around 1¼ miles, then past spherical concretions lying loose in the tidal zone. These "bowling balls," which gave the beach its name, are best viewed at low tide.

CCT continues along the beach to the mouth of Galloway Creek at 1½ miles. The beach angles south to an impassable rocky point. Just beyond the creek the Coastal Trail veers left to climb a narrow path to the blufftop and a junction at 1⅝ miles. The left fork contours east to Highway 1. CCT takes the right fork along the bluff edge. Near the southern tip of the bluffs around 1¾ miles, your trail turns east to drop past an outhouse to a junction overlooking the sheltered sandy cove of Schooner Gulch Beach.

At the junction you can turn left to climb east along the verdant gulch to Highway 1 at 1⅞ miles, a route ¼ mile longer. You can instead turn right on a rougher route to reach the highway south of the narrow bridge over the gulch. To do that, descend 175 feet to the logjam at the mouth of the creek, then go south for 125 feet, cautiously crossing the logjam. At the first head-high rock, turn left on the path climbing the bluff. It's easy at first, then climbs steeply where trees lie across the trail. When you reach the highway at 1⅞ miles, turn right and walk the shoulder.

Before 2⅝ miles the Coastal Trail leaves the highway, heading out to the point north of Saunders Landing. You can walk the bluff edge or follow a paved road that ends on the point at 2¾ miles. Either way leads to headlands with sweeping vistas up the coast to Point Arena. Take a break to savor the view because CCT heads east around the south rim of the headland to return to the highway above a cove, the site of Saunders Landing.

Private property now forces the Coastal Trail to follow the highway shoulder south along a splendid coast of sparkling blue coves and wooded points. You have limited chances to see the beauty as you carefully walk the often narrow road shoulder through gulches and around numerous curves. The road walking isn't too bad until 3⅜ miles where you dip, twist and rise through Walker Gulch. Then contour along the highway across wooded headlands, crossing Morrison Gulch, then Slick Rock Creek at 4⅜ miles where white Sail Rock stands ¾ mile offshore.

Highway 1 straightens out past Steens Landing and across Signal Port Creek around 5¼ miles. Look south for views of the prominent peninsula called Havens Neck. From 5⅞ miles to 7¼ miles the highway winds and stays near the shore as it crosses Roseman Creek, Triplett Gulch and other small streams. Then a broad terrace occupied by private residences forces the road inland past Havens Neck around 7½ miles.

Continue along the winding highway shoulder with Fish Rocks towering 120 feet high offshore. Wind past several ocean-view lodgings and across Ferguson Gulch before 8¼ miles where the highway narrows and winds east into Fish Rock Gulch and past Anchor Bay Campground (fee for access to Fish Rock Beach) at 8½ miles. Follow the highway out of the gulch and into the small town of Anchor Bay at 8⅝ miles where a store, restaurant and laundromat offer services. The final Mendocino County section of CCT starts here.

**ALTERNATE ROUTE:** When the tide is too high to round the point at one mile on Bowling Ball Beach, you must detour east at ¾ mile along the Ross Creek Trail and follow Highway 1 to the Schooner Gulch access.

**SUGGESTED ROUND TRIPS & LOOPS:** Whether you start from Moat Creek on the north or Schooner Gulch on the south, the beach and bluffs in between offer a pleasant and scenic round trip hike.

**HOW TO IMPROVE CCT HERE:** Extend the Whiskey Shoals blufftop trail north at least to north end of subdivision, ideally all the way to Arena Cove. Acquire a trail corridor south of Saunders Landing that keeps hikers off the highway.

## SECTION 19
# Anchor Bay to Gualala Point Regional Park Visitor Center

DISTANCE: 5¾ miles (9.3 kilometers).

OPEN TO: Hikers. Bicyclists on road.

SURFACE: Highway shoulder, road shoulder, trail.

ACCESS POINT: Anchor Bay.

HOW TO GET THERE: On Highway 1 north of Gualala at Milepost 4.45, park near the commercial center of the small community of Anchor Bay.

OTHER ACCESS: Anywhere along highway.

DIFFICULTY: Easy.

ELEVATION GAIN/LOSS: 350 feet+/370 feet-.

CAUTIONS: Stay on road shoulder. Watch for traffic. Use extreme caution crossing highway.

FURTHER INFORMATION: Gualala Point Regional Park (707)785-2377.

FACILITIES: Restrooms, phone, water at access point. Gualala Point Regional Park has restrooms, phone, water, picnic area.

CAMPGROUNDS: Gualala Point Regional Park has a small campground near section's end along the river east of Highway 1. Salt Point State Park has campgrounds 18 miles south.

LODGING: Many in Gualala and Anchor Bay.

MAP: See page 164.

The final Mendocino County section primarily offers yet another span of road walking, most of it along the shoulder of busy Highway 1. But we'll stick our necks out to say that the worst of the highway walking is over as the highway from Anchor Bay to the Sonoma County line has fewer curves and broader shoulders than previous sections. You're even able to get off the highway on several lengths of quiet side road, mostly through residential neighborhoods where the ocean glimmers close by.

Follow the wooded highway shoulder southeast out of Anchor Bay, crossing Quinliven Gulch and climbing over a small rise before descending to cross Getchell Creek at ½ mile where the ocean is once again just west of the highway. Walk the shoulder across gullies, then across St. Orres Creek at one mile. Then walk past the distinctive onion-dome architecture of Saint Orres Inn & Restaurant and dip across Glennen Gulch. You leave the pine forests here for mostly open grasslands.

At 1⅜ miles where unmarked Old Coast Highway forks right, take it for a short but quiet respite from highway walking. It passes sheltered Cooks Beach and climbs over the point that held the 1870 lumber loading chute called Bourn's Landing. A wide gauge railroad ran from Bourn's to the Gualala sawmill, and the CCT follows much of its route for the next 2 miles.

The side road ends by 1¾ miles, returning you to the highway shoulder. Follow it around a curve, along a straightaway and down to another unmarked fork on the right at 2¼ miles. There you veer right on sleepy Old Coast Highway. Walk it to 2⅜ miles where you must turn left to climb quickly back to the highway. Turn right and walk the shoulder over deep Big Gulch.

At 2⅞ miles the Coastal Trail again veers right, following suburban Robinson Reef Road out onto Robinson Point. Beyond 3⅛ miles you must turn left on Westward Ho Road, then go right on Pacific Drive until it returns you to the highway before 3½ miles. Walk the highway shoulder as it dips across Robinson Gulch, then turn right and follow Sedalia Drive to 3¾ miles. Go right at Hubert Drive on the continuation of Sedalia to unmarked Ocean Drive where you can again go right, staying near the coast to the end of Ocean Drive at 4 miles. Then you must return to Highway 1.

Turn right and follow Highway 1 as it passes through the center of the town of Gualala. After you pass the landmark 1903 Gualala Hotel on the left, the town quickly thins out. By 4⅜ miles you've left town and now overlook the broad estuary of the Gualala River. From here you can follow a wide highway shoulder to the river bridge at 4⅞ miles. Parking is available on the left at the north end of the bridge.

Cautiously cross the narrow bridge, entering Sonoma County about half way across. Just 60 feet from the south end of the bridge, the Coastal Trail veers right to descend a rudimentary trail down a steep embankment. At the bottom you pass through a break in the fence and meet the River Trail in Gualala Point Regional Park. A right turn would lead to the park campground, but the Coastal Trail goes left, crossing the river flat briefly, then ascending the face of the bluff by two switchbacks. When you reach the blufftop at 5⅛ miles, turn right and walk the trail between the park road and the bluff's edge. You pass a pleasant picnic area in ⅛ mile, then come to the parking lot with the visitor center just beyond. Welcome to Sonoma County, Coastwalk's home base.

**ALTERNATE ROUTE:** None, unless you stay on the highway shoulder and avoid the quieter side roads.

**SUGGESTED ROUND TRIPS & LOOPS:** The side trails to the shoreline at Collins Landing and Gualala are short pleasant detours to explore the spectacular coast. Longer loops and round trips are available in Gualala Point Regional Park. See Sonoma County Section 1.

**HOW TO IMPROVE CCT HERE:** Develop a trail off the highway.

# Sonoma County

**S**ONOMA COUNTY TEETERS ON THE BRINK of the San Francisco Bay Area's urban growth, but the Sonoma coast's light population clusters in small villages and isolated developments, leaving most of the scenic shoreline wild and pastoral, much of it protected in parks, enhancing the CCT experience here. It could easily have been much different. On the Sonoma coast occurred one of the earliest battles over the public's right to coastal access versus developers' efforts to remold the coast exclusively for private use. This fight began in the 1960s when the developers of Sea Ranch announced plans to keep the public off the northernmost ten miles of the Sonoma coast. See the feature *The Battle for the Sea Ranch Coast*.

While the public won that struggle, preserving the right of coastal access generally, coastal access remains a mixed bag along the Sonoma shore. About 60 percent of the Coastal Trail in Sonoma County follows trails and beaches, but that leaves 40 percent of CCT here on roads, mostly Highway 1. We can all visit the spectacular coast at Gualala Point Regional Park and the three miles of Sea Ranch coast next to it, but the next seven miles of Sea Ranch are only open to residents and guests. Then for the next six miles, a large private ranch keeps the public from using the scenic coast.

Fortunately Sonoma's fine state parks begin right beyond this look-but-don't-touch splendid shoreline. Salt Point State Park, the Sonoma coast's largest park, protects eight miles of coastline with a spectacular trail right along the bluffs exploring the rocky collision of land and sea. Then private lands hold sway, except for the short, lovely shoreline of Stillwater Cove Regional Park, until Fort Ross State Park protects almost nine miles of gorgeous and wild shore, including Sonoma's rugged Lost Coast where the shoreline remains thoroughly wild and raw.

Directly south of the Lost Coast, Sonoma Coast State Beach protects most of the gentle coastline all the way south to dramatic Bodega Head, although several private inholdings and preexisting subdivisions share some of this coast. The town of Bodega Bay provides the Sonoma coast's biggest commercial and residential enclave, plus a busy fishing port. However, the Coastal Trail winds its way through parks along the coastline west of town until the upscale Bodega Harbour subdivision south of town forces the CCT inland along Highway 1. South of the subdivision, once again ranches keep the Coastal Trail off the coast and along the highway shoulder until the south county line.

The Sonoma coast offers some of the most pleasing seaside vistas in the state and many opportunities still exist to save more of this gorgeous shoreline for public access. Like so many parts of the California coast however, public acquisitions need to occur soon before population and development pressures subvert the essentially pastoral nature of this coast.

## SECTION 1
# Gualala Point Regional Park Visitor Center to Sea Ranch Lodge

DISTANCE: 9¼ miles (14.9 kilometers).

OPEN TO: Hikers. Bicyclists on highway.

SURFACE: Trail, highway shoulder.

ACCESS POINT: Gualala Point Regional Park Visitor Center.

HOW TO GET THERE: Turn west off Highway 1 .25 mile south of the Gualala River bridge and drive .5 mile to the visitor center.

OTHER ACCESS: Via Salal Trail and at Walk-on Beach, Shell Beach, Stengel Beach, Pebble Beach, and Black Point Beach trailheads.

DIFFICULTY: Easy.

ELEVATION GAIN/LOSS: 230 feet+/190 feet-.

CAUTIONS: Sea Ranch is closed to the public except for the northern Blufftop Trail, Salal Trail and the five access trails and the beaches they reach, plus any of the tideline you can walk below the mean high tideline. Wandering off the trails is trespassing. Blufftop Trail south of Walk-on Beach is closed to the public, but open to anyone staying in Sea Ranch lodgings.

FURTHER INFORMATION: Gualala Point Regional Park (707)785-2377.

FACILITIES: Park's visitor center has water, restrooms, picnic tables. The five beach trailheads have chemical toilets. Sea Ranch Lodge has a restaurant and small store.

CAMPGROUNDS: Gualala Point Regional Park Campground is east of the highway.

LODGING: Sea Ranch has a lodge and many houses for rent (800)732-7262. If you stay in Sea Ranch lodging, you have the right to walk the non-public trails of Sea Ranch.

This first walk in Sonoma County traverses a part of the coast that gave birth to the modern coastal protection movement. See the feature *The Battle For the Sea Ranch Coast.* Though Sea Ranch has many houses, you'll enjoy its gorgeous shoreline. Consider staying overnight in Sea Ranch accommodations, which gives you the right to walk private trails at Sea Ranch, including the southern six miles of the Blufftop Trail to Sea Ranch Lodge.

This walk starts at the visitor center with dramatic views overlooking the Gualala River and Mendocino shore to the north. Take the paved trail northwest then southwest for about 450 feet, then go left on the dirt path where the paved trail swings to the right. You follow a row of cypress trees and the fence marking the Sea Ranch boundary. At ¼ mile turn left through the fence and trees onto the Blufftop Trail which meanders along the convoluted, rugged bluffs. At 1¼ miles you drop down to a small creek and meet Salal Trail which loops back to the visitor center.

Blufftop Trail climbs out of the ravine and crosses flat headlands with the stylish Sea Ranch houses arranged in clusters. Pass a cypress windrow, then cross

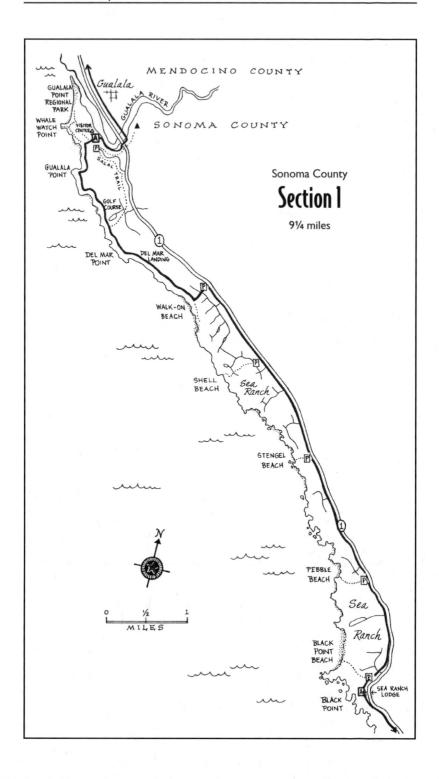

MENDOCINO COUNTY

Gualala

GUALALA RIVER

SONOMA COUNTY

GUALALA
POINT
REGIONAL
PARK

WHALE
WATCH
POINT

VISITOR
CENTER

GUALALA
POINT

SALAL TRAIL

GOLF
COURSE

Sonoma County
**Section 1**
9¼ miles

DEL MAR
POINT

DEL MAR
LANDING

WALK-ON
BEACH

SHELL
BEACH

Sea
Ranch

STENGEL
BEACH

N

PEBBLE
BEACH

Sea
Ranch

0      ½      1
MILES

BLACK
POINT
BEACH

SEA RANCH
LODGE

BLACK
POINT

# The Battle for the Sea Ranch Coast

Looking back at the history of how the public's right to coastal access was won, the battle between Sonoma County environmentalists and a huge corporation backed by local elected officials and news media is now recognized as a seminal event.

In 1963 Oceanic Properties bought about ten miles of undeveloped coast at the northern end of Sonoma County. Their plan: an exclusive 5200-home development called Sea Ranch, carefully designed to blend with the environment and open exclusively to the homeowners. Their intended result: permanent closing of the coastline to public enjoyment and use. In exchange for this, Sea Ranch offered Sonoma County 120 acres beside the mouth of the Gualala River to become park land, with less than a mile of shoreline available to the public. Local coast lovers objected to this giveaway of our right to coastal access, guaranteed by the state constitution, to no avail.

In 1968 these coastal activists formed an environmental organization called COAAST, Californians Organized to Acquire Access to State Tidelands. COAAST first pushed for a citizens' initiative to require the county supervisors to provide coastal access through Sea Ranch. When the supervisors refused to put the measure on the ballot, COAAST sued, taking the case to the state supreme court, which forced the county to do so. The initiative lost after a long, expensive and dishonest campaign against it by the developers (outspending environmentalists 30 to 1), the Santa Rosa Press Democrat, and the business community.

The initiative's defeat caused other communities along the coast to realize they were facing the same kinds of problems. They sensed with growing alarm that the coast would be closed to public use if something were not done. They created the Coastal Alliance, a group of 105 organizations concerned about coastal protection and access. After unsuccessfully lobbying the state legislature for relief, the Coastal Alliance tackled the statewide initiative process with a different outcome. In 1972 California voters passed Proposition 20, the Coastal Protection Act. This set up a statewide zoning process directed by the new Coastal Commission. The law required that zoning laws protect public access in any development proposed on the coast.

The Sea Ranch scheme, still in the planning stages, reached deadlock with the developers refusing to allow access and the Coastal Commission denying building permits. Thus in 1980 the Legislature stepped in and passed the Bane Bill which required Sea Ranch to grant five trails across Sea Ranch to the beaches and to set aside three miles of public blufftop trail along the Sea Ranch coast in exchange for allowing homes to be built without Coastal Commission permits. It also decreased the number of homes allowed from 5200 to 2500.

This solution was not satisfactory to Sea Ranch which appealed the bill to the state appeals court and lost. Nor was it OK with COAAST because it allowed the public on part of the development but not what the Sonoma County Coastal plan called for, a trail the entire length of the Sea Ranch coast.

The battle for the Sea Ranch coast in the '60s, '70s and '80s had a major effect on the right of the citizens to enjoy their coast. Without the passage of Proposition 20, the California coast would undoubtedly have many more large, exclusive developments than it has today.

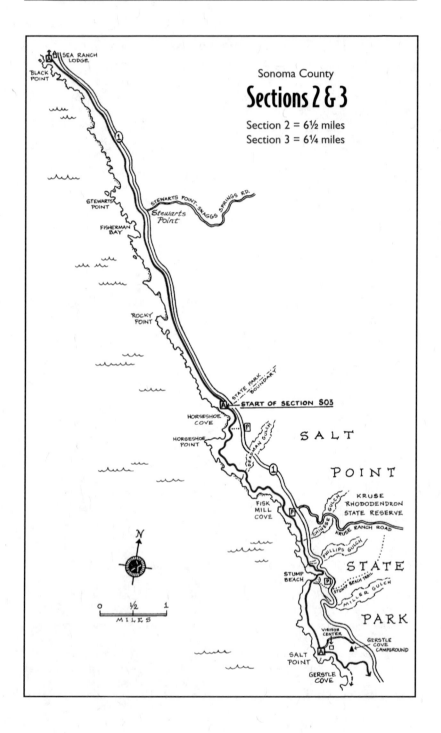

Sonoma County

# Sections 2 & 3

Section 2 = 6½ miles
Section 3 = 6¼ miles

a small creek at 1⅝ miles. At 2 miles you pass through another windrow, this one marking the boundary of the Del Mar Landing Ecological Reserve set aside to protect marine invertebrates. Take the right fork and pass the site of the lumber schooner landing. Little remains but a wooden beam and a rusty spike sticking out of the ground.

The trail continues along the bluff, passing through two more cypress windbreaks and crossing two creeks. Meet the junction with the Walk-on Beach Trail at 3¼ miles. You can take the side trail down to the beach for a break. Head northeast from the junction to find the parking area and highway at 3½ miles.

The next 6 miles to Sea Ranch Lodge follow the shoulder of Highway 1. You can break up or lengthen the walk by taking any of the four public trails down to scenic pocket beaches along the rugged, rocky tideline. Pass the first side trail, Shell Beach, at 4⅝ miles. It offers a 1¼-mile round trip. Stengel Beach Trail at 6 miles makes a ⅜-mile side trip. Pass the Pebble Beach Trail at 7⅝ miles, a round trip of ⅝ mile. At 9 miles, just before reaching the lodge, you'll find the Black Point Beach Trail, a ⅝-mile round trip. The hike ends at 9¼ miles at Sea Ranch Lodge where you'll also find a store, restaurant and post office.

**SUGGESTED ROUND TRIPS & LOOPS:** From the visitor center take the Blufftop Trail and loop back on the Salal Trail for a 2½-mile hike. From the visitor center to Walk-on Beach is 6½ miles round trip. For a great short walk, take the 1¼-mile loop from the visitor center to the beach at the river mouth and back along the bluff.

# SECTION 2
# Sea Ranch Lodge to Salt Point State Park North Boundary

**DISTANCE:** 6½ miles (10.5 kilometers).

**OPEN TO:** Hikers, bicyclists.

**SURFACE:** Highway shoulder.

**ACCESS POINT:** Sea Ranch Lodge.

**HOW TO GET THERE:** Turn west off Highway 1 10 miles south of Gualala and 30 miles north of Jenner into Sea Ranch Lodge parking lot.

**OTHER ACCESS:** Anywhere along highway.

**DIFFICULTY:** Easy.

**ELEVATION GAIN/LOSS:** 240 feet+/240 feet-.

**CAUTIONS:** Private property lines both sides of the road for the entire section.

**FURTHER INFORMATION:** None.

**FACILITIES:** Restaurant and small store at Sea Ranch, store at Stewarts Point.

**CAMPGROUNDS:** Gualala Point Regional Park to the north and Salt Point State Park to the south have camping.

**LODGING:** Sea Ranch Lodge.

For all the public coastal land in Sonoma County, this piece of coast represents, along with southern Sea Ranch, a real barrier to the public entitlement of access to the state tidelands. The huge Richardson Ranch spans almost the entire length of this walk, so watch for numerous "NO TRESPASSING" signs. The rugged indented low bluffs, the marine terrace, and rich intertidal zone are off limits. The dramatic views from the road shoulder only hint at a better hike.

Follow the highway shoulder across the gently sloping marine terrace, leaving Sea Ranch before one mile to walk through scenic rural land. The highway skirts the forested hills rising to the east, staying roughly ¼ mile in from the shore until around 2 miles where the land form of Stewarts Point slopes westward ½ mile.

Descend to the settlement called Stewarts Point at 2½ miles. Founded in 1857, it was a major doghole lumber port. This area, a designated historical district, presents an excellent example of a 19th-century coastal settlement. The Richardson family still operates their fine general store in an 1868 building.

Continue south on the highway, watching for the old one-room schoolhouse west of the road. After you dip across Stewarts Creek, good views of points and coves open up, first of Fisherman Bay, then Sandy Point around 3 miles. The road rolls through hilly terrain around 4 miles where Rocky Point juts west. Continue to the walk's end at 6½ miles where a large turnout is on the west side of the road with a grove of Bishop pines just over the fence. A sign for Salt Point State Park is up the road several hundred feet.

> **HOW TO IMPROVE CCT HERE:** The ideal would be to acquire all the land west of the highway and lay the Coastal Trail across it, but any trail off the road would greatly improve this section.

## SECTION 3
# North Boundary to Salt Point, Salt Point State Park

DISTANCE: 6¼ miles (10.1 kilometers).

OPEN TO: Hikers.

SURFACE: Trail.

ACCESS POINT: North boundary of Salt Point State Park.

HOW TO GET THERE: Park in the wide shoulder on the west side of Highway 1 at Milepost 44.54, 4.6 miles north of the Gerstle Cove Campground entrance.

OTHER ACCESS: Fisk Mill Cove and Stump Beach parking areas.

DIFFICULTY: Easy.

ELEVATION GAIN/LOSS: 260 feet+/380 feet-.

**CAUTIONS:** This trail is mostly unmarked.

**FURTHER INFORMATION:** Salt Point State Park (707)847-3221.

**FACILITIES:** Restrooms, water and picnic tables at Fisk Mill Cove, Stump Beach, and Salt Point parking areas.

**CAMPGROUNDS:** Salt Point State Park has Gerstle Cove and Woodside Campgrounds, plus a group camp and hike and bike camps.

**LODGING:** Salt Point Lodge is just south of the park on the next section.

**MAP:** See page 176.

In contrast to the last section's highway walk past privately owned coastal property, this fine walk unfolds entirely within Salt Point State Park, exploring a saw-toothed coast of jutting promontories and rocky inlets. It's one of the most dramatic and scenic walks in Sonoma County and for this author's money, in the state.

This hike begins at the turnout just north of the Salt Point State Park boundary, which is marked by a sign. Walk the shoulder south briefly past the sign, then locate an unmarked trail plunging down slope through the brush. If it's too overgrown, continue ⅜ mile on the shoulder, then turn right where a well-worn trail heads straight down to the shore from a wide shoulder parking area. To hike the first trail, drop from the road and head south through a stand of trees, across a small gully before ¼ mile, and gently downhill past more trees. Cross a wide grassy area, then meet the second trail from the road. You can turn right and descend to the bluff's edge to overlook steep Horseshoe Point and the dramatic cove.

Walk east along a ravine, then cross it heading south on the first obvious path. Then cross the sloping terrace above dense bush lupines and head for the notch in the ridge defining the point. Top the notch at one mile. Before you descend, consider a short climb to the point for a great view. Then follow the old ranch road south, soon leaving the ridge to drop to the blufftop at 1¼ mile. The big rock outcrop jutting seaward invites exploration of its nooks and crannies carved by the surf. The trail meanders south past fantastically shaped sandstone.

Round a point and turn east to the north end of Fisk Mill Cove at 2¼ miles. As you follow the bluff overlooking the cove, watch for a heavy ring attached to the rocks. This 19th century relic moored the lumber schooners that called at this small cove. As you round the cove, cross a small gully, then meet a trail from the highway. Stay to the right and reach a steep banked gulch at 2¾ miles. A path near the bottom forks right, descending to a rocky beach. The Coastal Trail climbs out of the gulch, through an old fence and into a grassy area. After several hundred feet a side trail forks right to a cemetery for the Fisk family who settled here in 1860, operating a ranch for many years.

The main trail soon merges with the spur and passes another trail from the road. Turn right, pass through another fence, and dip through another steep gully. Ascend through lovely Bishop pine forest. Reach an unmarked trail junction at 3 miles. Left leads ⅛ mile to Fisk Mill parking area with water, picnic tables and restrooms. CCT takes the right fork 150 feet to another junction. The spur climbs

**The Russian Orthodox chapel is Fort Ross's most distinctive building.**

steeply to the viewing deck atop Sentinel Rock overlooking the cove 120 feet below, Horseshoe Point to the north and Salt Point to the south.

The Coastal Trail turns left to descend south. It then contours above the bluff's edge through magical forest, crossing two bridges and passing two rock outcrops. After the second rock, descend to a picnic table with a grand coastal view south. (Fisk Mill South parking area lies just east.) Follow the wooded bluff past another rock outcrop, cross a bridge and leave the forest for open headlands at 3⅝ miles. Follow the bluff's edge to ford Chinese Gulch Creek before 3⅞ miles. It cascades over rock shelves with flowers sprouting from cracks and clear pools to cool your weary feet. Across the creek, step carefully to the cliff edge to view the mossy waterfall.

Climb the bank, wind past a brushy hill almost to the highway, then drop south to follow the bluff's edge. At 4⅛ miles you ford Phillips Gulch Creek above another waterfall. Climb a steady incline along bluff's edge to an overlook high above dramatic, deep Stump Beach Cove. The trail skirts the cliff, enters forest at 4⅜ miles, then drops into a gully. Descend steeply to Stump Beach at 4½ miles. Walk across the beach, ford the creek, and climb west up the steep eroded track to a grassy terrace.

CCT follows the main track veering left toward Gerstle Cove, or you can follow a lesser path along the bluff edge, pausing to explore the bizarre eroded rocks called tafoni, most impressive around 5¼ miles. Both paths ford Warren Creek around 5¾ miles, then pass rocks quarried in the 1870s to supply San Francisco with stone. Reach the large Salt Point parking area at 6¼ miles.

**SUGGESTED ROUND TRIPS & LOOPS:** From Fisk Mill Cove, Stump Beach or Salt Point parking areas, walk the trail out and back on a hike suited to your time and energy. Or get the park map and take either the 2⅝- or 5-mile loop up to the Pygmy Forest east of the highway.

# SECTION 4
# Salt Point, Salt Point State Park, to Fort Ross

**DISTANCE:** 8¼ miles (13.7 kilometers).

**OPEN TO:** Hikers. Bicyclists on road.

**SURFACE:** Trail, highway shoulder.

**ACCESS POINT:** Salt Point parking lot.

**HOW TO GET THERE:** Turn west off Highway 1 at Milepost 39.9 (signed Gerstle Cove Campground). Go straight for .5 mile, then take right fork to its end.

**OTHER ACCESS:** Either of Salt Point's campgrounds, Stillwater Cove Regional Park, or anywhere along the highway.

**DIFFICULTY:** Moderate.

**ELEVATION GAIN/LOSS:** 720 feet+/600 feet-.

**CAUTIONS:** The trail from Salt Point to the highway is mostly unmarked.

**FURTHER INFORMATION:** Salt Point State Park (707)847-3221. Stillwater Cove Regional Park (707)847-3245.

**FACILITIES:** Water, restrooms, and picnic tables at access point, Gerstle Cove and Fort Ross. Latter two also have visitor centers.

**CAMPGROUNDS:** Salt Point State Park campgrounds, Stillwater Cove Regional Park campground, two private campgrounds south along the highway.

**LODGING:** Several lodges are on the route along Highway 1.

This hike leads from one of the most scenic state parks on the coast to one of the most dramatic historic parks in the state, Fort Ross. Here the CCT offers a mixed bag of unmarked trails and highway shoulder with intriguing stops along the way.

From the trailhead at the south end of the lot, walk south onto the point and head northeast toward Gerstle Cove. You soon cross the paved access road to the cove. Climb north on a dirt road, then turn right on a path paralleling a paved road and reach the A-framed visitor center at ¼ mile.

The Gerstle Cove Visitor Center overlooks the placid cove often busy with skin and scuba divers. Since the cove is a marine reserve, divers can look but not take. The trail leads from the front of the visitor center southeast into the trees, then crosses a bridge over a gully and follows the bluff above the cove. A wildfire burned this entire area in 1995. It's a good place to watch this forest and terrace recover.

The CCT meanders along the marine terrace, coming to a parking area at the end of the road at ⅝ mile. From here a dead-end side trail explores the shore to the south. It passes a gate, dips through a gully and crosses the terrace. Around ⅝ mile, the path ends at steep cliffs overlooking a rugged coast. You can turn inland here and hike cross-country to the highway about ⅜ mile uphill. It's easy to get

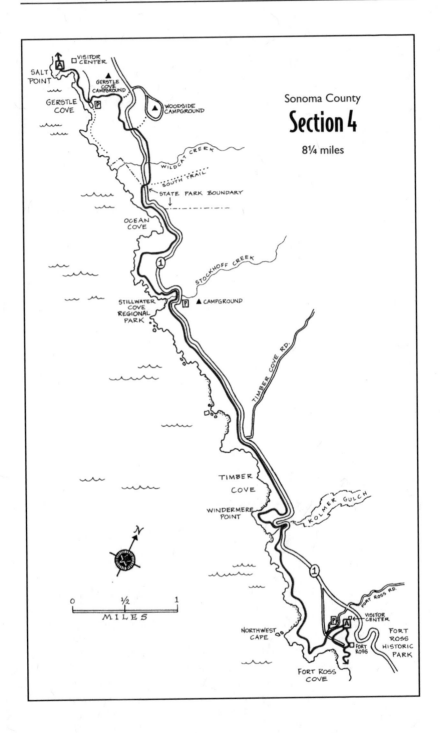

Sonoma County
# Section 4
8¼ miles

lost in the thick undergrowth and drift onto adjacent private property, so we don't recommend this route.

From the parking area at the end of the road, walk a few yards up the road and take the trail climbing northeast through more burned-over forest. At an unmarked junction at one mile, turn right and follow the path through the woods, coming to the highway at 1⅜ miles. Cross the highway and take the path uphill toward Woodside Campground. At 1⅝ miles you reach another unmarked junction just before the campsites. Turn right and follow the trail below the power lines through thick Bishop pine forest. That trail ends at a fire road at 2 miles. Turn right on the fire road, quickly descending to the highway where you turn left to follow its shoulder. Use extreme caution walking this narrow section of highway. At 2⅝ miles reach the Ocean Cove Store, a good place for a break.

You can pay an entrance fee here and walk through the private campground to the Stillwater Cove Park boundary at 3 miles. Otherwise, walk the road ⅛ mile, then turn right after passing the private land, descending toward the shoreline at 3 miles. An informal trail follows the bluff overlooking a rugged series of points and coves and returns to the highway at 3½ miles.

CCT follows the narrow highway shoulder down to the Stillwater Cove short-term parking area. A short side trail on the right heads down past a grove of fantastically gnarled redwoods to the restroom and picnic tables beside the cove. From the short-term parking, cross the highway, then ascend the stairs up the canyon wall to the parking lot, then take the entrance drive out to the highway. If the stairs are closed you must cautiously walk the narrow highway shoulder.

From the park south the land is part of the Timber Cove subdivision and posted "NO TRESPASSING." At 5 miles Timber Cove Lodge perches on a point. Behind the lodge on the tip of the point sits California's smallest state park. It's ¼ acre holds a 100-foot-tall Benny Bufano statue. You can reach the statue by taking the access road that rounds the lodge's north end and turns south behind it, leading to the statue. Return the same way.

CCT continues south on Highway 1's shoulder past a private campground. After passing the Fort Ross Store at 5⅞ miles, take the gravel road on the right that heads out to Windermere Point, once the site of a lumber mill but now vacant and publicly owned with a great view north. Swing around the point and return to the highway at 6⅜ miles. Cautiously follow the narrow shoulder down to Kolmer Gulch.

As you climb out of the gulch, the highway reaches a graded notch in low hills. Step over the old fence here around 6⅝ miles and descend the faint trail angling south to the bluffs. Then follow the bluff's edge toward Fort Ross. The trail winds over the grassy terrace past scenic points and coves and wind- and wave-carved tidal rocks. It heads south to Northwest Cape at 7¾ miles, then turns east and traces the edge of the cliffs overlooking Fort Ross Cove. The trail rises through low, rounded hillocks to a gate at 8 miles, crosses the fort's access road, then runs along the edge of the large parking lot, arriving at the Fort Ross Visitor Center at 8¼ miles.

SUGGESTED ROUND TRIPS & LOOPS: For an easy round trip of about 1¼ miles, walk south from South Gerstle Cove to the southern park boundary and back. Stillwater Cove Park has a nice short trail up Stockhoff Creek, a fine coastal creek lush with redwoods and ferns. From Fort Ross you can walk the Coastal Trail northwest to the highway and back, 3¼ miles round trip.

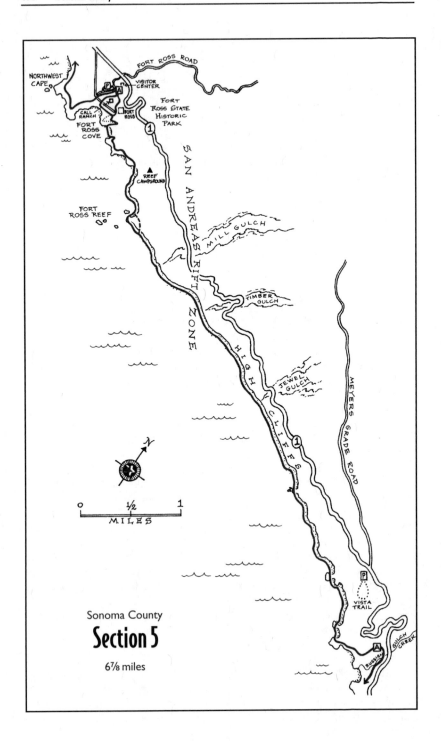

NORTHWEST CAPE

FORT ROSS ROAD

VISITOR CENTER

CALL RANCH

FORT ROSS

FORT ROSS COVE

FORT ROSS STATE HISTORIC PARK

1

SAN ANDREAS RIFT ZONE

REEF CAMPGROUND

FORT ROSS REEF

MILL GULCH

TIMBER GULCH

HIGH CLIFFS

JEWEL GULCH

MEYERS GRADE ROAD

1

N

0    ½    1
M I L E S

VISTA TRAIL

RUSSIAN GULCH CREEK

Sonoma County
**Section 5**

6⅞ miles

# SECTION 5
# Fort Ross State Historic Park to Russian Gulch

**DISTANCE:** 6⅞ miles (11.1 kilometers).

**OPEN TO:** Hikers.

**SURFACE:** Trail, beach, rocky tideline.

**ACCESS POINT:** Fort Ross Visitor Center.

**HOW TO GET THERE:** Turn west off Highway 1 12 miles north of Jenner at Milepost 33.00 into Fort Ross entrance and park at the visitor center lot.

**OTHER ACCESS:** Fort Ross Reef Campground.

**DIFFICULTY:** Difficult.

**ELEVATION GAIN/LOSS:** 470 feet+/560 feet-.

**CAUTIONS:** Hike requires boulder hopping, walking uneven beaches, and steep climbs and descents. It is only passable at a 3.0 foot or lower tide in calm weather. Wear sturdy boots and don't go solo.

**FURTHER INFORMATION:** Fort Ross State Historic Park (707)847-3286.

**FACILITIES:** Fort Ross has water, phone, restrooms and picnic tables. Chemical toilets at Fort Ross Cove, Reef Campground (water too), and Russian Gulch.

**CAMPGROUNDS:** Reef Campground is 1.6 miles south of the Fort Ross entrance.

**LODGING:** Several motels are north of Fort Ross.

This hike begins with an easy walk through the historic Russian fort to scenic Fort Ross Cove, gets rougher climbing over bluffs to Reef Campground, then explores one of the roughest and most remote areas on the California shore, Sonoma's Lost Coast. This dramatic terrain results from the proximity of the San Andreas Fault, which comes ashore amidst these high bluffs, causing this land to rise steeply from the sea. Most of the hike follows the base of cliffs far below the highway where you must scramble over rocks, walk on slippery, uneven cobbles, and make several steep climbs and descents. It's a stimulating trek for fit hikers, passable only in calm weather when the tide is ebbing. Sonoma's Lost Coast has a wilderness feeling. An Alternate Route follows the highway.

Start at the Fort Ross Visitor Center where excellent displays discuss the Kashaya Pomo, Russians and Americans who lived on and worked this land. Walk through the museum if it's open, or around to its right if it's closed and descend the paved path through a cypress grove past historic Call Ranch buildings to the fort at ¼ mile. Fort Ross testifies to the hardships and ingenuity, but ultimate failure, of the Russians who tried to settle here.

From the fort's southwest corner, the trail winds down the bluff to Fort Ross Cove beyond ½ mile. Walk the cove's beach, passing a side trail on the left to the old Russian cemetery. CCT climbs the narrow path up the bluff, reaching the top at ¾ mile. Follow the trail along the bluff's edge, descending to the end of the Reef Campground road before 1⅛ miles where you'll find water and an outhouse, the last of civilization for the next 5¾ miles. Cross the small dirt parking area, hop over the stile and descend the trail to the rocky beach.

At 1¼ miles you reach a rocky point impassable at high tide. If this is the case, climb the crumbly bluff 80 feet to a broken down fence along a hogback. Walk up the fenceline to the top of the bluff at 1½ miles and find the rough trail angling back down to the beach. Use caution on this detour. Head south along a beach of large rocks. Beyond piles of driftwood around 1⅞ miles, walk a beach of smaller rocks. Round a sandstone shelf and pass the mouth of Mill Gulch. The beach narrows at 2⅛ miles.

The beach turns east to meet the heart of the San Andreas fault at 2½ miles,

## The Russians at Fort Ross

One of the most unusual places in California perches atop a bluff overlooking the wild and scenic Sonoma coast beside a small sheltered cove. Fort Ross State Historic Park takes you back to March 1812 when 25 Russians and 80 native Alaskans dropped anchor in the cove and established what they hoped would be a permanent colony for czarist Russia. The Russians also hoped to compete with the Spaniards for the territory, establish trade with the Spaniards, and produce enough food in northern California to supply their struggling Alaska colonies.

The Russians had been visiting the region for 40 years to hunt sea otter pelts, the softest, densest and most valuable furs on the market. They paid the local residents, the Kashaya Pomo, trade goods for the right to build the fort at the Pomo village of May-tee-nee, then built their sturdy fort at a great defensive location and guarded it with 41 cannons before the Spaniards at the Presidio in San Francisco were aware of the Russian settlement.

The Russians hurried to solidify their California position, starting farms at Bodega, Freestone and Willow Creek. Fort Rossiya grew to a population of 300 to 400 with 50 or 60 buildings. Europeans even used the fort as a meeting place when exploring the wild California landscape. The efficient native Alaskan hunters gathered about 200,000 otter pelts, ranging as far as Baja California, but after just twenty years, the economic viability of the fort had declined with the otter population — the sea otter was nearing extinction — and the failure of food crops due to harsh coastal weather and persistent gophers, insects and deer.

The Russians put the fort up for sale in 1839. After the Spaniards declined to buy it, John Sutter (who later figured prominently in the California gold rush) bought the fort for 30,000 pesos. By 1842 the Russians were gone from California. Sutter moved equipment and livestock to his Sacramento Valley ranch, leaving the fort to the Pomos, who reclaimed the land and occupied it for another 30 years.

In 1873 the Call family bought the fort and 15,000 acres, ranching and logging the area well into the 20th century. The Call House sits next to the fort today. The state bought the remains of the fort in 1906, and over the years has carefully reproduced the fort and buildings. To vividly experience this unique slice of California history, don't miss visiting the restored fort and its excellent museum and bookstore.

marked by the huge slide of gray mud on the cliff. The rock is fractured so severely here it's reduced to pulverized clay called mylonite. You leave the Pacific Plate for the North American Plate in the next ¼ mile as the sand becomes dark. Pass Timber Gulch at 2¾ miles.

Reach a narrow spot beyond 3 miles passable only at tides less than 4.5 feet. The dark sandy beach offers welcome relief from rock hopping. The sand ends around 3⅝ miles, and at 3⅞ miles a steep side trail climbs to the highway far above. Scramble over a jumble of rocks at 4 miles, then descend to a rocky beach. The beach provides easy walking to 4⅜ miles, where you need a medium tide to proceed. Then walk a broad sandy beach past seeps and a steep gulch.

At 4¾ miles you must scramble over a rocky point. Pick your way to the top, then scramble down large rocks to the beach. More easy beach walking ends at a narrow spot where cliffs crowd the beach at 5¼ miles. Climb over a rock shelf and walk a gravelly beach. Where you pass two gigantic sea stacks at tideline around 5⅜ miles, pick your way over uneven terrain, scrambling between massive rocks and hopping over tidepools.

Walk the beach to a huge, domed rock outcrop jutting seaward at 5¾ miles. To continue you must carefully scramble up the steep chute between the outcrop and the precipitous headlands. Reach the top 75 feet above the beach on a narrow hogback (see photograph on page 171), then use extreme caution scrambling steeply down the other side. Though not a technical climb, we don't recommend it for anyone afraid of heights.

Walk a small rocky beach briefly followed by a long sandy one, interspersed with short rock scrambles. After a big sea stack at 6¼ miles, pass a beautiful sandy-bottomed tidepool. You can explore it at low tide or take a cooling dip on a warm day.

The beach ends at 6⅜ miles at the south end of the cove. The trail climbs a steep crumbly 200-foot bluff on an informal but well-used trail. To get to it, walk 100 feet on tidal rocks from the end of the cove to where the cliff is sloughing, less steep than the surrounding slope. Stay on the path others have created. At the top the views of the coast you just walked and south to Bodega Head are stunning. The well-worn trail follows bluff's edge overlooking a pocket beach, then turns inland at 6 miles, angling downhill toward the gravel Russian Gulch parking area. The trail passes a grassy area above the beach then goes through coastal scrub thick with poison oak, ending at the parking lot at 6⅞ miles.

ALTERNATE ROUTE: From the end of the Reef Campground road walk up the canyon one mile to Highway 1, then turn right and walk the highway shoulder. It climbs to 600 feet above the water for stunning views, passing the ¾-mile wheelchair-accessible Vista loop Trail at 5¾ miles, then drops to Russian Gulch at 7½ miles.

SUGGESTED ROUNDS TRIPS & LOOPS: From the visitor center explore the fort and Fort Ross Cove, then walk south to Reef Campground and return for an easy 1½ miles round trip. A short side trail leads from Fort Ross Cove uphill to the historic Russian cemetery.

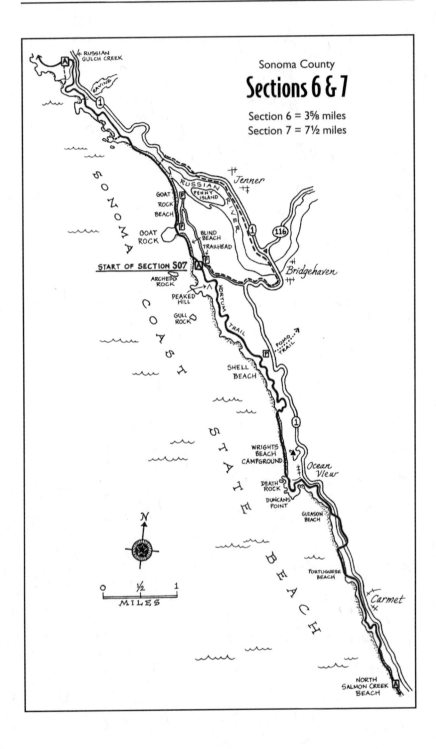

Sonoma County
# Sections 6 & 7
Section 6 = 3⅝ miles
Section 7 = 7½ miles

## SECTION 6
# Russian Gulch to Blind Beach Trailhead, Sonoma Coast State Beach

**DISTANCE:** 3⅝ miles (5.8 kilometers).

**OPEN TO:** Hikers.

**SURFACE:** Trail, beach, highway shoulder.

**ACCESS POINT:** Russian Gulch.

**HOW TO GET THERE:** Turn west off Highway 1 3 miles north of Jenner into the Russian Gulch parking lot.

**OTHER ACCESS:** Several points along Highway 1.

**DIFFICULTY:** Easy.

**ELEVATION GAIN/LOSS:** 360 feet+/200 feet-.

**CAUTIONS:** Several very steep trails on Alternate Route. Very narrow shoulder for short walk on Highway 1.

**FURTHER INFORMATION:** Sonoma Coast State Beach (707)875-3483.

**FACILITIES:** Chemical toilet at Russian Gulch. Chemical toilet and water at Goat Rock Beach parking lot.

**CAMPGROUNDS:** Willow Creek and Pomo Campgrounds south of Russian River.

**LODGING:** Jenner Inn Bed and Breakfast (707)865-2377.

This short, dramatic section takes you from a pocket beach, along a high marine terrace full of wildflowers onto a broad beach where you cross the Russian River mouth, finishing up at a dramatic overlook of Goat Rock and Blind Beach.

From the parking lot at Russian Gulch, CCT heads for the highway and climbs south on its west shoulder. Near the top of the hill, just past where the highway barrier ends around ⅜ mile, climb the 10-foot embankment and look for an old railroad bed that heads west along the base of the little knoll. When the huge redwood trees were being stripped from the hills, this old railroad ran up Russian Gulch and delivered logs to a mill and landing site overlooking Russian Gulch Beach. Follow the bed west, watching for ties buried in the dirt, to the point high above the ocean for great views. The road returns to the highway at ¾ mile, where it's necessary to walk a very narrow shoulder for a few hundred feet.

After you pass the "MUNIZ RANCH" sign east of the highway, watch for the informal trail around ⅞ mile made by past explorers. It leaves the highway, dropping down the ravine to a culvert, then climbs south to the marine terrace. Follow the bluff edge to 1⅛ miles and look for a path coming straight down from the highway. It leads to a rugged path that drops down to the beach. If you aren't afraid of a fairly steep trail, and if the tide is low, you can walk a beautiful rocky shore for ½ mile, climbing another steep trail just before the "no-pass" at the other end. The trail is accessible but tricky so use caution. The other choice is to return to the highway to avoid three steep and deep ravines that cut through the terrace.

Walk the shoulder to 1½ miles where the vegetation ends and leave the highway for another volunteer path. Follow it a few hundred feet to the trail that climbs from the tideline. Cross this trail and continue to the bluff's edge. Watch for the path at 1¾ miles that drops to the beach at the mouth of the Russian River. In summer when a sandbar closes off the river mouth, descend this trail to hit the beach before 2 miles. If the river is not crossable, take the Alternate Route.

Walk down the beach, often littered with driftwood, to the mouth of the river at 2½ miles. The large colony of harbor seals living on the sand bar should not be approached or disturbed. Keep a distance of at least 150 feet between you and the seals. If the sand bar is in place, walk south onto popular Goat Rock Beach and continue toward Goat Rock, the huge flat-topped rock to the south.

At 3⅛ miles the beach ends at the parking lot. Climb the riprap, cross the lot, and walk down to Blind Beach, which may be closed during high surf. If so, retreat north to the road and follow it south to the Blind Beach parking area. If the beach is open, follow it south and take the maintained trail up the bluff around 3½ miles. It climbs the 170-foot bluff and arrives at the lot at 3⅝ miles.

## The Russian River

World class salmon fishery, vacation playground for San Francisco, giant redwoods, Stumptown, and sewer discharge all help describe the beautiful river that flows 110 miles from the hot inland Mendocino County hills before pouring into the ocean near the village of Jenner in Sonoma County. This diverse river flows through chaparral and oak woodlands, fir and redwood forests, drains the second largest freshwater marsh in northern California, the Laguna de Santa Rosa, and provides drinking water for most of Sonoma County as well as receives treated wastewater.

Historically, the Pomo people lived along the river. The Russians explored the area in the early 1800s, and the Mexican government claimed the land for their own, dividing the area into large ranchos in the 1840s. In the 1850s the lumber industry moved in, building a mill on the river at Bridgehaven in 1860. The present town of Guerneville was known as Stumptown because the lush groves of immense redwoods growing on the river bank were cut. In 1887 the North Coast Pacific Railroad was extended from Sausalito to Duncans Mills four miles upriver from the coast, making it an important rail center. Tourists soon started arriving on the railroad, and resort camps and hotels were built. Today the railroad is gone but little Duncans Mills is an historic district with several old buildings housing tourist businesses and a small railroad museum.

The quality of the river has declined steadily over the years because of logging, farming, and sewer discharge. Tourism declined from its heyday of big band dances and big hotels to the point that the small towns became somewhat decrepit. In the 1980s, however, tourism made a comeback, and the river towns are reviving along with it. The salmon and steelhead have been declared endangered, prompting local and state agencies to pay more attention. Plans are in the works to protect the river and begin restoration. Huge stubborn problems remain, but the State Legislature passed a budget in 1997 that included $1 million for the Coastal Conservancy to work on access and restoration projects along the Russian River.

*CCT hikers approach the mouth of the Russian River.*

**ALTERNATE ROUTE:** If you can't cross the Russian River, find the steep trail from the beach just north of the mouth climbing the bluff to the highway. Walk the shoulder south through the quaint town of Jenner, cross the river bridge, and climb west then north to the Blind Beach parking lot, about 3½ miles total.

**SUGGESTED ROUND TRIPS & LOOPS:** You can reach ¼-mile long Russian Gulch Beach, rimmed by cliffs, via the ⅜-mile trail from the corner of the parking lot through the willows. In winter the creek runs high at times and may be hard to cross, but it's dry in summer. From the Goat Rock Beach parking lot walk about ¼ mile north to the river mouth to check out the harbor seals, or walk south over Goat Rock onto Blind Beach and continue to the south end, 1½ miles round trip.

## SECTION 7
## Blind Beach Trailhead to Salmon Creek, Sonoma Coast State Beach

**DISTANCE:** 7½ miles (12.1 kilometers).

**OPEN TO:** Hikers. Bicyclists on road.

**SURFACE:** Trail, beach, tidal rocks, highway shoulder.

**ACCESS POINT:** Blind Beach Trailhead.

**HOW TO GET THERE:** From the junction of Highway 116 (River Road) and Highway 1, go south one mile to Goat Rock Road. Follow it west .5 mile to the trailhead.

**OTHER ACCESS:** Shell Beach, many parking spots along Highway 1.

**DIFFICULTY:** Easy.

**ELEVATION GAIN/LOSS:** 280 feet+/480 feet-.

CAUTIONS:Watch for dangerous surf and highway traffic.

FURTHER INFORMATION:Sonoma Coast State Beach (707)875-3483.

FACILITIES:Chemical toilets at access point, Shell Beach and Salmon Creek. Restrooms, picnic area and water at Wrights Beach.

CAMPGROUNDS:Willow Creek and Pomo walk-in Campgrounds are just east. Wrights Beach Campground is on route.

LODGING:Bodega Bay has lodges, motels and B&Bs.

MAP:See page 188.

Here the CCT offers a great combination of views, wildflowers, rocky tidal areas, and short sandy beaches. From the Blind Beach Trailhead 200 feet above the beach, you can see north to Jenner, the Russian River mouth, and Salt Point.

From the parking area, walk south 300 feet to the Kortum Trail. Follow it down through a broad swale then up to a notch between two hills at ¼ mile. The view opens out to the marine terraces with Bodega Head ten miles south and Point Reyes beyond. For even better views, take the short spur west to Peaked Hill.

The trail descends east and south to the tabletop flat marine terrace. At ⅝ mile you pass a huge rock outcrop used regularly for rock climbing. This rock was a sea stack jutting from the ocean, just like the ones offshore now, before being drylanded by the rising wave-cut terrace. The trail follows the bluff's edge past more sea stacks both on and offshore. At one mile it cuts inland to wind through a gully. Continue across the level terrace, jogging east to cross a bridge over a creek at 1½ miles. Return to bluff's edge and follow it to Shell Beach at 1⅞ miles. A short side trail on the right deadends at rocky Shell Beach.

Cross the parking area to find the trail south. It crosses a bridge over a creek to traverse headlands with thick coastal scrub. During spring and summer wildflowers bloom profusely here. After following the bluff's edge, the trail turns east and crosses a bridge over another gully. Traverse the headlands until 2⅜ miles where the trail drops into Furlong Gulch to cross its creek. A dark sand beach lies at its mouth. CCT climbs out of the gulch to follow the bluff edge. The trail soon turns inland to a paved road end at 2⅞ miles, one of several roads built for a subdivision halted by coastal advocates, who saved this beautiful area for public use.

Head south across a bridge over a gully and veer toward the bluff. At 3 miles the trail drops to Wrights Beach. Walk the sand south past a campground, picnic area and restrooms around 3¾ miles. Continue along the beach, which ends before 4¼ miles at Death Rock, so named because of huge waves that sometimes break over the rocks and wash people into the dangerous, sometimes deadly surf. Climb the trail to Duncan's Point and follow the one lane road circling around the point. On the south side a trail drops to a small beach and protected cove, but even at low tide you cannot walk the tideline to Portuguese Beach. The Coastal Trail reaches Highway 1 at 4⅝ miles. From here to section's end, the road hugs the blufftop, with trails dropping to the beach in several places. At low tide you can explore the rocky tidal zone, but beware of large waves.

Continue south on the narrow highway shoulder, watching for places to walk off the shoulder. After passing houses hanging precariously on the cliff (as of this writing three of them are starting to slip off), the road descends to Portuguese Beach at 5½ miles. Walk this short beach for almost ½ mile, then climb a trail to a point before 6 miles. Just across the point is Schoolhouse Beach. Since there's no safe way down, walk the highway past the vacation subdivision of Carmet. Around 6½ miles an unmarked but official trail descends to the rocks 40 feet below. You can take this route ¼ mile before coming back to the road, or just stay

## Why It's Called the Kortum Trail

For the past forty years, virtually every time Sonoma County's environment or public access has been threatened, Bill Kortum has been there fighting for the earth and for your rights. When PG&E started building a nuclear power plant atop the San Andreas fault on Bodega Head in the early 1960s, no environmental movement was fighting local issues. Bill Kortum joined with a coalition to scuttle the project. In the mid-60s he worked to establish Salt Point State Park, now the largest natural area protected on the Sonoma coast.

In 1968 Bill Kortum and other Sonoma County activists founded COAAST, Citizens Organized to Acquire Access to State Tidelands, to fight plans for the Sea Ranch development which tried to close ten miles of the coast to public access. See Section 1 feature for that story. His Sea Ranch experience led Bill to become the chair of a coalition of 105 organizations to put Proposition 20, the Coastal Protection Initiative, on the 1972 California ballot. They fought to get it passed, despite intense opposition and spending from development interests, and won. The Coastal Initiative affirmed the public's right to coastal access and established the Coastal Commission.

In 1976 Kortum won a seat on the Sonoma County Board of Supervisors, making an environmentalist majority. Because the new supervisors made land use decisions based on ecology, conservation and controlled growth, several groups launched a recall campaign. The environmental majority was removed from office in one of the county's most disastrous episodes for the environment.

Still, Kortum continued his selfless service to the county. In 1982 he dreamed up the idea of Coastwalk, thereby launching a long-term commitment to establishing the California Coastal Trail. When Coastwalk planned the CCT Whole Hike of 1996, Bill Kortum not only helped it happen, he went along, walking 450 miles from Oregon to San Francisco and celebrating his 69th birthday on the trek. As we walked, Bill was there encouraging Richard and Bob to write this book.

Bill Kortum has been active in public transit issues and in deciding how Santa Rosa and other cities should dispose of wastewater. His influence, based on honesty, principals and well thought ideas, has been enormous. Without his work, and that of many others in COAAST, our coastline would be crowded with development and access would be negligible. He's earned the title "Dean of Sonoma County environmentalists."

So after State Parks established a trail across the dramatic headlands south of the Russian River from Blind Beach to Wrights Beach, they named the path for lifetime Sonoma County resident and environmental legend, Bill Kortum, honoring the man who has helped saved so much of the Sonoma County and California coast for public access.

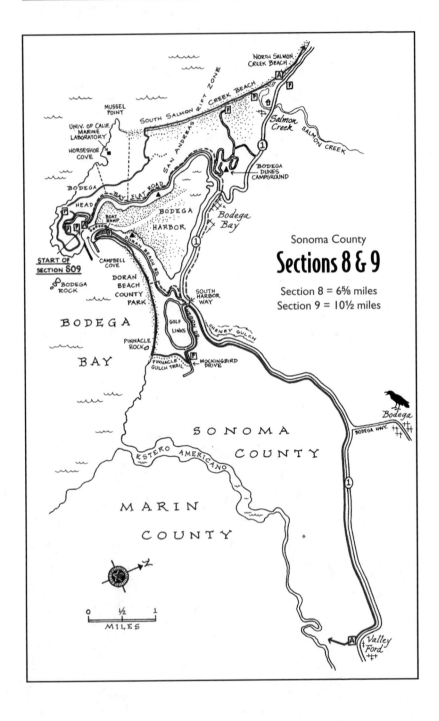

NORTH SALMON
CREEK BEACH

SOUTH SALMON CREEK BEACH

SAN ANDREAS RIFT ZONE

MUSSEL
POINT

Salmon
Creek

UNIV. OF CALIF.
MARINE
LABORATORY

SALMON CREEK

HORSESHOE
COVE

BODEGA
DUNES
CAMPGROUND

BODEGA
HEAD

BAY FLAT ROAD

BOAT
RAMP

BODEGA
HARBOR

Bodega
Bay

Sonoma County
# Sections 8 & 9

Section 8 = 6⅝ miles
Section 9 = 10½ miles

START OF
SECTION S09

DORAN BEACH RD.

CAMPBELL
COVE

BODEGA
ROCK

DORAN
BEACH
COUNTY
PARK

SOUTH
HARBOR
WAY

BODEGA

GOLF
LINKS

NELSON DR.

CHENEY GULCH

BAY

PINNACLE
ROCK

PINNACLE
GULCH TRAIL

MOCKINGBIRD
DRIVE

Bodega

BODEGA HWY.

S O N O M A
C O U N T Y

ESTERO AMERICANO

M A R I N

C O U N T Y

0    ½    1
M I L E S

Valley
Ford

on the road. At 7 miles look for a trail down to rocky Coleman Beach. You can usually walk from here onto Salmon Creek Beach. If the tide is too high, continue on the road. Either way, walk to the mouth of Salmon Creek at 7½ miles where a parking lot and outhouse are on the bluff near a short trail to the beach.

**SUGGESTED ROUND TRIPS & LOOPS:** From Shell Beach walk the Pomo Trail over the ridge to Pomo Campground, then loop back to Highway 1 on one-lane, lightly used Willow Creek Road. Walk the highway south to Goat Rock Road, turn right and follow it to the Blind Beach Trailhead, then take the Kortum Trail south to Shell Beach, a loop of 8 miles. A good 4-mile round trip hike from Shell Beach takes Pomo Trail to Pomo Campground and back. From Shell Beach explore the coastal terrace, 4 miles round trip either north or south.

## SECTION 8
# Salmon Creek Beach to Campbell Cove, Bodega Head, Sonoma Coast State Beach

**DISTANCE:** 6⅝ miles, or 5¼ miles without Bodega Head Loop (10.7 or 8.4 kilometers).

**OPEN TO:** Hikers. Equestrians on part.

**SURFACE:** Beach, trail.

**ACCESS POINT:** North Salmon Creek Beach parking lot.

**HOW TO GET THERE:** Turn west off Highway 1 2 miles north of Bodega Bay, ¼ mile north of the Salmon Creek bridge into North Salmon Creek parking lot.

**OTHER ACCESS:** For South Salmon Creek parking lot, turn west at the south end of the Salmon Creek bridge. Also access from Bodega Dunes or Bodega Head.

**DIFFICULTY:** Moderate.

**ELEVATION GAIN/LOSS:** 240 feet+/160 feet-.

**CAUTIONS:** Dangerous surf at Salmon Creek Beach. Please stay on trail through Marine Reserve.

**FURTHER INFORMATION:** Sonoma Coast State Beach (707)875-3483.

**FACILITIES:** Chemical toilets at both ends and at South Salmon Creek parking area.

**CAMPGROUNDS:** State Park's large Bodega Dunes Campground is near the route.

**LODGING:** Several lodges and B&Bs in the Bodega Bay area.

This wonderful walk explores sandy beach, windswept dunes and Bodega Head hard by the San Andreas fault. The Head offers dramatic views of forty miles of coastline, while Sonoma County's longest sandy beach offers great beachcombing, surf fishing, surfing and family outings. Our description begins at Salmon Creek, but look at the creek's mouth to decide exactly where. In the winter it usually flows into the surf, and in summer a sand bar usually forms. If the mouth is flowing, walk or drive to the South Salmon Creek parking lot.

Coastwalk, CalTrans, the Bodega Bay Grange and Sonoma County are exploring the possibility of building a walking path from the north end to the south end of town. Such a route would be an good Alternate Route for CCT since, in addition to serving the town, it would not require a boat shuttle as the current CCT route does south of Campbell Cove.

Walk the beach south toward Mussel Point, the northern end of Bodega Head in the distance. In winter the beach narrows so that waves may run to the base of the dunes. In that case you must retreat to the dunes to pass. In summer a wide flat beach makes passage easy.

Around one mile from Salmon Creek, a wheelchair-accessible ramp crosses the dunes to a parking area. You pass through the San Andreas Rift Zone here as it comes ashore to cross the dunes. As you approach Mussel Point start looking for a notch in the dunes. Find the notch at 2¼ miles, about ¼ mile before the beach ends at cliffs. The trail through the notch, often unmarked, is the third trail into the dunes south of the ramp. Before taking it, consider a side trip to explore the end of the beach, which has a cave with a freshwater spring and three narrow low-tide channels.

Take the trail into the dunes. If you've found the right trail it soon comes to a low structure of peeled logs marking a junction. Go straight, heading toward tall dunes in the distance. The shifting sand can make the trail tricky to follow so watch for the most trodden trail, marked with green posts with an angled top. At the base of the dune, the trail veers to the right and climbs the face of the dune.

Climb to a saddle between the high dunes, then descend to another junction at 3 miles. Take the trail straight ahead marked "BODEGA HEAD – 1.7 MILES." The other trails return to the beach or lead to Bodega Dunes Campground. At 3⅛ miles you pass through a stile in the fence marking the University of California Marine Lab property. Please stay on the trail here to avoid disturbing research projects in the area. Follow the trail winding through the dunes, crossing a narrow paved road to the lab around 3⅞ miles.

This road marks a transition from dunes to the soil and rocks defining Bodega Head's hilly terrain. Climb the trail south to a junction at 4¼ miles. The short side trail on the right climbs to a hilltop for a view of the marine lab beside scenic Horseshoe Cove, with green Mussel Point stretching seaward and Salmon Creek Beach beyond. CCT follows the trail on the left, descending to the main parking area on Bodega Head at 4⅝ miles. This popular spot set high on cliffs overlooking a rocky shoreline has great gray whale viewing.

From the parking area you have two choices. One choice is to walk down the road to Campbell Cove, ending the walk at 5¼ miles. The longer choice follows the spectacular trail around the perimeter of Bodega Head. To do so, take the trail that climbs gently south along the edge of the cliffs. It circles the Head's high bluffs, with great views south to Bodega Rock, Tomales Point and Point Reyes and east to Bodega Bay. At 5⅞ miles you come to the east parking lot. From here you must follow the road, snaking downhill to Campbell Cove at 6⅝ miles. It passes the "Hole in the Head," a massive excavation for the foundation of a nuclear power plant that was never built. In one of California's first major environmental battles, outraged citizens effectively organized to scuttle the project.

**SUGGESTED ROUND TRIPS & LOOPS:** From Salmon Creek walk Salmon Creek Beach south to its end and back, about 5 miles. From either Bodega Head parking area, walk the loop trail around Bodega Head, 1¾ miles.

## SECTION 9
# Campbell Cove, Bodega Head, to Valley Ford

DISTANCE: 10½ miles (16.5 kilometers).

OPEN TO: Hikers. Bicyclists on road.

SURFACE: Beach, trail, highway shoulder.

ACCESS POINT: Campbell Cove at Bodega Head.

HOW TO GET THERE: Turn west off Highway 1 at the north end of the town of Bodega Bay onto Eastside Road, then turn west on Bay Flat Road and go 3 miles to the Campbell Cove parking lot where the road makes a sharp turn uphill.

OTHER ACCESS: Doran Regional Park, Pinnacle Gulch Trailhead, along Highway 1.

DIFFICULTY: Easy.

ELEVATION GAIN/LOSS: 420 feet+/380 feet-.

CAUTIONS: It is best to arrange a boat ride across Bodega Harbor ahead of time. The south end of Doran Beach may be flooded at high or medium tide.

FURTHER INFORMATION: Sonoma Coast State Beach (707)875-3483. Doran and Westside Regional Parks (707)875-3540.

FACILITIES: Picnic tables at Campbell Cove, water and restrooms at Doran Regional Park, store and restaurants at Valley Ford.

CAMPGROUNDS: Doran and Westside Regional Parks and Bodega Dunes State Campground are all nearby.

LODGING: Lodges and B&Bs in Bodega Bay and Valley Ford.

MAP: See page 194.

The CCT's final Sonoma County leg offers a walk first on a beach with calm surf, then up a small creek. The last portion requires a long highway walk. We advocate public purchase of the undeveloped headlands between Bodega Bay and Dillon Beach so hikers can experience this dramatic landscape and CCT users can avoid the long highway walk. For now the only way to finish Sonoma County without trespassing across uninhabited, open farmland is to walk the highway.

To do this section as described, you must arrange a boat ride across the harbor mouth. Ask some fishermen at the Westside County Park boat ramp for a lift. Without a boat ride, through-hikers must follow the **Alternate Route**, while day hikers can start at Doran Regional Park.

Our walk starts at Campbell Cove on the leeward side of Bodega Head and just inside the harbor jetty. Take the ¼-mile boat ride across Bodega Harbor to the dock at Doran Regional Park. CCT crosses the sand spit to the beach on the ocean side, but consider the ¼-mile side trip to the end of the spit. From there you can walk east along the entire ocean shore of Doran Spit.

Walk east along the ocean shore, usually very calm here and safe for swimming. Gradually the beach curves southeast and south. After you leave Doran Park, continue south until you come to large rocks at 2 miles. If the tide is too high to get through a low tunnel in the rocks, you must retrace your steps about ½ mile, cross the low dunes to the road, walk it south to Highway 1, and turn right to walk the highway shoulder to Valley Ford. Otherwise continue past the tidal rocks.

At 2¼ miles you need to find Pinnacle Gulch Trail where a few wooden steps climb from the beach. Take this trail, climbing gradually up the gulch. Large houses perch above the gulch on both sides. After a short steep climb, the trail ends at the county parking lot at 2⅞ miles. Walk the road north briefly and turn right on Heron Drive, the main road through the upscale Bodega Harbour subdivision and golf course. At 3⅝ miles turn right on South Harbor Way, descend to Highway 1 at 3⅞ miles, and turn right. From here to Valley Ford CCT follows the highway shoulder.

Follow the highway up Cheney Gulch, then through rolling farm lands. At 7 miles Bodega Highway forks left ½ mile to the little village of Bodega, famous mostly as the location for Alfred Hitchcock's "The Birds." Coastwalk's home base, Sebastopol, lies ten miles farther inland. CCT continues along the highway shoulder through pastoral hills all the way to Valley Ford at 10¼ miles.

**ALTERNATE ROUTE:** Without a boat ride, through-hikers must walk Bay Flat Road to the village of Bodega Bay and walk Highway 1 all the way to Valley Ford.

**SUGGESTED ROUND TRIPS & LOOPS:** Walk Pinnacle Gulch Trail to the beach. If the ocean is calm and you know the tide is ebbing, with caution you can walk north or south along the coast to wonderful pocket beaches. At very low tides it's possible to get around cliffs to the Estero Americano and the Marin County line, about 1¾ miles from Pinnacle Gulch. At low tide you can also walk north and west 2½ miles to the end of Doran Spit. Don't get trapped by the rising tide.

---

**HOW TO IMPROVE CCT HERE:** Acquire the undeveloped headlands south from Pinnacle Gulch to Estero Americano in Sonoma County, and the Marin headlands between Estero Americano and Dillon Beach, then route the CCT along these dramatic bluffs and get the CCT off the highway.

---

# Marin County

**M**ARIN COUNTY IS BLESSED with 40 percent of its land protected in parks. Along its magnificent Pacific coastline, nearly all the land has been protected except in the far north. Because of the historic foresight of citizens and government here, the public can walk almost the entire Pacific coast of Marin County plus hundreds of miles of inland trails. In Marin County's 72¾ miles of Coastal Trail from Tomales Point to the Golden Gate Bridge, the CCT follows trails and beaches for almost 59 miles, more than 80 percent of the total. Of the 14 miles that CCT follows roads in Marin, only a quarter mile is on a highway.

You'll find startling views from many points along Marin's Coastal Trail. Marin County has more than its share of dramatic landforms: the drowned valleys of Tomales Bay, Drake's Estero and Bolinas Lagoon, old-growth-forest draped Inverness Ridge, the immense marine terrace of

Point Reyes, the steep slopes of Mount Tamalpais and the Marin Headlands. Beyond the Marin mainland you'll often see San Francisco Bay or the Farallon Islands in the distance. Sometimes surprising vistas of the San Francisco skyline appear from atop a remote windblown hill. At other times you'll see the north bay hills or mountains far to the south.

Marin's Coastal Trail begins in the tiny village of Valley Ford, following county roads through ranch land before reaching the coast at Dillon Beach. This inland route detours around steep rugged headlands held by ranchers and a mostly impassable tidal zone. After crossing Tomales Bay by boat, the Coastal Trail enters magnificent Point Reyes National Seashore to explore some of the most remarkable coastline in California. The CCT runs the length of Tomales Point, passing through lovely Tomales Bay State Park, then over Mount Vision. Then the Coastal Trail traverses designated wilderness in Point Reyes National Seashore for 15 miles, visiting some of the most spectacular scenery along the CCT. After visiting the small coastal villages of Bolinas and Stinson Beach, the CCT ascends the steep western slopes of Mount Tamalpais State Park. It then enters the Golden Gate National Recreation Area, climbing over three ridges with stunning views of the Bay Area. Marin's Coastal Trail concludes by dropping dramatically from the Marin Headlands to the north portal of the Golden Gate Bridge.

Did we mention the herds of tule elk and deer and abundant populations of birds of all shapes and sizes? What about the low-tide Alternate Route along one of the world's great tidepooling areas, Duxbury Reef? Altogether the trek through Marin County must be considered among the highlights of the California Coastal Trail.

# SECTION 1
# Valley Ford to Lawson's Landing, Dillon Beach

DISTANCE: 8 miles (12.9 kilometers).

OPEN TO: Hikers. Bicyclists on road.

SURFACE: Beach, road shoulder.

ACCESS POINT: Valley Ford.

HOW TO GET THERE: Take Highway 1 to Valley Ford just north of the Sonoma-Marin County line.

OTHER ACCESS: Anywhere along route.

DIFFICULTY: Easy.

ELEVATION GAIN/LOSS: 860 feet +/900 feet-.

CAUTIONS: Watch for vehicle traffic on road.

FURTHER INFORMATION: Lawson's Landing (707)878-2443.

FACILITIES: Store, gas station, restaurant in Valley Ford and Dillon Beach.

CAMPGROUNDS: Lawson's Landing is a private campground at the mouth of Tomales Bay.

LODGING: West Marin has several B&Bs.

Through most of Marin County a hiker can walk the CCT all the way to the Golden Gate on trails and beaches. However, this first Marin County CCT section requires the only significant road walking in the entire county. Narrow county roads roll through dairy land with occasional farmsteads dotting the hills. The road crosses the upper watersheds of the wildlife-rich Estero Americano and Estero de San Antonio. Paddlers launch canoes and kayaks at these crossings and boat down to the beaches at the mouths of the isolated and beautiful marine estuaries.

Valley Ford, where this walk begins, is noted for Christo's monumental artwork, *Running Fence*. Made of big nylon panels stretched between posts, it swept across Sonoma and Marin counties for 25 miles and through Valley Ford. *Running Fence* made a dramatic statement about both art and the environment as it billowed in the wind, reflecting light, and wound over hills and across valleys, finally dropping into the ocean west of Valley Ford. It made an important artistic and political statement in these parts in the 1970s because Christo considered the planning, public meetings, and differences of opinion part of the art process. After months securing county permits and permission from dozens of land owners to cross their land, Christo assembled a large team of volunteers to erect and take down the fence. The final product was up for only two weeks.

Valley Ford is only a block long so it isn't hard to find Valley Ford-Franklin School Road at the north end of town in front of Dinucci's Italian Dinners. At the street sign "VALLEY FORD ESTERO," head southwest on the road, crossing the Estero

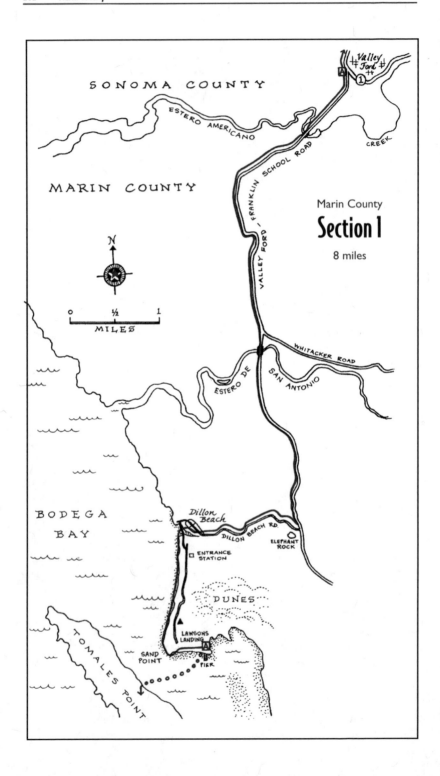

SONOMA COUNTY

ESTERO AMERICANO

CREEK

Valley Ford

MARIN COUNTY

Marin County
**Section 1**
8 miles

VALLEY FORD - FRANKLIN SCHOOL ROAD

N

0   ½   1
MILES

WHITACKER ROAD

ESTERO DE SAN ANTONIO

BODEGA
BAY

Dillon
Beach

DILLON BEACH RD.

ELEPHANT
ROCK

ENTRANCE
STATION

DUNES

LAWSONS
LANDING

SAND
POINT

PIER

TOMALES POINT

Americano at ¾ mile and entering Marin County. Continue 5 miles through rolling hills to Dillon Beach Road, dipping across the Estero de San Antonio at 4⅛ miles. Turn right on Dillon Beach Road at 5¾ miles. Elephant Rock near the junction has fine views of Bodega Head, Bodega Bay, Tomales Bay and Tomales Point. Descend to the small village of Dillon Beach at 6¾ miles. Pass the small store and restaurant on the left and walk to the beach. Cross the parking lot and walk south on the beach. This sand-dune backed beach rims the south end of Bodega Bay. Walk around Sand Point on the beach and come to hike's end at Lawson's Landing around 8 miles, depending on how much sand has piled up on the point. Lawson's is a funky fishing camp with a pier and boat rentals. They run a barge to the clam beds in season.

ALTERNATE ROUTE: Walk the road from the beach parking area at Dillon Beach through the Lawson's Landing entrance station and campground. Day use fee for Lawson's is $5. If you intend to continue south on Marin Section 2, you need to either arrange in advance a boat shuttle from Lawson's to Tomales Point or walk the Highway 1 shoulder south from Dillon Beach Road on a long but scenic detour.

## SECTION 2
# Lawson's Landing to Heart's Desire Beach, Tomales Bay State Park

DISTANCE: 9¾ miles by trail plus a ½-mile boat ride (15.7 + .8 kilometers).

OPEN TO: Hikers.

SURFACE: Trail, paved road, gravel road.

ACCESS POINT: Lawson's Landing.

HOW TO GET THERE: From the town of Tomales on Highway 1 go west on Dillon Beach Road 4 miles to Dillon Beach. Turn left at the beach and drive 1.1 miles to Lawson's Landing.

OTHER ACCESS: Pierce Point Ranch.

DIFFICULTY: Moderate.

ELEVATION GAIN/LOSS: 860 feet +/900 feet-.

CAUTIONS: To avoid a long detour on Highway 1 you must arrange in advance a boat ride from Lawson's Landing across to Tomales Point. Lawson's has told some hikers that a boat shuttle is no longer available from them. Be aware that the often calm bay can be windy and rough. You'll find no services before Upper Pierce Ranch. On the trail, avoid poison oak and don't approach the tule elk living on the point. Beyond Upper Pierce Ranch, the route follows ranch roads through grazing areas. Even though the ranch land is leased from the park and open to the public, respect the dairy operation and the privacy of farm buildings and residences.

FURTHER INFORMATION: Point Reyes National Seashore (415)464-5100, Tomales Bay State Park (415)669-1140, Lawson's Landing (415)878-2443 for a boat ride.

FACILITIES: Chemical toilets, water, camping (no showers) at Lawson's. Chemical toilet, phone and water at Upper Pierce Ranch. Restrooms, water at Tomales Bay State Park.

CAMPGROUNDS: Lawson's Landing, Tomales Bay State Park (hike and bike only).

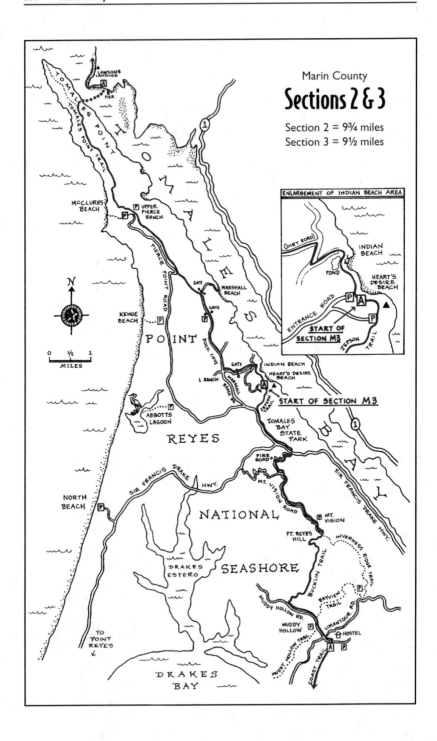

Once you have found a boat ride across Tomales Bay, you enter Phillip Burton Wilderness Area, part of Point Reyes National Seashore. Little used and lightly populated, Tomales Bay is 13 miles long by one mile wide, a flooded rift valley on the San Andreas fault, a scenic and biological wonder. Great white sharks, harbor seals (shark food), halibut, sting rays, a herring run, and small commercial oyster farming are just a sample of its resources.

Ask your boat captain to drop you at Blue Gum Beach directly across from Lawson's. Eucalyptus trees line the base of the hill. Find the trail leading up the bluff on the north end of the beach. In ⅜ mile you meet the main trail about 100 feet north of Lower Pierce Ranch site, where only a row of trees and a pond remain. The pond often attracts the tule elk herd. Take the path as it passes the pond and heads south. This is the Tomales Point Trail, actually the old ranch road, which follows the ridge with views of the Pacific to the west and Tomales Bay east. At 3⅝ miles the trail ends at the historic Upper Pierce Ranch, one of the original 19th century dairies on Point Reyes. A short interpretive trail explores the numerous old farm buildings, creamery, one-room school, a huge barn, and the ranch house.

Come to the Tomales Point Trailhead and a small parking area in front of the ranch buildings. An outhouse, water and a phone are down the road ⅝ mile toward the ocean at the McClures Beach parking area.

A few yards from the Pierce Ranch parking lot, pick up an unofficial and obscure trail starting by a guard rail. (The alternative is to walk the road, but the old farm roads and open land CCT follows are much safer and more pleasant.) Follow the trail up the west slope of the draw. At the top it turns left across the top of the draw, then goes to the right, descending gently to the elk fence at 4⅝ miles. Cross the fence at the cattle guard. Walk the farm road paralleling the main road. At 5⅜ miles you continue straight as the paved road swings sharply west. Walk the ranch road downhill. Around 6¼ miles you pass through a farm gate. The side trail east through the stile ends at secluded Marshall Beach, about one mile round trip from here. Continue straight ahead to a gravel road and the Marshall Beach parking lot at 6⅞ miles.

Our trail continues south on the gravel road for 1¼ miles to a road at 8⅛ miles. A park service sign identifies it as the "Historic L Ranch, established 1885." Turn left here and come to a locked gate at the top of the rise at 8⅜ miles. Duck under the fence. The trail drops steeply down the road through Bishop pine forest. Shortly beyond the sign marking the Tomales Bay State Park boundary at 9 miles, make a hard right turn onto a road with a pipe gate. At 9⅛ miles turn left onto a service road and soon come to Indian Beach. Three re-creations of bark dwellings used by the original inhabitants, the Coast Miwoks, sit near the shore. Walk south on the beach briefly, cross the bridge, and walk up the hill through a lovely forested area. At 9¾ miles you'll find the parking area for Heart's Desire Beach.

**SUGGESTED ROUND TRIPS & LOOPS:** Start at Heart's Desire Beach and walk CCT north to

Marshall Beach, 8 miles round trip. Start at Upper Pierce Ranch and walk CCT north to Blue Gum Beach or Tomales Point, 7¼ or 9⅜ miles round trip.

**HOW TO IMPROVE CCT HERE:** Sign the trail from Upper Pierce Ranch to Tomales Bay State Park.

## Tomales Bay

Tomales Bay exists as a feature of the San Andreas fault. Here two huge plates of the earth's crust move against each other, the Pacific plate west of the bay and the North American plate to the east. The crack in the earth's surface between the plates sinks in some locations, forming what geologists call a rift valley. Tomales Bay is a flooded rift valley, the deepest part of a valley that continues south for ten more miles to return to the ocean at Bolinas Lagoon. In the San Francisco earthquake of 1906, the greatest movement occurred in this lightly populated area, moving Point Reyes north as much as 16 feet in one dramatic shift.

Tomales Bay is sandy bottomed and shallow, although the main channel depth ranges to 60 feet. The bay, 13 miles long by one-half to one-and-a-half miles wide, nestles in a dramatic setting with the high hills of Tomales Point and Inverness Ridge rising abruptly on the west, and the more gradual rise of Bolinas Ridge to the east punctuated by numerous points and bays along the bayshore. Jewel-like, placid white-sand pocket beaches dot the western shore. Both Point Reyes National Seashore and Tomales Bay State Park encompass much of the shoreline.

The name Tomales probably originated from the Coast Miwok tribe's name for bay, tamal. Some say it's from the Coast Miwok word for westerner. The bay's eastern shore was well populated with Coast Miwok villages, the westernmost settlements of the Tamal Miwok who lived primarily near the western shore of northern San Francisco Bay. Still others claim the Mexican food tamales as the source.

The many piles of discarded shells, called middens, left by the Coast Miwok at villages along the bayshore attest to its abundant marine life. More than 1000 species of worms, clams, crabs and other invertebrates inhabit the bay. Fish include perch, flounder, sting rays, leopard sharks, sand dabs and herring. Almost 100 species of water associated birds have been identified here. Harbor seals also frequent the bay and the ocean just outside the bay is a major breeding area for great white sharks.

Today Tomales Bay is popular for boating, fishing, and clamming. Clams are harvested on the sand flats during low tides. Rock crabs and Dungeness crabs are netted off the bottom from skiffs. Commercial uses include robust oyster growing operations in the bay's clean water and herring netted for their prized roe which is shipped to Japan.

Marin County residents consider conservation of Tomales Bay very important. Bay waters are nearly pristine, while the few towns are small. The ranch lands east of the bay, although ringed by considerable public land, have been dogged by proposals for developments and dumps. The U. S. Congress is considering establishing a buffer zone from the bayfront to the ridgeline which would encourage ranchers to sell development rights, allowing them to continue owning the land while including it in Point Reyes National Seashore. If the owner eventually became a willing seller, the federal government would purchase the land for the park. We hope with time that everyone will see the wisdom of preserving this national treasure.

## SECTION 3
# Heart's Desire Beach, Tomales Bay State Park, to Hostel, Point Reyes National Seashore

DISTANCE: 9½ miles (15.3 kilometers).

OPEN TO: Hikers. Bicyclists on Pierce Ranch Road and Mount Vision Road.

SURFACE: Trail, road shoulder.

ACCESS POINT: Heart's Desire Beach at Tomales Bay State Park.

HOW TO GET THERE: From the junction of Sir Francis Drake Blvd. and Highway 1 at Point Reyes Station, turn west on Sir Francis Drake Blvd. Continue straight through Inverness, and at 6.4 miles turn right on Pierce Point Road. At 7.65 miles turn right into Tomales Bay State Park entrance. Pay a fee at the kiosk about half way down the .75 mile road to parking at Heart's Desire Beach.

OTHER ACCESS: At top of Mount Vision on Mount Vision Road.

DIFFICULTY: Strenuous.

ELEVATION GAIN/LOSS: 1680 feet+/1520 feet-.

CAUTIONS: The hostel is closed during the day and facilities are not available.

FURTHER INFORMATION: Tomales Bay State Park (415)669-1140, Point Reyes National Seashore (415)464-5100.

FACILITIES: Restrooms and water at Heart's Desire Beach.

CAMPGROUNDS: Tomales Bay State Park has hike and bike camping, no cars overnight.

HOSTEL: Point Reyes Hostel (415)663-8811.

LODGING: The Inverness area has B&Bs and motels.

MAP: See page 204.

Inverness Ridge is the defining feature of this hike from the gentle shore of Tomales Bay to within a mile of Drakes Bay. You must climb from sea level to the top of the ridge, more than 1300 feet. The Bishop pine forests and the sweeping views from the ridge make it worthwhile.

Tomales Bay State Park is one of the prettiest places in California. Located on the east slope of the ridge defining Tomales Point, the park spans from the bay to the ridgetop. It features a virgin Bishop pine forest and a rich variety of plants and animals. Along the water's edge a series of stunning little white sand beaches have shallow water safe for swimming, Slopes plunging to the shore have flora hanging over the water, reminiscent of a Buddhist ink drawing. The Coast Miwok Indians lived here for centuries.

From the south end of Heart's Desire Beach, climb the short set of steps to the bluff above. Walk through the picnic area and past the restroom to the parking lot

# The Coast Miwok and Their Neighbors

As we move south along the California coast, the fate of its native cultures grows increasingly harsh. While all native cultures suffered from white settlement, some of the northern tribes like the Tolowa and Yurok discussed earlier were able to maintain sufficient population to retain much of their cultural identity. North of the Russian River, the majority of native cultures along the coast survived at least partially intact, although many smaller groups like the Mattole, Sinkyone, and Coast Yuki had few survivors let alone any surviving cultural integrity.

Historically, the Pomo people of modern Mendocino, Sonoma, and Lake counties were, after the Chumash of the Santa Barbara area, the second most populous native group along the California coast. The Pomo culture has survived and even prospered despite the unsympathetic modern society.

The Coast Miwok people were the Pomo's immediate neighbors to the south, inhabiting the region from Bodega Bay south to the Golden Gate and east into Sonoma Valley. They visited and traded regularly with their Pomo neighbors. Sadly, the fate of the Coast Miwok culture was far worse than their Pomo neighbors with whom they shared many cultural traits.

The Coast Miwok people prospered in their territory for at least 5000 years. Before the Spaniards established missions in the San Francisco Bay Area in the late 18th century, the Coast Miwok population numbered between 2000 and 4000 individuals. Roughly 113 Miwok villages lined the shores of Tomales Bay alone, mostly along the sunnier eastern shore. They fared well in this abundant land of mild climate, subsisting by a combination of marine fishing and gathering, acorn collecting, and game hunting. They were a peaceful culture, although ritual wars did occur.

The Miwok's robust society survived the initial encounters with the Spaniards, but was doomed with the coming of the Spanish missionaries in 1776. Sixty years after the Spaniards established a mission at San Rafael, 90 percent of the Miwoks were dead from European diseases and the depredations of slavery in the mission system. The Miwoks were so devastated that they barely survived as a culture. Today a group of descendants have formed an association, holding ceremonies and dances at the reconstructed Miwok village of Kule Loklo near the Point Reyes National Seashore Visitor Center at Olema.

Linguistically the Coast Miwok are closely related to the Ohlone people who inhabited the coast south of the Golden Gate all the way to Point Sur. The Miwok probably traded with the nearby Ohlone by sailing their tule boats across San Francisco Bay.

The even more numerous Ohlone also fared poorly under the mission system with very few surviving. In the last half of the 19th century, surviving Ohlone people began to once again practice their traditional culture, holding dances, building sweathouses, and reviving shamanic practices. However, the Anglo-American population of the Bay Area grew too fast for this cultural renaissance to survive. The last Ohlone sweathouse was torn down in 1900, the last speaker of an Ohlone language died in 1935, and the last full-blooded Ohlone died in the 1970s. Today descendants of the Ohlone Indians still live in the region of their ancestors, but their language and most of their culture has died.

Still, California's natural landscape sings the heritage of its extinguished native cultures. Many of the place names we use today stem from these cultures. Modern Petaluma and Cotati took the names of nearby Coast Miwok villages, today's Olema was once Olema-loke and Bolinas was Bauli-n.

around ¼ mile, then turn left onto the driveway. As it circles around watch for the Jepson Trail on the west side. Follow the trail up through enchanting Jepson Memorial Grove. Around one mile you come to a junction. Turn right on the short trail marked "Pierce Point Road." At 1¼ miles turn left onto the road. Walk its broad, grassy shoulder to Sir Francis Drake Blvd.

Carefully cross busy Sir Francis Drake Blvd., turn left and walk its shoulder for ⅜ mile to 2¼ miles. Turn right onto a fire road marked by a split rail fence on the south side of the boulevard. Follow the fire road as it climbs southwest up Inverness Ridge through more Bishop pine forest. Of the three intersections on this stretch, go straight past the first one, then go left at the other two. At 3⅛ miles you meet paved, one-lane Mount Vision Road. Turn left and ascend the paved road. As you gain elevation, the views open up to Point Reyes. Continue up the road through the parking lot and past the gate. As you approach the top of Point Reyes Hill, watch for the radio range station behind a fence at 5¼ miles. Take the marked Bucklin Trail which begins here and skirts the north edge of the station for 200 feet across the crest of Point Reyes Hill. On clear days the views of the Point and Drakes Beach are stunning. The summit offers a great but often windy place for lunch.

The trail drops off the hill and descends sharply to the west, passing burnt trees from the 1995 Vision Fire. Bishop pines depend on fire for regeneration. When the trees were destroyed here, the cones burst from the heat reseeding a new forest. Ghostly blackened trees rising from an intensely green undergrowth with countless little pine trees provide a striking scene. At 7⅝ miles go south on the dirt Muddy Hollow Road, reaching the Muddy Hollow parking lot at 9 miles. Continue up the road, carefully cross Limantour Road, and follow the one-lane paved road to section's end at the Point Reyes Hostel at 9½ miles.

**ALTERNATE ROUTE:** To use the Johnstone Trail instead of the Jepson continue along the bluff past the restroom to a junction at ⅜ mile. A left turn follows a short trail to quiet Pebble Beach, but you go right, climbing gradually. It's 2 miles to Pierce Point Road and the junction with the Jepson Trail.

**SUGGESTED ROUND TRIPS & LOOPS:** Jepson Trail and Johnstone Trail combine for a wonderful 3¼-mile loop from Heart's Desire Beach. Heart's Desire Beach to Shell Beach at the south end of Tomales Bay State Park makes a day hike of about 8 miles round trip. You can combine it with the Jepson/Johnstone loop.

**HOW TO IMPROVE CCT HERE:** Build a connecting trail between the Tomales Bay State Park trail and Point Reyes National Seashore to eliminate walking on Pierce Point Road. This would ideally connect to a trail that is needed from Sir Francis Drake Blvd. to Point Reyes Hill to eliminate walking on Mount Vision Road.

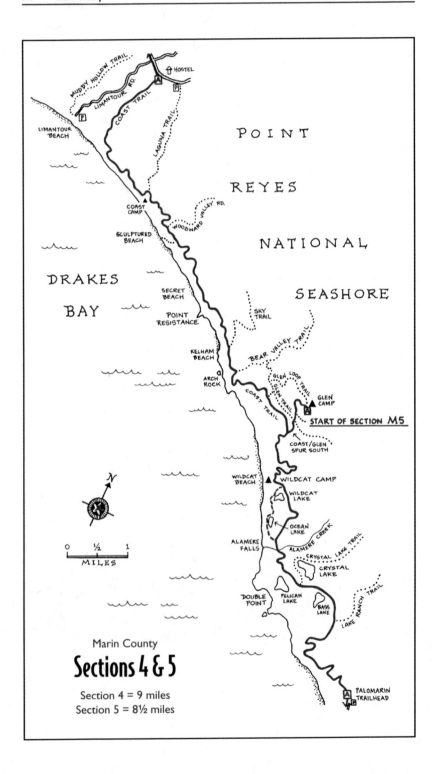

MUDDY HOLLOW TRAIL

HOSTEL

LIMANTOUR RD.

COAST TRAIL

LAGUNA TRAIL

LIMANTOUR
BEACH

POINT

REYES

COAST
CAMP

WOODWARD VALLEY RD.

SCULPTURED
BEACH

NATIONAL

DRAKES

BAY

SECRET
BEACH

POINT
RESISTANCE

SKY
TRAIL

SEASHORE

KELHAM
BEACH

BEAR VALLEY TRAIL

ARCH
ROCK

GLEN LOOP TRAIL

GLEN TRAIL

COAST TRAIL

GLEN
CAMP

START OF SECTION M5

COAST/GLEN
SPUR SOUTH

N

WILDCAT
BEACH

WILDCAT CAMP

WILDCAT
LAKE

OCEAN
LAKE

ALAMERE CREEK

ALAMERE
FALLS

CRYSTAL LAKE TRAIL

CRYSTAL
LAKE

0      ½      1
M I L E S

DOUBLE
POINT

PELICAN
LAKE

BASS
LAKE

LAKE RANCH TRAIL

Marin County

# Sections 4 & 5

Section 4 = 9 miles
Section 5 = 8½ miles

PALOMARIN
TRAILHEAD

## SECTION 4
# Hostel to Glen Camp, Point Reyes National Seashore

DISTANCE: 9 miles plus a ⅞-mile side trip to Glen Camp (14.5 + 1.4 kilometers).

OPEN TO: Hikers. Bicyclists to Coast Camp only.

SURFACE: Trail.

ACCESS POINT: Point Reyes Hostel.

HOW TO GET THERE: From the junction of Highway 1 and Sir Francis Drake Blvd. in Olema, take Bear Valley Road one mile, turn left onto Limantour Road and go 9 miles to the hostel.

DIFFICULTY: Moderate.

ELEVATION GAIN/LOSS: 1060 feet+/640 feet-.

CAUTIONS: Reservation and fees are required for backcountry camps. Some of the trail is in poor condition. No services along trail. Watch for ticks and poison oak.

FURTHER INFORMATION: Point Reyes National Seashore (415)464-5100.

FACILITIES: The hostel has bunk beds, showers, a kitchen and phone. Coast Camp and Glen Camp have tables, chemical toilets and water.

CAMPGROUNDS: Glen Camp is walk-in only and Coast Camp is hike and bike. A private campground is in Olema.

HOSTEL: Point Reyes Hostel (415)663-8811.

LODGING: Olema and Point Reyes Station have inns and B&Bs.

When you leave the hostel heading south on CCT, you are leaving civilization for two days. For the next 16 miles to Palomarin (Sections 4 and 5), the trail traverses the 25,370-acre Phillip Burton Wilderness Area. This wilderness leg of CCT is marked as "Coast Trail," a name chosen in the 1960s before the idea of a California Coastal Trail was born. Whatever you call it, the trail explores some of the most dramatic terrain on the entire California coast. Unless you intend to hike the 16 miles in one long day, you must reserve a site at Wildcat Camp or Glen Camp and bring a backpack.

From the hostel walk west on the road for ⅛ mile to find the Coastal Trail. Head west to descend along a creek with thick marshy riparian forest. By 1⅜ miles the sound of breakers becomes evident as you swing south and parallel the beach behind the dunes. After passing a marshy lagoon on the right, your alternative to the trail here is to find a gap through the dunes and walk the beach. If you do, watch for the big eucalyptus tree marking where you must return to the trail at Coast Camp. Coast Camp has a pleasant beach with curious rock formations jutting into the surf farther south. The trail reaches Coast Camp 2⅞ miles from the hostel, about the same as the beach route. Coast Camp has water and chemical toilets.

After you pass the group camp, climb to the marine terrace. The trail follows the terrace, meandering through small ravines on the way to Arch Rock. A good side trip at 4⅛ miles descends to geologically unique Sculptured Beach, ⅜ mile round trip. Continue along the terrace above the spectacular coast, at 7¼ miles meeting the popular Bear Valley Trail which leads 4½ miles east to the Bear Valley Visitor Center. Another good short side trail on the right leads to Arch Rock which thrusts out into the surf, affording sweeping views north and south and a good place for lunch.

The Coastal Trail crosses Coast Creek and starts climbing, the beginning of a stiff and steep 800-foot ascent on an eroded trail for about 1⅜ miles. Great views reward you. Climb past a spur trail at 8⅜ miles, and around 9 miles, find the spur

## Point Reyes National Seashore

Farming, logging and development have severely altered much of California's coast, so to experience the coast in a relatively original and unaltered condition, visit Point Reyes National Seashore. The United States Congress recognized the extraordinary value of this wild and scenic place, creating the National Seashore in 1962, preserving it permanently for public recreation and protecting its wonderful wildlife. Today the National Seashore protects 71,000 acres of the Point Reyes Peninsula, with almost 40 percent of it in the Phillip Burton Wilderness Area and numerous privately operated ranches within the remaining acreage.

Wide beaches, protected bays, open ocean, salt marshes and esteros, grasslands, brush covered hills, creeks and forested ridges harbor 56 species of land mammals and 24 of marine mammals. About 425 species of birds have been sighted here, as many as any area of similar size in North America. Fish, shellfish and sharks jam the oceans and bays. You can see California gray whales cruising the coast, a sea lion colony recently re-established at Drakes Bay, and a tule elk herd on Tomales Point. Several creeks even have small runs of ocean-going steelhead trout.

The park and its large wilderness area provide a hiker's and equestrian's paradise with miles of backcountry trails and four walk-in campgrounds. While beach and backcountry hiking through spectacular scenery in this pristine environment are a primary feature, many fascinating educational activities exist for non-hikers. The Bear Valley Visitor Center has a fine introductory exhibit to the area. From there the short wheelchair-accessible Earthquake Trail leads you along the fracture zone of the 1906 quake for a dramatic look at a fence moved sixteen feet by the temblor. Nearby are Kule Loklo, an authentic re-creation of a Coast Miwok village, and the Morgan Horse Ranch where gentle Morgan horses are trained for national park use.

Try not to miss the long drive out to the Point Reyes Lighthouse in one of the harshest and most dramatic locations on the west coast. It's the windiest point on the Pacific Coast and second foggiest place on the North American continent. Winds to 133 miles per hour have been recorded, with 60 m.p.h. winds common. In summer, fog shrouds the point for weeks on end. In winter and spring, the lighthouse provides a great spot for whale watching. The lighthouse was built in 1870 to warn ships away from the point, which juts 10 miles into the ocean. The light station was retired in 1975, but most of the buildings and equipment are intact, including the original Fresnel lens.

trail on the left that leads to Glen Camp. CCT continues straight on Coast Trail as described in the next section. If you have a reservation tonight at Glen Camp, go left on the spur. At 9⅜ miles it meets a dirt service road. Take this road to reach Glen Camp at 9⅞ miles. The alternative to Glen Camp would be to continue to Wildcat Camp in the next section.

**SUGGESTED ROUND TRIPS & LOOPS:** From the Point Reyes Hostel take the Coast Trail to Coast Camp and beyond to Sculptured Beach. Return to the hostel via the Laguna Trail. You can make several other excellent loops from the hostel.

# SECTION 5
# Glen Camp to Palomarin Trailhead, Point Reyes National Seashore

**DISTANCE:** 8½ miles plus ⅞-mile side trip from Glen Camp (13.7 + 1.4 kilometers).

**OPEN TO:** Hikers.

**SURFACE:** Trail.

**ACCESS POINT:** Glen Camp.

**HOW TO GET THERE:** Walk in from Palomarin Trailhead (south), Five Brooks or Bear Valley Trailheads (east), or from Point Reyes Hostel (north) along the Coastal Trail, or you can start from the south end (see next section, How to Get There).

**DIFFICULTY:** Moderate.

**ELEVATION GAIN/LOSS:** 1140 feet+/1500 feet-.

**CAUTIONS:** Reservations and fees are required for backcountry camps. Some of the trail is in poor condition. No services along trail. Watch for ticks and poison oak.

**FURTHER INFORMATION:** Point Reyes National Seashore (415)464-5100.

**FACILITIES:** Water, tables and chemical toilets at Wildcat Camp and Glen Camp. Chemical toilet at Palomarin.

**CAMPGROUNDS:** Wildcat Camp and Glen Camp, backpacking only.

**MAP:** See page 210.

Prettiest of the Point Reyes backcountry camps, Glen Camp sits smack in the middle of the most remote part of the Burton Wilderness, offering plenty of great day hikes as well as a good stopover for people hiking the Coastal Trail. The camp nestles in a small meadow surrounded by oak and fir covered hills. If you're staying more than one night, explore old growth fir forest on the Greenpicker or Stewart Trails, take the short Glen Camp Loop or the longer Glen-Baldy-Sky Loop to the north. The final leg of Coast Trail to Palomarin Trailhead packs loads of scenery in a few miles.

If you stayed overnight at Glen Camp, make your way ⅞ mile back to the Coastal Trail. From the junction (the mileage counts from here), head south on the track variously called Coast Trail, Coastal Trail, and CCT. You begin a long descent to Wildcat Camp with expansive views from the top. As you descend, Wildcat Camp comes into view far below. At ¾ mile, the Coastal Trail meets Stewart Trail from Five Brooks Trailhead. Turn right and continue down to Wildcat Camp at 1⅝ miles. The camp sits on a grassy bluff beside a creek. You might take the short side trail down to Wildcat Beach.

**Point Reyes' wilderness coastline holds many surprises.**

The Coastal Trail from Wildcat Camp departs near the privies. It crosses the small creek and climbs to a fork above Wildcat Lake. You can take either the trail above the lake or the trail that skirts the west shore of the both Wildcat Lake and Ocean Lake. The trails come back together in about one mile. These are the first of five small, picturesque lakes which resulted from a massive ancient landslide. Four of the lakes can be seen from the trail as it climbs through rolling hills.

Dip across Alamere Creek around 3¼ miles, then climb to meet a spur trail on the right. It drops ½ mile to overlook Alamere Falls which tumble to the beach. A second spur 150 feet beyond leads out to sweeping views up and down the coast from a hilltop above Double Point, ¾ mile round trip. At 3⅜ miles dramatic Pelican Lake, in a hanging valley at the edge of the coastal cliffs, comes into view. Continue through the coyote brush prevalent in this region, and you soon enter forest.

At 5⅞ miles Bass Lake lies below the trail. Dense vegetation shrouds the hills surrounding this small lake, a setting reminiscent of a Zen ink drawing. Just before you get to the lake, take the unmarked spur west (you may have to retrace a few steps to find this spur). In several hundred feet it comes to a small meadow by the lake, the best and only place to swim. The swimming hole is popular, so expect a crowd on warm days and/or weekends.

From Bass Lake, it's 2⅝ miles to the Palomarin Trailhead. Climb gently along the base of the hill where springs pour from the hillside to feed the lake. Before 6½ miles, you pass a series of small, quiet ponds which resulted from the same ancient landslide that formed the lakes to the north.

Past the ponds, the trail turns west and drops sharply down a rocky ravine, descends the hill, and turns south. Traverse the hillside well above the tideline with grand views north and south. Dip through several small creek canyons. After the last creek, pass a stand of enormous eucalyptus trees. In the eucalyptus grove you meet the newly rerouted Palomarin Beach Trail, which descends about ¾ mile to a low-tide Alternate Route. The parking area and section's ends are just a short walk past the trees at 8½ miles.

**SUGGESTED ROUND TRIPS & LOOPS:** From Palomarin, day hike north to Bass or Pelican Lake or go overnight to Wildcat or Glen Camp. Most loops in the southern national seashore are quite rugged, but the little 2-mile loop around Wildcat and Ocean Lakes is gentle.

# SECTION 6
# Palomarin Trailhead, Point Reyes National Seashore, to Bolinas

**DISTANCE:** 5 miles (8 kilometers).

**OPEN TO:** Hikers. Bicyclists on road.

**SURFACE:** Trail, road shoulder. Alternate Route on beach and tidal rocks.

**ACCESS POINT:** Palomarin Trailhead.

**HOW TO GET THERE:** Five miles north of Stinson Beach on Highway 1, turn west on unmarked Bolinas Road. Go 1½ miles to Mesa Road. Turn right and go 5 miles to the trailhead.

**OTHER ACCESS:** Along Mesa Road and in Bolinas.

**DIFFICULTY:** Easy for uplands route, moderate for beach route.

**ELEVATION GAIN/LOSS:** 240 feet+/480 feet-.

**CAUTIONS:** Don't disturb cows on the grazing land. Leave the ranch gates just like you find them. Dangerous surf and slippery rocks on beach route.

**FURTHER INFORMATION:** Point Reyes National Seashore (415)464-5100.

**FACILITIES:** Palomarin has chemical toilets. Bolinas has the usual small town services.

**CAMPGROUNDS:** Olema has a private campground and Samuel P. Taylor State Park, 6 miles east, has camping.

**LODGING:** Bolinas has Thomas' White House Inn. Olema and Stinson Beach have choices.

The Coastal Trail from Palomarin to Bolinas offers a choice of two very different routes. The alternate beach hike is a spectacular low-tide-only route. The Bolinas Mesa route crosses rolling headlands over ranch lands recently acquired for the national seashore, then winds into town, getting you there without wet feet.

From the Palomarin parking lot, take the gravel road south. Follow it past the Point Reyes Bird Observatory (visitors welcome, restroom open to the public), cross the bridge over wooded Arroyo Hondo, then pass the Ridge Trailhead.

At 1¼ miles you meet a driveway marked "COMMONWEAL 451." A few steps west on the driveway, go left through a gate into a new addition to Point Reyes

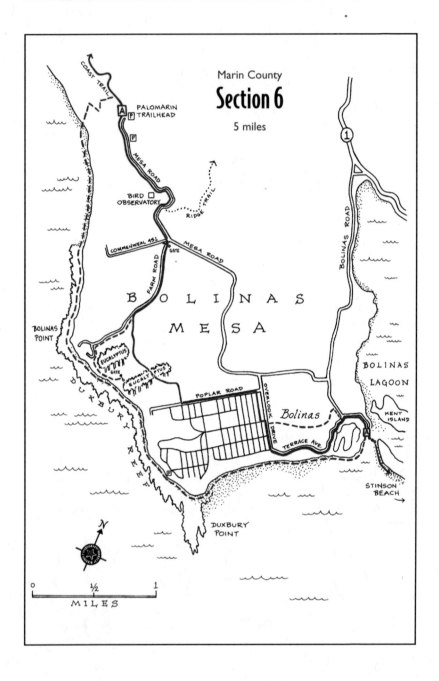

Marin County
**Section 6**
5 miles

leased to a rancher. Please don't disturb his cattle. Follow the farm road southwest. Look south to see the first of two rows of eucalyptus trees ¾ mile away.

Around 1¾ miles, turn off the road and head south across the trailless pasture toward the upper end of the trees. Pass to the left of the trees and angle southeast toward the second row of trees. Find and pass through a gate in the fence paralleling the tree line at 2¼ miles. Beyond the gate your route angles east downhill towards the upper end of the second set of trees. Cross the ravine at 2½ miles on rough tread where the trail cuts deeply into the creek bank. Hop across the creek and climb up the other side.

The overgrown trail follows the side of the ravine, turns uphill to pass through a gate and reach the top of the hill. Before 3 miles you go through another gate to Poplar Road. You leave Point Reyes National Seashore and enter the residential part of Bolinas with its grid of mostly unmarked roads in varying states of disrepair, from completely overgrown and impassable to paved and potholed, and an eclectic and charming mix of houses. Go left on Poplar to its end beyond 3½ miles.

Turn right on Beach Street for a few blocks. After it jogs to the left and ends, turn right and walk Overlook Drive to its end. Turn left on Terrace Avenue and walk ¾ mile to Bolinas Road at 4¾ miles. Left leads off Bolinas Mesa to Highway 1. Turn right and walk through the funky commercial center of Bolinas. Only a few blocks long, it includes a grocery store, bakery, bar, local museum, some tourist stores, and a gas station. Soon the wildlife-rich Bolinas Lagoon will be on the left with houses built on pilings in the channel. Both road and trail end at Bolinas Beach at the mouth of the lagoon around 5 miles.

**LOW TIDE ALTERNATE ROUTE:** This is a great walk at low tide but not recommended if the tide has turned. Allow about 2½ hours to do the 5-mile walk. From the Palomarin Trailhead, follow Coast Trail northwest for about ⅛ mile to find the newly rerouted Palomarin Beach Trail. Turn left and follow the trail about ¾ mile down the bluff to the beach.

The tidal area below the bluffs, only 2 miles from Bolinas, feels wild and remote. Most of the route south is easy going on sand and rocks, but for several hundred yards north of Duxbury Reef you walk on slick tidal rocks. Low tides expose a wide area of tilted and wave-cut sedimentary rocks great for tidepooling. The reef stretches about 2 miles between Bolinas Point and Duxbury Point.

You can leave the beach at several places if the tide is too high. Beyond 2 miles a trail cuts up to Agate Beach County Park, and beyond 4 miles, short steps from a residential street reach the beach. Take care if attempting to climb the steep and crumbling bluffs anywhere else. The walk ends at the mouth of Bolinas Lagoon, with downtown Bolinas only a short walk up the road.

**SUGGESTED ROUND TRIPS & LOOPS:** Combine the Mesa route and beach route for a great 10-mile loop. Time your beach walk to make sure the tide is out or going out.

**HOW TO IMPROVE CCT HERE:** Build a trail off road from Palomarin to Commonweal 451.

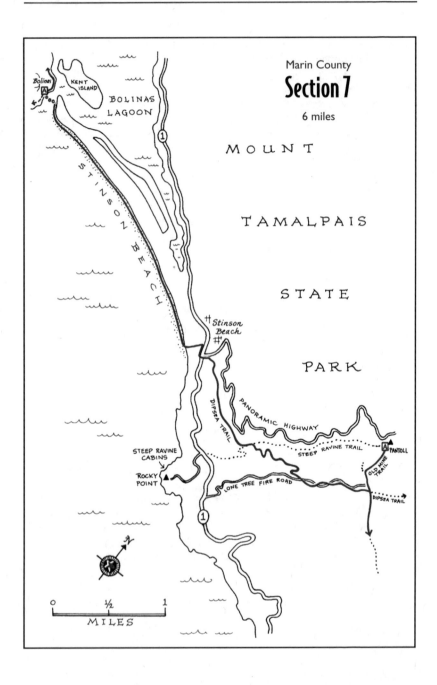

Marin County
# Section 7
6 miles

## SECTION 7
# Bolinas Beach to Pantoll, Mt.Tamalpais State Park

DISTANCE: 6 miles. Alternate A: 10 miles. Alternate B: 16¾ miles (9.7 or 16.1 or 27 kilometers).

OPEN TO: Hikers.

SURFACE: Beach, trail.

ACCESS POINT: Bolinas Beach.

HOW TO GET THERE: From Stinson Beach, drive 5 miles north on Highway 1. Turn west on unmarked Bolinas Road just beyond Bolinas Lagoon. Drive two miles and through Bolinas to road's end at the beach. Parking is restricted here, so parking in town might be easier.

OTHER ACCESS: Stinson Beach.

DIFFICULTY: Strenuous.

ELEVATION GAIN/LOSS: 1500 feet+/80 feet-.

CAUTIONS: Use caution boating across the lagoon which has strong currents.

FURTHER INFORMATION: Mount Tamalpais State Park (415)388-2070.

FACILITIES: Full services are available at Bolinas and Stinson Beach.

CAMPGROUNDS: Pantoll Campground at Mount Tamalpais State Park.

LODGING: Stinson Beach and Bolinas have several choices. State Parks' Steep Ravine Cabins and Environmental Camps are superb, but usually require advance reservations.

To continue along the coast, you need to arrange a boat ride across the mouth of Bolinas Lagoon. If you can't get a ride, you have two alternate routes to choose from. All the routes lead high onto the flanks of Mount Tamalpais.

One hundred yards across the lagoon's mouth, Seadrift subdivision sits atop the sand spit defining the lagoon, the scene of a long-time battle over beach access. The public claimed the beach as public, the homeowners said it wasn't. Finally in 1998 the courts decided that you cannot be stopped from walking the tideline the length of the beach.

After the boat drops you east of the lagoon's mouth, walk the tideline southeast. At 2¼ miles the beachfront houses end and Stinson Beach Park, part of Golden Gate National Recreation Area, begins. Turn inland before 2⅝ miles to walk through the parking lot to Highway 1 and the middle of the village of Stinson Beach with its stores and restaurants, a good place to buy lunch.

Walk south along often busy Highway 1, then turn left on Panoramic Highway briefly to the Dipsea Trailhead on the right around 2¾ miles. Follow the Dipsea Trail on a stiff 1400-foot climb up the west flank of Mount Tamalpais. It climbs a hill, flattens out on a rolling terrace, and drops down to Steep Ravine

Trail at 3¾ miles. Turn left and after a few yards, continue up the Dipsea Trail on the south side of the ravine.

Climb steeply to Cardiac Hill at 5¼ miles. Beyond 4¾ miles the trail braids with a fire road so that either the road or the trail gets you to the same place. Bikes are allowed on the fire road but not the single track path. At the top, where several paths converge at 5¼ miles, look for the trail sign to Pantoll. In 500 feet you can veer right on the parallel Old Mine Trail to get off the road. Continue ¾ mile up the hill to Pantoll and the end of the section.

**ALTERNATE ROUTE A:** The road route offers a pleasant walk albeit in the company of cars — use extreme caution. From downtown Bolinas walk 2 miles along Bolinas Road to Highway 1. Turn south and walk 5 miles to Stinson Beach, much of it along the shore of Bolinas Lagoon where wildlife abounds including wading birds, a harbor seal colony on a sand bar just off the road, and nesting egrets and blue herons at Audubon Canyon Ranch just across Highway 1 from the lagoon. If Audubon is open, consider it for a rewarding stop. Pick up the Dipsea Trail in Stinson Beach as described above and continue to Pantoll.

**ALTERNATE ROUTE B:** This inland route is much longer and more challenging but the fantastic scenic views from the ridge in every direction are worth it. From this trail you can see Bolinas, Stinson Beach, San Francisco Bay, San Francisco and the three highest peaks in the Bay Area: Mount Tamalpais, Mount Diablo, and Mount Saint Helena. If you do this all-day route, it replaces Sections 6 and Section 7 in one hike.

From the Palomarin Trailhead, walk ¾ mile south on the road and take the Ridge Trail on the left. At 2⅜ miles, turn right on the Teixeira Trail and descend into scenic Olema Valley along the infamous San Andreas Rift Zone. The trail ends at Highway 1 at 4⅝ miles. Find the McCurdy Trail directly across the road. It climbs 1200 feet in 1¾ miles to gain the top of Bolinas Ridge. Make a right on the Ridge Trail (a wide fire road, watch for mountain bikes) and walk 3 miles to Bolinas-Fairfax Road.

Cross the road and pick up the Coastal Trail. Bikes are not allowed on this single track trail and rangers actively cite illegal bike use. The trail traverses the west flank of Mount Tamalpais for 6⅜ miles. Around 2 miles the trail circles the head of a steep ravine on a road for 100 yards before dropping back below the road. Take the trail that angles slightly downhill. A side trail goes sharply down the slope here. Continue on the trail as it contours across a steep hillside. The trail ends at the Pantoll parking lot.

**SUGGESTED ROUND TRIPS & LOOPS:** Walk Stinson Beach north to the end of the spit, 5⅛ miles round trip. From Stinson Beach take the Dipsea Trail to Pantoll and return to Stinson down the Steep Ravine Trail, a rewarding 5¼ miles round trip.

## SECTION 8
# Pantoll, Mt. Tamalpais State Park, to Muir Beach, Golden Gate National Recreation Area

DISTANCE: 5 miles (8 kilometers).

OPEN TO: Hikers. Bicyclists on part.

SURFACE: Trail.

ACCESS POINT: Pantoll, Mount Tamalpais State Park.

HOW TO GET THERE: From Highway 101 at Tamalpais Valley Junction take Highway 1 for 3 miles to Panoramic Highway and turn right. Continue 5 miles to Pantoll.

OTHER ACCESS: Muir Woods Road, Pelican Inn.

DIFFICULTY: Moderate.

ELEVATION GAIN/LOSS: 40 feet+/1500 feet-.

CAUTIONS: Take it easy on the steep descents.

FURTHER INFORMATION: Mount Tamalpais State Park (415)388-2070. Golden Gate National Recreation Area, Marin Headlands (415)331-1540, ask for a TDD line if you need one.

FACILITIES: Water, restrooms and visitor center at Pantoll. Water, toilets at Muir Beach.

CAMPGROUNDS: Pantoll Campground and various campgrounds in the GGNRA.

LODGING: Pelican Inn, Muir Beach.

This section of the Coastal Trail starts high on the flank of Mount Tamalpais, dropping dramatically down to sea level at popular Muir Beach. The trail provides exceptional views when it's clear, but be prepared for wind and fog. Mount Tamalpais State Park, Muir Woods and surrounding lands have been attracting visitors for years because of the beautiful scenery and stunning views from the top of the mountain. Weekends find the extensive trail system full of hikers.

From the main parking area at Pantoll, follow the paved road south past the famous Steep Ravine Trailhead for about 200 feet. Go left down the Old Mine Trail. At ¾ mile you cross the Dipsea Trail. Continue south downhill on the wide Coastal Trail as it follows the ridgetop through grasslands and coyote brush. This fire road trail allows bicycles. Just before 2⅝ miles turn left on the Heather Cutoff. This single-track, carefully constructed trail snakes down a steep hill to Frank's Valley and Muir Woods Road. At 4 miles at the bottom of the hill, turn right past the corrals and large group picnic area, cross the creek on a foot bridge up the driveway, and cross Muir Woods Road. Across the road and a short way uphill turn right on Redwood Creek Trail. The trail parallels above the road before dropping down to the pavement just before the intersection with Highway 1 at 4½ miles. Carefully cross the road and walk the shoulder for about ¼ mile to

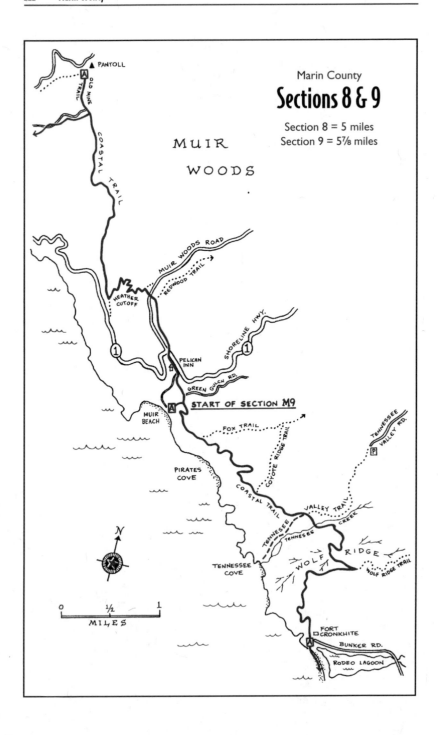

PANTOLL

OLD MINE TRAIL

COASTAL TRAIL

MUIR WOODS

Marin County
# Sections 8 & 9

Section 8 = 5 miles
Section 9 = 5⅞ miles

MUIR WOODS ROAD

REDWOOD TRAIL

HEATHER CUTOFF

SHORELINE HWY.

1

1

PELICAN INN

GREEN GULCH RD.

START OF SECTION M9

MUIR BEACH

FOX TRAIL

COYOTE RIDGE TRAIL

TENNESSEE VALLEY RD.

P

PIRATES COVE

COASTAL TRAIL

VALLEY TRAIL

TENNESSEE CREEK

TENNESSEE

N

TENNESSEE COVE

WOLF RIDGE

WOLF RIDGE TRAIL

0    ½    1
MILES

FORT CRONKHITE

BUNKER RD.

RODEO LAGOON

Muir Beach Road. The Pelican Inn, fashioned after an English country pub, is on the corner if you are thirsty or want a place to sleep. Walk down Muir Beach Road about 300 feet to a gated and unsigned fire road on the left. Go around the gate and walk down the fire road to scenic Muir Beach. The road ends at 5 miles at a bridge over Muir Creek. Walk across the bridge to find picnic tables and a parking area. The beach is a few yards away over the low dunes.

SUGGESTED ROUND TRIPS & LOOPS: From Pantoll, trails radiate in every direction, providing many enjoyable hiking routes on Mount Tamalpais.

## SECTION 9
# Muir Beach to Rodeo Beach, Golden Gate National Recreation Area

DISTANCE: 5⅞ miles (9.5 kilometers).

OPEN TO: Hikers. Bicyclists and equestrians on part.

SURFACE: Trail, paved trail.

ACCESS POINT: Muir Beach.

HOW TO GET THERE: Exit Highway 101 at Tamalpais Valley 3 miles north of Golden Gate Bridge onto Highway 1, follow it 6 miles to Muir Beach and turn left into parking area.

OTHER ACCESS: Tennessee Valley Trailhead.

DIFFICULTY: Strenuous.

ELEVATION GAIN/LOSS: 1700 feet+/1700 feet-.

CAUTIONS: Part of this walk is very steep.

FURTHER INFORMATION: Golden Gate National Recreation Area (415)331-1540, ask for a TDD line if you need one.

FACILITIES: Water, chemical toilets, and picnic tables at Muir Beach and Rodeo Beach.

CAMPGROUNDS: Several backpack and group camps are located in the Marin Headlands. Contact the GGNRA for more information.

LODGING: Mill Valley, Sausalito and other towns along Highway 101 have plenty.

This challenging section of the Coastal Trail features remarkably steep climbs through wild coastal hills for rewarding ocean and urban views, solitude, and fine coastal sage scrub. Although you can see San Francisco from the ridgetops, the trail has a wilderness feeling. Here the CCT starts a lengthy run through the Golden Gate National Recreation Area. See the feature on the next page. From here the Coastal Trail also follows the shoreline of the Monterey Bay National Marine Sanctuary for the next 360 miles. The feature on page 297 describes the marine sanctuary.

From the south end of the Muir Beach parking lot, walk across the bridge over Redwood Creek. The Coastal Trail sign informs you that it's 5⅞ miles to Rodeo Beach. The trail heads inland, meeting the Green Gulch Trail on the left at ⅛ mile. Up Green Gulch Trail ¾ mile east, the renowned Green Gulch Farm shelters a Zen Meditation Center and an organic produce garden. Green Gulch Trail bisects the gardens and continues up into the hills.

Continue on the Coastal Trail, climbing steeply. You ascend 500 feet to the Fox Trail intersection at ¾ mile, where the views of San Francisco and Mount Tamalpais are stunning. Hikers want the Coastal Trail on the right. Bicyclists, not

## The Golden Gate National Recreation Area

*The Golden Gate National Recreation Area (GGNRA) is not only the largest urban park in the world at 74,000 acres but also one of the most dramatic meetings of land and sea on the planet. GGNRA grew out of years of efforts to save open space in urban San Francisco and neighboring Marin and San Mateo Counties. The resulting park spans from urban waterfront to the boundaries of wilderness Point Reyes National Seashore, covering nearly every gradation in between.*

*The creation of GGNRA connected existing park lands in Point Reyes National Seashore, Mount Tamalpais State Park and Marin Municipal Water District to make an enormous open space area of more than 120,000 acres. Included in the park are Alcatraz Island, Fort Point, Muir Woods National Monument, the Presidio of San Francisco, and much more. More than 20 million people visit the park every year, making it the most visited park under the National Park Service.*

*This might never have happened if much of the land wasn't already claimed by the military in the 1850s, if William Kent hadn't donated land to create Muir Woods National Monument in 1903, and if the National Park Service hadn't recommended the creation of Point Reyes National Seashore in 1958. This set the stage in 1970 for the final push for GGNRA*

*when citizens called for creating the park to link all the other parks and military reservations. In October 1972 President Richard Nixon signed the bill creating GGNRA.*

*The wonder of GGNRA and the surrounding parks and open spaces is that hundreds of miles of trails connect their many features. GGNRA's 28 miles of outer coastline accommodate one of the most diverse and scenic portions of the California Coastal Trail. The 34 miles of the Coastal Trail from Bolinas to Fort Funston seldom follows roads. Features along the trail are boundless, and many more miles of trails web out into the region connecting even more features. The Coastal Trail in GGNRA will take you from Bolinas over the shoulder of Mount Tamalpais, past historic military batteries, across the Golden Gate Bridge to the Presidio of San Francisco (the newest addition to GGNRA), onto the scenic San Francisco Headlands, past the famous Cliff House and Sutro Baths and down Ocean Beach to Fort Funston. From the Coastal Trail you can connect with trails to the top of Mount Tamalpais, Muir Woods National Monument with its glorious virgin redwoods, Civil War era Fort Point National Historic Site, and miles of other pleasant hikes. If you love hiking in great surroundings, don't miss GGNRA.*

allowed on the narrow steep section ahead, can pedal above it on the Fox and Coyote Ridge Trails. The Coastal Trail contours high above the surf across steep slopes with views down plunging cliffs as it winds through deep drainages. Descend into the largest drainage where tiny Pirates Cove is tucked at the base of rugged cliffs. A spur on the right drops 100 feet to an overlook.

Stay to the left to climb steeply, gaining 450 feet before you meet the Coyote Ridge Trail at 1¾ miles. You have more great views at the junction, or can take the short spur on the right to a bluff overlooking vast ocean. The Coastal Trail veers left, descending steeply on a wide trail (bikes allowed) to the popular Tennessee Valley Trail at 2½ miles. A right turn leads ⅝ mile to Tennessee Cove Beach. Turn left and follow the Tennessee Valley Trail for 200 feet to another fork. Left leads to the Tennessee Valley Trailhead in 1⅜ miles.

Turn right and descend the Coastal Trail through a meadow. Cross the footbridge over Tennessee Valley Creek at 2⅝ miles and contour along the base of the hill before climbing steeply to Wolf Ridge. At the top at 3⅞ miles, the trail makes a hard right turn to the west. The Wolf Ridge Trail which forks east on pavement climbs ¼ mile to a derelict Nike missile base atop Hill 88 with grand 360-degree vistas. Follow the Coastal Trail, which mostly follows an old paved military road from here, along the ridge towards the ocean. You drop down the ridge past several World War II gun emplacements. At 4⅜ miles the paved road ahead has been closed by a major slide. Take the path down the stairs through dense coastal scrub. Rejoin the paved road by 4¾ miles and descend past another defunct battery to the parking area at Rodeo Beach and this section's end at 5⅞ miles.

Across the road, Rodeo Lagoon backs up behind the beach. This valley, site of the former military installation Fort Cronkhite, now hosts peaceful uses in the renovated buildings, including the Headlands Institute Conference Center and the Marine Mammal Center.

SUGGESTED ROUND TRIPS & LOOPS: The choices are too numerous to mention. Get the trail map available at the Marin Headlands Visitor Center on Bunker Road near Rodeo Beach. It shows loops and round trips you can make from Pantoll, Muir Beach, Tennessee Valley, Rodeo Beach and other locations.

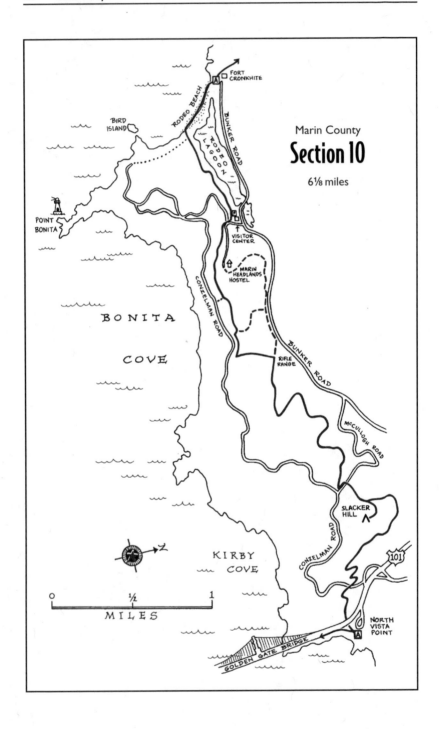

FORT CRONKHITE

RODEO BEACH

BIRD ISLAND

RODEO LAGOON

BUNKER ROAD

Marin County
## Section 10
6⅛ miles

POINT BONITA

VISITOR CENTER

MARIN HEADLANDS HOSTEL

CONZELMAN ROAD

BONITA COVE

RIFLE RANGE

BUNKER ROAD

McCULLOGH ROAD

SLACKER HILL

101

CONZELMAN ROAD

KIRBY COVE

N

0    ½    1
MILES

NORTH VISTA POINT

GOLDEN GATE BRIDGE

## SECTION 10
# Rodeo Beach to Golden Gate Bridge North Vista Point, Golden Gate National Recreation Area

DISTANCE: 6⅛ miles (9.9 kilometers).

OPEN TO: Hikers. Bicyclists on part.

SURFACE: Trail.

ACCESS POINT: Rodeo Beach.

HOW TO GET THERE: From Highway 101 take the Sausalito exit at the north end of the Golden Gate Bridge. Go north towards Sausalito .5 mile then left on the road marked "MARIN HEADLANDS VISITOR CENTER." Drive through the tunnel and go about 4 miles to Rodeo Beach.

OTHER ACCESS: Along Conzelman Road.

SOUTH END ACCESS: Across Highway 101 from the Golden Gate Bridge North Vista Point is a little used parking area just off Conzelman Road. The CCT crosses this lot and goes under the bridge on a catwalk to the Vista Point.

DIFFICULTY: Moderate.

ELEVATION GAIN/LOSS: 940 feet+/820 feet-.

CAUTIONS: Dangerous surf at Rodeo Beach.

FURTHER INFORMATION: Golden Gate National Recreation Area (415)331-1540, ask for a TDD line if you need one.

FACILITIES: Water and restrooms at Rodeo Beach and the Golden Gate Bridge Vista Point.

CAMPGROUNDS: GGNRA has several campgrounds. Call (415)331-1540.

HOSTELS: Marin Headlands Hostel (415)331-2777.

LODGING: Many accommodations available in Sausalito and San Francisco.

This hike starts from a popular beach at a former military base and ends at one of the world's great tourist attractions. Expect variety and dramatic views as you traverse the steep hills of the Marin Headlands. Unless the fog is in, you'll see the entire San Francisco peninsula, San Francisco Bay with Angel and Alcatraz Islands, Oakland and Berkeley on the east shore, and the hills ringing the bay.

From the parking lot at Rodeo Beach, walk south on the sand, or over the bridge if the lagoon mouth is open to the ocean, to the far end of the beach at ¼ mile. Turn inland to a junction. The side trail on the right climbs past World War II military fortifications to the Point Bonita Lighthouse, 3¾ miles round trip. Go left on the Lagoon Trail along the south shore of Rodeo Lagoon at the base of the hill. You climb slightly on sandy tread, then drop back near the lagoon shore and come to the parking lot for the Marin Headlands Visitor Center around one mile.

Across the lot, Field Road and Bodsworth Road intersect. Walk up Bodsworth for 200 feet to find the trail as it climbs steps through an often muddy area. The trail contours along a sidehill then makes a steep but short ascent to a trail junction at 1¾ miles. Turn left and descend. At 2 miles turn right, climbing steeply for less than ¼ mile. Just before a gravel road, the trail turns left and parallels the road ⅛ mile before coming to another junction at 2⅜ miles.

The trail drops downhill to intersect a wide gravel multi-use trail at 2¾ miles. Turn right to follow edge of the old military rifle range then climb gently through coastal scrub behind the range. Watch for fast bikes coming down the hill for the next 1½ miles. At the top at 4¼ miles, the tread ends at the corner of McCullogh Road and Conzelman Road. Step carefully across Conzelman Road for the spectacular views of San Francisco Bay and its entrance, the Golden Gate Bridge, and San Francisco spread out below. The bridge presents one of the world's greatest meetings of a human structure with the natural landscape.

Recross Conzelman Road and walk north down McCullogh Road for a few yards. Take the Coastal Trail (a fire road) on the right to climb steeply. At 4⅞ miles leave the fire road, turning left onto a trail. (The fire road continues to the top of Slacker Hill where vistas include Marin Headlands, Berkeley and Oakland across the bay, and Highway 101 at the bottom of the ridge.) CCT takes the well graded trail, descending a sidehill toward the bridge, coming to Conzelman Road at 5⅝ miles. Cross the road and descend to 6 miles. At the bottom cross a parking area and take the stairway that leads to a catwalk under the bridge. Cross the catwalk to the Golden Gate Bridge North Vista Point at 6⅛ miles, the end of the Marin County chapter of the California Coastal Trail. Visitors from all over the world usually crowd the vista point, and for good reason. The views of the bridge, the Bay, and San Francisco are fantastic.

**ALTERNATE ROUTE:** This route replaces a short section from the Marin Headlands Visitor Center to the rifle range and eliminates several short steep climbs and good views, but involves a little road walking. From the visitor center walk up Bodsworth Road and instead of taking the Coastal Trail, continue on the road. At ¼ mile pass the Marin Headlands Hostel. Continue along the road as it curves around old military buildings and a parade ground. Come to Bunker Road at ¾ mile. Cautiously walk the road for ¼ mile, then go right on the Coastal Trail along the rifle range as described above.

**SUGGESTED ROUND TRIPS & LOOPS:** The side trail to Point Bonita offers a good hike. Get a map at the visitor center to find more of the abundant trails and loops in the Marin Headlands portion of Golden Gate National Recreation Area.

# San Francisco

S AN FRANCISCO COUNTY covers a mere 46.4 square miles, by far the
smallest county in California. Only in San Francisco do the city
and county governments exist as one entity, with about half of
the land publicly owned. San Francisco County hosts the only fully complete Coastal Trail of all fifteen coastal counties in California, a mere 10¾
miles long. You can easily walk it in a day or two, but the attractions are
so great and numerous that it takes days to do it justice. The Coastal Trail
through San Francisco is one of the world's greatest urban trails.

CCT begins its city trek by crossing the Golden Gate Bridge, among
the great human architectural achievements and most beautiful structures
in the world. From the 220-foot height of the bridge's deck, you'll have
breathtaking views of one of the planet's most dramatic coastlines. The
vistas on the clearest days range up to 80 miles. Countless people have

driven over the Golden Gate Bridge and stopped at the vista points for the fabulous views, and millions have walked on the bridge. Relatively few people have experienced these riches by walking the length of the bridge and continuing along water's edge either east along the bayshore or west to the Pacific. The Golden Gate Bridge has become an important trail junction, with four long-distance trails now crossing the bridge. See the feature article on page 233. All of these trails lead to San Francisco's many natural and cultural features.

After crossing the bridge, you'll walk through a gorgeous and dramatic urban landscape. The trail out to Land's End follows the edge of the cliffs overlooking the outer San Francisco Bay, the bridge and the Marin Headlands, then traverses the affluent neighborhood of Seacliff before continuing high along the cliffs to pass within sight of an excellent art museum. After reaching the historic Cliff House, the trail runs the length of expansive Ocean Beach before visiting Fort Funston where some of the sand dunes that once covered almost half of San Francisco remain in a natural state. Most of the Coastal Trail, except for the bridge and Seacliff, traverses the Golden Gate National Recreation Area.

## SECTION 1
# Golden Gate Bridge North Vista Point to the Cliff House, Golden Gate National Recreation Area

DISTANCE: 5½ miles (8.8 kilometers).

OPEN TO: Hikers. Bicyclists on the bridge.

SURFACE: Sidewalk, trail.

ACCESS POINT: Golden Gate Bridge North Vista Point.

HOW TO GET THERE: From San Francisco take the Vista Point exit at the north end of the Golden Gate Bridge into the parking area for the North Vista Point. From Marin County, take the last exit, Golden Gate National Recreation Area, before the bridge. Make an immediate left, and then another left into a parking area. Walk the catwalk underneath the bridge to the North Vista Point.

OTHER ACCESS: Golden Gate Bridge Toll Plaza, Seacliff Avenue, Camino del Mar.

DIFFICULTY: Easy.

ELEVATION GAIN/LOSS: 300 feet+/425 feet-.

CAUTIONS: Cyclists must use the sidewalk on the west side of the bridge on weekends and holidays.

FURTHER INFORMATION: Golden Gate National Recreation Area (415)331-1540 (ask for a TDD line if you need one), Presidio (415)561-4323, TDD (415)561-4314.

FACILITIES: Restrooms, water, picnic tables, telephones at access point.

CAMPGROUNDS: Pantoll Campground on Mt. Tamalpais has walk-in sites. Marin RV Park in San Rafael for RVs.

HOSTEL: San Francisco Hostel at Fort Mason (415)771-3645.

LODGING: Many choices in San Francisco.

As you begin this dramatic walk into a dramatic city, you'll walk across one of the greatest tourists attractions anywhere. The Golden Gate Bridge not only provides the route of the California Coastal Trail across San Francisco Bay, but also the route for three other major trails. See the feature article. San Francisco City and County has both the shortest Coastal Trail and the only fully complete Coastal Trail of California's fifteen coastal counties. San Francisco's Coastal Trail is also one of the most diverse trails, going from a world renowned bridge, through un-developed park land, into one of the most expensive neighborhoods in California, past historic and military sites, and on to the windswept Ocean Beach. The trail has all of this plus easy access to one of the most exciting cities in the world.

Begin at the North Vista Point of the Golden Gate Bridge. Mingle with tour-ists from around the world as they stand in awe of the views of the bridge, San

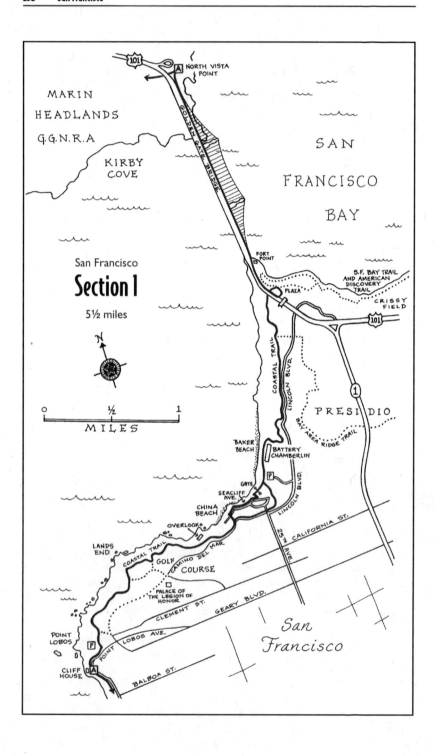

San Francisco
## Section 1
5½ miles

# The Golden Gate Bridge:
# A Magnet for Trails

San Francisco is among the world's most popular tourist attractions and the Golden Gate Bridge is the City's biggest attraction. Millions of people come to marvel at this astounding man-made feature in its dramatic natural setting. So far, however, few people know that four different long distance trails cross the Golden Gate Bridge en route to far-flung locations. The Bay Area Ridge Trail, California Coastal Trail, San Francisco Bay Trail, and American Discovery Trail all cross the bridge. A fifth, the De Anza Trail, terminates at the Presidio overlooking the Bridge. All of the trails are currently works in progress. When these trails are completed, it will be the most dynamic convergence of trails ever, a huge testament to the popularity of hiking in America. We'll look at them in the order in which they were conceived.

The idea of a trail along the ridges encircling San Francisco Bay was conceived by the legendary park advocate and land use visionary William Penn Mott Jr. almost 40 years ago. Since 1988 an advocacy nonprofit group called the Bay Area Ridge Trail Council has taken solid root, enthusiastically promoting the Ridge Trail. To date 225 miles of the Ridge Trail have been signed, 56 percent of the planned 400-mile trail through nine counties connecting 75 parks and open space districts.

The idea of a California Coastal Trail came out of the state's coastal protection movement of the 1970s. While many agencies have helped build the CCT, no one agency has taken charge. Still, the 1200-mile trail currently stands somewhere between two-thirds and three-quarters complete. Now that the state of California has officially recognized the CCT, with Coastwalk advocating and working for completing the trail, and the Coastal Conservancy making it a priority, the Coastal Trail is progressing rapidly.

The San Francisco Bay Trail is another work in progress. A dream of Senator Bill Lockyear, he first proposed the trail in 1986 as a multiple use path that would circle the bay's shoreline. It's administered by the Association of Bay Area Governments and funded largely by the Coastal Conservancy. Nearly 200 miles of the 400-mile trail are complete.

America's first coast-to-coast trail was proposed by the American Hiking Society and Backpacker Magazine in 1989. The 3000-mile American Discovery Trail will lead from Delaware's Cape Henlopen State Park on the Atlantic shore to San Francisco and Point Reyes National Seashore on the Pacific, connecting cities, villages, rural areas and wilderness areas as well as linking together the Appalachian Trail, Continental Divide Trail, Pacific Crest Trail, and California Coastal Trail in one huge network.

The De Anza Trail traces the route taken by Spanish explorer Juan Bautista de Anza from Mexico to the Presidio of San Francisco in 1775–76. The idea for the trail grew from the 1975–76 bicentennial reenactment of the 1200-mile expedition. Through the efforts of the Heritage Trails Fund, the trail was included in the National Trails System Act in 1990. Still in the planning stages, it is administered by the National Park Service from San Francisco.

Next time you're on the Golden Gate Bridge, imagine walking one trail to the east coast, another to Mexico and Oregon, or taking a high or low route around the entire San Francisco Bay. The idea, whether or not you ever do it, stretches the imagination and warms you to a sense of adventure and freedom. The individuals, nonprofit groups, and public agencies working to complete these five trails deserve our thanks and support.

Francisco, Angel and Alcatraz Islands, and the cities of Oakland and Berkeley below the East Bay hills. As you begin your walk across the bridge, its overwhelming size and elegant design become apparent. In the middle of the bridge the immense cables sweep down to the walkway with the bay's water moving 220 feet below and the towers 526 feet overhead. Before you reach the south end, look over the railing and straight down on Fort Point, a Civil War era (1861) fort built to guard the entrance to San Francisco Bay. Reach the Toll Plaza at 1½ miles with several interpretive displays about the bridge, the visitor/gift center, and more great views looking back across to the Marin Headlands.

From the plaza CCT passes just east of the visitor/gift center back towards the bridge and drops down an incline for 100 feet to a trail intersection. The Coastal Trail turns left here and heads west under the bridge. Meet the bike path climbing on the left as the Coastal Trail turns right on a dirt path into the Golden Gate National Recreation Area. In the next ⅜ mile, the trail traverses high on the bluffs past several concrete coastal defense batteries from the 1890s. The trail climbs

## The Presidio of San Francisco

In 1776 Juan Bautista de Anza arrived at the tip of the San Francisco Peninsula. His party camped for two nights at Mountain Lake. De Anza pounded a cross into the earth on the bluff overlooking the Golden Gate, claiming it for Spain. Soldiers and settlers followed, establishing the Presidio (it means garrison or fort) and Mission San Francisco de Asis and starting a 200-year history of military occupation at this strategic location overlooking the bay entrance. The occupation happily ended with the conversion of the Presidio Army Base into part of Golden Gate National Recreation Area in 1996 when President Bill Clinton signed the bill into law. With his signature he transformed the place army personnel considered the best duty on U.S. soil into one of the world's most dramatic and scenic urban parks.

The 1446-acre Presidio offers many attractions, from natural history to military architecture to great scenery. Start your exploration at the Resource Center to learn more about the Presidio and ask about the guided tours. You can bicycle the miles of roads, go fishing at Baker Beach, Crissy Field or Fort Point, or try world class board sailing in the bay off Crissy Field.

To best explore the Presidio, walk some of the more than 10 miles of trails and many miles of sidewalks and informal paths. The park invites meandering, intrigue waiting at every turn. Presidio trails will take you to military buildings dating from the 1860s to the 1970s in a range of styles from Victorian Gothic, French Second Empire, Colonial Revival to Spanish Colonial Revival. Most striking is Civil-War-era Fort Point, built in 1861 and saved from destruction when the Golden Gate Bridge was designed to avoid the fort. The fort sits under the south end of the bridge. Other features are the Presidio Army Museum and the Main Post with the parade ground used since 1776.

The Presidio does have its problems. Only about 10 percent of the land remains in a natural state, containing several endangered species. Plans to restore the landscape were initiated with restoration of the 100 acres that once held Crissy Field, an historic airfield, to a wetlands, a grassy meadow, and a shoreline walkway. The Army has budgeted $100 million to clean up the many contaminated sites within the park. A trust board oversees the Presidio's economic survival, renting many of the buildings and using the funds for restoration and maintenance.

*San Francisco's Coastal Trail provides great vistas of the Golden Gate.*

wooden steps and passes two informal parking areas. At the second parking area the Bay Area Ridge Trail branches left to head inland. Around 2 miles the Coastal Trail parallels Lincoln Boulevard along the guard rail.

At 2½ miles the trail turns right on a red gravel-surfaced road and winds down to Baker Beach. Around 2⅝ miles CCT passes through Battery Chamberlin. If the gate is locked, walk a few yards to the beach to walk around the installation. Just beyond 3 miles, leave the beach and pick up the path as it heads up steps and meets a gate to 25th Avenue North, a dead end street. If the gate is unlocked, walk 25th Avenue North to Seacliff Avenue, turn right and follow it to El Camino del Mar. If the gate is locked, backtrack about ⅛ mile and walk south along the parking lot, then follow the sandy path through the cypress trees up to Lincoln Blvd. Hop the low traffic barrier, and turn right on the sidewalk. You can also follow the driveway from the parking lot to Lincoln Blvd. In either case you come to Lincoln Blvd. Walk Lincoln west to 25th Avenue. There it becomes El Camino Del Mar, the main street through Seacliff, one of San Francisco's most exclusive neighborhoods with many elegant mansions.

At 3¾ miles Seacliff ends and the trail returns to the GGNRA. Turn right to leave the street, coming immediately to a viewing deck. The deck affords another stunning view of the bridge and the Marin Headlands. Continue west on the trail as it parallels a fairway of the Lincoln Park Golf Course. Soon the trail follows the edge of the bluff, climbing up and over several landslides before dropping back down to follow the route of the Ferries and Cliff House Railway. Around 4¼ miles a broad side trail on the left leads uphill to the Palace of the Legion of Honor, a museum designed like the Napoleonic Legion of Honor in Paris, and home to a fine collection of Rodin sculptures and the largest collection of French art in the U.S.

The Coastal Trail continues on the roadbed, following it high above the coastline. Just before the trail swings south it passes a stairway leading to a World War II memorial. Five hundred feet past the stairs take the unmarked trail west as it cuts into the trees and in about ⅛ mile comes out at a large gravel parking lot at mile 5, overlooking Point Lobos and the Cliff House. The ruins of the gigantic Sutro Baths lie below just above the tidal rocks. You can explore them via a side trail dropping down from the parking area. The bathhouses accommodated up to 24,000 people at a time before falling into disuse by 1937, eventually burning in 1966. Another interesting side trip is the walk through Sutro Heights Park just across Point Lobos Avenue. Here on the grounds of the Sutro mansion, all that remain are some statues, overgrown gardens and a big rock deck overlooking the ocean. The main entrance is at the intersection just uphill from the parking area. To finish the section, walk the path in front of the parking area and turn right on Point Lobos Avenue/Geary Boulevard and walk the sidewalk down to the Cliff House at 5½ miles.

At the Cliff House you can have a drink or eat at the restaurant, or check out the GGNRA Visitor Center and Camera Obscura on the lower deck and the free museum full of hundreds of antique and curious mechanical games, many of which were acquired from the Sutro amusement palace when it closed.

SUGGESTED ROUND TRIPS & LOOPS: Take the San Francisco Bay Trail from the bridge east along the waterfront to the Marina District, Fort Mason and Fisherman's Wharf. Take the side trail down to the rugged coast to explore the ruins of the Sutro Baths or walk through Sutro Heights Park.

## SECTION 2
# Cliff House to Fort Funston, Golden Gate National Recreation Area

DISTANCE: 5¼ miles.

OPEN TO: Hikers. Bicyclists on part.

SURFACE: Beach, sidewalk.

ACCESS POINT: Cliff House.

HOW TO GET THERE: Head west on Geary Blvd., a major thoroughfare that crosses San Francisco from downtown to the ocean. Drive to its end and veer right on Point Lobos Avenue to the Cliff House.

OTHER ACCESS: Anywhere along the Great Highway.

DIFFICULTY: Easy.

ELEVATION GAIN/LOSS: 170 feet+/80 feet-.

CAUTIONS: Watch for big waves when walking Ocean Beach.

FURTHER INFORMATION: Golden Gate National Recreation Area, Cliff House (415)556-8642.

FACILITIES: Restrooms, water, and picnic tables at each end.

CAMPGROUNDS: Pacific Park RV Resort is on San Mateo County Section 2.

HOSTELS: San Francisco Hostel at Fort Mason (415)771-3645 or San Francisco Downtown Hostel (415)788-5604.

LODGING: San Francisco has thousands of hotel and motel rooms.

The hike begins at the Cliff House, a San Francisco landmark. Today's Cliff House is the third structure on that site to serve as a visitor destination for people from all over the world. The first, a huge Victorian affair built in 1863, served visitors who came to what was then a rural beach far from the city. Just offshore, Seal Rock was long a haul-out for noisy sea lions. They recently moved to Pier 39 at Fisherman's Wharf, becoming tourist attractions in a place full of attractions.

Beginning in fall 2002, the Cliff House and surrounding buildings will undergo a major renovation. The National Park Service expects the remodelling to be completed by spring 2004. The restaurant and some of the other facilities will be closed during much of that period.

From the Cliff House, walk south down the sidewalk. Across the road cliffs of fake rock, used for erosion control, rise to Sutro Heights Park. Ahead Ocean Beach stretches south more than three miles.

At the bottom of the hill you can take either of two routes. The Esplanade offers a wide sidewalk between the seawall and the Great Highway, or you can walk across the wide beach and follow the tideline south. The beach, often windy and pounded by rough surf, is a beachcomber's paradise. At ½ mile watch for the

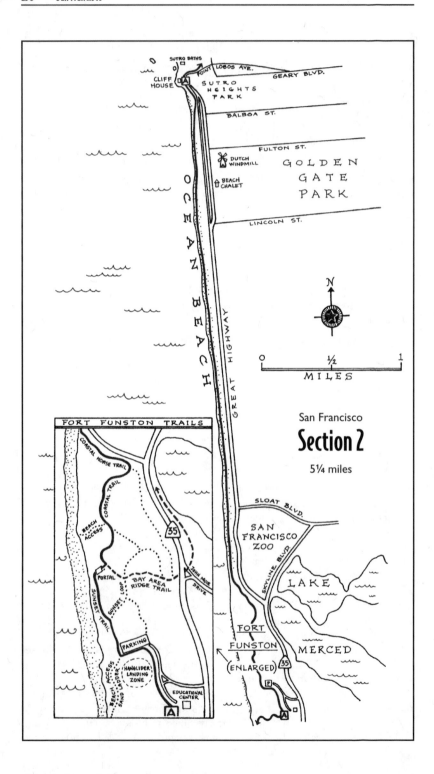

SUTRO BATHS

POINT LOBOS AVE.

GEARY BLVD.

CLIFF HOUSE

SUTRO HEIGHTS PARK

BALBOA ST.

FULTON ST.

DUTCH WINDMILL

BEACH CHALET

GOLDEN GATE PARK

LINCOLN ST.

OCEAN BEACH

GREAT HIGHWAY

N

0    ½    1
MILES

San Francisco

## Section 2

5¼ miles

FORT FUNSTON TRAILS

COASTAL HORSE TRAIL

COASTAL TRAIL

BEACH ACCESS

35

BAY AREA RIDGE TRAIL

PORTAL

JOHN MUIR DRIVE

SUNSET TRAIL

SUNSET LOOP

PARKING

BEACH ACCESS SAND LADDER

HANGLIDER LANDING ZONE

EDUCATIONAL CENTER

SLOAT BLVD.

SAN FRANCISCO ZOO

SKYLINE BLVD.

LAKE

FORT FUNSTON

(ENLARGED)

35

MERCED

# The Many Attractions of San Francisco

San Francisco's staggering number of attractions invite foot-powered exploration with many of them near the California Coastal Trail. Whether you want to learn about military or maritime history, walk around quiet lakes, visit a Dutch windmill, or dine overlooking the ocean, it's all close by. If you choose to walk to a destination and return by public transit, San Francisco's transit system is excellent.

A remarkable slice of history sits beneath the south end of the Golden Gate Bridge. Fort Point's massive brick edifice shows the importance the U.S. government placed on San Francisco Bay as a strategic harbor. The Army Corps of Engineers took eight years to build the fort starting in 1853. It housed 126 huge cannons and 500 soldiers during the Civil War. The fort never fired a shot before its decommissioning in 1900. Today the fort, part of the GGNRA, has free admission, tours by historically uniformed guides, museum displays and a bookstore. Exploring the three story maze of rooms, stairwells, and cannon bays is fascinating, with the Golden Gate Bridge looming overhead.

The Golden Gate Promenade, part of the San Francisco Bay Trail, runs three miles east along the bay from the bridge. It passes the Palace of Fine Arts, designed by Bernard Maybeck, where the Exploratorium has one of the world's best science museums for kids, then makes its way to the San Francisco National Maritime Historic Park. This park near Fisherman's Wharf has a museum of West Coast maritime history and the Hyde Street Pier, where eight historic ships dock including the Balclutha, a three-masted vessel that sailed around Cape Horn in 1886 and the ferry Eureka which carried cars and people over the bay from 1922 to 1941.

From the bridge to the northwest corner of San Francisco, the dramatic Coastal Trail itself is a big attraction. It passes the Palace of the Legion of Honor, a fine art museum, on its way to the Cliff House, a City attraction since the 1870s. This eatery and nearby attractions like the Musee Mechanique, Camera Obscura, and GGNRA Visitor Center overlook nearby Seal Rocks and miles of coastline. Nearby the ruins of Sutro Baths occupy a dramatic rocky cove reached by a trail.

Three-mile-long by half-mile-wide Golden Gate Park offers enough to keep you busy for days. Across the Great Highway from Ocean Beach a garden full of tulips surrounds an authentic Dutch windmill built in 1903. You can see its 75-foot tower from the beach. Nearby on the Great Highway, the recently restored Beach Chalet's glass enclosed restaurant overlooks the ocean. The first floor houses the Golden Gate Park Visitor Center with wonderful murals and mosaics created in the 1930s by Works Progress Administration artists. By walking inland on miles of park trails, you can discover three major museums, the Japanese Tea Garden, Strybing Arboretum with plants from around the world, several small formal gardens including the Shakespeare Garden, a rose garden, and the ornate Victorian Conservatory of Flowers full of tropical plants. You can rent a boat on Stow Lake, one of the park's ten artificial lakes, or a horse or carriage to tour the park. Other features include a restored antique carousel, children's playground, ball fields, bowling green, tennis courts, archery range, horseshoe pits, and a small herd of American bison.

Out beyond the CCT, San Francisco awaits exploration on foot. Across the street from the CCT in the City's southwestern corner is the fine San Francisco Zoo. You can easily walk or take public transit to many other attractions like Little Italy in North Beach, Chinatown, Pier 39, and Coit Tower on Telegraph Hill.

tall renovated windmill to the east at the northwest corner of Golden Gate Park. To reach the park, cross the Great Highway at the Fulton Street crosswalk. Across the Great Highway south of the windmill, the newly refurbished Beach Chalet houses the Golden Gate Park Visitor Center. Stop in for ideas of what to visit in the park. The Chalet also features 1930-era murals of life in San Francisco, plus a new micro brewery and restaurant upstairs. The historic structure, designed by Willis Polk, opened in 1925, but was closed for many years.

Continue walking south. The Sunset District, a residential area laid out on top of sand dunes, fronts the Great Highway for sixteen blocks. At 3 miles the San Francisco Zoo across the highway can be reached via the crosswalk at Sloat Blvd. Continue south to 3½ miles where sand dunes rise from the beach. The Great Highway turns inland and ends here.

The Coastal Trail heads up the dunes into Fort Funston, a former Nike missile base and now part of the GGNRA. Turn left here and leave Ocean Beach, climbing alongside the Great Highway on a sandy horse trail. Pass an area fenced to protect a bank swallow nesting area. At the top of the ridge at 3¾ miles, turn right and follow an old asphalt road which winds south through some of San Francisco's last dune habitat. Just past 4 miles, a trail heads west to the beach and another forks left. The Coastal Trail takes the right fork.

At 4⅜ mile make a sharp right turn and pass through a tunnel that is part of Battery Davis. After the tunnel, the trail turns left. At 5 miles you come to a large parking lot near a viewing platform on the bluff edge. Most likely you'll see a hang glider swooping along the cliff. The nearby hang glider launch site takes advantage of the strong winds that always seems to blow here, creating a favorable updraft in front of the cliffs. Take the path paralleling the driveway southeast to section's end at the Environmental Education Center at 5¼ miles.

**SUGGESTED ROUND TRIPS & LOOPS:** Huge Golden Gate Park, three miles long by a half mile wide, has many long and short loops you can take from the beach. You can walk the length of the park and ride the Fulton Street bus back to the beach.

# San Mateo County

**S**PECTACULAR CLIFFS and prominent points interspersed with secluded pocket beaches characterize the San Mateo County coast. The cliffs range from the towering, unstable precipices at Daly City and Devil's Slide in the north to the low, erodable sandstone palisades south of Half Moon Bay. Along the varied San Mateo coast, you'll also find some of California's best tidepools, attractive beaches, fascinating geology, and the expansive dunes of Año Nuevo where the immense and once again abundant northern elephant seals merit a visit.

The San Mateo coastline presents a remarkably rural face for most of its 55 miles considering it's so close to the metropolitan San Francisco Bay Area. The towns of Daly City and Pacifica bordering San Francisco have given in to the pressures of development, and Half Moon Bay has grown in recent years, but the southern half of the coast and the hills that separate it from the bayside cities are distinctly undeveloped. Here the public beaches and parks dotting the coastline and the hills to the east are interspersed with large private ranch holdings. Such a large amount of open space is extraordinary considering that the Ocean Shore Railroad ran between San Francisco and Santa Cruz from 1908 to 1920. The railroad's owners held large tracts of land which they wanted to develop as the "Coney Island of the Pacific Coast."

On the San Mateo coast's urban northern part, the CCT starts out on a remote sandy beach below steep cliffs, then follows streets and beaches and ascends headlands before climbing the shoulder of Montara Mountain on a historic wagon road. Returning to the coast, the CCT rolls through the little town of Moss Beach and past Fitzgerald Marine Reserve before reaching Pillar Point Harbor, the only anchorage on the San Mateo coast. From here the trail follows the curving shore of Half Moon Bay where hikers can walk the beach or take the paved Coastside Trail along the bluffs.

South of Half Moon Bay, the Coastal Trail follows Highway 1 and other coastal byways, bypassing privately owned land and tidal areas at the base of tall cliffs. The CCT returns to the immediate coast for stretches south of San Gregorio, but either irregular terrain or private land keeps forcing the CCT route back along the highway. Here one has access to gorgeous isolated beaches with several intriguing small villages just inland.

The coastline at the county's southern end seems so far from the bustle of the Bay Area only 50 miles north. The CCT returns to an enchanting shoreline between Gazos Creek and Cascade Creek. Then, after one more highway stint, the San Mateo coast climaxes at Año Nuevo State Reserve, which provides a wondrous and diverse natural area most famous for its abundant elephant seals, but also notable for other marine mammals, excellent birding, ample dunes and beaches, and fractured geology.

## SECTION I
# Fort Funston, Golden Gate National Recreation Area, to Mussel Rock City Park, Daly City

DISTANCE: 4 miles (6.4 kilometers).

OPEN TO: Hikers.

SURFACE: Sandy trail, beach.

ACCESS POINT: Fort Funston Environmental Education Center.

HOW TO GET THERE: Fort Funston is in the very southwestern corner of San Francisco, west of Highway 35 (Skyline Blvd.) 1.5 miles south of Sloat Blvd. and 1 mile north of Alemany Blvd. Turn west and park in the Environmental Education Center parking lot.

DIFFICULTY: Easy.

ELEVATION GAIN/LOSS: 175 feet+/ 200 feet-.

CAUTIONS: Watch for high waves on beach.

FURTHER INFORMATION: Golden Gate National Recreation Area, Fort Funston (415)331-1540, ask for a TDD line if you need one. Bay Area District, California State Parks (415)330-6300.

FACILITIES: Restrooms, water, picnic tables at Fort Funston.

CAMPGROUNDS: Pacific Park RV Resort is on the next CCT section.

LODGING: Pacifica, Daly City and San Francisco all have choices.

Even though the long beach on this walk borders a major urban area, it seems nearly as remote and distant from city bustle as a deserted island. The beach walk follows the base of high, steep eroding cliffs. Although houses perch on the cliff top, the beach usually draws only a few solitude seekers.

After a visit to the Fort Funston Environmental Education Center or a look at the hang gliders soaring gracefully just off the cliff edge taking advantage of the strong winds around the high cliffs, find the sandy trail near the west end of the Education Center buildings. The trail meanders south and west as it drops 200 feet down the dunes. At the bottom at ¼ mile, you come to the Phillip Burton Memorial Beach, named for the legendary congressman who sponsored the Golden Gate National Recreation Area enabling legislation in the 1970s.

As you walk south on the beach, the cliff gets higher, more unstable and eroded, soon towering 400 feet. The cliff looks unstable because the San Andreas Rift Zone comes onto the beach just north of Mussel Rock, causing extreme up-lifting of the land. Most visitors north of Mussel Rock are surf fishermen seeking striped bass.

As you approach Mussel Rock at 3¾ miles, riprap at the top of the beach shores up the base of the slope. Climb up the rocks to some wooden steps, then

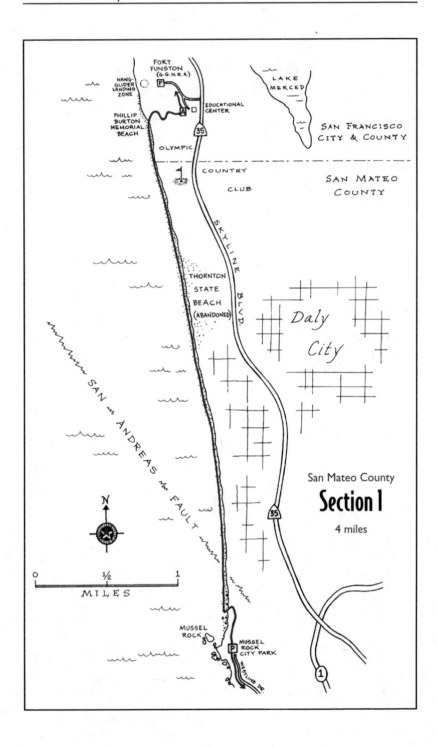

FORT
FUNSTON
(G.G.N.R.A.)

HANG-
GLIDER
LANDING
ZONE

EDUCATIONAL
CENTER

PHILLIP
BURTON
MEMORIAL
BEACH

OLYMPIC

COUNTRY

CLUB

35

LAKE
MERCED

SAN FRANCISCO
CITY & COUNTY

SAN MATEO
COUNTY

SKYLINE BLVD.

THORNTON
STATE
BEACH
(ABANDONED)

Daly
City

SAN ANDREAS FAULT

N

35

San Mateo County
# Section 1
4 miles

0          ½          1
M I L E S

MUSSEL
ROCK

MUSSEL
ROCK
CITY PARK

WESTLINE DR.

1

cross an old landfill to the Mussel Rock City Park parking lot and the end of this short section.

SUGGESTED ROUND TRIPS & LOOPS: Take a pleasant beach walk from either end and back, up to 8 miles round trip.

## SECTION 2
# Mussel Rock City Park, Daly City, to Pacifica State Beach

DISTANCE: 5¼ miles (8.4 kilometers).

OPEN TO: Hikers, bicyclists.

SURFACE: Road shoulder, sidewalk, trail, beach.

ACCESS POINT: Mussel Rock City Park.

HOW TO GET THERE: South of San Francisco, exit Highway 1 in Pacifica at Palmetto Avenue. Go north on Palmetto, turn left on Westline Drive and drive to the city park at the end of the road.

OTHER ACCESS: Anywhere along the route.

DIFFICULTY: Easy.

ELEVATION GAIN/LOSS: 175 feet+/250 feet-.

CAUTIONS: Watch for traffic on roads and big waves on the beach.

FURTHER INFORMATION: Bay Area District, California State Parks (415)330-6300.

FACILITIES: Restrooms, water at Sharp Park. Pacifica has stores and cafes.

CAMPGROUNDS: Pacific Park RV Resort on this section.

HOSTELS: Montara Lighthouse Hostel (650)728-7177 is on San Mateo Section 4.

LODGING: Pacifica has several motels.

This short section of the Coastal Trail passes from Daly City through the seaside town of Pacifica. Daly City, renowned for the near incessant fog that blows in from the sea, was made famous by the song "Little Boxes." The rows of uniform houses lining Daly City's coastal bluffs inspired Malvina Reynolds to write this satirical song because the dwellings seemed ticky-tacky in this fine coastal area.

Pacifica encompasses nine small communities which joined together in 1957. Pacifica's coastline is broken by ridges, with small beaches at the mouths of valleys in between. The Ohlone tribe lived here before the Spaniards arrived in 1769.

This section has notable changes since this book's first edition. Mori Point's 105 acres, purchased for public use in September 2000, will one day allow the CCT to stay on the coast from Mori Point to Rockaway Beach. Between Rockaway and Pacifica State Beach, a ¾-mile wheelchair-accessible CCT link is being built.

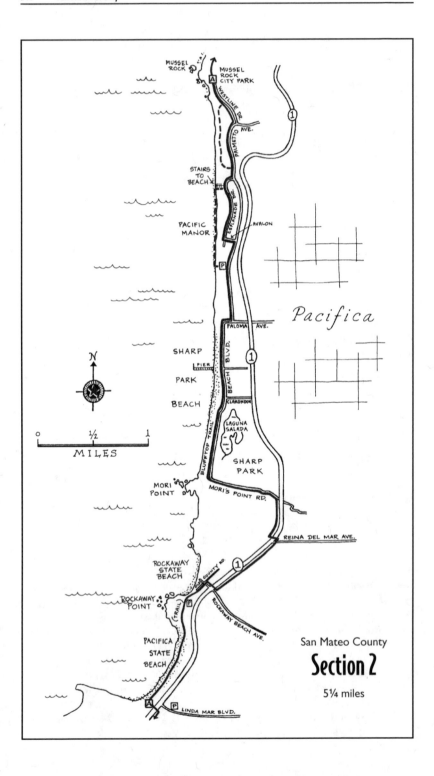

MUSSEL ROCK

MUSSEL ROCK CITY PARK

WESTLINE DR.

PALMETTO AVE.

STAIRS TO BEACH

PACIFIC MANOR

ESPLANADE DR.

AVALON

P

PALOMA AVE.

Pacifica

SHARP

PIER

PARK

BEACH

BEACH BLVD.

CLARONDON

LAGUNA SALADA

SHARP PARK

N

MILES

0     ½     1

BLUFFTOP TRAIL

MORI POINT

MORI'S POINT RD.

REINA DEL MAR AVE.

ROCKAWAY STATE BEACH

COUNTY RD.

ROCKAWAY POINT

TRAIL

ROCKAWAY BEACH AVE.

PACIFICA STATE BEACH

A     P     LINDA MAR BLVD.

San Mateo County

## Section 2

5¼ miles

# The Spaniards Colonize California

In the 18th century, the colonial powers considered the California coast hot property. The Spaniards, English, and Russians all wanted the vast resources of this bountiful land. The Spaniards launched expeditions from their colony in Mexico, claiming California for the Spanish crown. The Spaniards worried about the Russian presence in California, with the czar's men ranging as far as Baja California in search of sea otter pelts. Francis Drake had landed in northern California in 1579, presumably at Point Reyes, claiming the area for Queen Elizabeth I.

In 1769 the Spaniards sent Captain Gaspar de Portola on a colonial mission up the California coast to establish a settlement at Monterey. They chose Monterey because 150 years earlier Sebastian Vizcaino had sailed into Monterey Bay and returned to Spain with a glowing report of its safe and secure harbor, a gross exaggeration at best. Vizcaino evidently liked the area, painting a favorable picture in hopes of returning.

Portola departed San Diego in July 1769 with 64 people including soldiers, Indian servants, priests and others. They traveled up the coast until the steep Big Sur coastline forced them inland. Reaching the upper Salinas Valley in late September, they then followed the Salinas River to the coast. They searched for the fine harbor at Monterey described by Vizcaino, but found no protected harbor because it didn't exist. Portola, determined to keep looking despite low supplies and illness, led the expedition north. The group soon camped near the mouth of San Pedro Creek at Pacifica. On October 11, Portola rode up Sweeney Ridge and discovered the huge San Francisco Bay.

The expedition returned to San Diego. Despite the report of no secure harbor at Monterey, Portola planned their return to found a mission and presidio there. Father Junipero Serra, in charge of setting up missions, sailed to Monterey while Portola led the overland expedition, reaching Monterey in just 36 days. They soon established the first mission and presidio at Monterey. Then Serra moved his mission south to Carmel for the fresh water and fertile soil. In official ceremonies on June 3, 1770, Portola claimed the land for Spain, beginning the Spanish settlement of California.

Meanwhile, in Sonora, Mexico, Captain Juan Bautista de Anza was fighting Apache Indians on behalf of the Spanish crown. Rumors circulated that the Portola expedition had succeeded, igniting the idea that a trail could link Sonora to the new colony. De Anza, who had heard of the vast bay fed by a big river (the Sacramento) north of Monterey, was given the job. He mounted the expedition in October 1775 with 300 people and six tons of food. The group traveled through Arizona and southern California, arriving in Monterey in March 1776. De Anza then left for San Francisco Bay with a smaller group. They stopped at the bay's entrance and established the Presidio, while Father Serra established a mission a few miles south.

Today significant historical parks and buildings remain marking California's Spanish era. These include presidios at San Francisco and Monterey, the 21 missions, and the buildings of Monterey State Historic Park. While we celebrate these events as important parts of California history, we must also note that the colonization of California took a tremendous toll on native Americans. The Spaniards exploited the resources and people, with the mission system enslaving the natives to work the farms, leading to the destruction of native culture.

From the Mussel Rock City Park parking lot, walk south up Westline Road. You soon enter Pacifica. You might consider an informal, unsigned trail that crosses open, sloping land west of the road for about ⅝ mile. CCT continues along Westline through a residential area. At ¼ mile turn right on Palmetto Avenue, the frontage road for the freeway. Follow Palmetto to ⅝ mile, turn right and follow Esplanade Drive. The all-tides CCT continues along Esplanade, a quiet residential street, to its end.

If the tide is low, consider dropping to the beach by the stairs at the north end of Esplanade or a trail opposite the end of West Manor Drive. You can walk the beach south for about ⅜ mile from the stairs. If the tide is low enough to continue south around the rocky point, you can walk the beach another ⅜ mile, then climb the cement steps to a parking lot just south of Pacific Park RV Resort.

At the end of Esplanade, the all-tides route of CCT turns left on Avalon. This ends at Palmetto Avenue at 1¼ miles. Turn right and continue south along Palmetto past Pacific Park RV Resort.

At 2 miles turn right and walk Paloma Avenue two blocks to Sharp Park Beach. Turn left and follow the walkway beside Beach Boulevard overlooking the beach. Pass the Pacifica Pier at 2½ miles where fisherfolk usually cast for perch, bass, smelt or shark. Restrooms and a small store are at the foot of the pier.

Continue south on the walkway. After the street ends, the path continues as the wide Promenade past the freshwater Laguna Salada and the Sharp Park Golf Course just over the low dunes. If the tide is out you can walk the beach here. Just before rocky Mori Point, turn left and head inland on the dirt Mori's Point Road to Highway 1 at 3¾ miles. Walk the sidewalk on the west side of the two lane roadway to Reina Del Mar Avenue at 4 miles. Cross the highway and follow the east sidewalk south.

At 4¼ miles cross the highway again at Rockaway Beach Avenue. Continue briefly to Old County Road, turn left and walk to the parking area. Take the path across the undeveloped headlands of Rockaway Point. At 4¾ miles it drops down onto pleasant Pacifica State Beach, protected by rocky headlands at both ends and with a good break for surfers. Walk to the south end at 5¼ miles to complete the section. Highway 1 and a business district are adjacent to the beach.

**SUGGESTED ROUND TRIPS & LOOPS:** Rockaway Beach to the south end of Pacifica State Beach and back is 2 miles round trip.

# SECTION 3
# Pacifica State Beach to Montara State Beach

DISTANCE: 6⅝ miles (10.7 kilometers).

OPEN TO: Hikers. Bicyclists on part.

SURFACE: Trail, road shoulder, beach.

ACCESS POINT: Pacifica State Beach.

HOW TO GET THERE: Turn west off Highway 1 in Pacifica at Linda Mar Blvd. into Pacifica State Beach parking lot .

OTHER ACCESS: McNee Ranch State Park, Montara Beach.

DIFFICULTY: Moderate.

ELEVATION GAIN/LOSS: 900 feet+/900 feet-.

CAUTIONS: Steep climb over Montara Mountain. Watch for bicyclists descending San Pedro Mountain Road.

FURTHER INFORMATION: Bay Area District, California State Parks (415)330-6300.

FACILITIES: Water, restrooms, picnic tables at both ends.

CAMPGROUNDS: Pacific Park RV Resort on previous section.

HOSTELS: Montara Lighthouse Hostel (650)728-7177.

LODGING: Pacifica has several motels.

This unforgettable hike starts at the beach, climbs over the flank of wild and un-developed Montara Mountain, runs through McNee Ranch State Park, and drops down to another beach. You walk an historic road through the site of a long-term controversy over plans to build a freeway over the mountain.

In 1769 the Gaspar de Portola expedition camped beside an Ohlone village by the mouth of San Pedro Creek where this section begins. From there they climbed east up Sweeney Ridge and discovered San Francisco Bay. See the feature article.

From the south end of Pacifica State Beach, walk east across Highway 1 at Linda Mar Boulevard and follow the highway south. Cross the bridge over San Pedro Creek before ¼ mile and turn left on San Pedro Terrace Road. You can walk on the road or follow the path north of the road along the channeled brushy creek, returning to the road before Peralta Road. Go right on Peralta for a block, left on Rosita Road to Adobe Drive, where you go right to narrow Higgins Way. Walk east on Higgins to its end where a gate blocks the road at 1¼ miles. Behind the gate follow the historic Old San Pedro Mountain Road. This fire road climbs through steep and rugged terrain, winding through a rich coastal scrub plant community full of wildlife, including the endangered peregrine falcon and San Bruno elfin butterfly.

You reach the top at 3¼ miles after a 900-foot ascent. The fire road crosses a

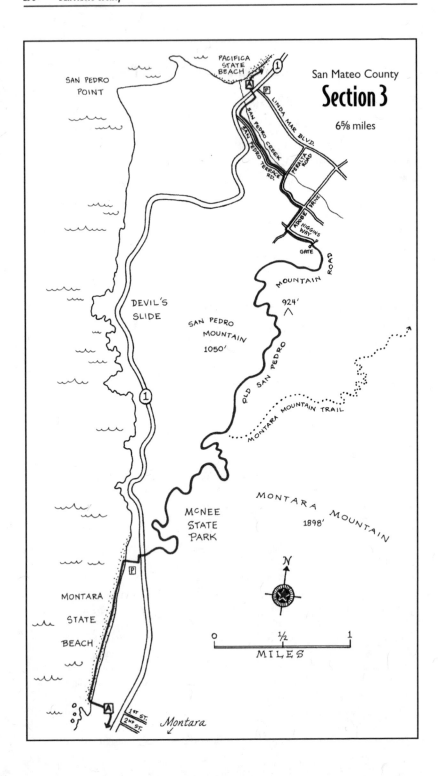

SAN PEDRO POINT

PACIFICA STATE BEACH

San Mateo County
**Section 3**
6⅝ miles

LINDA MAR BLVD.

SAN PEDRO CREEK

SAN PEDRO TERRACE RD.

PERALTA ROAD

ADOBE DRIVE

HIGGINS WAY

GATE

MOUNTAIN ROAD

924'

DEVIL'S SLIDE

SAN PEDRO MOUNTAIN
1050'

OLD SAN PEDRO

MONTARA MOUNTAIN TRAIL

1

McNEE STATE PARK

MONTARA MOUNTAIN
1898'

N

MONTARA STATE BEACH

P

0    ½    1
M I L E S

1ST ST.
2ND ST.

*Montara*

saddle between Montara Mountain and San Pedro Mountain to the west. Take a few minutes to absorb the breathtaking views north and south. Imagine that the California Department of Transportation planned an 80-foot wide reroute of Highway 1 climbing the ridge and passing over this saddle. Thanks to the protests of San Mateo County residents, this plan was withdrawn, and twin tunnels through the mountain are being built. When it is closed to vehicles, the old highway will provide a dramatic route for the Coastal Trail.

From the saddle, CCT descends to Montara Beach. Follow the main fire road, ignoring any side trails as it snakes its way down a series of switchbacks into McNee Ranch State Park. At the bottom pass the old McNee farm house and follow the dirt road out to the highway at 6 miles. Be especially careful crossing the highway since the traffic descending from Devil's Slide goes very fast here. Walk south ⅛ mile on the shoulder to a parking area and take the stairway down to the beach. Walk this quiet beach popular for fishing, surfing and picnicking to its south end at 6⅝ miles where this section ends. A parking area and restrooms are on the bluff beside Highway 1.

SUGGESTED ROUND TRIPS & LOOPS: From the north end of Montara Beach, walk into McNee State Park and up the Old San Pedro Mountain Road to the ridge and back, 5¾ miles round trip.

# SECTION 4
# Montara State Beach to Pillar Point Harbor

DISTANCE: 4½ miles (7.3 kilometers).

OPEN TO: Hikers. Bicyclists on road.

SURFACE: Highway shoulder, trail.

ACCESS POINT: Montara State Beach.

HOW TO GET THERE: Turn west off Highway 1 at the north end of the town of Montara into Montara State Beach parking area.

OTHER ACCESS: Fitzgerald Marine Reserve in Moss Beach.

DIFFICULTY: Easy.

ELEVATION GAIN/LOSS: 100 feet+/100 feet-.

CAUTIONS: Watch for traffic on highway. Stay back from cliff edge.

FURTHER INFORMATION: San Mateo State Parks (415)330-6300. Fitzgerald Marine Reserve (650)728-3584.

FACILITIES: Water, restrooms, picnic tables at both ends and at Fitzgerald Marine Reserve.

CAMPGROUNDS: Francis Beach Campground at Half Moon Bay State Park.

HOSTELS: Montara Lighthouse Hostel (650)728-7177.

LODGING: Montara and Half Moon Bay have motels.

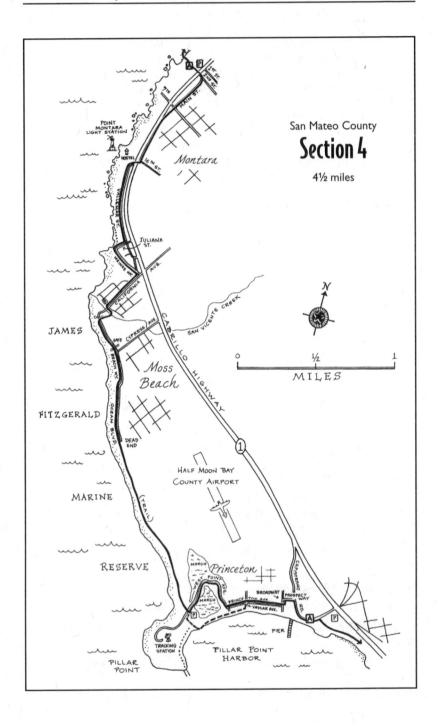

San Mateo County
# Section 4
4½ miles

POINT
MONTARA
LIGHT STATION

HOSTEL

*Montara*

7TH

MAIN ST.

1ST ST.
2ND ST.

16 TH ST.

JULIANA
ST.

WIENKE WY.

CALIFORNIA

VALLEMAR ST.

AVE.

GATE

CYPRESS AVE.

BEACH WY.

JAMES

San Vicente Creek

*Moss
Beach*

FITZGERALD

OCEAN BLVD.

DEAD
END

CABRILLO HIGHWAY

N

0        ½        1
MILES

MARINE

(TRAIL)

HALF MOON BAY
COUNTY AIRPORT

1

RESERVE

MARSH

*Princeton*

WEST POINT

MARSH

CAPISTRANO

BROADWAY

PRINCETON AVE.

PROSPECT WAY

CAPISTRANO RD.

VASSAR AVE.

PIER

PILLAR
POINT

TRACKING
STATION

PILLAR POINT
HARBOR

**CCT overlooks Fitzgerald Marine Reserve from wooded bluff.**

In contrast to the mountainous nature of the previous section, this walk follows flat coastal terraces, passes through one of the most significant intertidal areas in California, and ends at the town of Princeton at Pillar Point Harbor.

From the parking area at the south end of Montara Beach, carefully cross Highway 1 at 2nd Street, walk to Main Street and follow it south to 11th Street. At the end of Main, step around the barrier to follow the abandoned roadway which now serves as an informal walkway. When this ends at 14th Street, walk the highway shoulder to 16th Street around ¾ mile.

Cross the highway to the driveway for Montara Lighthouse and Hostel. Take a look around the grounds and lighthouse. If you plan to stay, remember the hostel is closed during the day.

Turn left and walk the side road running along the chain link fence. Just past the Sanitary District office the road ends, and the path continues past a few trees before ending at the Vallemar Street cul-de-sac before one mile. Walk Vallemar Street to Juliana Street, where you go right one short block to the bluff edge, and turn left on Weinke Way. The bluff on your right has a public trail and a few benches.

At 1½ miles Weinke Way ends at the intersection of California Street and Highway 1. Turn right on California Street and walk a few blocks to its end. On your right are parking, picnic tables and toilets, plus an information kiosk for Fitzgerald Marine Reserve. To reach the reefs, which are exposed during low tide and offer excellent tidepooling, go down to the tidal zone. CCT crosses North Lake Street and follows the footpath down and across the small creek. Continue for about 100 feet and take the trail to the right. Go 300 feet to where the CCT switches back to the left and uphill. CCT passes through a forested area atop steep cliffs overlooking the reef 100 feet below.

The trail ends at the corner of Cypress Avenue and Beach Street overlooking the ocean at 2 miles. Walk down Beach Street in this quiet residential area (quiet because it's caving into the sea due to an earthquake fault, and the residents are nervous!) past the Moss Beach Distillery Restaurant. Continue on Ocean Boulevard, walking to the end of the street at 2⅝ miles. Follow the trail there that continues south along the open, undeveloped bluff. The huge Air Force tracking station looms prominently on Pillar Point in the distance.

The trail comes to a paved road at 3½ miles which serves the tracking station. Step around the gate and continue down the road to the parking lot. Here you

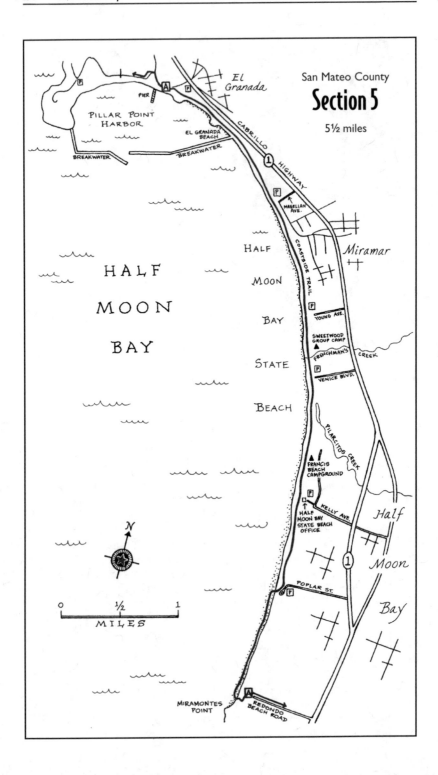

San Mateo County
## Section 5
5½ miles

El Granada

PILLAR POINT HARBOR

PIER

EL GRANADA BEACH

BREAKWATER

BREAKWATER

CABRILLO HIGHWAY

1

MAGELLAN AVE.

COASTSIDE TRAIL

Miramar

HALF

MOON

BAY

STATE

BEACH

HALF

MOON

BAY

YOUNG AVE.

SWEETWOOD GROUP CAMP

FRENCHMAN'S CREEK

VENICE BLVD.

PILARCITOS CREEK

FRANCIS BEACH CAMPGROUND

KELLY AVE.

HALF MOON BAY STATE BEACH OFFICE

Half

Moon

1

Bay

POPLAR ST.

N

½    1

MILES

MIRAMONTES POINT

REDONDO BEACH ROAD

have two choices to reach Princeton. At low to medium tides walk down to the beach, turn left and walk the beach ¼ or ⅜ mile, then take either West Point Avenue or Vassar Avenue up to Princeton Avenue. The other route follows the road around the north side of the marsh, then goes left to follow Princeton Avenue.

Take Princeton Avenue to its end, then jog left on Broadway for a half block, go right on Prospect Way for another short block, turn right and follow Capistrano Road another block to the harbor parking area and the end of this section at 4½ miles. The harbor facilities here include restaurants, stores, a pier and marina.

**ALTERNATE ROUTE:** The beach from Fitzgerald Marine Reserve to the north end of Pillar Point is passable at low tide. From there it's a scramble up the bluff to the trail described above.

**SUGGESTED ROUND TRIPS & LOOPS:** From Fitzgerald Marine Reserve walk to Pillar Point Harbor and back.

## SECTION 5
# Pillar Point Harbor to Redondo Beach Road, Half Moon Bay

**DISTANCE:** 5½ miles (8.9 kilometers).

**OPEN TO:** Hikers, bicyclists. Equestrians on part of the beach.

**SURFACE:** Beach, paved trail.

**ACCESS POINT:** Pillar Point Harbor.

**HOW TO GET THERE:** Turn west off Highway 1 at the well marked exit to Pillar Point Harbor and Princeton, 2.5 miles south of Moss Beach and 4 miles north of Half Moon Bay. Take Capistrano Road to the harbor parking lot.

**OTHER ACCESS:** Parking lots along this route at the ends of Young Avenue, Venice Avenue, Kelly Avenue and Poplar Avenue.

**DIFFICULTY:** Easy.

**ELEVATION GAIN/LOSS:** 50 feet+/50 feet- (depending how often you climb the bluff).

**CAUTIONS:** The trail exiting the beach at Redondo Beach Road is steep and undeveloped.

**FURTHER INFORMATION:** Half Moon Bay State Beach (650)726-8819.

**FACILITIES:** Store, restrooms, water at Pillar Point Harbor. Toilets and water at several locations along the route, but not at the end.

**CAMPGROUNDS:** Francis Beach Campground at Half Moon Bay State Beach. Group Camp at Sweetwood.

**HOSTELS:** Montara Lighthouse Hostel on previous section (650)728-7177.

**LODGING:** Half Moon Bay has several motels.

In sharp contrast to the last two sections, this section offers an easy, flat walk which follows the beach and bluff forming the gentle curve of Half Moon Bay. The route is really two parallel paths: one on the beach and the other on the paved Coastside Trail on the low bluff above. If the tide is in and blocking the way, simply walk on the multi-use Coastside Trail.

Start the walk at the harbor and walk southeast along the waterfront, passing the pier and boat ramp and an RV park before reaching the east breakwater at ½ mile. Surfers use the beach here because of the shore break created by the breakwater. The bluff has been eroding at a fast rate since the harbor breakwater was built in 1959. See the feature article.

Continue south along the beach or on the bluff. El Granada Beach was once a popular vacation destination for San Franciscans who rode the Ocean Shore Railroad here in the early 1900s. Around 1½ miles you reach Miramar Beach. The odd, driftwood looking A-frame building peering over the low bluff is the Miramar Beach Health Club.

At 2¼ miles the Sweetwood Group Camp is sheltered behind a row of Monterey pines on the bluff. You'll find an outhouse and water at the camp. The Coastside Trail goes through the middle of the camp. If Frenchman's Creek, and

## How To Wreck a Beach

It's easy to destroy the natural processes of beach formation with enough large rocks and money. That's what the U.S. Army Corps of Engineers did in 1959 when they built the long planned Pillar Point Harbor breakwater. Before the breakwater, waves from the northwest bent around the point and lost much of their energy, and waves from the south broke on the broad sandy beach south of the point, seldom affecting erosion of the bluffs. Fishing boats, however, were subject to the powerful waves and were regularly dragged off anchor and wrecked on the beach. Locals started asking the federal government for a breakwater as early as 1911.

After the breakwater was built, waves deflected off the breakwater and were forced to smash onto El Granada and Miramar Beaches. Within ten years the beaches were virtually gone. Without the sand as a buffer, the waves quickly eroded an astounding 150 feet of bluff along the length of the beach. It's still receding about five feet a year. Instead of a broad beach serving as a natural barrier to the ocean's power, only a steep, narrow bluff armored with rock remains. In the early 20th century El Granada Beach was touted as "The Coney Island of the West, the most remarkable stretch of clean, sandy, safe beach in the world." Now the narrow beach is walkable only at low tide.

Any attempt to armor the shoreline will likely fail. Coastside residents had used the old Mirada Road since the 1850s. After the breakwater was built, the San Mateo County government tried to save the road from the invading ocean by armoring it with riprap, but the effort failed. Now at low tide you can see the riprap in the surf 150 feet from the bluff and historic Mirada Road is entirely gone.

Thanks for help from The Coastside Trail Guidebook by Barbara Vander Werf.

Pilarcitos Creek a little farther along the beach, are flowing heavily into the surf, the paved trail has bridges over the creeks. Pass Francis Beach Campground, then the headquarters for Half Moon Bay State Beach at the end of Kelly Avenue at 3½ miles. The old downtown section of Half Moon Bay can be found ¾ mile inland on Kelly. You can continue down the beach or the Coastside Trail. Beyond Poplar Avenue around 4½ miles, the Coastside Trail hasn't yet been completed, but a broad dirt path continues south for another 1¾ miles. As you walk south the bluffs get higher, reaching over 40 feet high at Miramontes Point. Around 5¼ miles just before Redondo Beach Road, walk up a ravine to find the dead end of the dirt Redondo Beach Road at 5½ miles where this section ends. There are no services here. Highway 1 is ¾ mile inland.

SUGGESTED ROUND TRIP & LOOPS: You can reach this walk from several State Park parking lots and public streets along the route presenting numerous possibilities for short or long round trip beach strolls.

## SECTION 6
# Half Moon Bay to San Gregorio State Beach

DISTANCE: 10¼ miles (16.5 kilometers).

OPEN TO: Hikers, bicyclists.

SURFACE: Highway shoulder, road shoulder.

ACCESS POINT: Redondo Beach Road.

HOW TO GET THERE: Turn west off Highway 1 1.5 miles south of Half Moon Bay on Redondo Beach Road. Go .75 mile and park at the end of the road.

DIFFICULTY: Easy.

ELEVATION GAIN/LOSS: 490 feet+/450 feet-.

CAUTIONS: Beware of speeding traffic when walking Highway 1.

FURTHER INFORMATION: San Mateo Coast State Beaches (650)879-2170.

FACILITIES: Store in San Gregorio. Chemical toilets at San Gregorio Beach.

CAMPGROUNDS: Francis Beach Campground at Half Moon Bay State Beach on previous section. Pelican Point RV Park (650)726-9100 on this section.

HOSTELS: Pigeon Point Lighthouse Hostel (650) 879-0633 at end of Section 8.

LODGING: Half Moon Bay area has several motels.

This stretch of the San Mateo coast has the potential for some excellent coastal hiking, but unfortunately for now, nearly all the 10¼-mile walk follows roads. The good news is that it's mostly through scenic rolling agricultural land.

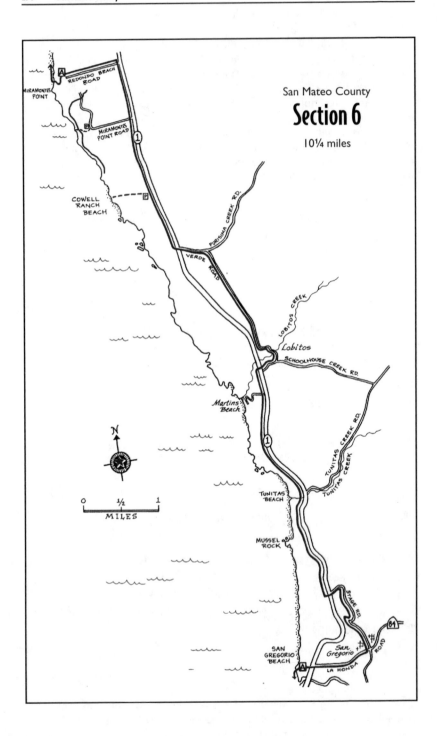

San Mateo County
**Section 6**
10¼ miles

Eventually the Coastside Trail will extend farther south where impassable rocky tidelands will keep the trail on the bluffs. The two golf courses just south of Redondo Beach Road now have new a link in the Coastal Trail, but the CCT there has not yet been connected with the CCT north or south, essential for that path to truly become a link in the Coastal Trail. When the trail is done, it will connect the beach ending at Miramontes Point beyond Redondo Beach Road to the Cowell Ranch land purchased in 1996 by the Coastal Conservancy. This will add 2½ miles to the trail, eliminating some highway walking.

In the meantime, CCT follows Redondo Beach Road east to the highway at ¾ mile. Turn south and walk the highway shoulder. At the traffic light for Miramontes Point Road beyond 1⅜ miles, one can turn right and go ⅜ mile to walk the new ¾-mile link in the Coastal Trail, which leads north and south for about ⅜ mile from the parking lot. (It hasn't yet been connected to the main CCT. Watch for flying golf balls and speeding golf carts if you go.) For now, CCT continues along the highway shoulder to Verde Road at 3¼ miles. The Cowell Ranch trail will end here when done. Turn left and follow Verde Road as it heads inland to 3½ miles then turns south. This quiet rural road provides relief from walking the busy highway. The road veers inland briefly to cross Lobitos Creek, passing a few houses in the tiny historic settlement of Lobitos, eucalyptus groves, and a pumpkin farm before returning to the highway at 5½ miles.

As you follow the highway south, you can only wish CCT took you across the coastal bluffs now privately owned and down to some of the pristine beaches hiding below the bluffs. At 5¾ miles Martin's Beach Road leads down to the beach. Open year round, a parking fee is charged. The little store only opens in summer.

At 7¼ miles you pass Tunitas Creek where private property blocks access to the inviting beach. You overlook the beach and cliffs as you walk south along the highway up a hill. At the top of the long grade around 9¼ miles, Stage Road heads east. Take this road to avoid a long highway descent. Stage Road soon swings south and snakes down the hill. At the historic little village of San Gregorio at the bottom, stop in at the general store for almost anything you want, from sunscreen to a glass of wine. After you visit the store, walk La Honda Road west ¾ mile down to Highway 1. Take extreme care crossing the highway to San Gregorio Beach since the traffic goes very fast. This section ends here at 10¼ miles.

**SUGGESTED ROUND TRIP & LOOPS:** You can drive to the new parking lot on Miramontes Point Road and walk the new, still disconnected link in the Coastal Trail through the golf courses of the otherwise gated Spyglass and Ocean Colony subdivisions. It leads north and south with ocean views for about ⅜ mile each, meaning a 1½-mile round trip if you do it all.

**HOW TO IMPROVE CCT HERE:** Connect the new Ocean Colony/Spyglass link of CCT with Redondo Beach Road or the adjacent beach on the north end and with the Cowell Ranch property to the south. Open the Cowell Ranch and Purisima Farms properties to public access with a fully completed Coastal Trail there. Build a trail off the highway south of Cowell Ranch.

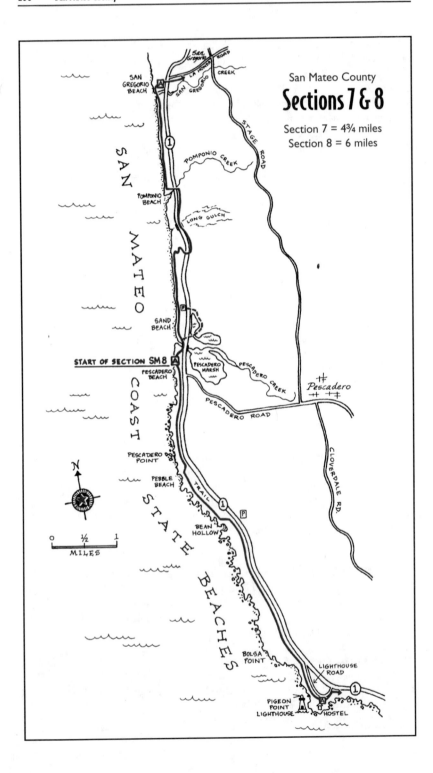

San Mateo County
# Sections 7 & 8

Section 7 = 4¾ miles
Section 8 = 6 miles

SAN GREGORIO BEACH

San Gregorio Road
La Honda Road
SAN GREGORIO CREEK

STAGE ROAD

POMPONIO CREEK

POMPONIO BEACH

LONG GULCH

SAND BEACH

START OF SECTION SM8

PESCADERO BEACH

PESCADERO MARSH

Pescadero Creek

Pescadero

PESCADERO ROAD

PESCADERO POINT

PEBBLE BEACH

SAN MATEO COAST STATE BEACHES

TRAIL

BEAN HOLLOW

CLOVERDALE RD.

N

0  ½  1
MILES

BOLSA POINT

LIGHTHOUSE ROAD

PIGEON POINT LIGHTHOUSE

HOSTEL

## SECTION 7
# San Gregorio State Beach to Pescadero State Beach

DISTANCE: 4¾ miles (7.6 kilometers).

OPEN TO: Hikers. Bicyclists on road.

SURFACE: Beach, highway shoulder.

ACCESS POINT: San Gregorio State Beach.

HOW TO GET THERE: Turn west off Highway 1 just south of Highway 84/La Honda Road into San Gregorio State Beach parking area.

OTHER ACCESS: Pomponio State Beach.

DIFFICULTY: Easy.

ELEVATION GAIN/LOSS: 160 feet+/300 feet-.

CAUTIONS: Don't get trapped by rising tides. Use caution on the tricky, short descent to the beach.

FURTHER INFORMATION: San Mateo Coast State Beaches (650)879-2170.

FACILITIES: Chemical toilets at San Gregorio, Pomponio, and Pescadero State Beaches.

CAMPGROUNDS: San Mateo County Memorial Park 10 miles east of Pescadero Beach on Pescadero Road has many sites.

HOSTELS: Pigeon Point Lighthouse Hostel (650)879-0633 is at end of next section.

LODGING: Half Moon Bay to the north and Davenport to the south have lodging.

At low to medium tides, this piece of coast offers some fine walking on isolated beaches at the base of steep cliffs. Although the highway is near, you can't see it for the 100-foot-high cliffs, and the crashing surf blocks most highway sounds. At high tide, you must walk the highway or wait for the tide to recede. State Parks owns the beach and bluffs west of the highway from San Gregorio Beach all the way to Pescadero Beach, but the bluffs have no official trail and the marine terrace is deeply cut by ravines.

From the San Gregorio State Beach parking lot, drop down to the beach south of San Gregorio Creek. The beach from here to Pomponio Beach is almost always open except at the highest tides. Since the beach backs against high cliffs, don't go unless you're sure of the tides. If you have doubts, don't do it. CCT follows the beach south. Since most people stay near the parking lots, you'll probably find solitude quickly. Walk an open beach for ¾ mile. Just before you reach Pomponio Beach, big rocks on the beach may block your way at very high tides. If it's blocked, find a safe way up the bluff to the highway and walk the shoulder. Otherwise, walk Pomponio Beach to Pomponio Creek around one mile.

South of Pomponio Creek, rocks, cliffs and surf block the beach, so you must turn east and walk the highway shoulder. It climbs a hill, then drops across Long

Gulch. Part way up the next rise around ½ mile from the Pomponio Beach parking lot, look for a casual trail west across the bluffs before 3¼ miles. It's marked by three creosote posts with a barren patch of ground behind them. Unless it's high tide, take this trail down toward the beach. In about ⅛ mile the trail drops into a small gully, crossing the creek on a short, narrow board bridge, then heads for the beach. Descend the final fifteen feet to the beach by handholds and steps cut into the sandstone. It's fairly safe if you're careful, unless you have a fear of heights. You come to an isolated beach with few visitors. Unless the tide is high, walk the beach south all the way to Pescadero Beach.

You reach the first parking area for Pescadero Beach at 4½ miles. Continue down the beach to Pescadero Creek. Follow the creek up to the highway bridge. Walk the pedestrian path on the bridge to the parking lot on the west side of the highway and section's end at 4¾ miles. You can see Pescadero Marsh across the highway.

**SUGGESTED ROUND TRIPS & LOOPS:** From any of the four state park parking lots, you can take short strolls to explore the beaches. Pescadero Marsh, one of the most important freshwater/brackish coastal marshes in California, has three short trails into it. It's an important stop on the Pacific Flyway and home to many resident birds. One trail starts across the highway from the north parking lot. Another follows Pescadero Creek's north bank under the highway bridge, and the third starts from Pescadero Road.

*Surf, rocks and wildflowers grace the San Mateo coast.*

# SECTION 8
# Pescadero State Beach to Pigeon Point Lighthouse

DISTANCE: 6 miles (9.7 kilometers).

OPEN TO: Hikers. Bicyclists on road.

SURFACE: Beach, trail, highway shoulder, road shoulder.

ACCESS POINT: Pescadero Beach.

HOW TO GET THERE: Turn west off Highway 1 about 15 miles south of Half Moon Bay and .25 mile north of Pescadero Road into Pescadero State Beach south parking lot.

OTHER ACCESS: Bean Hollow Beach.

DIFFICULTY: Easy.

ELEVATION GAIN/LOSS: 60 feet+/40 feet-.

CAUTIONS: The hostel closes during the day from 10 AM to 4:30 PM.

FURTHER INFORMATION: San Mateo Coast State Beaches (650)879-2170.

FACILITIES: Chemical toilets at Pescadero Beach. Water at Pigeon Point Lighthouse.

CAMPGROUNDS: Butano State Park in hills east of section has camping. San Mateo County Memorial Park 10 miles east of Pescadero Beach on Pescadero Road has many sites.

HOSTELS: Pigeon Point Lighthouse Hostel (650)879-0633.

LODGING: Half Moon Bay to the north and Davenport to the south have lodging.

MAP: See page 260.

The California coastline is ever changing as one proceeds down the coast. The previous section was all rolling hills and steep cliffs. This one is on a gentle marine terrace with low bluffs overlooking an extensive area of tidal rocks. Much of this walk follows the highway through agricultural land, presenting many opportunities to explore the intertidal zone and some pocket beaches.

From the Pescadero Beach south parking lot, walk the highway shoulder south. For the 2 miles to Pebble Beach, the highway is on the low bluff, offering many places to drop down to the rocky tidal zone and explore. While the rugged tidal zone makes for slow going, if you're up to it, it can be negotiated at low to medium tide.

At Pebble Beach, a short side path from the parking area drops to the beach, so named because of its colorful, pea-sized quartz rocks. You'll also find a curious rock formation called tafoni. The Coastal Trail south from the parking area follows the nature trail right along the edge of the bluff. Since State Parks is restoring this coastal bluff plant community, hikers should stay on the path. Watch for harbor seals resting on the offshore rocks.

At 2¾ miles the nature trail ends at another pocket beach, Arroyo de los Frijoles, or as it is marked, Bean Hollow. You can explore the tidal area south from Bean Hollow Beach for about 2 miles to Bolsa Point but may not be able to reach Lighthouse Road. Since a hiker may be trespassing when he steps onto the bluff from the tidal zone, the Coastal Trail returns to the highway.

For now the CCT follows the highway shoulder south from Bean Hollow Beach. As you walk south, the Pigeon Point Lighthouse, second tallest on the west coast at 115 feet, comes into view. The highway rolls past Bolsa Point around 4¾ miles, then dips across a creek. At 5¼ miles you want to turn right onto Lighthouse Road. You can reach the sandy beach across the bluff. Walk the narrow road along the bluff between the highway and the shore. You'll see some informal paths along the bluff edge. Artichoke fields are east of the road and the lighthouse looms large as you approach it. The section ends at the hostel entrance at 6 miles. A fence separates the grounds of the lighthouse and hostel. The hostel closes during the day, reopening at 4:30. The lighthouse merits a look, perched above the churning ocean on picturesque Pigeon Point.

SUGGESTED ROUND TRIPS & LOOPS: From either Pebble Beach or Bean Hollow, take the nature trail and return, 1½ miles round trip.

## Coastal Agriculture

Giant thistles and a mustard that looks like a miniature cabbage are two important crops growing along the coasts of San Mateo and Santa Cruz counties. While walking this stretch of California Coastal Trail, you'll walk among artichokes and Brussels sprouts which thrive in the cool summer fog and rich, sandy alluvial soils of the marine terraces. So perfect is the moist, temperate climate for these crops that 90 percent of the 1996 U.S. harvest of 35,000 tons of artichokes and 28,000 tons of Brussels sprouts grew in San Mateo, Santa Cruz and Monterey counties.

The artichoke, a perennial plant of the thistle family originally imported from Italy, grows 20 to 30 globes over the season. Then it's cut down to the ground, growing a new crop in about six months. Artichoke plants take year-round care but are so hardy that one coastal farm reports having some plants that have been producing since 1924! The spine-tipped edible part of the plant hides at the base of the flower bud's bracts (usually called leaves) and in the heart of the globe above the stem. Artichoke fanciers steam or boil the globe, then peel off the bracts one by one, dipping the base into melted butter or mayonnaise and scraping the edible part off the otherwise tough and stringy bract. After the time-consuming task of eating the leaves, you get to devour the meltingly tender, buttery and nutty heart.

Brussels sprouts were first cultivated in 13th-century Belgium and aren't very popular in the U.S. The little one to two inch cabbage-like balls grow in rows on a tall, thick stalk and are very high in iron and vitamins A and C. Cook fresh Brussels sprouts quickly to release their sweet, nutty flavor.

Stop by one of the many produce stands along the central coast to get some artichokes or Brussels sprouts for dinner. You may also find the apples, squash, tomatoes, strawberries, olallieberries, loganberries and salad vegetables for which the area is also known.

# SECTION 9
## Pigeon Point Lighthouse to Año Nuevo State Reserve

DISTANCE: 8¼ miles (13.3 kilometers).

OPEN TO: Hikers. Bicyclists on road.

SURFACE: Beach, trail, highway shoulder.

ACCESS POINT: Pigeon Point Lighthouse.

HOW TO GET THERE: Turn west off Highway 1 about 20 miles south of Half Moon Bay onto Pigeon Point Lighthouse Road and go .75 mile to hostel.

OTHER ACCESS: Gazos Creek Coastal Access.

DIFFICULTY: Moderate.

ELEVATION GAIN/LOSS: 80 feet+/60 feet-.

CAUTIONS: Beware of the poison oak at Franklin Point.

FURTHER INFORMATION: Año Nuevo State Reserve (650)879-2025.

FACILITIES: Water at Pigeon Point. Chemical toilet at Gazos Creek. Water, restrooms, picnic tables, visitor center at Año Nuevo State Reserve.

CAMPGROUNDS: Butano State Park, about 4 miles east off Gazos Creek Road, has campsites in a beautiful redwood forest.

HOSTELS: Pigeon Point Lighthouse Hostel (650)879-0633.

LODGING: Davenport and Santa Cruz to the south and Half Moon Bay to the north have lodging.

Although half of this section follows the shoulder of Highway 1, the highway stints are interspersed with pleasant walks on beach, dunes, bluffs and sleepy secondary roads. The section's best part falls smack in the middle where from Gazos Creek to Cascade Creek you'll walk a splendid little-used beach past intricately etched pockets of sandstone at the base of low cliffs, climb through dunes over rocky Franklin Point, then wind through more dunes along natural bluffs to overlook the rocky tidal zone of Año Nuevo Reserve, where elephant seals have full access and hikers are restricted or prohibited depending on the time of year. If you stay overnight at Pigeon Point Lighthouse Hostel, the thundering surf will lull you into a deep sleep, especially if you've had a soak in the hot tub there.

From the lighthouse, walk the narrow road east to the highway around ⅛ mile. Heading south, you can walk the low, vehicle-damaged bluff to about ⅜ mile, or just walk the wide shoulder of the highway. The rutted bluff soon gives way to agricultural fields. Around 1¼ miles, a farm produce stand beckons you to buy some fresh food. Continue on the shoulder, passing a mushroom farm east of the highway.

At 2½ miles turn right into the Gazos Creek Coastal Access where parking

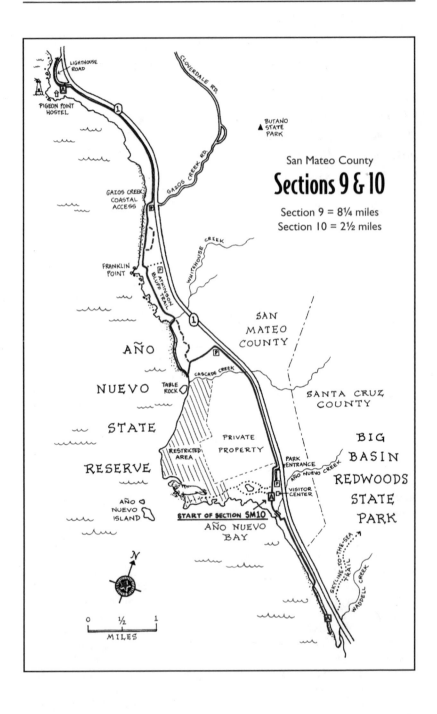

and a privy are available. Take the short trail through a thick patch of poison oak down to the beach, leaving the highway behind. To the south Franklin Point juts out to sea. Walk the beach towards the point. In summer you can walk to the end of the beach on the sand. In winter, part of the sand washes away, so around 3 miles you must take a short trail up through the dunes. Where a small creek reaches a widening sandy area, look for the white plastic pipe marking the trail into the dunes. After about ¼ mile the trail returns to the beach. Follow it south past eroded pockets of sandstone at the base of the low cliffs.

Just before Franklin Point at 3¾ miles, watch for the unmarked but wide and distinct trail heading up into the dunes. Stay on the most-used track, following it as it winds through dunes, willows and poison oak. The trail comes to rocky Franklin Point overlooking the tidal rocks, then winds through more dunes. Around 4¼ miles the trail forks at the ravine of Whitehouse Creek. The left fork turns inland, leading to a parking lot on the highway. Turn right and descend the trail into the ravine, across the creek and out to the beach.

During most tides the beach south is passable. If it's not, ascend the trail on the south side of the ravine and walk the blufftop south to Cascade Creek. Otherwise, walk the beach south to Cascade Creek at 5⅛ miles. Unless the creek is high, it doesn't cascade, but mostly disappears under the sand as it flows out of the marsh up from the beach.

As inviting as the rocks south beyond the beach look, they are off limits. From here to Año Nuevo Point the shoreline and the land about ½ mile inland from it are restricted breeding grounds of the Northern Elephant Seal (See feature article in the next section). A few hundred feet north of Cascade Creek, find and take the path climbing up onto the marine terrace. This trail meets the blufftop trail and leads to Highway 1 and a parking area at 5¾ miles. Turn right and walk the highway shoulder for about 2 miles, passing the historic Año Nuevo Ranch.

Beyond 7¾ miles, find the driveway into the parking lot for Año Nuevo State Reserve. Walk down this road to the visitor center and section's end at 8¼ miles where you will find water and privies.

**SUGGESTED ROUND TRIPS & LOOPS:** From the Gazos Creek Coastal Access walk south on the beach, across Franklin Point and down to the beach north of Año Nuevo Point. Turn around at Cascade Creek and return, a pleasant 6 miles round trip.

## SECTION 10
# Año Nuevo State Reserve to Waddell Creek

DISTANCE: 2½ miles for CCT plus 3 or more miles round trip at Año Nuevo (4.0 + 4.8 kilometers).

OPEN TO: Hikers. Bicyclists on road.

SURFACE: Trail, highway shoulder.

ACCESS POINT: Año Nuevo State Reserve Visitor Center.

HOW TO GET THERE: Turn west off Highway 1 19 miles north of Santa Cruz or 30 miles south of Half Moon Bay into Año Nuevo State Reserve.

OTHER ACCESS: Along highway portion.

DIFFICULTY: Easy.

ELEVATION GAIN/LOSS: 50 feet+/130 feet-.

CAUTIONS: Año Nuevo State Reserve has restricted access. During elephant seal breeding season from December 15 to March 31 access is by reservation only.

FURTHER INFORMATION: Año Nuevo State Reserve (650)879-2025.

FACILITIES: Water, restrooms, picnic tables and visitor center at Año Nuevo. Chemical toilets at Waddell Beach.

CAMPGROUNDS: Butano State Park east of Pigeon Point has camping.

HOSTEL: Pigeon Point Lighthouse Hostel (650)879-0633 is 8 miles north.

LODGING: Davenport and Santa Cruz to the south have lodging.

MAP: See page 266.

Año Nuevo State Reserve, one of the most fascinating and popular wildlife areas on the California coast, is home to a large and very active colony of northern elephant seals. From December through March, you can only visit the breeding area on a guided tour. From April through November, you must get a permit available at the park. The walk out to the point and a visit to Cove Beach are worth the effort, one of the great side trips on the California Coastal Trail. See the feature article for more information.

From the visitor center, head south on the New Years Creek Trail. Pass the handsome old farmhouse and descend stairs around ¼ mile. At the bottom of the stairs, the trail turns right and descends to Cove Beach. If you don't want to visit the beach, head straight for an old bridge over Año Nuevo Creek just ahead. Cross the bridge and follow the old roadbed of Highway 1 past a stand of Monterey pines to reach the current Highway 1 at ½ mile.

Walk the shoulder south, reaching the Santa Cruz County line at 1¼ miles. Soon the highway follows right along the shoreline at the base of the steep eroding Waddell Cliffs. Riprap has been dumped on the beach to protect the highway from the strong surf, but the riprap has nearly destroyed the beach. In summer and at low tides, you may be able to follow the beach if you can get down to it. Watch for a safe place to get on the beach if it looks passable. Whether on the beach or the highway, the section ends at the big dirt parking lot on the west side of the highway overlooking Waddell Beach and the mouth of Waddell Creek at 2½ miles.

SUGGESTED ROUND TRIPS & LOOPS: Of course the first suggestion is to take the guided tour out to Año Nuevo Point during elephant seal breeding season, a trip unlike any other along the California Coastal Trail. From April through November it's still a great hike. You'll have more freedom to roam but less elephant seal action. If you've done all that, consider taking the easy Waddell Creek Trail east up the creek into the southwest corner of Big Basin State Park, up to 9 miles round trip.

## The Northern Elephant Seals of Año Nuevo

Largest of the world's seals, the elephant seal's name derives from the male's huge size, up to 22 feet long and four tons in weight, and long drooping nose, or proboscis. The females weigh up to 2000 pounds and grow to 10 feet long.

By 1868 the scientific community thought the northern elephant seal was extinct, wiped out by sealers hunting for the valuable oil rendered from their blubber. Their range had been from the Pacific coast of Baja all the way to the Gulf of Alaska. In 1892 a small remnant colony of between 20 and 100 elephant seals was found on Guadalupe Island off Baja California. In 1922 the Mexican government protected the colony. The U.S. government followed suit a few years later when the seals reappeared in southern California waters.

In an astounding reversal, the northern elephant seal now numbers around 160,000. Healthy breeding colonies have established themselves in several places including Año Nuevo State Reserve, the Farallon Islands and Point Reyes National Seashore. They first returned to Año Nuevo Island just offshore in 1955, then came to the mainland and started pupping in 1975. In 1995, 2000 pups were born on the mainland beach.

The seals come to Año Nuevo to pup and then breed in the winter months from December to March. In December the males arrive, fighting for dominance over groups of females, or harems. The bulls have fierce and bloody battles with the strongest winning the harem. When the bulls aren't breeding or fighting, they loll about conserving their energy. The females arrive in January to give birth to 50 to 75 pound pups conceived the previous year. The new pups can get lost in the stormy ocean conditions and ferocious male disputes. Mother and pup find each other with distinctive vocalizations. Feeding on rich mother's milk, pups are weaned within a month, growing to between 250 and 500 pounds. By mid-March the mothers mate and leave. The weaners remain, learning to fend for themselves, then head to sea by the end of April.

For much of the rest of the year, elephant seals live alone in the open ocean diving up to 1000 feet for rays, skates, small sharks and squid. They add the blubber they'll live on for the three months they don't feed during breeding.

To witness the winter breeding season at Año Nuevo, make reservations for the docent-led tours of the breeding area. From April to November you can observe the elephant seals and other residents by obtaining a permit to walk out to the point.

# Santa Cruz County

O NCE AGAIN A CALIFORNIA COUNTY'S COASTLINE provides amazing variety in a relatively short length of shore. Walking the 42-mile-long Santa Cruz County coastline will take you from secluded sandy beaches facing the open ocean and backed by low cliffs, through bustling urban Santa Cruz and Capitola as you round the gracefully curving arch of northern Monterey Bay, ending in the south county on the isolated dune-backed beaches at the base of the broad Pajaro River Valley flood plain.

Santa Cruz County begins just south of Año Nuevo Point, where the untrammeled, convoluted shoreline shelters at the base of the rugged and wild Santa Cruz Mountains. On this northern shore, eroded and geologically twisted sandstone cliffs rise above numerous pocket beaches. Wise planning has kept Santa Cruz County's north shore rural in character with agricultural lands predominating adjacent to the coast.

Recently 7000 acres of the north county with 7 miles of coastline was acquired for public access and resource protection. The purchase of the Coast Dairies lands, stretching from Scott Creek to Wilder Ranch, will open another 13 percent of the county's coast to public access and the California Coastal Trail. Until the Coast Dairies aquisition opens to the public, probably by 2004, much of northern Santa Cruz County's CCT remains along the highway shoulder and secondary roads with the recently opened Wilder Ranch State Park a pleasant exception. Even newer is the Coastal Trail link between Wilder Ranch and the city of Santa Cruz.

Santa Cruz has been a tourist attraction for more than 100 years. Today it remains a popular year-round destination thanks to its scenic coastline, mild climate, great swimming and surfing beaches, parks, and laid back ambiance. Upon reaching the city limit, the Coastal Trail leaves Highway 1 behind, returning to the coast at Natural Bridges State Beach. From there the CCT follows a popular multiple-use path along the urban waterfront. At Point Santa Cruz in Lighthouse Field State Beach, the shoreline makes an abrupt left turn as the CCT heads due north then east to follow Monterey Bay's sheltered coast. The Coastal Trail follows the bluff, then the beach or the famed amusement park Boardwalk before taking to city streets through east Santa Cruz, circling the small craft harbor and passing lagoons with important bird habitat.

The CCT follows a residential shoreline into Capitola, another long-standing seaside resort town before reaching twelve miles of continuous beach at New Brighton State Beach. The Coastal Trail follows this long sandy beach through three more state park units with progressively fewer visitors as it follows the curve of the bayshore all the way to the Pajaro River and the Monterey County line.

The challenges for completing Santa Cruz County's Coastal Trail rest mainly in the north county where several gaps remain. The urban part of the CCT through Santa Cruz and Capitola will remain a mix of blufftop, beach and street because of the densely developed nature of the coastal bluffs.

# SECTION I
# Waddell Creek to Davenport

DISTANCE: 7⅝ miles (12.3 kilometers).

OPEN TO: Hikers. Bicyclists on road.

SURFACE: Beach, highway shoulder, road shoulder.

ACCESS POINT: Waddell Creek parking lot.

HOW TO GET THERE: Turn west off Highway I about 17 miles north of Santa Cruz into Waddell Creek parking lot.

OTHER ACCESS: Greyhound Rock, Scott Creek Beach, Davenport Landing, or anywhere along highway.

DIFFICULTY: Easy.

ELEVATION GAIN/LOSS: 320 feet+/240 feet-.

CAUTIONS: Watch for big waves when walking beach. Watch for traffic on highway.

FURTHER INFORMATION: Wilder Ranch State Park (831)423-9703.

FACILITIES: Food, gas, water in Davenport. Chemical toilets at Waddell Creek, Greyhound Rock, and Davenport Landing.

CAMPGROUNDS: Butano State Park east of Pigeon Point has car camping. Waddell Creek has both hike-in and equestrian campgrounds, but you must call for reservations, hike-in: (831)338-8861, horse: (831)425-1218.

HOSTELS: Pigeon Point Lighthouse Hostel (650)879-0633 is 11 miles north. Santa Cruz Hostel (831)423-8304 is 17 miles south.

LODGING: Davenport has a few choices with many more in Santa Cruz.

This hike begins on Waddell Beach, the terminus of the Skyline-to-the Sea Trail, and ends at the historic little town of Davenport. Much of the route follows the highway and several small rural side roads, but the scenic shoreline and agricultural character of the area make the walk pleasant.

From the parking area on the north side of Waddell Creek, step down to the beach and head south. If the creek is too high to cross, use the highway bridge and then drop to the beach. Soon steep cliffs border the beach. At ⅝ mile tidepools invite exploration. Because the highway runs far above across the marine terrace, this beach feels remote and wild.

As you round a point above the tidepool area, Greyhound Rock comes into view. At 1½ miles an access trail comes down to the beach at the smooth gray sandstone rock, a popular fishing spot. CCT heads up this trail, but first consider exploring the rock and the pleasant beach beyond, blocked at the south end by a steep promontory. Climb the trail to the parking lot at the top of the 160-foot cliff at 1⅝ miles.

Follow the highway south for the next 3 miles as it hugs the very edge of the

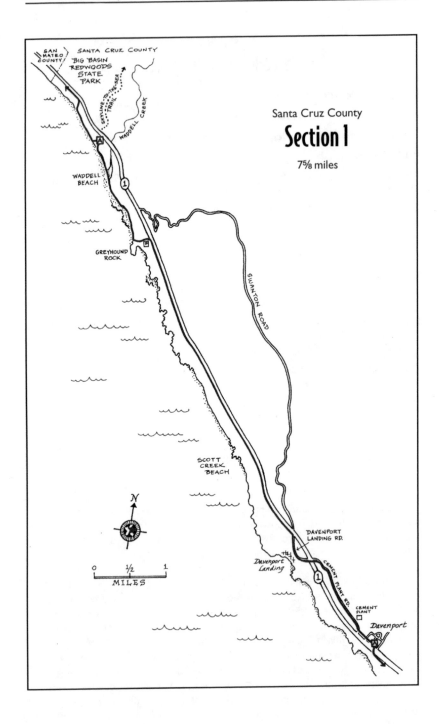

SAN MATEO COUNTY

SANTA CRUZ COUNTY

BIG BASIN REDWOODS STATE PARK

SKYLINE-TO-THE-SEA TRAIL

WADDELL CREEK

WADDELL BEACH

Santa Cruz County

# Section 1

7⅝ miles

GREYHOUND ROCK

SWANTON ROAD

SCOTT CREEK BEACH

N

0    ½    1

MILES

DAVENPORT LANDING RD.

Davenport Landing

CEMENT PLANT RD.

CEMENT PLANT

Davenport

marine terrace. The land west of the highway is public, but the cliffs are steep, and in places the highway follows the cliff edge. Watch for places where you can walk off the shoulder.

At 4⅝ miles the highway drops down off the terrace to cross Scott Creek. To the west accessible Scott Creek Beach, now part of Santa Cruz County's park system, offers a good place to take a break but no through passage south along the shore. Continue along the highway shoulder, traversing a wide marine terrace dedicated to agricultural crops. At 5⅞ miles turn right and walk Davenport Landing Road to the little settlement of Davenport Landing at 6⅛ miles, site of an historic whaling community built in 1870. A stairway and ramp lead to the beach and chemical toilets are available. The pleasant and popular beach is blocked by vertical cliffs at its south end. Continue along the side road as our route swings back up to the highway at 6⅜ miles.

Cross the highway and follow Cement Plant Road as it parallels the highway and passes an old farm building, then a small settlement of worker housing. After you pass the cement plant, the road comes out on the highway at 7½ miles. Walk the shoulder briefly into the tiny town of Davenport at 7⅝ miles where this section ends. The town has a deli, a restaurant and a store. The point out on the bluffs across the highway offers an excellent vantage point to watch for gray whales on their twice yearly passage between Mexico and Alaska.

SUGGESTED ROUND TRIPS & LOOPS: Park at either Waddell Creek or Greyhound Rock and walk out and back for a pleasant 3-mile round trip on a beach with tidepools.

On the east side of the highway at Waddell Creek you'll find the western end of the Skyline-to-Sea Trail, a 38-mile-long hiking and horse trail that starts high in the Santa Cruz Mountains, passing through virgin redwood forests in Big Basin Redwoods State Park. Most people who hike it start at the other end, but it offers pleasant walks up Waddell Creek before it starts climbing steeply.

*One of many sheltered coves hiding along the northern Santa Cruz coast.*

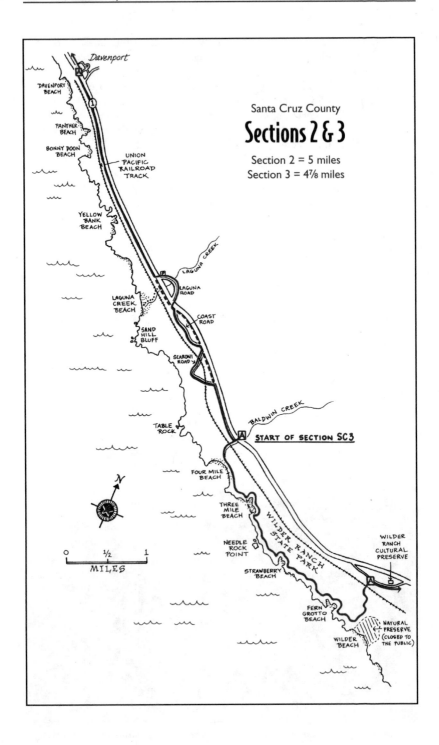

Davenport

DAVENPORT
BEACH

PANTHER
BEACH

BONNY DOON
BEACH

UNION
PACIFIC
RAILROAD
TRACK

YELLOW
BANK
BEACH

Santa Cruz County

# Sections 2 & 3

Section 2 = 5 miles
Section 3 = 4⅞ miles

LAGUNA CREEK

LAGUNA
ROAD

LAGUNA
CREEK
BEACH

COAST
ROAD

SAND
HILL
BLUFF

SCARONI
ROAD

BALDWIN CREEK

TABLE
ROCK

START OF SECTION SC3

FOUR MILE
BEACH

N

THREE
MILE
BEACH

WILDER RANCH STATE PARK

NEEDLE
ROCK
POINT

WILDER
RANCH
CULTURAL
PRESERVE

STRAWBERRY
BEACH

0        ½        1
MILES

FERN
GROTTO
BEACH

NATURAL
PRESERVE
(CLOSED TO
THE PUBLIC)

WILDER
BEACH

# SECTION 2
# Davenport to Four Mile Beach Trailhead

DISTANCE: 5 miles (8 kilometers).

OPEN TO: Hikers. Bicyclists on road.

SURFACE: Paved road, highway shoulder, trail.

ACCESS POINT: Davenport.

HOW TO GET THERE: Davenport is on east side of Highway 1 about 10 miles north of Santa Cruz.

OTHER ACCESS: Anywhere along Highway 1.

DIFFICULTY: Easy.

ELEVATION GAIN/LOSS: 20 feet+/80 feet-.

CAUTIONS: Stay back from cliff edges. Watch for traffic on Highway 1.

FURTHER INFORMATION: Wilder Ranch State Park (831)423-9703.

FACILITIES: Davenport has restaurants, a deli and a store. Four Mile Beach has chemical toilets.

CAMPGROUNDS: Butano State Park east of Pigeon Point has car camping. Waddell Creek has both hike-in and equestrian campgrounds, but you must call for reservations, hike-in: (831)338-8861, horse: (831)425-1218.

HOSTELS: Santa Cruz Hostel (831)423-8304 is 10 miles south.

LODGING: Davenport has a few choices and Santa Cruz has many.

Probably by 2004 the huge ranch known as the Coast Dairies will open to the public. In September 1997, the Save-the-Redwoods League, Trust for Public Land and Santa Cruz Land Trust negotiated a deal to purchase the 7000-acre ranch for permanent open space and park land. We anticipate that the public will have access to the entire coastline under the jurisdiction of State Parks. Many of the historic farm uses will likely remain, and about 7 miles of coastal bluffs north and south of Davenport will become accessible. At present many of the pocket beaches are accessible by legal easements on paths from informal parking areas along the highway.

For now however, this CCT section requires walking the highway shoulder to get along the coast. Many people, from farmworkers to surfers, walk the railroad tracks paralleling the highway to get along the coast. Technically that's trespassing but it is commonly done without repercussions. We must emphasize that the only legal routes for now are the highway shoulder or adjacent side roads. Before leaving Davenport, check out the old jail built in 1906 and the Catholic church built in 1915 and still in use.

CCT follows the highway shoulder and three side roads from Davenport to

Four Mile Beach, rolling through farmland and skirting the base of the hills. Deeply cut arroyos descend from the Santa Cruz Mountains on the inland side. West of the highway, the flat marine terrace grows abundant artichokes and Brussels sprouts.

All along this stretch of the coast, hidden pocket beaches are tucked between spectacular wave- and wind-cut cliffs. Very popular with Santa Cruz surfers, swimmers and sun worshipers, most of these beaches are unmarked or cryptically marked. The best way to find them is to watch for clusters of cars parked along the highway, then follow the well-worn paths across the railroad tracks and down to the beaches. Spacious and tranquil Davenport Beach nestles at the base of the bluffs just south of town. To the south, Panther Beach, Hole in the Wall Beach and Bonny Doon Beach are all in the first mile from Davenport. Yellow Bank Beach is at 1¾ miles, Laguna Creek Beach is around 2¾ miles, and Red, White, and Blue Beach is at 3½ miles.

Several portions of old highway still intact along this stretch get you off busy Highway 1. At 2¾ miles from Davenport, turn left for a ⅜-mile stroll on quiet Laguna Road. After a brief highway walk, veer right onto Coast Road around 3⅛ miles. It comes back to the highway at 3½ miles. Then follow the highway to Scaroni Road, veer right and walk Scaroni across the tracks out onto the marine terrace, looping back to Highway 1 around 4 miles. The mileage listed here is for the main highway. If you take all these scenic detours add about ¼ mile to the total. These loops take you by historic farms for a more intimate look at this picturesque area.

The highway reaches the parking area for Four Mile Beach about 5 miles from Davenport. Watch for asphalt turnouts adjacent to each other on both sides of the highway. Just a few yards beyond, CCT climbs to a rutted parking area on the coastside perched above the highway. The turnout has a pipe gate and (as of this writing) a well-grafittied state park sign. This section ends here and the next section descends to Four Mile Beach.

**SUGGESTED ROUND TRIPS & LOOPS:** The pocket beaches along this route are well worth exploring. Park on the highway and walk the short paths leading over the tracks and through agricultural fields to the beaches.

# SECTION 3
# Four Mile Beach Trailhead to Wilder Ranch, Wilder Ranch State Park

**DISTANCE:** 4⅞ miles (7.8 kilometers).

**OPEN TO:** Hikers, bicyclists.

**SURFACE:** Trail, dirt road, beach.

**ACCESS POINT:** Four Mile Beach Trailhead.

**HOW TO GET THERE:** From Santa Cruz go north on Highway 1. In 4 miles from the city limits, watch on the left for an unmarked rutted parking area on the coastside of the highway. The entrance is at the top of a little rise just before the highway crosses Baldwin Creek. Park above the highway where the road drops toward the wide arroyo.

DIFFICULTY: Easy.

ELEVATION GAIN/LOSS: 120 feet+/60 feet-.

CAUTIONS: Stay back from steep, crumbly cliff edge. Watch for big waves on the beach.

FURTHER INFORMATION: Wilder Ranch State Park (831)423-9703.

FACILITIES: Chemical toilet at Four Mile Beach. Restrooms and water at Wilder Ranch State Park parking lot.

CAMPGROUNDS: Henry Cowell Redwoods State Park is 3 miles inland from Santa Cruz.

HOSTELS: Santa Cruz Hostel (831)423-8304.

LODGING: Many lodgings are available in Santa Cruz.

MAP: See page 276.

Finally we once again get to leave the highway behind and enjoy great blufftop walking, secluded pocket beaches and fascinating geology. This walk, entirely within Wilder Ranch State Park, hints at what Santa Cruz County's entire north coast could one day be like for the Coastal Trail. Wilder Ranch State Park allows historic use on its 5000 acres, in this case the growing of Brussels sprouts and other cool climate crops. As stewards of the natural resources, California State Parks encourages organic practices on land they manage for farming.

From the turnout parking area walk around the pipe gate and follow the well-traveled trail down Baldwin Creek to Four Mile Beach at ¼ mile. You might take a break on the pleasant beach. The Coastal Trail continues south on a path climbing up to the bluff on the south side of the creek canyon. At the top, the trail follows the bluff edge down the coast.

You overlook Three Mile Beach around one mile. It's a steep descent down the bluff if you want to get to the beach. Otherwise, take the trail around the arroyo and continue along the blufftop track. After you pass Needle Rock Point, follow the bluffs to the next cove at 1¾ miles. You look down on the deeply indented cove of Strawberry Beach. Beware of the sheer cliffs here. The cliffs all along the trail consist of sedimentary rock that's been bent and tilted by earthquakes and exposed to the wave action.

Continue along the bluff edge track, following the coastline as it heads almost due east. At 2⅜ miles you skirt the rim of the deeply indented cove of scenic Fern Grotto Beach. Continue along the bluffs. Around 4⅛ miles the trail comes to a viewing platform overlooking Wilder Beach and a marsh. They have been closed to protect snowy plover nesting sites and other important habitat. The trail turns inland and follows the edge of a wide arroyo. Cross the railroad tracks at 4¾ miles and follow the road to the parking lot for Wilder Ranch State Park at 4⅞ miles.

SUGGESTED ROUND TRIPS & LOOPS: From either end of this section, walk out and back, up to 9¾ miles for the round trip.

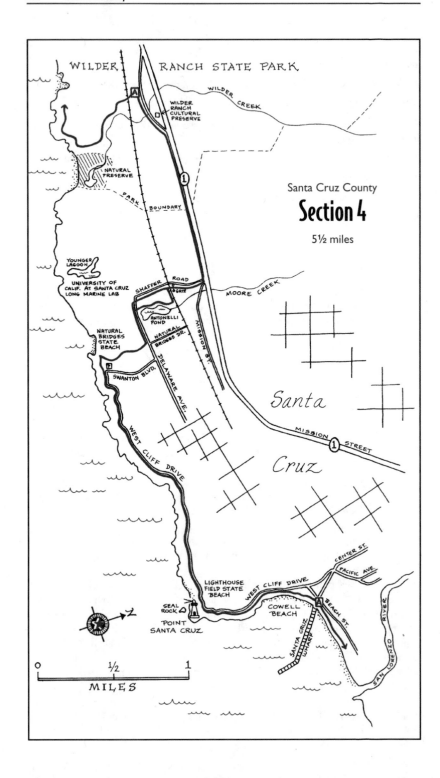

WILDER RANCH STATE PARK

WILDER CREEK

A
WILDER RANCH CULTURAL PRESERVE

NATURAL PRESERVE

PARK BOUNDARY

1

Santa Cruz County

## Section 4

5½ miles

YOUNGER LAGOON

UNIVERSITY OF CALIF. AT SANTA CRUZ LONG MARINE LAB

SHAFFER ROAD

MOORE CREEK

GATE

ANTONELLI POND

NATURAL BRIDGES DR.

MISSION ST.

NATURAL BRIDGES STATE BEACH

SWANTON BLVD.

DELAWARE AVE.

*Santa*

WEST CLIFF DRIVE

MISSION 1 STREET

*Cruz*

CENTER ST.

PACIFIC AVE.

LIGHTHOUSE FIELD STATE BEACH

WEST CLIFF DRIVE

COWELL BEACH

BEACH ST.

SEAL ROCK

SANTA CRUZ WHARF

SAN LORENZO RIVER

POINT SANTA CRUZ

N

0          ½          1

MILES

# SECTION 4
# Wilder Ranch State Park to Santa Cruz Wharf

DISTANCE: 5½ miles (8.9 kilometers).

OPEN TO: Hikers. Bicyclists on most.

SURFACE: Trail, highway shoulder, paved trail, beach.

ACCESS POINT: Wilder Ranch State Park parking lot.

HOW TO GET THERE: Turn west off Highway 1 one mile north of the Santa Cruz city limit.

OTHER ACCESS: Natural Bridges State Beach, anywhere on north Santa Cruz city shoreline.

DIFFICULTY: Easy.

ELEVATION GAIN/LOSS: 100 feet+/160 feet-.

CAUTIONS: Watch for speeding bicyclists and skaters on the multi-use trail.

FURTHER INFORMATION: Santa Cruz State Parks (831)429-2850, Natural Bridges State Beach (831)423-4609.

FACILITIES: Restrooms, water, picnic tables at several points along route.

CAMPGROUNDS: Henry Cowell State Park 3 miles east of Santa Cruz has camping.

HOSTELS: Santa Cruz Hostel (831)423-8304.

LODGING: Santa Cruz has abundant motels, hotels and B&Bs.

Along this walk you'll see many contrasts, from the rural agriculture north of town to suburbia to the bustle of the wharf area. The busy multiple-use trail explores a spectacular shoreline. Plenty of interesting things to do and see along the way can make this short hike an all day affair.

From the Wilder Ranch State Park parking lot, walk east down the park road to the historic center of the ranch. This is the real thing — restored ranch houses, buildings, and artifacts from the 1850s through the 1890s. Docents lead tours on weekends, and visitors are welcome to wander among the buildings or hike the miles of trails inland.

Continue on the road to reach Highway 1 at ⅜ mile. Walk the new trail off the road along the highway right of way. The latter is heavily used by mountain bikers going to Wilder Ranch State Park. At 1⅝ miles turn right on Shaffer Road and walk to the railroad tracks at 1⅞ miles.

From here you have a choice. Go left along the tracks for a short distance and turn right just before the little bridge onto a trail skirting Antonelli Pond, coming to Delaware Street at 2⅛ miles. Alternately continue across the tracks on Shaffer Road and turn left on Delaware. Either way continue on Delaware a short way.

Watch on the right for the wide paved trail entering Natural Bridges State Beach at the intersection with Natural Bridges Drive. Walk the paved trail into the park and find the visitor center around 2⅝ miles. The visitor center emphasizes the thousands of monarch butterflies which migrate here, overwintering in eucalyptus trees from September through March. A short wooden ramp trail leads into the butterfly resting area.

Walk across the parking lot and take the trail leading down to the beach around 2¾ miles. The rock bridge that once graced the main beach is gone, washed away by the waves. Only one of the original three natural bridges for which the park was named remains.

From the beach, walk up the bluff stairway to West Cliff Drive and the beginning of the busy paved multi-use trail. As you follow the trail east, watch for runners, bicyclists and inline skaters. The trail stays near the bluff's edge overlooking the churning surf crashing against the cliffs. Houses line the other side of the street. All along here board surfers and boogie boarders enjoy some great breaks.

Point Santa Cruz at Lighthouse Field State Beach at 4⅝ miles defines the northern tip of Monterey Bay. On the point a building designed to look like a lighthouse now houses a surfing museum and store. The point offers good

## The Monarch Butterfly

The fragile and beautiful monarch butterfly, brightly orange and black with white spots, makes a journey as long as 3000 miles from the eastern seaboard to wintering sites in central Mexico where they escape harsh winters. The west coast population doesn't have to make it all the way to Mexico in winter because the central California coast's mild Mediterranean winters suit the monarch just fine.

In spring the monarchs individually migrate north as far as Canada to lay eggs on milkweed plants. The eggs hatch into larval caterpillars with bright yellow, black and white vertical bands, feeding on the milkweed before metamorphosing into butterflies. At least four generations will live and die before autumn. Then the monarchs rise en mass and head south to find the same trees their ancestors visited in previous years. There they pack together by the thousands, hanging from branches in a state of dormancy. These winter adults live up to eight months. Certain eucalyptus, cypress and pine trees are so thickly populated that they take on the orange hue of the monarchs.

Although monarchs congregate in their favored groves along the California coast from Bodega Bay to Santa Monica, one perfect place to see this monarch butterfly display is Natural Bridges State Beach. From October through February the monarch winters here in a grove of eucalyptus. You can also see monarchs wintering in Pacific Grove on the Monterey Peninsula, where they inhabit trees throughout the town and are protected by city ordinances.

The monarchs have natural protection against bird predation because many milkweed species are poisonous, making the butterflies and their larva toxic to birds. The viceroy and queen butterflies not only share the monarch's coloration, they're also poisonous to birds. This mimicry increases the degree of protection for each species.

How the tiny one-ounce monarchs make the long journey to arrive precisely at their ancestral home was long a mystery, but recent scientific breakthroughs have illuminated, if not fully answered the puzzle. Not only do the monarch's wings contain traces of magnetite that somehow act as an internal compass, the butterflies also home in on the chemical odor of billions of fallen butterfly scales at their ancestral destination.

*This secluded cove near Santa Cruz has a natural bridge.*

viewing of sea otters, whales and brown pelicans. Steamer Lane, a world famous big-wave surf break, rolls along just off the east side of the point. As you round the point and head north, you can see the Santa Cruz Wharf ahead. Follow the wooded path winding along the bluff. Above Cowell Beach it leaves West Cliff Drive and descends to the foot of the wharf and section's end at 5½ miles. The ½-mile-long wharf is worth a look with fisherfolks, boat and sea kayak rentals, restaurants and shops.

SUGGESTED ROUND TRIPS & LOOPS: Starting at either the Wharf or Natural Bridges State Beach, walk out and back on the multi-use trail for a fine urban waterfront 6-mile round trip. From Wilder Ranch State Park, several long and short loops climb into the low hills across the highway from the historic ranch buildings. This area is heavily used by mountain bikers, so hikers should use caution walking the inland areas. The park also has docent led tours of the extensive and historically significant farm buildings.

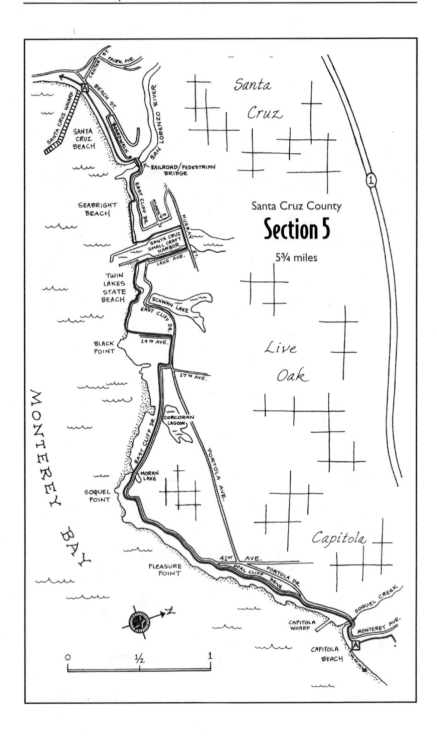

Santa Cruz County
# Section 5
5¾ miles

# SECTION 5
# Santa Cruz Wharf to Capitola

DISTANCE: 5¾ miles (9.3 kilometers).

OPEN TO: Hikers. Bicyclists on most.

SURFACE: Beach, sidewalk.

ACCESS POINT: Santa Cruz Wharf.

HOW TO GET THERE: Turn east off Highway 1 west of downtown Santa Cruz onto Laurel Street. Go downhill and across the railroad tracks, then turn right on Washington Street and follow it to the Wharf at its end.

OTHER ACCESS: The entire route is accessible by city streets.

DIFFICULTY: Easy.

ELEVATION GAIN/LOSS: 60 feet+/70 feet-.

CAUTIONS: Watch for traffic.

FURTHER INFORMATION: Santa Cruz County Department of Parks and Recreation (831)454-7900.

FACILITIES: Restrooms, water, picnic tables at wharf, Capitola and several places on route.

CAMPGROUNDS: Henry Cowell Redwoods State Park 3 miles inland has camping.

HOSTELS: Santa Cruz Hostel (831)423-8304.

LODGING: Abundant in area.

This pleasant urban walk leads from one interesting beach town to another, both with wharves and tourist attractions. The Coastal Trail here will likely remain mostly on residential streets far into the future since most of the bluffs are developed, and negotiating the rocky tideline is impossible in places.

From the wharf you can either walk down to the beach and follow the tideline or walk along the street and through the Boardwalk amusement park, one of the oldest in California. For a thrill, catch a ride on the 1924-vintage wooden roller coaster. Both routes bring you to the San Lorenzo River at ⅝ mile. If you're on the beach, walk a block up river to the old railroad bridge. Cross the railroad bridge on the pedestrian walkway on the inland side and turn right on East Cliff Drive. Follow the sidewalk a short block, then follow the street as it turns left overlooking the beach. A short side trip is the walk out to San Lorenzo Point, the rock spit jutting into the surf on your right. Continue down the coast along East Cliff to one mile. At the sign "SEABRIGHT BEACH," walk out along the beach.

At 1⅜ miles you reach the mouth of the Santa Cruz Small Craft Harbor where you can walk out on the jetty if the surf is quiet. The Coastal Trail heads inland on the path along the harbor. Walk the sidewalk through the harbor parking area and climb the steps to the bridge at 1½ miles. Turn right and cross the bridge over the harbor, and after a few hundred feet, turn west and drop down into another parking lot. Skirt the harbor with its thicket of sail boat masts and come to a row of shops and a restaurant just up from the beach at 1⅞ miles. You might visit the interpretive display in front of the Crows Nest Restaurant for information about the Monterey Bay National Marine Sanctuary.

## The Loma Prieta Earthquake of 1989

If you had been walking the Santa Cruz coastline at 5:04 P.M. on October 17, 1989, a powerful earthquake would have jolted you from your revelry with nature. The strong quake, measuring 7.1 on the Richter scale, shook the entire central California coast. It hit during the third game of baseball's World Series between San Francisco and Oakland, bringing the big earth tremor to a national television audience and the game to a dramatic and sudden end.

The quake was centered northeast of Santa Cruz on the San Andreas Fault near a mountain peak named Loma Prieta (small dark hill). Although not considered the "big one" — the San Francisco Earthquake of 1906, magnitude 8.3, was 16 times more powerful — the Loma Prieta temblor nonetheless killed 62 people, destroyed 367 businesses, and left an estimated 12,000 people homeless when it damaged 18,000 homes, totally destroying 1000 of them. Structural damage and business interruption estimates were as high as $10 billion. Structures alone accounted for $6.8 billion. All that damage happened in a scant 20 seconds.

Press coverage centered on the freeway collapse in Oakland that killed 42 people, the destruction in San Francisco, and the collapse of a portion of the San Francisco-Oakland Bay Bridge. Although some of the most dramatic damage happened in the Bay Area, the shaking there was less severe than near the epicenter. Much of the Bay Area damage occurred to structures built on filled-in marshland.

The more severe destruction that fell upon the towns of Santa Cruz, Watsonville and other communities near the epicenter was less publicized. The old downtown Santa Cruz, revitalized and turned into the pedestrian friendly Pacific Garden Mall, suffered major damage. A number of unreinforced brick buildings and historic structures collapsed or suffered terminal damage. Today lots still stand empty where businesses once stood, but much of the downtown has been rebuilt. In Watsonville almost 40 percent of pre-1940s frame houses were destroyed or badly damaged. People camped out for weeks in the parks, afraid to return to their damaged homes.

Many people felt that the inevitable "big one" had occurred, but that was not the case. Not only was it less severe than the 1906 quake, the Loma Prieta temblor didn't even relieve the possibility of a major quake happening soon. A study released after Loma Prieta by the U.S. Geological Survey concluded that the possibility of another quake of 7 or greater within 30 years is 67 percent. It also predicts the epicenter will likely be closer to Bay Area populations centers, resulting in a much higher loss.

Disaster preparedness officials are concerned that because most buildings in the Bay Area escaped with no damage, owners have concluded that their structures are earthquake proof. Experts say that if the epicenter of the next quake is near San Francisco, many of these building could fail. The potential for major disruption is 10 times greater ($100 billion) than in 1906 because of economic development and a much larger population.

Walk down to the beach and turn left, walking the tideline of Twin Lakes State Beach past the mouth of Schwan Lake. Before you come to impassable Black Point, turn left on a dirt trail between cypress trees that heads inland to 14th Avenue.

From here to Capitola, the trail follows city streets because years ago the bluffs were intensely developed with housing subdivisions with little respect for public access or views. Walk 14th to East Cliff Drive and turn right, then follow East Cliff as it jogs right for one block, then turns left to stay within sight of the ocean. Pass a couple of short side trails to the beach and walk the shoulder of East Cliff around Soquel Point to Pleasure Point at 4⅛ miles. You pass several overlooks and accesses to rocky beaches along this blufftop road. Pleasure Point has some benches overlooking this popular surfing spot.

Continue along East Cliff Drive to 41st Avenue, then veer right onto Opal Cliff Drive at 4¾ miles. The homes here block your ocean views along this stretch. For a side trip look for a gap between the houses marked by a chain link fence and a sign. It leads to an ocean view and access to several pocket beaches. At about 5⅜ miles the houses end and the road follows the edge of a steep eroding cliff overlooking a rocky beach and the Capitola Wharf. One wonders how long the houses built on the bluff edge can last after looking at the street breaking off into the surf here.

At 5⅝ miles you arrive at the bridge crossing the shallow estuary of Soquel Creek. A restored and oddly designed old motel of Italian motif faces the estuary. Take Wharf Road one block to the Capitola Wharf. Just over the bridge turn onto Esplanade, passing bars, restaurants, and shops before coming to City Beach and section's end at 5¾ miles. This popular beach has benches and restrooms.

SUGGESTED ROUND TRIPS & LOOPS: From the Santa Cruz Wharf, walk north over Beach Hill to overlook historic downtown Santa Cruz. It's less than a mile to the heart of town. Downtown Capitola fronting the beach is full of restaurants and shops.

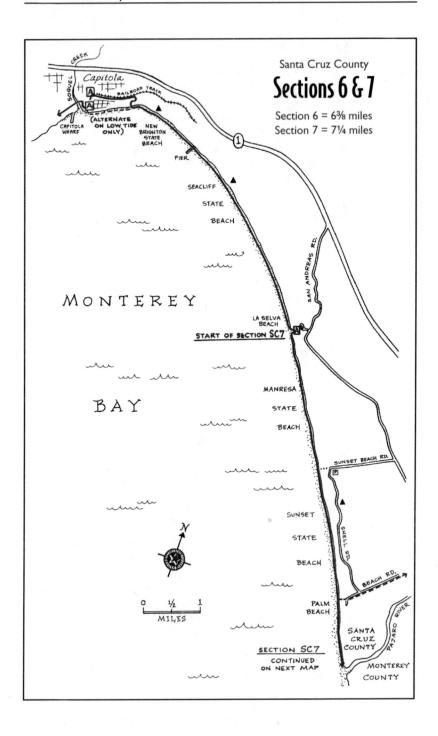

Santa Cruz County

# Sections 6 & 7

Section 6 = 6⅜ miles
Section 7 = 7¼ miles

Capitola

CREEK

SOQUEL

RAILROAD TRACK

A

A

(ALTERNATE ON LOW TIDE ONLY)

CAPITOLA WHARF

NEW BRIGHTON STATE BEACH

1

PIER

SEACLIFF

STATE

BEACH

SAN ANDREAS RD.

M O N T E R E Y

LA SELVA BEACH

START OF SECTION SC7

MANRESA

STATE

BEACH

B A Y

SUNSET BEACH RD.

P

SUNSET

STATE

BEACH

SHELL RD.

BEACH RD.

N

0   ½   1

MILES

PALM BEACH

SANTA CRUZ COUNTY

PAJARO RIVER

SECTION SC7
CONTINUED
ON NEXT MAP

MONTEREY COUNTY

# SECTION 6
# Capitola to Manresa State Beach

DISTANCE: 6⅜ miles (10.3 kilometers).

OPEN TO: Hikers.

SURFACE: Beach, short road shoulder stretch.

ACCESS POINT: Capitola.

HOW TO GET THERE: From Highway 1 east of Santa Cruz, take the Bay Avenue exit. Head west, then turn right onto Capitola Avenue, or continue straight. Both will bring you to the beach before one mile.

OTHER ACCESS: New Brighton State Beach, Seacliff State Beach.

DIFFICULTY: Easy.

ELEVATION GAIN/LOSS: 60 feet+/60 feet-.

CAUTIONS: Parking is a problem at Capitola on weekends and in summer. Take the free shuttle. Low tide required to walk first ⅝ mile of beach. Much of the walk is on soft sand.

FURTHER INFORMATION: New Brighton State Beach (831)464-6330. Seacliff State Beach (831)685-6500.

FACILITIES: Restrooms and water at both ends, New Brighton State Beach and Seacliff State Beach.

CAMPGROUNDS: New Brighton State Beach and Seacliff State Beach have campgrounds.

HOSTELS: Santa Cruz Hostel (831)423-8304.

LODGING: Available in Capitola and throughout the area.

This section of the CCT and the next are all sandy beach, miles of it, except for the rocky tidal zone just south of the Capitola City Beach. Before you leave Capitola, check out the several blocks of quaint shops specializing in mostly tourist items from trinkets and T-shirts to shoes and seascapes, with plenty of places for a drink, ice cream and food.

Before attempting the rocky shore at the base of the cliffs, first make sure the tide is low or going out. If you try it, you will soon discover if it's passable. It's a nice walk at the base of fossil laced vertical cliffs for ⅝ mile to the sand at New Brighton Beach. If the tide is in, then from City Beach walk uphill on the sidewalk along Monterey Avenue until you reach the railroad tracks around ¼ mile. The locals use the track shoulder as a path to get from Capitola to New Brighton. You can either take the tracks or walk a few more yards and turn right on Park Avenue.

Either way, you end up overlooking New Brighton Beach. An informal trail that descends the bluff can be very slippery. It's best to continue to the parking lot around ⅞ mile and use the stairway down to the beach.

Walk the beach south, all sand walking to the section's end at Manresa State

Beach. Notice an odd shaped pier ahead jutting into the surf. Walk the beach to the pier and Seacliff State Beach at 2⅜ miles. The pier extends toward an old ship, a rare supply ship built of cement for World War I but never used and later towed here in 1929. It served as an amusement center with a dance floor, swimming pool and arcade before falling into disrepair after several years. Now it is at the end of a public fishing pier. You'll find restrooms and a small store at the foot of the pier. Nearby is the Seacliff Visitor Center, open in summer, which has exhibits on fossils and a history of the ship.

Walk south along the beach or the road that extends along the base of the cliffs. The pavement is lined with State Park campsites, then private houses beyond the park boundary. These days it's almost impossible to build houses right on the beach.

Continue down the long beach. After the last of the houses, 100-foot high cliffs block views of most development and the beach is quiet and secluded.

## The California Brown Pelican

You'll see them all along the California coast, crashing into the ocean and gracefully gliding just above rolling waves. They, along with the less common white pelican, are the biggest flying critters on the coast. Brown pelicans boast a wingspan up to 6½ feet, with white pelicans reaching an astounding 9½ feet. The browns breed only on offshore islands from the Channel Islands south to Baja California, but they migrate north from May or June until December. The whites breed on islands of landlocked lakes and mostly visit the coast near Point Reyes in autumn. If pelicans look a little prehistoric, it's because the breed began at least 30 million years ago.

You can easily observe brown pelicans on the coast because of both their large size and unusual social and feeding characteristics. Flying in long lines, sometimes fifty feet in the air, sometimes gliding inches above a wave as it rolls towards shore, flapping their wings a few times before gliding, pelicans apparently use the slight updraft created by the wave to maintain the glide. They may be the only bird that synchronizes wing beats on a cue from the leader.

In a dramatic feeding technique a single brown pelican will suddenly peel off from the line and plunge beak first into the surf for a fish. Protective air sacks in the skull protect the pelican from the shock of the collision. The white pelican doesn't dive. Instead groups float on the surface, herding fish together before scooping them up. The large pouch fills with water and fish, the water ejected and the fish swallowed whole when the pelican reaches the surface.

The tale of the pelican must include the harrowing events that led to its near extinction. DDT, an extremely toxic insecticide used widely in agriculture, was the culprit. The chemical didn't break down in the environment but instead polluted streams and rivers from runoff, which eventually reached the ocean. The fish in the coastal zone absorbed the toxins and were then eaten by pelicans. The pollutants affected the metabolism of the birds, resulting in thin shelled eggs easily broken by the incubating bird inside, causing the failure of a timely hatch. This caused the brown pelican population to decrease by about 90 percent over twenty years. The U.S. government finally banned DDT in 1971 and the pelican population has rebounded. Although the pelican was saved, pollutants in the runoff from towns and farms remain a problem for the overall health and water quality of the coastal zone.

Manresa State Beach is about 4 miles down the coast, plenty of distance to stride out and work out the kinks, or run, or go for a lazy stroll. At 6⅜ miles watch for a steep, long stairway coming down the bluff. It marks the end of this section. The next section continues along the beach. If you're day hiking and have left a car at Manresa, take the stairs to the Manresa State Beach parking lot at 6½ miles.

SUGGESTED ROUND TRIPS & LOOPS: Start from either New Brighton, Seacliff or Manresa State Beaches to explore miles of beach.

# SECTION 7
# Manresa State Beach to Pajaro River

DISTANCE: 7¼ miles (11.7 kilometers).

OPEN TO: Hikers.

SURFACE: Beach.

ACCESS POINT: Manresa State Beach.

HOW TO GET THERE: Take the San Andreas Road exit from Highway 1 south of Aptos. Head southwest to beach parking around 2 miles.

OTHER ACCESS: Sunset Beach Road leads to the Sunset State Beach Access. Beach Road ends at the Palm Beach access. Continue south on San Andreas Road to intersect these roads.

SOUTH END ACCESS: End of Beach Road.

DIFFICULTY: Easy.

CAUTIONS: Stay off private property east of the beach.

FURTHER INFORMATION: Santa Cruz District State Parks (831)429-2850, Manresa State Beach (831)724-3750.

FACILITIES: Restrooms, water at Manresa State Beach (at top of stairs), Sunset State Beach entrance station and at Palm Beach.

CAMPGROUNDS: Sunset State Beach has camping.

LODGING: Aptos and Watsonville have several choices.

MAP: See page 288.

The last walk in Santa Cruz County follows a tranquil stretch of the California coast. This gentle, remote area contrasts vividly with the hills, high bluffs and cliffs of the north county and the urban landscape of Santa Cruz.

From the Manresa State Beach stairway simply head south on the wide beach at the base of low bluffs. You have miles of sand, crashing waves, shells, solitude and peace. The Monterey Bay National Marine Sanctuary offshore teems with birds, sea mammals and fish.

At 2¾ miles you arrive at the access path from the Sunset State Beach parking lot. Up the path you'll find the park headquarters, campground, picnic tables and water. From here to the mouth of the river, the bluffs give way to the largest dunes system in the county. The dunes rise steeply off the beach, and the campground is on the sheltered east side of the dunes.

Continue down the beach on this sandy stroll. You reach the Palm Beach Access of Sunset State Beach beyond 5 miles, the southernmost vehicle access for this section. It's located at the north end of the Pajaro Dunes condominium development built right on the dunes. The development seems ill advised since it not only sits on dunes but also at the mouth of a river.

To finish this section, walk the beach down to the mouth of the Pajaro River around one mile. If you are not continuing into Monterey County, return the way you came. If you want to continue south, in summer you can usually wade the river and continue down the beach to the Zmudowski State Beach parking lot and section's end at 7¼ miles. The lot lies inland from the beach behind the low dunes. When the river is too deep to ford, follow the Alternate Route.

**ALTERNATE ROUTE:** If you can't ford the Pajaro River, from the Palm Beach access, follow Beach Road northeast. Then turn right and go south on Thurwachter Road. After crossing the river it continues as McGowan Road. Turn right and follow Trafton Road, then go left on Bluff Road, then left on Jensen Road to Highway 1. Follow the highway shoulder about 1½ miles south. Turn right and walk Struve Road to Giberson Road, then go right on Giberson to its end.

**SUGGESTED ROUND TRIPS & LOOPS:** From Manresa, Sunset, or Palm Beach you can have a fine sandy day hike as long as you'd like.

# Monterey County

**M**ONTEREY COUNTY, the most popular tourist destination on the California coast, may have the most beautifully diverse and interesting coastline in the state. It offers abundant wildlife, scenic points, early California history, pricey resorts, and the wild and legendary Big Sur.

Monterey County's coastline begins at the mouth of the Pajaro River, roughly at the midpoint of Monterey Bay. From there the north county shore sweeps gracefully in a grand sandy arc right to the foot of the bulging Monterey Peninsula. The clenched-fist-shaped peninsula thrusts seaward against the open ocean currents, a dynamic meeting of rocky coastline and wild Pacific. The tiny Monterey Peninsula holds about one quarter of this immense county's population and much of its commercial activity.

The Monterey County coastline continues south another 121 miles, climaxing in the steep and convoluted Big Sur coast, one of the most majestic areas on the entire California coast. Altogether, the 144 miles of the Monterey County coast makes it the second longest county coastline in California, nearly as long as Humboldt and longer than Mendocino. Having covered slightly more than half the distance of the 1197-mile CCT, however, this volume of *Hiking the California Coastal Trail* ends at the doors of the world famous Monterey Bay Aquarium not far from the northern tip of the Monterey Peninsula. The rest of Monterey County's Coastal Trail is detailed in Volume Two of this guide.

The three sections of Monterey County's coast covered in this volume span 22 miles of the 144-mile coast. The Coastal Trail has no gaps in this 22 miles, unlike much of the rest of the CCT through Monterey County. From the remote windswept beach at the mouth of the Pajaro River, the CCT follows the beach, except for a detour around the mouth of Moss Landing Harbor, for 21 miles before reaching the urban waterfront of Monterey. This wild but gentle shore fronts one of the largest dune systems in the state. Birds abound at the Salinas River National Wildlife Refuge and in the Moss Landing-Elkhorn Slough area.

Once the Coastal Trail reaches Monterey at Municipal Wharf #2, the emphasis changes from windswept isolation to urban bustle. At the wharf, the CCT joins the Monterey Peninsula Recreation Trail, following the old railroad right-of-way right through the busy waterfront. As it slices through the heart of Monterey, the trail passes two more public wharves and Monterey State Historic Park which preserves buildings from the era of Spanish and Mexican rule of California as well as the site of the founding of the California Republic in 1849.

The CCT soon comes to Cannery Row, made famous by John Steinbeck in his novels *Cannery Row* and *Sweet Thursday*. The bounty from one of the world's great fisheries was processed here for 40 years until the sardine schools disappeared in 1951. At the end of Cannery Row, the northern half of the California Coastal Trail ends at David Avenue just before the Monterey-Pacific Grove city line. Just a half block downhill on the right you'll find the world famous Monterey Bay Aquarium in the old Hovden Cannery.

# SECTION 1
# Pajaro River to Moss Landing

DISTANCE: 4⅞ miles (7.8 kilometers).

OPEN TO: Hikers. Equestrians allowed on beach August 16 to April 14.

SURFACE: Beach, highway shoulder, road shoulder.

ACCESS POINT: Zmudowski State Beach.

HOW TO GET THERE: On Highway 1, 1.5 miles north of Moss Landing, take Struve Road west, then turn west onto Giberson Road and go about 2 miles to the parking lot for Zmudowski State Beach.

OTHER ACCESS: Moss Landing State Beach. In summer when you can ford Pajaro River, Palm Beach on Beach Road north of river in Santa Cruz County has access.

DIFFICULTY: Easy.

ELEVATION GAIN/LOSS: Negligible.

CAUTIONS: If hiking from Palm Beach, you must be able to ford Pajaro River to continue south.

FURTHER INFORMATION: Monterey State Parks (831)649-2836.

FACILITIES: Moss Landing has a few stores and restaurants. Chemical toilets at Zmudowski State Beach and Moss Landing State Beach.

CAMPGROUNDS: Sunset State Beach on previous section has 90 sites.

LODGING: Watsonville has several choices.

The extraordinary and complex Monterey coastline begins in the north with a long sandy beach covered in two CCT sections. The fishing boat harbor at Moss Landing, with the adjacent bird-rich Elkhorn Slough to its east, separates the two long beach walks. This sandy and remote area contrasts sharply with the sophisticated urban environment on the scenic and rocky Monterey Peninsula. All of this gives way in the southern two-thirds of Monterey County to the wildly steep mountains and rugged coastline of legendary Big Sur.

From the parking area follow the boardwalk west through the dunes to the sandy beach. This first section of Monterey begins on the quiet, undeveloped Zmudowski State Beach with only farmland and dunes in the area. If you are on a quest to walk every foot of the California coast, walk the beach north from the parking lot for ¾ mile to the mouth of the Pajaro River, then backtrack south to the parking area. Add 1½ miles to the book's mileage if you go to the river.

Walk south along the tideline of this lightly visited broad beach. The sand dunes back up against extensive wetlands with good birding, but the land behind the dunes is privately owned.

Around 1¾ miles you leave Zmudowski State Beach for Moss Landing State

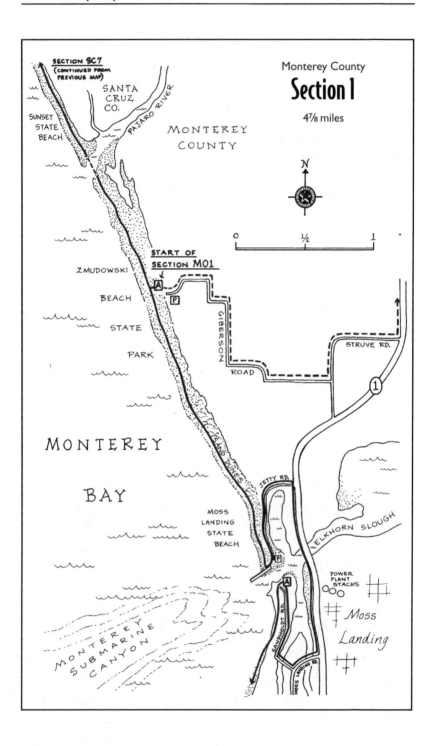

SECTION SC7
(CONTINUED FROM
PREVIOUS MAP)

SANTA
CRUZ
CO.

SUNSET
STATE
BEACH

PAJARO RIVER

MONTEREY
COUNTY

Monterey County
**Section 1**

4⅞ miles

N

0      ½      1

START OF
SECTION M01

ZMUDOWSKI

BEACH

STATE

PARK

GIBERSON

ROAD

STRUVE RD.

1

A

P

SAND DUNES

MONTEREY

BAY

JETTY RD.

MOSS
LANDING
STATE
BEACH

P

A

ELKHORN SLOUGH

POWER
PLANT
STACKS

*Moss*

*Landing*

SANDHOLDT RD.

MOSS LANDING RD.

MONTEREY
SUBMARINE
CANYON

Beach. Jetty Road which lies to the east is part of the route of the Coastal Trail. First CCT continues south to the end of the beach at 2¼ miles, marked by the jetty at the mouth of Moss Landing Harbor. A half mile offshore begins one of the great canyons on the planet, the Monterey Submarine Canyon, rivaling the Grand Canyon in depth. Find the State Park access road at the jetty and follow it back to the north to 2¾ miles. If you're day hiking you might want to return to the Zmudowski parking lot from here. The Coastal Trail route follows Jetty Road east

## The Monterey Bay National Marine Sanctuary

Monterey Bay holds the closest-to-shore deep ocean environment in the continental U.S. and one of North America's largest submarine canyons, but it was the threat of offshore oil development that in 1992 led to the creation of the Monterey Bay National Marine Sanctuary, the nation's largest. This huge preserve covers 5312 square miles including 360 miles of coastline from the Marin Headlands to Cambria in San Luis Obispo County. It protects the coast from the high tideline to about 50 miles offshore. In addition to sheltering the Monterey Submarine Canyon, the sanctuary protects the entire habitat of the endangered southern sea otter, one of the most important marine estuaries in California, Elkhorn Slough, and the most diverse algal community in the nation.

One of the four sanctuaries on the California coast administered by the National Oceanic and Atmospheric Administration, the Monterey Bay National Marine Sanctuary protects the marine environment and encourages and coordinates research and education activities. The sanctuary permits traditional uses such as fishing and recreation, but bans oil and gas development and seabed mining. It requires high treatment levels for sewage before discharge, and generally discourages activities that damage the marine environment. The sanctuary ranges from the shallow land-wrapped waters of Elkhorn Slough to the depths of Monterey Canyon.

Monterey Canyon rivals Arizona's Grand Canyon in size, but it's submerged and difficult to see. The canyon's shallow end begins just offshore from Elkhorn Slough and plunges to almost two miles deep at its western end. Inhabitants include giant squid, the great white shark, and blue, gray, sperm, finback and humpback whales. In the spring, water begins upwelling from deep in the canyon, bringing nutrients to the surface which feed the phytoplankton to begin the food chain, the basis of the rich marine environment.

Elkhorn Slough is an extension of Monterey Canyon. It was an ancient river valley flooded by the rising ocean that has since filled with sediment. Today this important marsh and tidal flat reaches seven miles inland, encompassing 2500 acres. Human activity has heavily impacted the area, including the dredging of Moss Landing Harbor in 1947 which created an opening to the ocean where none existed before. Still, the marsh remains a vital habitat for marine invertebrates, fish, shorebirds and five endangered species: the brown pelican, least tern, Santa Cruz long-toed salamander, southern sea otter and peregrine falcon.

The Monterey area has long attracted scientists because of the diversity of its habitats and variety of living organisms. Five marine research stations study wetlands, sandy beaches and sea floor, rocky shorelines, extensive kelp forests, and Monterey Canyon. These habitats are home to 27 species of marine mammals, 94 species of seabirds, 345 species of fishes, and a diverse and rich population of marine invertebrates.

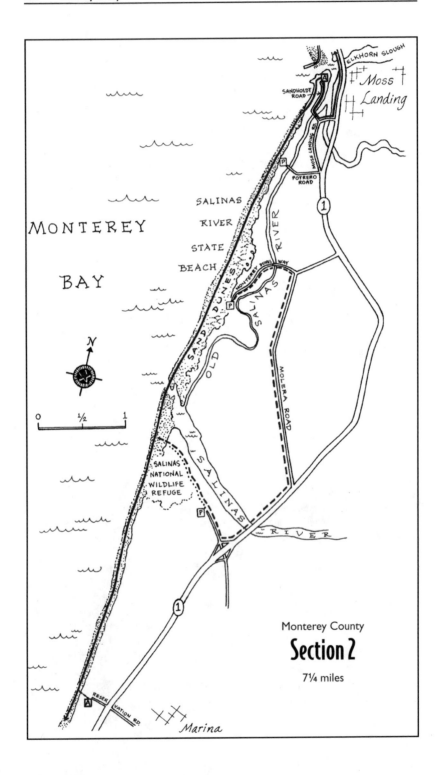

ELKHORN SLOUGH

*Moss Landing*

SANDHOLDT ROAD

MOSS LANDING RD.

POTRERO ROAD

SALINAS RIVER STATE BEACH

MONTEREY BAY

SALINAS RIVER

OLD SAND DUNES

MONTEREY DUNES WAY

MOLERA ROAD

N

0    ½    1

SALINAS

SALINAS NATIONAL WILDLIFE REFUGE

RIVER

1

Monterey County
**Section 2**
7¼ miles

RESERVATION RD.

*Marina*

to Highway 1 at 3 miles. Turn right and walk the highway shoulder south, crossing the bridge over Elkhorn Slough at 3½ miles. The power plant stacks just ahead rise several hundred feet into the air, a landmark all around Monterey Bay. Continue along the highway shoulder past the power plant. Before 4¼ miles, turn right onto Moss Landing Road which leads into the little port town full of fishing boats, funky buildings, antique stores, and eating establishments. Cross the bridge over the bay. The road turns north and becomes Sandholdt Road. You'll pass marine supply stores, the ocean research facility for the Monterey Bay Aquarium, a deli/fish market, and the fleet of boats docked in the harbor. Complete the walk on the beach at the mouth of the bay at 4⅞ miles.

**SUGGESTED ROUND TRIPS & LOOPS:** From either Zmudowski or Moss Landing State Beaches, walk out and back on the beach for a serene 4½-mile round trip. Moss Landing State Beach at the end of Jetty Road north of the harbor has a parking fee.

# SECTION 2
# Moss Landing to Marina State Beach

**DISTANCE:** 7¼ miles, plus ½ mile to South End Access (11.7 + .8 kilometers).

**OPEN TO:** Hikers.

**SURFACE:** Beach.

**ACCESS POINT:** Moss Landing.

**HOW TO GET THERE:** From Highway 1 north of Monterey, turn west on Moss Landing Road, cross the bridge, then take Sandholdt Road to its end at .6 mile.

**OTHER ACCESS:** Salinas River National Wildlife Refuge.

**DIFFICULTY:** Moderate.

**ELEVATION GAIN/LOSS:** Negligible.

**CAUTIONS:** Salinas River may be unfordable in winter. Soft sand makes this walk more strenuous than a typical beach walk. Watch for big waves on the beach.

**FURTHER INFORMATION:** Salinas River State Beach (831)649-2836, Marina State Beach (831)384-7695, Salinas River National Wildlife Refuge (510)792-0222.

**FACILITIES:** Chemical toilets at each end. Water at Marina State Beach.

**CAMPGROUNDS:** Marina Dunes RV Park (831)384-6914 is near end of section. Sunset State Beach is about 10 miles north.

**LODGING:** Available in the city of Marina.

This long, quiet, serene and scenic beach walk features extensive dunes, big surf, a national wildlife refuge and soft sand that makes you work harder for each mile.

If you like quaint port towns, Moss Landing Harbor merits a look at its cluttered fishing port: fishing and pleasure boats both in their prime and derelict, old buildings, seafood restaurants, and marine supply stores.

Inland from the harbor, Elkhorn Slough covers 2500 acres of salt marsh, mudflats, channels and salt ponds. This tidal embayment provides important habitat for the hundreds of thousands of shorebirds, more than 250 species, that reside or migrate here. It's also a major nursery for myriad sea and land creatures, including the diverse invertebrates that feed the abundant birds. The endangered brown pelican and California clapper rail nest here, and the golden eagle and peregrine falcon are also seen. Consider a side trip to explore Elkhorn Slough either by kayak or canoe, or on the more than five miles of trails that wind through the reserve.

Historically the Salinas River emptied into the sea at Moss Landing, four miles north of its present mouth. Then in 1909 locals redirected the river by excavating a channel through the sand dunes where the river meets the ocean today. This decreased flooding and made the rich soil of the old riverbed available for farming. Moss Landing's present entrance and harbor were dredged in 1947 to take advantage of the deep waters of the Monterey Submarine Canyon offshore which keeps the mouth free of sandbars. The sand slides into the deep marine canyon instead of piling up along the shore.

From the south side of the harbor entrance at the end of Sandholt Road, head south along the tideline of the beach. First the southern arm of Moss Landing Harbor lies to the east, then you parallel the Old Salinas River channel. Shorebirds and quiet are the norm here. Not many people make this trek in the soft sand. Beyond one mile you pass the access trail from the end of Potrero Road.

Keep walking south with the dunes above the tideline becoming larger as you go. Around 2⅞ miles another access path runs from the beach to the end of Monterey Dunes Way off Molera Road. At 4 miles you reach the mouth of the Salinas River. The mouth is blocked by a sandbar in summer and may be open or closed in winter, depending on river flow and storms. If the sandbar is in place, or when the river is shallow enough to ford, you can continue south along the beach. Otherwise you must retreat to the last access path and follow the **Alternate Route**.

South of the river mouth you walk through the Salinas River National Wildlife Refuge, an area of beach, dune and estuary alive with wildlife including endangered terns, snowy plovers, brown pelicans and many other birds. Take care not to disturb the birds here, especially the snowy plover which nests on the dry upper beach and is very hard to see. A 200-foot long derelict barge resting in the surf creates its own unique habitat with barnacles, mussels and seaweed clinging to the hull, and eddies of sand forming inside the hull. Eventually rust, the pounding waves and sand will claim this derelict.

After lunch and wildlife observation, continue the march down the beach. Keep an eye to the ocean for sea otters and gray whales. Around 5 miles, large dunes rise steeply from the beach. As you continue south, you may see hang gliders launching from the dunes ahead.

At 7¼ miles a long boardwalk reaches the beach. This section of CCT ends here, but the next one continues along the beach. If you're not continuing south, either return the way you came or follow the boardwalk east ⅜ mile to the Marina State Beach main parking lot at the end of Reservation Road.

**ALTERNATE ROUTE:** When you can't ford the Salinas River, leave the beach at 2⅞ miles to walk Monterey Dunes Way to Molera Road, go south to Highway 1, walk the highway shoulder across the river, turn right into Salinas River National Wildlife Refuge and follow road and trail to the beach south of the river.

**SUGGESTED ROUND TRIPS & LOOPS:** A walk around Moss Landing followed by a walk on the beach is a pleasant way to spend the day. Walking the beach to the Salinas River and back is 8 miles. Starting at Marina State Beach and walking to the Salinas River and back is about 7 miles. Also consider a walk along the trails at Elkhorn Slough. Call (831)728-2822 for information.

## SECTION 3
## Marina State Beach to Monterey Bay Aquarium

**DISTANCE:** 10¼ miles (16.5 kilometers).

**OPEN TO:** Hikers. Bicyclists on the Monterey Peninsula Recreation Trail.

**SURFACE:** Beach, paved trail.

**ACCESS POINT:** Marina State Beach.

**HOW TO GET THERE:** Take Reservation Road exit from Highway 1 at the north end of the city of Marina. Drive west to the parking area at the end of Reservation Road.

**OTHER ACCESS:** Monterey Beach Hotel has public parking and beach access adjacent to it. Anywhere along the Monterey Peninsula Recreation Trail. The waterfront district of Monterey has abundant parking.

**DIFFICULTY:** Moderate.

**ELEVATION GAIN/LOSS:** Negligible.

**CAUTIONS:** Some of the beach may be impassable at high tide.

**FURTHER INFORMATION:** Monterey State Beaches, Monterey State Historic Park (831)649-2836, Monterey Bay Aquarium (831)648-4888.

**FACILITIES:** Marina State Beach has restrooms, water. Monterey has all services.

**CAMPGROUNDS:** Veterans Memorial County Park is in Monterey. Laguna Seca Recreation Area 7 miles east has 183 sites.

**LODGING:** Abundant in Monterey area.

The shoreline of Monterey Bay sweeps magnificently along the sandy shore of Marina, Sand City, Seaside, and the great Monterey dunes system, then hooks westward to the rocky points of the Monterey Peninsula. This walk offers a great

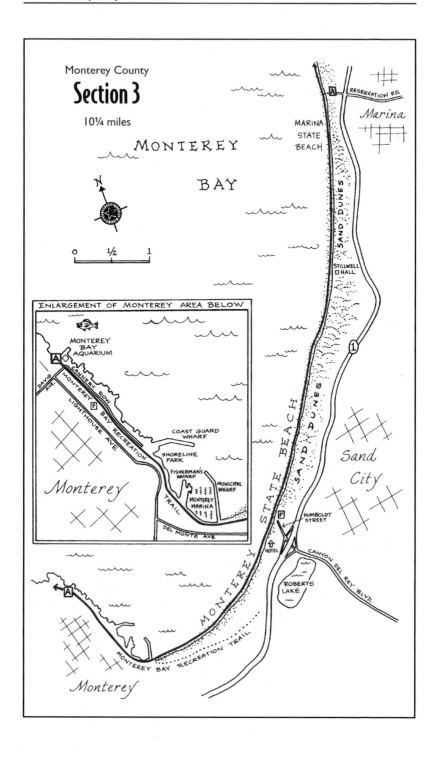

Monterey County
# Section 3
10¼ miles

MONTEREY

BAY

MARINA
STATE
BEACH

Marina

RESERVATION RD.

SAND DUNES

STILLWELL
HALL

1

ENLARGEMENT OF MONTEREY AREA BELOW

MONTEREY
BAY
AQUARIUM

CANNERY ROW

DAVID AVE

MONTEREY BAY RECREATION

LIGHTHOUSE AVE

Monterey

COAST GUARD
WHARF

SHORELINE
PARK

FISHERMAN'S
WHARF

MUNICIPAL
WHARF

TRAIL

MONTEREY
MARINA

DEL MONTE AVE

MONTEREY STATE BEACH

SAND DUNES

Sand
City

HUMBOLDT
STREET

HOTEL

CANYON DEL REY BLVD.

ROBERTS
LAKE

MONTEREY BAY RECREATION TRAIL

Monterey

place to stretch out the legs on some very soft sand and observe the Monterey Peninsula as you approach it. The last 1½ miles follows the paved and popular Monterey Peninsula Recreation Trail along Monterey's waterfront full of California history and tourist attractions. We end the first volume of *Hiking the California Coastal Trail* at the splendid Monterey Bay Aquarium where you can experience all the different habitats hiding beneath the ocean's surface as well as some of the onshore habitats you've walked past.

To reach the Coastal Trail from the access point at the main Marina State Beach parking area, walk the boardwalk ⅜ mile to the beach. If the winds are favorable you might be entertained by hang gliders taking off from the deck built for their launching. The Coastal Trail heads north and south along the tideline. As you head south, the beach quickly becomes more quiet and remote as beach strollers turn back and high dunes isolate the area.

Beyond 1⅛ miles you pass the boundary of the former Fort Ord Military Reservation, now providing miles of open space plus places for a new state college and state park. Continue down the beach. At 2½ miles a large wall of riprap drops off the dunes into the surf. It protects the closed enlisted men's club, Stilwell Hall. Unless the tide is very low, you must carefully climb over the rocks, walk in front of the hall, then find and take the unmarked trail leading south and gently downhill through iceplant to a road. Walk the road to return to the beach around 2⅞ miles.

Continue along the beach through an area once used for war games. Ahead the Monterey Peninsula grows large as you draw near. You finally leave the former fort and reach the badly degraded dunes of Sand City around 5⅜ miles. This whole area has been mined for its fine beach sand.

At 6¾ miles you'll see the tall Monterey Beach Hotel sitting on the dunes to your left. California State Parks has restored the adjacent dunes of Monterey State Beach to illustrate how beautiful the dunes will look after more extensive restoration plans are completed. You can walk on a boardwalk to observe the area. As you continue south, freshwater Roberts Lake sits about ¼ mile inland. A side trail leads from the beach to the lake. Adjacent to the lake at Roberts Avenue, the Monterey Peninsula Recreation Trail reaches its northern terminus. One could follow that paved path all the way to the Monterey Bay Aquarium at this section's end, but for now the Coastal Trail continues along the beach.

As CCT continues down the coast, the beach remains wild but the buildings and bustle of the Monterey area become more prominent. The beach angles southwest then west, aiming for the Monterey Peninsula. As you pass more access ways, you'll find more people enjoying the beach. Finally you walk the narrow strand along the Window on the Bay portion of Monterey State Beach. As the sand ends at 8¾ miles, you come to the Municipal Wharf #2. At the wharf you'll find a popular cafe if you need a lunch break.

After you leave the Municipal Wharf, Monterey State Historic Park nearby on your left features buildings surviving from Monterey's early days. You pass Fisherman's Wharf before 9¼ miles, the Coast Guard Pier around 9⅜ miles, then continue on the busy paved trail for nearly a mile, the last half of it through Cannery Row made famous by John Steinbeck. The sardine canneries closed long ago, but their remnant buildings today house restaurants, bars and abundant gift shops of every kind. The paved trail follows the old railroad right-of-way over-looking the waterfront, paralleling the street called Cannery Row downhill on the right.

When you reach David Avenue just before the Monterey-Pacific Grove city line at 10¼ miles, the northern half of the California Coastal Trail has nearly reached its end. Turn right and follow the sidewalk of David Avenue a half block

## The Monterey Bay Aquarium

Complementing the wonders of the immense Monterey Bay National Marine Sanctuary is one of the world's great aquariums and interpretive centers. The Monterey Bay Aquarium, located at the end of the last hike in this book, presents a living representation of the many habitats in and around the bay in more than a hundred innovative habitat galleries and exhibits.

The kelp forest exhibit alone merits a visit. It's 28 feet deep and holds 335,000 gallons of water open to the sky. You can watch sardines, sharks and many other kinds of fish swim among the giant kelp which grows as much as eight inches a day.

Another exhibit explores Monterey Bay habitats. A 90-foot long tank recreates four distinct habitats: deep reef, sandy sea floor, shale reef and wharf pilings. Large sharks, salmon, striped bass, albacore, bat rays, halibut and other fish species inhabit the exhibit along with the tiny crabs, barnacles, urchins and other tidal creatures.

In the Outer Bay Wing, a million gallon exhibit, currently the world's largest aquarium tank (35 feet deep, 90 feet long and 52 feet front to back), holds seven-foot long ocean sunfish, yellowfin tuna, green sea turtles, barracuda and other ocean swimmers. Visitors view this world, suspended far from shore and above the sea floor, through the largest window on the planet — 54 feet long by 15 feet tall. Other exhibits in the wing bring drifters of the open ocean close to viewers. These drifters range from plants and animals too small to see without a microscope to the elegant, hypnotic jelly fish that come in an amazing variety of shapes and sizes, many pulsing with bright electric currents.

The two-story sea otter exhibit is among the most popular with visitors and also an important research facility. The exhibit approximates the wild near-shore habitat and gives visitors a close look at these curious, playful creatures. The aquarium runs a research and conservation program to help the wild otter population recover from near extinction by hunters in the 18th and 19th centuries. Sea otters were hunted because their fur is the thickest of any animal at a million hairs per square inch. For years scientists thought the southern sea otter was extinct until a small group was found at the mouth of Bixby Creek in Big Sur in 1938. The aquarium staff rescues and rehabilitates sea otter pups with the goal of returning them to the wild. The effort has resulted in a deeper understanding of how to care for otters in the event of an oil spill or other disaster. Today more than 2300 otters live along the central coast, an astounding rebound from the 50 that survived hunting.

The Monterey Bay Aquarium also serves as a major educational institution. More than 70,000 school children visit the aquarium each year participating in tours, laboratories and presentations. Around 1500 teachers attend programs designed so they can bring marine science and environmental topics back to their students.

The Monterey Bay Aquarium in the old Hovden Sardine Cannery on Cannery Row is open 10 AM to 6 PM daily. For information, call 1-831-648-4888.

downhill to end your hike at the wonderful Monterey Bay Aquarium at the northwest end of Cannery Row. The aquarium, which so eloquently displays the California coast's natural abundance, marks the official midpoint of the nation's most fascinating and diverse trail, the California Coastal Trail. CCT has traversed 600 miles from the Oregon border, and it continues 597 miles more along the coast to the California–Mexico border.

The Monterey Peninsula Recreation Trail continues into the town of Pacific Grove, following the waterfront about another mile to Lovers Point. From there a waterfront path continues most of the way around the peninsula. We tell you all about the second half of the trail in *Hiking the California Coastal Trail, Volume Two: Monterey to Mexico*.

*The gorgeous shore of Point Lobos State Reserve is explored in* **Hiking the California Coastal Trail, Volume Two: Monterey to Mexico.**

**SUGGESTED ROUND TRIPS & LOOPS:** From Marina State Beach south to Stilwell Hall and back makes a pleasant 5¼-mile round trip on a seldom walked beach. From around the Municipal Wharf in Monterey, walk north for miles on the beach and return, or follow the Monterey Peninsula Recreation Trail to explore the many attractions of the Monterey waterfront. Another nice town walk, the Path of History, branches off the Recreation Trail at Monterey State Historic Park.

# More about the California Coastal Trail

*"California's beautiful coastline serves as a commons for all the people."*
—Bill Kortum, Coastwalk founder

The California Constitution guarantees the public's right to access to the state's navigable waters. Courts have ruled that this includes the state's tidelands. In fact, the State of California owns the tidelands and submerged lands seaward of the mean high tideline.

The State Lands Commission has administered the state's tidelands since 1938. They use the average of normal tides over the past 19 years and an analysis of what causes shoreline changes over time to establish the mean high tideline. While this formula is complex, you can safely follow this general rule:

> **At the least you have the right to walk on the wet beach. Of course where lands are in public ownership you have the right to walk on a much larger area along the coastline.**

The California Coastal Trail matches any long distance trail in the country for scenic beauty, for diversity, for the countless features of human and natural history it encounters. The way the California coast unfolds along the CCT rivals the drama offered by any trail — redwoods to cactus on one trail, the Pacific Ocean nearly always in view.

The CCT is a state of mind as well as a physical path through the landscape. Even if you never walk the whole, only parts, you can envision the trail going beyond your last steps of a day hiking. You realize you could keep going, that tomorrow you could head on down the trail to Mexico or up to Oregon, alluring possibilities. Each day would bring a new beach, different dunes or bluffs, another river flowing into the ocean, or a new town.

The CCT may be the most diverse trail, and one of the most used trails on the planet. It traverses beaches, bluffs, marine terraces, rocky tidelands and mountains. The CCT is single track and multi-use, on sand and pavement, on rocks and sidewalks, through wilderness and cities. You can walk remote trails and beaches where few tread, or walk southern California beaches visited by millions annually. On given parts of it you will see backpackers, horse riders, bicyclists, runners, roller skaters and babies in strollers. The trail passes through federal, state, county and city parks, through special districts and military bases and in a few places crosses private land on easements. In some areas the trail is unbroken for many miles and in others it is broken up by barriers of private property and geological features. Now in 2002 the state is working with Coastwalk in a concerted effort to complete the CCT.

While Coastwalk and Bored Feet were encouraged by the outpouring of public, media and government support for the 1996 Whole Hike, we're even more excited by the trail's new official status. The time has come to spread the word. We wrote the first complete guide to the CCT so that hikers could negotiate the route successfully despite the trail's incomplete status. For hikers to have a complete guide, we've needed to include lengthy sections that can only be walked on road shoulders. Now we've fully updated and revised the guide for CCT's north half. The ultimate goal is to have the entire trail as close to the coast as possible on a designated pathway, even if it's a sidewalk through a town.

In the enlightened future of our nation, when hiking, whether in wilderness, through parks or greenways, in cities, towns or villages, is understood as both a physical and spiritual necessity for health and sanity, then these barriers will fall away and we Americans will understand the fullest and richest meaning of freedom, the freedom to experience fully the gifts of our magnificent planet earth.

## Chronology of the California Coastal Trail

**1972** California voters pass a citizen's initiative, the Coastal Protection Act, affirming the public's right to access to the coast. One of the manifestations of this right was public discussion of the idea of a California Coastal Trail.

**1975** The California Coastal Plan of 1975 identifies the Coastal Trail as part of the public's right to access to our coast. The Plan, drawn up and approved by the California Coastal Commission, includes Policy #145 calling for establishing a Coastal Trail for public access. The legislature approves this as part of the California Resources Code.

**1976** The California legislature passes the California Coastal Act which further details the public's right to access to the coast. The Act also establishes the Coastal Conservancy.

**1983** Coastwalk is founded in Sonoma County with the first hike including 70 people on a 60-mile walk from Gualala to Bodega Bay.

**1988** About 400 miles of CCT are complete and walkable thanks largely to efforts within the California State Parks Department, National Park Service and Coastal Conservancy.

**1990** The Coastal Trail includes 730 miles "providing public access and an unmatched experience of the state's natural and urban environments."

**1991** Coastwalk's Board of Directors officially states that one of the group's primary goals is to complete the California Coastal Trail.

**1992** The Coastal Conservancy and Coastwalk collaborate on a 36-page booklet, *The California Coastal Trail: Missing Links & Completed Segments.*

**1994** Coastwalk and the Coastal Conservancy produce a twenty minute slide-and-sound show, *Dream and Reality: The California Coastal Trail.*

**1996** Coastwalk and the Coastal Conservancy sponsor and Coastwalk leads the CCT Whole Hike, the first group walk of California's entire coast from Oregon to Mexico.

**1998** Coastwalk and Bored Feet co-publish Volume One of the first complete guide to the CCT. As of spring 1998, about 980 miles of the CCT are essentially complete, following existing trails and beaches or back roads reasonably safe for walking. The other 215 miles follow highways on provisional routes not recommended but possible to walk.

**1999** California Governor Gray Davis nominates the Coastal Trail as the state's Millennium Legacy Trail, and the federal Dept. of Transportation officially so designates the CCT.

**2000** Coastwalk and Bored Feet Press co-publish *Hiking the California Coastal Trail, Volume Two: Monterey to Mexico.* Voters pass Proposition 12, approving $2.1 billion for parks, coast and open space, including $5 million specifically for CCT.

**2001** California legislature passes and Governor Davis signs legislation to plan for completing the Coastal Trail. Coastwalk receives a $316,000 grant to map and plan the CCT.

**2001** Coastwalk accepts 38 OTDs in Mendocino County.

**2002** California voters pass Proposition 40, providing $2.6 billion for parks acquisitions and clean water. Coastwalk and Bored Feet publish this Second Edition of

*Hiking the California Coastal Trail, Volume One: Oregon to Monterey.*

**2003** Coastwalk plans another CCT Whole Hike.

## Help Complete the California Coastal Trail

Conservation and trails go hand in hand for many hikers. Most people hike both for health and to enjoy nature. To have pleasant places to hike, we must work to protect the environment. California is continually assaulted by development threats. Many elected officials seek office to support growth forces while others run to protect natural values. To support the Coastal Trail and the California environment, ask your candidates and officials these important questions:

*Will they support adequate funding for parks and trails?*
*Will they fight development in sensitive habitats and open space?*
*Will they support acquisition of parks, natural lands and open space?*
*Will they make parks, open space and trails a part of approved growth projects?*

Government cannot do it alone. Hundreds of organizations advocate for parks and recreation users. Support groups that help parks, develop urban parks and greenways, and protect habitat, plants and wildlife.

Other ways you can help complete the CCT:

❏ Tell your friends and co-workers about the CCT or present them this book as a gift.

❏ Contact your state legislators and officials and tell them you think it's high time the California Coastal Trail be completed and clearly signed.

❏ Talk to park rangers and tell them you care about the CCT.

❏ Volunteer for trail building and maintenance projects on the CCT.

❏ Organize some friends and spend a day picking up litter along the CCT.

❏ Support a coastal land trust and tell them you want to see completion of the California Coastal Trail in their area become one of their priorities.

❏ Become aware of and involved in coastal issues that threaten the natural splendor of California's coast.

❏ Contact your congressional representatives and tell them you want California's coastal military bases to allow the California Coastal Trail along their shorelines. Whenever such bases are decommissioned, work to insure that the new land use includes a route for the Coastal Trail.

❏ Sign up for a Coastwalk along the California Coastal Trail. Coastwalk leads CCT hikes every summer in each of California's fifteen coastal counties.

❏ Take a friend on a hike along the California Coastal Trail.

To support completion of the California Coastal Trail or get information on trail and conservation groups, contact Coastwalk at 1-800-550-6854 or on the web at www.coastwalk.org.

# Through-Hiking the CCT

If you're contemplating a long distance hike along the California Coastal Trail, you need to consider many things and do a lot of planning to prepare for your trip. If you plan to hike the entire CCT in one continuous trek, your planning and preparations must be particularly detailed. Coastwalk's 1996 "Whole Hike" took 96 hiking days plus 16 rest days to cover the entire 1194 miles. That amounts to an average of 12.4 miles per hiking day. That would be "The Journey of a Lifetime" for all but the most experienced long distance hiker.

The CCT covers many different kinds of terrain and passes through extremely remote, rugged country as well as urban landscapes. Different sections require extremely different levels of hiking ability. If you plan to hike the entire CCT, you need to start training unless you're already extremely fit.

You can conduct a long distance hike several ways. The most difficult is backpacking the entire trail. Perhaps the easiest would be to use lodgings along the way and eat out daily, but you'll find no lodgings or cafes for spans of 24 to 50 miles on the Lost Coast and at Point Reyes, so you'd need another way to cover those miles. If you plan your hike on lodgings, you'll need reservations for most places during summer. The lodging/cafe option requires a healthy budget.

However you do your long distance trek, here are some suggestions on possible ways to go, followed by some essentials to consider.

## Some Options

**Use a support vehicle:** Vans shuttled the Whole Hike group to the nearest campsite or hostel, returning them to the CCT the next day to resume the walk. A solo hiker or small group might find a friend to be driver, cook and/or errand runner. A larger group could use a van, hiring someone to provide support. People using a support vehicle will still need to backpack the Lost Coast and Point Reyes.

**Backpack:** The freedom of backpacking means you don't have to rely on any vehicle support, but the downside is carrying extra weight. Also, official campsites may not be available when you need them. In that situation, the options are staying in lodging or quietly finding a hidden spot to sleep.

**Hybrid Plan:** Combine various options into your own plan. Backpack areas requiring it and those with good camping. Use van support/lodgings elsewhere.

**A fourth option** is to do as much of the trail as time permits each year. This book serves as a handy way to keep track of progress over the years.

## Essentials

**Being prepared** is fundamental for any long distance hiking trip. We'll mention some of the most important essentials. Keep in mind, however, that entire books have been written on the logistics of such trips. For longer treks you should consult one. Several good books discuss planning through-hikes on the Pacific Crest and Appalachian trails. These aren't guidebooks, but books on how to make a long distance trek. Most of their planning information will be useful.

**Get in shape before you start.** While this isn't a mountain expedition, be prepared to hike some long days and rugged terrain. Parts of the CCT cross slippery tidal rocks and climb and descend steep hills. Walk every day starting several months before departure, and increase distances gradually. **Have the right gear, not just a lot.** Boots must be comfortable but not necessarily expensive. I wore out two pairs of $30 light hiking boots from Oregon to Mexico. Boots with good ankle support will pay off on rougher sections. Good socks, such as the new long wearing, comfortable socks of blended fibers are essential. Carry sandals for wading streams. Comfortable camp shoes are invaluable for resting boot-weary feet. Carry a fluorescent vest for times you must road walk.

**Bring clothes to dress in layers** to adjust for temperature and weather changes. See Preparing for Your Hikes on page 20. Bring two pairs of quick-drying long pants so you can switch when a pair gets wet.

**Carry a first aid kit** including any personal medicines you may need. Include an ample supply of moleskin to protect against blisters.

**A comfortable pack is essential.** Even with a support vehicle you'll need a sturdy day pack roomy enough for day gear and lunch. If you're backpacking and camping the entire way, you'll need an expedition pack for treks over 100 miles. If your backpack's only for sections requiring backpacking, a pack big enough for three-day trips is fine. Packs come in many sizes, shapes and suspension systems, but don't skimp if you'll be carrying it many miles. Before your trek, hike a long day or two with your pack loaded with the full weight you plan to carry.

**Depending on the nature of your trek,** you may want a sleeping bag, sleeping pad, lightweight backpacking stove, cookware, eating utensils, good light tent, ground cloth, clothesline, and numerous other items. In addition to this section, be sure to consult the list on page 20.

**When you're on your long distance trek,** pay close attention to weather and to ocean conditions. Don't get caught by a "sleeper wave."

**Plan boat crossings in advance** or plan on adding miles to walk around river mouths, bays and harbor entrances.

**On longer treks, always have a tentative plan** of what you can reasonably hike during the next two or three days, including where you'll spend the night. In the busy summer season, call ahead if you think a reservation might be needed.

# Further Reading

Adams, Rick and Louise McCorkle, *The California Highway 1 Book*, Ballantine Books, New York, 1985. (o.p.)

Berrill, N.J. and Jacquelyn, *1001 Questions Answered About the Seashore*, Dover Publications, New York, 1976.

Big Sur Land Trust, *Monterey Bay State Seashore, a Study for the Preservation of the Monterey Bay Dunes*, Big Sur Land Trust, Carmel, California, 1992.

Brown, Vinson and Douglas Andrews, *The Pomo Indians of California and their Neighbors*, Naturegraph Publishers, Happy Camp, California, 1969.

California Coastal Commission, *California Coastal Access Guide*, Fifth edition, University of California Press, Berkeley, 1997.

California Coastal Commission, *California Coastal Resource Guide*, University of California Press, Berkeley, 1987.

*California, A Guide to the Golden State*, Federal Writers Project, State of California, American Guide Series, Hastings House, New York, 1939. (o.p.)

*California Escapes, Handbook to California State Parks*, American Park Network, San Francisco, 1997.

Chase, J. Smeaton, *California Coast Trails: A Horseback Adventure from Mexico to Oregon*, Tioga Publishing, Palo Alto, California, 1987, reprint of 1913 edition. (o.p.)

*Citizen's Guide to Plastics in the Ocean: More Than a Litter Problem*, Fourth Edition, Center For Marine Conservation, Washington, D.C., 1994.

*Comprehensive Management and Use Plan*, de Anza National Historic Trail, 1996.

Donley, Michael W., and others, *Atlas of California*, Pacific Book Center, Culver City, California, 1979. (o.p.)

Doss, Margot Patterson, *New San Francisco At Your Feet*, Grove Press, New York, 1990.

Evens, Jules G., *The Natural History of the Point Reyes Peninsula*, Revised edition, Point Reyes National Seashore Association, Point Reyes, California, 1993.

*Explore*, a series of pamphlets for the Year of the Coast, U.S. Army Corps of Engineers, San Francisco, 1980. (o.p.)

Franks, Jonathan, *Exploring the North Coast: The California Coast from the Golden Gate to the Oregon Border*, Chronicle Books, San Francisco, 1996.

Gordon, Burton L., *Monterey Bay Area: Natural History and Cultural Imprints*, Revised edition, Boxwood Press, Monterey, California, 1996.

Griggs, Gary and Lauret Savoy, *Living with the California Coast*, Duke University Press, Durham, North Carolina, 1985. (o.p.)

Gudde, Erwin G., *California Place Names*, University of California Press, Berkeley, 1974.

Gustaitis, Rasa, ed., *San Francisco Bay Shoreline Guide*, Coastal Conservancy, University of California Press, Berkeley, 1995.

Hedgepeth, Joel, *Introduction to Seashore Life of the San Francisco Bay Region and the Coast of Northern California*, Fourth edition, University of California Press, Berkeley, 1970.

Heizer, R. F., and M. A. Whipple, eds., *The California Indians: A Source Book*, Second edition, University of California Press, Berkeley, 1971.

Iacopi, Robert, *Earthquake Country*, Fourth edition, Lane Publishing, Menlo Park, California, 1971. Reprinted by Fisher Books, 1996.

Jackson, Ruth, *Combing the Coast: Highway 1 from San Francisco to San Luis Obispo*, Chronicle Books, San Francisco, 1985. (o.p.)

Konigsmark, Ted, *Geologic Trips: San Francisco & the Bay Area*, GeoPress, Gualala, California, 1998.

Kroeber, A. L., *Handbook of the Indians of California*, Dover Publications, New York, 1976, reprint of 1925 edition.

Margolin, Malcolm, *The Ohlone Way: Indian Life in the San Francisco-Monterey Bay Area*, Heyday Books, Berkeley, 1978.

Martin, Don and Kay Martin, *Hiking Marin: 121 Great Hikes in Marin County*, Martin Press, San Anselmo, California, 1995.

Martin, Don and Kay Martin, *Mt. Tam: a Hiking, Running and Nature Guide*, Third edition, Martin Press, San Anselmo, California, 1987.

McConnaughey, Bayard H. and Evelyn, *Pacific Coast*, Audubon Society Nature Guide Series, Alfred A. Knopf, New York, 1985.

McKinney, John, *Walking the California Coast, One Hundred Adventures Along the West Coast*, Harper Collins, New York, 1994.

Nelson, Sharlene and Ted Nelson, *Umbrella Guide to California Lighthouses*, Epicenter Press, Seattle, 1993.

Neuwirth, Donald B., and John J. Osborn Jr., *The California Coast: A Traveler's Companion*, Countryman Press, Woodstock, Vermont, 1998.

Nisbet, Briggs, *The California Coastal Trail: Missing Links & Completed Segments: An Inventory*, Coastal Conservancy and Coastwalk, Oakland, 1992. (o.p.)

*Official Map and Guide to the Presidio*, Golden Gate National Park Association, San Francisco, 1992.

Olmstead, Nancy, *To Walk with a Quiet Mind: Hikes in the Woodlands, Parks and Beaches of the San Francisco Bay Area*, Sierra Club Totebook Series, Sierra Club Books, San Francisco, 1975. (o.p.)

Peterson, Roger Tory, *Field Guide to Western Birds*, Third edition, Peterson Field Guide Series, Houghton Mifflin, Boston, 1990.

*Pocket Guide to California's Public Piers*, Coastal Conservancy, Oakland, 1993. (o.p.)

Rusmore, Jean, *The Bay Area Ridge Trail*, Wilderness Press, Berkeley, 1995.

Rusmore, Jean, and others, *Peninsula Trails*, Third edition, Wilderness Press, Berkeley, 1997.

Vanderwerf, Barbara, *The Coastside Trail Guidebook*, Gum Tree Lane Books, El Granada, California, 1995.

Whitnah, Dorothy, *Point Reyes, A Guide to the Trails, Roads, Beaches, Campgrounds and Lakes of Point Reyes National Seashore*, Third edition, Wilderness Press, Berkeley, 1997.

## Photograph Credits

| PAGE | DESCRIPTION | SOURCE |
|---|---|---|
| 13 | Coastwalkers on Sonoma's Lost Coast | Simone Wilson |
| 21 | Whole Hikers approach Hunter Rock | Richard Nichols |
| 39 | Whole Hikers at Enderts Beach Trailhead | Richard Nichols |
| 53 | Agate Beach from Patrick's Point State Park | Richard Nichols |
| 68 | Whole Hike, Trinidad State Beach | Richard Nichols |
| 94 | Coastwalk hikes Lost Coast at Cape Mendocino | Richard Nichols |
| 111 | Bridge at Russian Gulch State Park from headlands | Bill Ring |
| 140 | Whole Hikers above Bromley Beach | Richard Nichols |
| 163 | Whole Hikers at Bowling Ball Beach | Richard Nichols |
| 171 | Hiker ascends hogback on Sonoma's Lost Coast | Bob Lorentzen |
| 180 | Chapel at Fort Ross | Bill Ring |
| 191 | Hikers approach mouth of Russian River | Richard Nichols |
| 199 | Brenda Nichols on CCT, Marin Headlands | Richard Nichols |
| 214 | Pt. Reyes National Seashore near Arch Rock | Richard Nichols |
| 229 | Golden Gate Bridge from Marin Headlands | Richard Nichols |
| 235 | CCT in San Francisco | Richard Nichols |
| 241 | Whole Hikers at Pacifica State Beach | Richard Nichols |
| 253 | Fitzgerald Marine Reserve | Bill Ring |
| 262 | Surf, rocks and wildflowers | Richard Nichols |

**Continued on page 313**

# Acknowledgments

We offer a robust and heartfelt thank you to the hundreds of people who helped create this book.  In particular we thank Donna Bettencourt for her meticulous and at times seemingly unending job of editing, Elizabeth Petersen for her elegant design and precise production, Marsha Mello for her beautiful, precise maps of the California coast, and the Coastwalk Board of Directors of 1996 through 2002 for their enthusiastic support and funding for the project.

The Whole Hikers of 1996 spent 16 weeks together exploring the glories of the California coast and persevering through long days on the trail, too many miles of highway, personality clashes, blisters, aches and pains, yet made it to the border in spite of everything. Without their efforts, we would not have undertaken this immense project. The Whole Hikers were Beverly Backstrom, Marilyn Goeller, Barbara Johnson, Fay Kelley, Al LePage and Richard Nichols. Two other Whole Hikers, Bob Cowell and Dinesh Desai, completed the San Francisco to Mexico portion with the group in 1996, after providing the essential service of scouting and pre-hiking the Oregon to San Francisco leg in autumn 1995 so that the 1996 hike could be successful.

Providing essential planning and support so that the Whole Hikers could complete the Whole Hike were Vivian McFarling, Tom McFarling, Emily DeFalla, Tim Reed and Brenda Nichols. The dozens of other individuals who guided, shuttled, fed and housed the hikers are too numerous to mention here, but we thank them heartily.

Many thanks to the people who reviewed chapters for accuracy: Sue Davis, Chuck Seward and Diane Seward for Del Norte County, Jon St. Marie for Humboldt County, Don Beers for Del Norte, Humboldt and Mendocino counties, Tim Reed for Sonoma County, Geoff White and Lou Wilkinson for Marin County, Ben Pease for San Francisco, Carl May for San Mateo County, Linda Locklin for Santa Cruz County, and Arlene Breise for Monterey County.

We thank all the people of the California State Parks Department who have kept open and maintained more than 60 coastal parks and beaches in the face of daunting budget cuts. Thanks also to all the other agencies, organizations, individuals and government entities that have worked so hard to create the California Coastal Trail.

For help with the second edition, we thank Don Beers, Ron Munson, Gary Shannon, Steve Fisher and Bob Culbertson of Californi State Parks, Dan Averill of BLM, Lynne Levi of Redwood National Park, Judy Tarbell, Marie Fostiniak, hikers Kent Bien and Wolfgang Rougle and other folks too numerous to mention.

With special thanks to Donald Murphy and Peter Douglas for providing their eloquent forewords, and to Liz Petersen, Eden Lorentzen and Brenda Nichols for putting up with our near total immersion in this project.

## Photograph Credits

### Continued from page 312

| PAGE | DESCRIPTION | SOURCE |
|---|---|---|
| 271 | Surfer memorial at Point Santa Cruz | Richard Nichols |
| 275 | Secluded cove, northern Santa Cruz coast | Richard Nichols |
| 283 | Natural bridge at sheltered beach, Santa Cruz | Richard Nichols |
| 293 | Hikers stride Monterey Peninsula Rec. Trail | Richard Nichols |
| 305 | Point Lobos State Reserve coastline | Liz Petersen |

COVER PHOTOS:

| | | |
|---|---|---|
| front, top | Whole Hiker Barbara Johnson walks Bowling Ball Beach | Richard Nichols |
| front, center | Whole Hikers approach Klamath River | Richard Nichols |
| front, bottom | Whole Hikers in the mist at Anson Grove | Richard Nichols |
| back , top | June wildflowers at Point Cabrillo | Bob Lorentzen |
| back, bottom | Tomales Bay | Bill Ring |

# Index

## About the Authors

*Bob Lorentzen* began writing and publishing in 1986 because the regional guide-books people wanted were not being published. His four *Hiker's hip pocket Guides* have set a new standard of excellence for trail guides. He's been an active Coastwalk volunteer since 1987. Bob and his family love to explore new country and find new trails, and sometimes to simply sit and contemplate nature. He hiked nearly 300 miles on the California Coastal Trail Whole Hike of 1996. On that trek Bob and Richard decided to write this book. Bob graduated from the University of California at Santa Cruz with a degree in Community Studies. This is Lorentzen's seventh book.

*Richard Nichols* has been the Executive Director of Coastwalk since 1991, a Coastwalk volunteer since 1983. Before that he worked as a carpenter. He led the CCT Whole Hike of 1996, walking almost 1200 miles from Oregon to Mexico in 112 days. Richard and his wife Brenda are enthusiastic hikers and explorers of the coast, deserts and mountains of California. He has worked on environmental issues in his home town of Sebastopol in western Sonoma County for 15 years, including instrumental work in wetlands preservation of the Laguna de Santa Rosa and other land use issues. Richard loves to read, watch movies, explore new territory, and create occasional pieces of assemblage art, several of which have been shown in galleries.

# About Coastwalk

In 1982 Bill and Lucy Kortum had an idea — walk the entire Sonoma County coast with 1000 people to emphasize the public's right to access and enjoyment of the California coastline. In 1983 that idea was implemented in a more manageable form by Tom and Vivian McFarling who organized a one time seven day walk with 70 people. The group walked the 60 miles from Gualala to Bodega Bay in a joyous celebration of the wonder and beauty of the Sonoma coast, also demonstrating that not all the coast was open to the public in spite of Article 10 of the California Constitution guaranteeing public access. Susan Swartz of the Santa Rosa Press Democrat came along and phoned in daily reports which the newspaper published with ample graphics and photos.

This "one time" event remains with us nineteen years later. Everyone had so much fun that it's been repeated every year since. Original Coastwalker Jon Toste exported the idea to Marin County in 1985. In that same year Coastwalk gained nonprofit status. By 1991 a paid part-time Director was added. In 1994 Coastwalk fulfilled a long held dream to conduct walks in all 15 coastal counties. The Kortums' original idea of 1000 walkers has multiplied as Coastwalk has led thousands along the coast. In 1996 Coastwalk realized yet another dream by conducting the first ever group walk of the entire coastline from the Oregon border to the Mexican border. During that walk the authors first realized that this book needed to be written.

Our "flagship" events, the annual summer walks in each of the fifteen coastal counties, are kept affordable, interesting and fun because of a large group of dedicated, talented and exceptional volunteers. They help for many reasons, but two stand out. First, they derive great pleasure in sharing our beautiful coast with fellow walkers. Second, they believe in Coastwalk's goal of completing the California Coastal Trail and protecting the coastal environment.

Because of Coastwalk activities and advocacy for the California Coastal Trail, over the years the realization of a completed CCT gained a major impetus in 2000 and 2001.

❏ In March 2000 voters passed a $2.1 billion parks bond act, which included $5 million specifically for the CCT.

❏ Governor Davis signed a Coastal Trail bill sponsored by senators Chesbro and Karnette and passed by the legislature in 2001. The bill officially recognizes the CCT, directs state agencies to cooperate in trail completion, and directs the Coastal Conservancy to take the lead in completing a trail implementation study. Coastwalk received a grant from the Conservancy for $316,000 to play a major part in the study and to prepare a program to sign the CCT.

To continue our work we depend on the continued support and participation of the public. We invite you to learn more about Coastwalk. We'd also like to hear about any long distance hikes along the California Coastal Trail, or other experiences you've had along the CCT.

Please write or call us at:

**Coastwalk**, 7207 Bodega Avenue, Sebastopol CA 95472, 1-800-550-6854.

Call us and leave your name and address for our free brochure of hikes.

Or contact us via e-mail at: coastwalk@coastwalk.org.

Our Web address is: www.coastwalk.org

# About Bored Feet

We began Bored Feet Press in 1986 to publish *The Hiker's hip pocket Guide to the Mendocino Coast*. We've grown our company by presenting the most accurate guidebooks for northern California and our two-volume series on the Coastal Trail.

We love to hear your feedback about this or any of our other products. Also, if you would like to receive updates on trails we cover in our publications, send your name and address, specifying your areas of interest.

We also offer lightning-fast mail order service offering more than 90 books and maps about California and the West. If you'd like a catalog and/or more of our guides please send name, address/check or money order, or call one of the numbers below.

| | |
|---|---:|
| Hiking the California Coastal Trail, Volume One: Oregon to Monterey, 2nd ed. | $19.50 |
| Hiking the California Coastal Trail, Volume Two: Monterey to Mexico | 19.00 |
| Mendocino Coast Bike Rides: Roads & Trails, Easy to Advanced / Lorentzen | 16.00 |
| Mendocino Coast Glove Box Guide, 2nd edition / Lorentzen | 16.00 |
| Hiker's hip pocket Guide to Sonoma County, 2nd edition / Lorentzen | 15.00 |
| Hiker's hip pocket Guide to the Humboldt Coast, 2nd edition / Lorentzen | 14.00 |
| Hiker's hip pocket Guide to the Mendocino Coast, 3rd edition / Lorentzen | 14.00 |
| Hiker's hip pocket Guide to the Mendocino Highlands | 16.00 |
| Trails & Tales of Yosemite & the Central Sierra / Giacomazzi | 16.00 |
| Great Day Hikes in & around Napa Valley, 2nd edition / Stanton | 15.00 |
| Geologic Trips: San Francisco & the Bay Area / Konigsmark | 13.95 |
| A Tour of Mendocino: 32 Historic Buildings / Bear | 7.00 |
| Wood, Water, Air & Fire: Anthology of Mendocino Women Poets/Doubiago,ed. | 19.00 |
| Napa Valley Picnic: CA Wine Country Travel Companion/Burton&Stanton | 15.00 |
| Sonoma Picnic: A CA Wine Country Travel Companion / Burton | 13.00 |
| Trails of the Lost Coast Map | 5.95 |

*Please add $3 shipping for orders under $30, $5 over $30 ($5 / 7 for rush)*
*For shipping to a California address, please add 7.25% tax.*
*PRICES SUBJECT TO CHANGE WITHOUT NOTICE.*

**BORED FEET PRESS**
P.O.Box 1832
Mendocino, CA 95460
888-336-6199
707-964-6629
Fax 707-964-5953
www.boredfeet.com